JOURNEYS DOWN THE ALBERNI CANAL TO BARKLEY SOUND

Journeys

Down the Alberni Canal to Barkley Sound

Jan Peterson

OOLICHAN BOOKS

LANTZVILLE, BRITISH COLUMBIA, CANADA

1999

Canadian Cataloguing in Publication Data

Jan Peterson, 1937-
    Journeys down the Alberni Canal to Barkley Sound
Includes bibliographical references and index.
ISBN 0-88982-178-X

    1. Alberni Valley (B.C.)—History. 2. Alberni Valley (B.C.)—Biography.
3. Barkley Sound Region (B.C.)—History. 4. Barkley Sound Region (B.C.)—Biography. 5. Coastwise shipping—British Columbia—Alberni Inlet—History. 6. Coastwise shipping—British Columbia—Barkley Sound Region—History. I. Title.
FC3845.A42P47 1999   971.1′2   C99-910648-1
F1089.A4P47 1999

We gratefully acknowledge the support of the Canada Council for the Arts for our publishing program.

THE CANADA COUNCIL | LE CONSEIL DES ARTS
FOR THE ARTS | DU CANADA
SINCE 1957 | DEPUIS 1957

Grateful acknowledgement is also made to the BC Ministry of Tourism, Small Business and Culture for their financial support.

We acknowledge the financial support of the Government of Canada through the Book Publishing Industry Development Program for our publishing activities.

Canadä

COVER IMAGE *City of Alberni, 1940* by Michael Dean

Published by
Oolichan Books
P.O. Box 10, Lantzville
British Columbia, Canada
V0R 2H0

Printed in Canada

ACKNOWLEDGEMENTS

This book is written for the enjoyment of all those who love the Alberni Inlet, the beautiful body of water that reaches from the Pacific Ocean to the centre of Vancouver Island. I have attempted to bring into focus the life and sea travels made by the early pioneers and the ships that connected them with the outside world. The history of the waterway is indicative of the technological change in shipping and fishing and how this affected the lives of those who chose to settle here.

Books are rarely the work of any one person. Many individuals and groups assisted me in this work and I thank them for their input. I could not have done this without the help of the volunteers with the Alberni District Historical Society and the staff of the Alberni Valley Museum. I also enlisted the help of the Ucluelet and Area Historical Society and welcomed the information contained in the Bamfield Oral History Project interviews. Reverend Oliver Howard kindly gave me access to his research notes on missionaries. Gordon Miller at the Pacific Biological Station library in Nanaimo guided me in researching fishing history at that facility. The Port Alberni Harbour Commission gave permission to use the Michael Dean drawings in its collection. Michael's talent added a nautical touch to the book. The Alberni Clayoquot Regional District supplied information and reports about the area.

I am grateful to friends and family who have remained supportive of my efforts, especially my husband Ray. Thanks to my son John for producing the maps of the area. I am indebted to friends Dorrit MacLeod and Frank Holm who scrutinized the manuscript and offered suggestions for improvement. Finally to all the people interviewed, I thank you for trusting me with your stories. To longshoremen, fishermen, boaters, and all those people who work on the waterfront in Port Alberni whom I met in the Donut Shop at Alberni Harbour Quay and who shared their knowledge of the area, a big thank-you.

I also would like to acknowledge the work of my editor Ursula Vaira and publisher Ron Smith of Oolichan Books who added their professional talent to the manuscript and published another regional history. There are too few publishers who will take a chance on regional histories.

Contents

Journeys

Down the Alberni Canal to Barkley Sound

Vancouver Island

Map of Loudon & Imperial Eagle Channel

Toquart
Bay

Pipestem
Inlet

Effingham
Inlet

Maggie
Lake

Vernon Bay

Barkley Sound

Tzartus I.

Fleming I.

Sandford I.

Helby I.

Diana I.

Trevor Channel

Edward King I.

Loudon Channel

Hand I.

Mence I.

Prideaux I.

Brabant
Is.

Nettle I.

Peacock   Channel

Jarvis I.

Erin I.

Reeks I.

Dodd I.

Hankin I.

Tiny
Group

Jacques I.

Willis I.

Gibraltar I.

Trickett I.

Keith I.

Turtle I.

Mullins
I.

Lovett I.

Thiepval

Onion I.

Dempster I.

Owens I.

Turret I.

Channel

Wiebe I.

Clarke
I.

Faber Its.

Benson
I.

Coaster   Channel

Cooper

Gilbert
I.

Camblain I.

Effingham I.

Batley I.

Bauke
I.

Wouwer
I.

Austin I.

Dicebox I.

Imperial Eagle Channel

Howell
I.

Cree I.

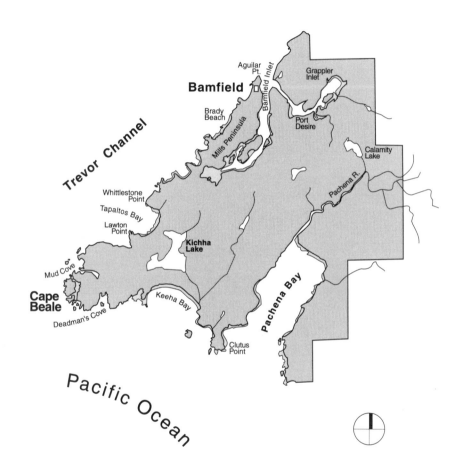

Trevor Channel & Pacific Ocean

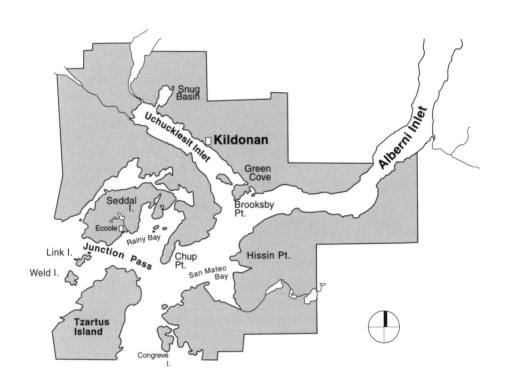

Uchucklesit Inlet & Alberni Inlet

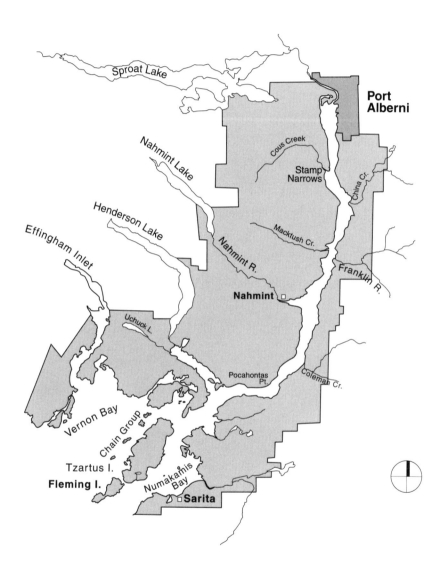

Alberni Inlet

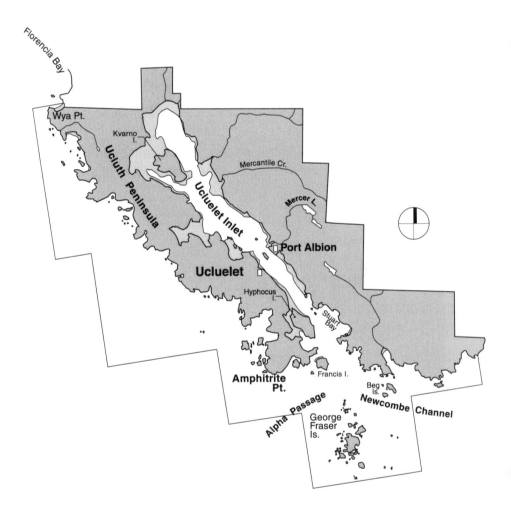

Ucluelet Inlet

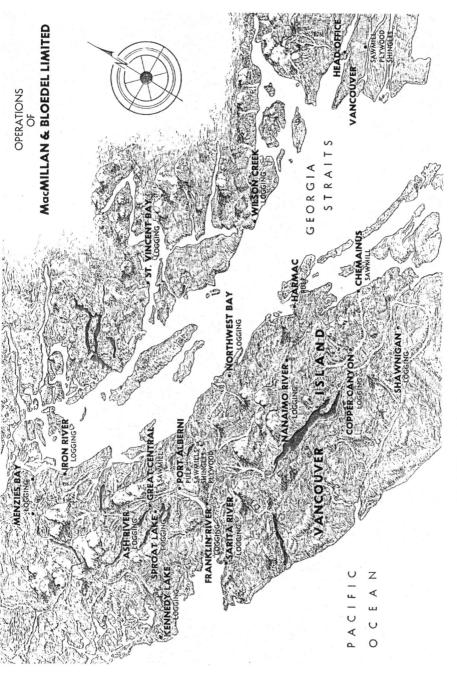

OPERATIONS
OF
MacMILLAN & BLOEDEL LIMITED

MENZIES BAY
LOGGING

IRON RIVER
LOGGING

ST. VINCENT BAY
LOGGING

ASH RIVER
LOGGING

GREAT CENTRAL
SAWMILL

SPROAT LAKE
LOGGING

PORT ALBERNI
PULP
SAWMILL
SHINGLES
PLYWOOD

KENNEDY LAKE
LOGGING

FRANKLIN RIVER
LOGGING

SARITA RIVER
LOGGING

WILSON CREEK
LOGGING

NORTHWEST BAY
LOGGING

HARMAC
PULP

NANAIMO RIVER
LOGGING

COPPER CANYON
LOGGING

CHEMAINUS
SAWMILL

SHAWNIGAN
LOGGING

HEAD OFFICE

VANCOUVER
SAWMILL
PLYWOOD
SHINGLES

VANCOUVER ISLAND

GEORGIA STRAITS

PACIFIC OCEAN

MacMillan & Bloedel Limited logging operations 1951

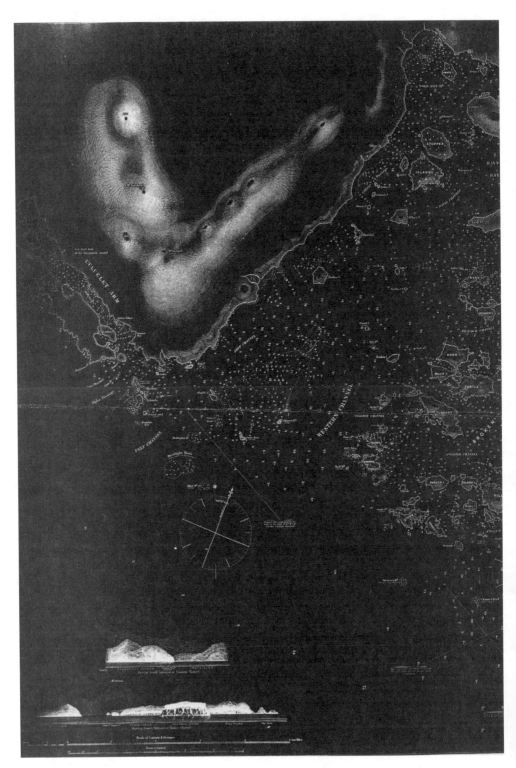

Capt. G. H. Richards 1861 Map

NORTH AMERICA-WEST COAST
SOUTH SIDE OF VANCOUVER I.

BARCLAY SOUND

SURVEYED BY CAPT.ᴺ G.H.RICHARDS, R.N.

Assisted by J.A.Bull, D.Pender & E.P.Bedwell, Masters, J.T.Gowlland &
G.A.Browning, Second Masters; & E.B.Blunden, Master's Assistant.

1861

INTRODUCTION

Vancouver Island is Canada's gateway to the Pacific. The island, approximately fifty miles wide and 280 miles long, is the largest island off the west coast of the Americas. This partially submerged mountain mass, with its mountainous peaks and glorious forest, fronts the Pacific Ocean like an impenetrable wall. Along the western coastline are narrow fiords, inlets and sounds, with partially sheltered coves and beaches where the surf pounds endlessly. The constant rise and fall of the tides, which together last about thirteen hours, produce strong currents in the inlets and channels.

The heavy rainfall supports the dense forest alive with Douglas-fir, hemlock, red cedar, yellow cedar, balsam, fir and yew trees. The salal clings to the edge of the rocky shoreline and grows so high it guards the edge of the forest with an almost impenetrable tangle. Moss covers every stone, fallen log and tree trunk, making travel difficult. Inland, the terrain is rugged and mountainous; what few settlements there are are dotted along the shoreline.

The landmass is equally blessed with a variety of wild animals such as deer, elk, black bear, cougar, wolves, and smaller animals such as mink, beaver, river otter and raccoons.

One of the most spectacular coastal regions on the island is the area encompassing Barkley Sound and the Alberni Inlet, the largest fiord on Vancouver Island. Salmon, herring, codfish, halibut, and shellfish such as prawns, shrimp, and clams are available at various times of the year. Seals, sea lions and porpoises frolic along the coastal waters, and each year, whales visit on their migratory route to Alaska.

Barkley Sound is the largest of the west-coast sounds. Roughly rectangular in shape, it is divided by island chains into three main channels: Loudoun Channel to the northwest; Imperial Eagle, the middle channel; and Trevor Channel to the southeast. The northern tip of Trevor Channel connects with Imperial Eagle and with the Alberni Inlet at Tzartus Island. The sound is dotted with the hundreds of islands in the Deer Group and Broken Group Islands. Five main rivers, the Effingham, the Maggie, the Henderson, the Toquart and the Sarita, flow into Barkley Sound.

Old documents often refer to it as "Barclay" Sound, but it was named for and by Captain Charles William Barkley of the British trading ship *Imperial Eagle*, when he sailed there in 1787 with his seventeen-year-old bride Frances Hornby Trevor. Mrs. Barkley noted in her journal that her husband named many of the places within the sound, including Trevor Channel, in her honour, and Imperial Eagle Channel after his ship.

The Alberni (Canal) Inlet was named by Lieutenant Francisco Eliza in 1791 to honour Don Pedro de Alberni, a lieutenant-colonel with the Spanish navy, who led the Spanish Catalonian troops to Nootka Sound. The waterway was known as the Alberni Canal until 1931 when the name was changed because of fears shipping companies would think it was a man-made canal requiring fees. For the purpose of this manuscript, the historical name will be used throughout. Today old-timers and residents along its shoreline still refer to the waterway as "the canal." A trip to Bamfield or Ucluelet from Port Alberni is referred to as going "down the canal."

The canal almost slices Vancouver Island in half and reaches into its very heart. Somass River, Cous Creek, China Creek, Macktush Creek, Franklin River, and Nahmint River are its major arteries. The canal begins at the mouth of the Somass River in Port Alberni and extends to Barkley Sound on the Pacific Ocean, a distance of about thirty miles. This important sheltered passage, about one mile in width, and the harbour at Port Alberni can accommodate the largest deep-sea vessels loading lumber for markets around the world. The Port Alberni Harbour Commission, incorporated in 1947, has jurisdiction from Chup Point, inside Barkley Sound, to the tidal waters of the Somass River at the head of the Alberni Canal.

Many communities share this common waterway. Ucluelet includes the reserves of the Ucluelet and Toquaht bands, plus the Village of Ucluelet; Bamfield includes the reserves of the Ohiaht and Nitinat bands plus the Village of Bamfield; the Uchucklesaht reserve is located at the head of Uchucklesit Inlet; the City of Port Alberni, the population centre of the region, includes the reserves of the Tseshaht and Opetchesaht bands. Beaver Creek, Cherry Creek and Sproat Lake are outlying rural communities.

Although each village and city has its own municipal government, the area has an elected governing body, the Regional District of Alberni-Clayoquot, located in Port Alberni. The Board's jurisdiction includes Tofino and the Clayoquot Sound areas to the north. The Nuu-chah-nulth Tribal Council looks after the affairs of the thirteen First Nations of the west coast from board offices on the Tseshaht Reserve in Port Alberni.

Today the Pacific Rim highway links Port Alberni to Ucluelet and Tofino, and a partially paved road connects Port Alberni to Bamfield. Logging roads, some open, some restricted, crisscross the mountains and valleys. For today's visitors and inhabitants the area seems idyllic, but it was not always so. Early pioneers suffered great hardships to build roads and communities and to harvest the resources. Many villages, fish canneries and logging camps that once dotted the Alberni Canal have disappeared with time, their presence but a memory with old-timers of the region. This is the story of the people and places of the Alberni Canal and Barkley Sound.

DISCOVERY

by Dick McMinn

Once by the rock-lipped ocean, many old moons ago,
a salt-skinned, brown-eyed people lived by the tidal-flo,
and the sea ran wide to the great moon-tide
till it met the sky where the old sun died.

Toopalth, the sea, they called it, from the edge of their mountain land.
It the home of the fish-people, who fed all the tribal band.
And over its edge, with cannon and kedge,
the sails of the white-man drove their wedge.

Swift came the tribes to behold them and *Coynee* the gull, marked their trails,
watching the white-winged monsters, swept by the Westerly gales.
Ucluelahts, Ohiats, and Sechants stood by the rock-ribbed sea—
Toquahts, Uchucklesahts, Opetchesahts, seeing the world to be.

They came with their pale-skinned faces, but their eyes burned bright with flame.
Theirs the scourge of the fire-urge, hot with the gain of the game.
Wider by far than *Eenuk,* the sky, the white-man's lodges spread,
And some were higher than *Nootchee,* the mountain, with glass eyes in their head.

But the white-man clutched his money, and the flame burned fiercer still,
and the creeks and rills of the high, clean hills grew slimy and muddy with swill.
These the wombs of the fish-people's young, these the life of the sea.
But the white-man's flame—the gain of the game was a fever that could not see.

And millions came across the sea, thicker than *Ootchkuk,* the fog,
till the fish-people died from a thousand hooks, the Tyee and the dog.
For no man greeted them in Spring, with the old words—*Kinatchluk*
And none said thanks, *Kleyhooee,* for food from the great salt-chuck.

The smoke of the Aht-people withered and died, and the eyeless totems were left
standing by *Toopalth* under *Eenuk,* where the stumps of the trees were reft,
regretting the white-wings of long ago, and the flame that burned so dry,
whispering one word, wood-lipped, unheard, the Aht *Tyoo* Goodbye!

CHAPTER ONE

FIRST EUROPEAN CONTACT

There is little written information about life on the west coast of Vancouver Island before the third decade of the nineteenth century, although there is a wealth of First Nations oral history passed down from generation to generation in story, song and dance. What is written comes from diaries and journals of visiting British, Spanish, American and Russian explorers who were viewed with suspicion and treated warily by the Nootka people.

Before these intruders arrived on the scene, west-coast people had already developed sophisticated systems of trade for food or goods. Shortages of food caused many intertribal wars, as did disagreements over territorial rights and attempts to gain rank within tribes. Over time, some of the original tribes were either annihilated or absorbed into larger groups.

This was the case with the Kiihin, who were annihilated by a neighbouring tribe, the Uchucklesaht. The Kiihin tribe of six hundred men lived on the seaward side of Uchucklesit Inlet where the Uchucklesaht, another tribe of eight hundred men lived. A Uchucklesaht chief and a Kiihin princess eloped, and when two boys were born to the young couple, the Uchucklesaht were given the Kiihin's drift-whale rights. This resulted in a shortage of food for the Kiihin, and some of their lower-ranking members plotted to kill their princess and her two sons to regain their old food supply. They ambushed the mother and her two sons but did not have the heart to kill them. The princess demanded her husband's tribe, the Uchucklesaht, take revenge for the attack on their two sons. She personally planned and guided the first raid, and in subsequent raids the entire Kiihin tribe was killed off with the exception of the immediate relatives of the princess. The Uchucklesaht took over the land and the water rights of the Kiihin on both sides of the Inlet.[1]

Another dispute over fishing rights almost annihilated the Ohiahts, whose small village was originally built on Keeshan, or Execution Rock, a huge rock separated from the main island a few miles west of Bamfield. A fight erupted when a few members of the Clallam tribe, from the other side of Juan de Fuca Strait, were caught fishing in Ohiaht waters. The Clallam chief's sons were killed in the incident. To add to the indignity, the Ohiahts displayed the severed heads of their victims. The Clallams vowed revenge and planned their attack carefully. They killed almost all the Ohiahts, but two boys and two girls escaped down a natural air shaft in the massive rock, where they stayed until the enemy left. The four left Keeshan in search of a new home. They came to a lovely river called Tsauk, which would later be named Sarita. As they paddled up the river, they reached the fork of another river, the Klesca-pois. Deciding this would make a good home, they named the place Kee-kee-in-coop. Each boy took the sister of the other for a wife, and the Ohiaht tribe was reborn.[2]

The first peoples planned their movements and activities according to the migratory patterns of fish or game and the harvest times of plants and trees. Winter and summer villages were dotted throughout the sounds and waterways of the coast; some sites were eventually included in the reservations, having passed down through generations. There were special places for berry picking and bark gathering, and beaches especially suited for launching canoes. Berries were an important part of diet; they were either eaten fresh or dried into cakes to be served later, at feasts hosted by the chief. Salmonberry patches were owned by families and harvested exclusively by them.[3] Cedar tree bark yielded fibre that was easily split and processed into woven blankets, capes and other items of clothing.[4] Cedar, being soft and resistant to decay, was also ideal for the construction of canoes.

A salmon-producing river was particularly prized. Such was the case when the Ucluelets seized Nahmint because it had the best salmon. The Ucluelets killed all the chiefs of the Nahmint and took their territorial and ceremonial rights.[5]

While France and England concentrated their efforts on the eastern seaboard of the continent, Spain claimed exclusive rights to the whole Pacific coast, settling mainly in Mexico and California. When Russia began expanding its territories, the worried Spanish began their exploration of the northwest coast. Soon the British arrived, intent on finding a northwest passage to the Orient. France, on hearing of the British exploration, soon sent its own explorers. The First Nations, using their skills as seasoned traders to their advantage, began trading with the visitors, exchanging sea otter pelts for European goods such as tobacco, alcohol and weapons.

The west coast and its vast resources had been discovered, and life for the aboriginal peoples would never be the same. At first they were eager to trade with the newcomers, but inevitably there were visiting traders who, anxious to drive a hard bargain, treated them with contempt. Word spread quickly and soon visitors were being threatened and even attacked. The first massacre occurred in March of 1803, when Captain Salter of the *Boston* and twenty-five of his crew were murdered near Friendly Cove. The ship burned and sank. Two men survived but were captured and made to serve as slaves to Chief Maquinna. John Jewitt, an armourer, and John Thomson, a sailmaker, were rescued by the Brig *Lydia* three years later. Jewitt later chronicled his time of captivity; he and Thomson, two of fifty slaves owned by Chief Maquinna, lived in fear, never knowing what would come first—rescue or death.[6]

The second incident happened in June, 1811, when the Boston ship *Tonquin*, under Captain Jonathan Thorn, was attacked at Village Island (Echatchis) in the Broken Group Islands. Only a Native interpreter survived.[7] There were other clashes, which signified the troubled relationships that had developed between the races. News of these incidents spread, and for a time white men were reluctant to venture to the west coast.

WILLIAM EDDY BANFIELD

One man who did was British sailor William Eddy Banfield, who, when discharged from HMS *Constance* at the Esquimalt station in 1849, settled in Victoria. With his friend Captain Peter Francis, who owned a small sloop named *Leonede*, he explored the west coast and immediately saw opportunities for trade. In the summer of 1858 he wrote a series of articles about the area and its people for the *Daily Victoria Gazette*. These articles provided the first reliable information about the inhabitants and the terrain of Barkley Sound and the Alberni Canal.

Banfield described Nitinat, midway between Port Renfrew and Cape Beale, as a thirty-mile area of rocky shore without a safe harbour of any kind. He estimated about five hundred people, not counting women and children, lived there under their forty-year-old chief Maacoola. They hunted whales, manufactured their own harpoons and gear, and fished for halibut and salmon.[8]

The Ohiaht tribe, with a similar population, lived on the eastern side of Barkley Sound under Chief Cli-shin. They, too, valued the fishing, and hunted whales, but they also rendered oil from dogfish and seals. They traded land animals such as bears, otters, martins, beaver, mink, raccoons and sea otters for blankets, tobacco, powder, shot and calico.

Banfield was especially impressed with the forests. "The timber is fine on this Sound and of large growth. It is the place best adapted on the Island for export of lumber mills and spar material."[9]

The Broken Group Islands, located between Cape Beale (Ohiaht Head) and Ucluelet (Youcloulyet) at the entrance to Barkley Sound, he described as "a group of small islands, with deep navigable channels between them, and forming shelter and good safe anchorage for any class of ships." The Tseshahts (Sheshats) tribe, estimated population of two hundred, inhabited the largest group of islands during the summer months. During the winter, the tribe migrated to the headwaters of the Alberni Canal. As with the other tribes, they relied on the sea for food, and had "developed a healthy trade in seal skins."

The Tseshahts were known to excel in "historical painting" on planks, which they sold for a high price to other tribes for their building lodges. Banfield noted these painted boards could be seen on the front boards of lodges. "The Macaws transport these planks across the open sea in their canoes—voyages frequently attended with much risk, the distance from Cape Classet to this sound being about 35 miles."

Another small tribe named the Taquats lived near the Tseshahts. They had once been a larger group, but intertribal warfare with the Nitinats had reduced their numbers considerably.

On the western side of Barkley Sound four hundred and fifty members of the Ucluelet (Youcloulyet) tribe resided near "a beautiful harbor, facing to the south but not at all exposed to the Pacific Ocean, equally sheltered, and five times as large as the estuary at Victoria." Here Banfield noted large patches of clear land in the immediate vicinity and thousands of acres of "good bottom land" extending from the village to Clayoquot Sound in the north.

Banfield raved about the Alberni Canal and the Alberni Valley, comparing them to his home in England. He was greatly impressed by the great depth of water cradled by mountains covered with forest. As he neared the end of the canal, he noted the land became less wooded, "a beautiful grazing country, or deer park, for miles." At the head of the canal, he found a small tribe of about twenty (the Opetchesahts) who hunted for a living and traded with the Ohiahts and the Uchucklesahts, as well as with the peoples of Nanaimo. He envisioned a great future for the area. He wrote:

> From the head waters of the Alberni Canal to the nearest point on the east side of Vancouver Island is not above 25 miles. Nanaimo is no considerable distance, an Indian trail connecting them. It would be no Utopean idea or absurd opinion to hazard the prediction that five years of the future will produce an Anglo-American Liverpool in the immediate neighborhood of this sound, connected by an iron road with Nanaimo, the Newcastle of the North Pacific, on which the swift wings of steam power will transport merchandise and mails from the headwaters of the Alberni to Nanaimo and thence across the Gulf of Georgia to the mouth of the Fraser, in the short space of eight hours. This scheme is nothing impracticable or improbable, but feasible in every shape.

He was so enthusiastic about what he saw on his journey that he declared the area to be the best on the island for exporting milled lumber and spars. He noted many other opportunities for industry, including copper mining and fishing the vast schools of herring, halibut and salmon in the sound.

Banfield soon learned the Native language and became acquainted with the different tribes. In 1859, when he was appointed Agent for the Colonial Secretary in the region, he moved permanently to live at Banfield Creek, so named for him by Captain G. H. Richards of HMS *Plumper*, when he surveyed Barkley Sound and published a navigational chart in 1861.[10] The creek empties into Bamfield Inlet. The name changed from "Banfield" to "Bamfield" through common usage. Richards' survey of the sound had been at the instigation of Banfield, who knew "a good chart would be of infinite service . . . and be a great benefit to the coast."[11]

Banfield purchased land from the Ohiaht band, but this location proved to be too close to the main village, and he moved to avoid being "pestered by curious Indians who probed into everything." He acquired another piece of land for the price of "six blankets, some beans and molasses"[12] at Grappler Inlet, opposite Port Desire. The title deed was signed by the chief and witnessed by three white men. He noted, "They put no value on land as they never cultivate."[13]

The land transaction with the Natives troubled Banfield as he knew it would never be recognised by the Colonial government. He wrote several letters to Victoria appealing for recognition of his land claim and became particularly alarmed when he heard the rumour that a Captain Edward Stamp had secured "a grant of the whole Sound" when all Banfield wanted was a small piece of land for his home. He thought his service to the Colony should account for something, but, always careful not to anger authorities, he broached the subject with some delicacy:

> I always had an intention of soliciting his Excellency the Governor by a humble memorial showing the many years I have lived and endured many privations and misfortunes on the south west coast for a grant of the little place immediately around and about my house. I humbly submit to you now Sir, whether it would be proper for me to do so.[14]

The following year Banfield informed the Colonial Secretary, W. A. G. Young, that he had staked another piece of land in Alberni.[15] He had purchased the land from the Opetchesaht band on the eastern bank of the Somass River for "the sum of five blankets and other small articles." The two joint chiefs of the Opetchesaht, Kal-wu-ish and Quite-chee-nam signed his written statement. The statement noted:

> The said Kal-wu-ish and Quite-chee-nam asserting solemnly that they are the present owners and that none others have a right to sell said ground and that they have done it willingly without fear or intimidation. They likewise solemnly guarantee to me that not any annoyance shall be given by any of their people. On these affirmations I have purchased this ground.[16]

Once again Banfield worried government would not recognise his title. Again he wrote to Victoria pleading for settlement. "I beg to inform you Sir, I have taken precautions to stake off my piece of land and put notices on it and I will be prepared to pay an instalment at any time—I have reference to that at the mouth of the River Somass."[17]

In Banfield's correspondence with the Colonial Government he was always careful to observe courtesy and rank as deemed appropriate in dealings with Victoria. This is evident in the way he signed his reports to Young: "Trusting that any indiscrete [*sic*] or improper language in this report will be forgiven as if such it is unintentional, I beg to subscribe myself. Your very humble Servant." In another letter he asks forgiveness for his blotted report: "But I have not paper enough to write a clean copy, trusting Sir to your generousness I shall continue to do my utmost to fulfill my trust."[18] Yet another report apologised for the "indistinctness of my writing but my ink is frozen and will scarcely mark, Sir, trusting to your forgiveness."[19]

Banfield may have felt some degree of ineptitude with his position, but the reports and ethnological information he sent to the Colonial government were extremely valuable. There is little doubt his information about the timber resource in the area influenced the decision to allow Captain Edward Stamp, an English shipmaster and commission agent for the Anderson Company in London, England, to locate a sawmill at Alberni, a move that greatly affected the west coast and significantly opened up the area for exploration and settlement.

On March 4, 1860, Banfield reported that Captain Charles Edward Stuart had joined him on the coast. Stuart, from Bristol, England, had joined the Hudson's Bay Company in 1842 and had served on many Company ships until he was appointed Officer-in-charge at Nanaimo in 1855. He was discharged four years later for "chronic drunkenness." He then moved to the Ucluelet area, where he opened his own trading post."[20]

On June 29, 1860, without navigational charts of Barkley Sound and the Alberni Canal, Banfield accompanied Captain Tom Pamphlet aboard the schooner *Meg Merrilies* to the head of the Alberni Canal, where they landed nine workmen who were to start work building a sawmill for Captain Stamp. In August, the machinery for the sawmill arrived from England aboard the *Woodpecker*. The *Meg Merrilies* returned on September 1 with Captain Stamp and another Anderson Company representative, Gilbert Malcolm Sproat, plus New Brunswick logger Jeremiah (Jerry) Rogers. The men recognised that they must come to some immediate arrangement with the Tseshaht people, many of whom lived on the site needed for the mill, the site known as Tlukwatkuuwis, or Wolf Ritual Beach. They agreed on a price of twenty pounds sterling plus fifty blankets, a musket, molasses, food and trinkets. The land transaction with the Tseshaht Natives for the mill site was reported "amicable and satisfactory."

The *British Colonist* reported on May 23, 1861, that Captain Stamp's place had been named Alberni. Soon after Stamp and Sproat's arrival, grants of land on the canal and sound were given to the Anderson Company to erect the sawmill and establish a fishing station. The fishing enterprise operated at Effingham Island (Village Island), where the *Tonquin* had been attacked years before. This was the first commercial fishing enterprise on the west coast.[21] The first shipment of cured fish was shipped to Callao, Peru.

Meanwhile, at Alberni, other workers, equipment, and oxen soon added to the growing sawmill village. The Opetchesaht and Tseshaht tribes viewed the newcomers with suspicion and anxiety as homes and buildings were erected. Banfield needed all his skills as negotiator to help lessen the impact of the newcomers on the Natives. He noted in his report:

The white men appear a decent class of men and have promised to abide by written instructions that I furnished their leading man with. The Natives have also promised not to annoy them but sir, I shall visit them at short intervals and use my influence with either party should any dispute take place.[22]

By the end of the year 1860, the first commercial logging was underway in Alberni.

CAPTAIN EDWARD HAMMOND KING

On March 8, 1861, every resident at the sawmill settlement attended the burial service of Captain King at the small cemetery on a bluff overlooking the Anderson mill and the Alberni Canal. King had been injured in a shooting accident on Barkley Sound and was brought to Alberni for medical attention. Unfortunately his injuries were so severe that he died before reaching the Anderson sawmill. He became the first white man to be buried in Alberni.

King was born in Devonshire, England on July 12, 1832. He joined the army at age seventeen, and become paymaster to His Majesty's 59th Regiment. He served with distinction in India and China. When his health deteriorated he was placed on sick leave. He retired from the army in 1857 and next held the appointment of Chief Constable of Carmarthen, South Wales, for one year until he left for Canada. On his arrival in Victoria, he was appointed the government printer. He is credited with establishing the *New Westminster Times* newspaper and later the *Victoria Gazette*. Both newspapers advocated the policies of the existing government and were successful for a time, but when the political climate changed, so too did their fortunes. This, combined with King's lack of knowledge of the printing business, forced his early retirement from the newspaper business.

King next worked for an insurance company, and after the wreck of the *Florencia* on November 14, 1860, near Ucluelet, he was sent to take charge of the wreck and to "inquire into the causes attending the sale of that wreck to Captain Stuart of Ucluelet."[23] The ship had been under tow by the steam gun boat HMS *Forward* and was cast adrift when the gun-boat developed boiler trouble. The sailing ship ended up on the rocks about five miles west of Amphitrite Point. It had been *en route* to Hawaii with a cargo of lumber. After the wreck of the ship, her crew went to Ucluelet and sought shelter with Captain Stuart. At Stuart's request, the mate of the *Florencia*, Mr. Lankenau, put the wrecked vessel and her cargo of lumber up for auction. He sold them at the ridiculously low price of one hundred dollars to Stuart, the only bidder there.[24] Eventually the crew arrived at Victoria on HMS *Hecate* and reported to authorities the wreck and the sale, which was immediately repudiated.[25]

After visiting the wreck and taking formal possession of it, King boarded the schooner *Saucy Lass* for a hunting and fishing trip. Aboard were King, his brother Joseph H. King, Captain Stuart, a Frenchman named Claude Devon, and a man named Charles Burnaby. For a time the occupants of the *Saucy Lass* visited the yacht *Templar*, also in the area.

On February 24, the two vessels parted company during a heavy gale. The *Saucy Lass* sheltered in a cove in Barkley Sound and lay there several weeks "dodging the weather." A year later, in 1861, Captain Richards would remember this incident while he was charting the waters of Barkley Sound. Captain Pamphlet would show him a sketch of the cove, which is a passage between two islands, and note, "It is a fine place to dodge in," thus drawing attention to the lengthy stay of the *Saucy Lass*. Captain Richards would reply, "That is so, and it will now for ever be known as Dodger Cove."[26]

Meanwhile the *Templar* left the *Saucy Lass* behind and reached Victoria safely eight days later. Captain Pamphlet, on the schooner *Meg Merrilies*, spoke with the members of the *Saucy Lass* as she lay in Barkley Sound only a few days after the gale. All was well with the ship at that point, so the *Meg Merrilies* continued on to Victoria as well.

Captain King and his party then sailed among the Broken Group Islands, enjoying the shooting and hunting possibilities of the area. On March 3, he and Charles Burnaby left the schooner, going ashore at a small island "near a larger island known then as Sechart," where mink were said to be plentiful. Both Burnaby and King carried guns. King had a double-barrelled English "fowling-piece with a hair trigger."

At the coroner's inquest held later, Burnaby explained what happened next. When they reached the beach, both stepped out and hauled the canoe to shore; as they did so, King reached down and grasped the gun by the barrel with his right hand, giving it a sudden jerk towards him. The cock may have caught on one of the stretchers of the canoe, for the gun discharged. King dropped it, turned and ran two or three paces from the canoe and fell on his face saying, "I am shot! I am shot!" Burnaby waved for help from the schooner. King was taken to the ship and placed on the cabin floor. Captain Stuart and King's brother Joseph examined the wound. The buckshot had passed through his left breast in a slanting direction and had entered the left shoulder, nearly tearing the arm from the socket.

They tried everything they could to stop the flow of blood. King, although in pain and distressed, continued to maintain his dignity. When King was brought alongside the *Saucy Lass*, Captain Stuart asked him what had happened. King replied, "Oh, I've only blown my arm off; I think Burnaby's gun must have gone off by accident." Burnaby's gun was examined and found to be loaded, whereas the barrel of King's weapon had been recently discharged. "It is all my own fault; I now believe my gun went off when I was pulling it out of the canoe," King said later.

The decision was made to send him by canoe to Victoria where he could be treated, but a southeast gale sprang up, compelling the party to return. The *Saucy Lass* then headed for "Capt. Stamp's settlement on Barclay Sound." King died about an hour before the schooner arrived. He had been conscious until the end, frequently begging for "opiate" to deaden the pain and allow him to stay alert enough to arrange his affairs before death. It seems King knew from the beginning that he would die from the wound.

On their arrival at the mill site, Captain Stamp took charge of the body and offered his home to the members of King's party. At the inquest held March 8, 1861, Stamp acted as coroner. The jury consisted of eleven men plus the foreman Charles Patch, who passed the verdict. "The jurors are all of (the) opinion, from the evidence we have heard, that the deceased (Edward Hammond King) came by his death in consequence of the accidental discharge of his gun by the hammer catching the gunnel of the canoe while in his own hand."

A few days after the burial, the schooner *Meg Merrilies*, arriving from Victoria, was ordered to return to that city immediately with details of the incident. The *Saucy Lass*, with King's brother Joseph and Captain Stuart, returned to the vicinity of the *Florencia* wreck where they continued on their hunting expedition. Captain Edward King left a wife and three young children. In recent years, his descendants from England visited his burial site. Edward King Island is named in his honour.

Another member of the hunting party met an untimely death two years later. In 1863, while Captain Stuart was on his way to do some exploratory work on Sangster Island, he became ill aboard his own boat. He died before a doctor arrived. He was buried in the old cemetery in Nanaimo.[27]

BANFIELD'S DEATH—WAS IT MURDER?

There were several occasions when William Eddy Banfield helped solve problems between the Native people and the workers at the Anderson mill. Captain Stamp even offered him a position as Government Agent, which, he was assured, would not interfere with his duties as Indian Agent. Banfield doubted this and stated so in his report of July 20, 1860. He felt he should maintain his independent position should other settlers arrive and have difficulty with the Natives.[28]

Banfield may have been encouraged by seeing all the activity on the canal and the emergence of a small sawmill community at Alberni. The first shipment of lumber went to Victoria in July, 1861, aboard the *Meg Merrilies*. The old *Woodpecker*, which had done yeoman's service by carrying the machinery from England for the mill, was now replaced by an eighty-seven-foot schooner named the *Alberni*, the first wooden ship constructed in Alberni.

Banfield's report of May 30, 1861, recorded the sawmill community's celebration of Queen Victoria's birthday:

Yesterday, the Birthday of our Queen was celebrated here in a marked, loyal, but exceedingly decorous manner. Some few citizens of the United States cheerfully participated with their British Colonial friends in their joyousness at another anniversary of the birthday of our Queen. The Indians too joined in the celebration with a hearty, goodwill, and drank no tangle-leg. The day was finished creditably; the last song sung was "Rule Britannia." Capt. Stamp's mill is in full operation. The summer weather and the beautiful vegetation of the plains combine to make Alberni vie with the best place in this Colony.[29]

Banfield's January 30, 1862 report stated that the Alberni Canal had frozen over with ice five inches thick for a distance of seven miles from the Alberni mill. The schooner *Meg Merrilies* and the ship *Pocahontas* were stranded, and all work at the mill suspended. It was on this date Banfield had trouble writing his report because the ink had frozen.

The winter of 1861-1862 was one of the coldest on record. Sproat later told his son Alex how he had walked seven miles down the canal on the ice. He said at one point he surprised some loggers who had gathered around a huge log fire outside their hut. He had left the ice and circled the shoreline in a biting cold wind to see whether they were all right. That winter oxen were used on the ice to haul sleds loaded with hay and supplies for the logging camps on the canal as far as they could go with safety.[30]

The story of the *Pocahontas* being frozen in is legendary. Skipper of the vessel, Captain Cyrus Sears, a retired resident of Baltimore, Md., fifty years later recalled the voyage to Alberni. The ship had been *en route* to Stamp Harbour to load spars for the English and French navies. Banfield again had acted as pilot for the vessel entering Barkley Sound until it reached its first anchorage. From there Sears proceeded up the sound trusting Captain Richards' new navigation chart. He had safely passed the rocky corners at the entrance to Barkley Sound and entered the canal when a wind storm battered the ship. As the ship neared Hell's Gate with no anchorage in sight, Sears managed to tie her to a tree and drop anchor in the channel. "We swung alongside the precipitous bank, where, after putting out fenders, we lay very safe. While lying there the ship was being painted, and one of the crew painted the ship's name, *Pocahontas*, on the rock."[31] The painted rock would be a landmark curiosity on the canal for many years to come. When weather conditions improved the next day, Sears continued on to Alberni. During the ship's stay in Stamp Harbour, the weather turned extremely cold and the canal froze over. The *Pocahontas* lay stranded for several weeks.

In 1862, the total value of export shipments from Alberni was $122,917. Included were: rough lumber, 7,804,000 feet valued at $85,844; dressed lumber, 270,000 feet at $5,400; four cargoes of spars at $28,673; five thousand gallons of oil at forty cents per gallon, $2000; and furs and skins valued at $1000.[32]

This same year, the small sawmill settlement at Alberni had a population of about two hundred. Stamp Harbour was a busy port, loading sailing ships with lumber for markets around the world. Letters and newspapers reported fourteen vessels loaded lumber or spars for export. The steam tug boat *Diana*, purchased by Stamp in San Francisco, was kept busy towing ships in or out of the canal, or making trips to Victoria.[33]

Captain Richards' navigational chart became a valuable document for ships entering the canal, for it eventually relieved Banfield of the chore of escorting those unfamiliar with the hazards of the waterway. By July, 1862, Banfield owned his own sailing boat which gave him a new freedom to sail farther north and explore Clayoquot Sound and other parts of the coast. His last report of August 24, 1862, described the Cape Beale headland and Pachena Bay, and the abundance of salmon, halibut, codfish, and whales. He suggested a whaling industry could possibly be established in the area.

On October 24, 1862, word reached Victoria of Banfield's death the previous Monday. He was reported to have gone around Aguilar Point in a canoe accompanied by a Native man named Klatsmick, to meet the schooner *Alberni*, which was *en route* to Alberni. Klatsmick, returning with the canoe, reported Banfield had accidentally upset the canoe and drowned, an incident difficult to believe considering Banfield's naval experience and his familiarity with the waters of the sound.

Many who knew Banfield doubted the story. The Colonial government sent the warship *Devastation* with the superintendent of police and an interpreter to investigate. The *Devastation* anchored in Numukamis Bay while the police superintendent, the ship's surgeon, and the interpreter rowed to Klatsmick's village. There they were threatened by Natives armed with muskets, knives, harpoons, and axes. One man had to be restrained from killing them.[34] When reason prevailed, the Natives allowed the delegation to return to their ship with Klatsmick, leaving the interpreter as hostage. The Natives soon realised the visitors meant no harm and were interested only in justice. Klatsmick was taken to Victoria to stand trial for Banfield's murder.

When the trial judge heard conflicting testimony, he dismissed the case. Banfield's friend Captain Peter Francis refused to believe the drowning had been accidental, and so did his own investigation. He returned the following spring to Victoria with more details of Banfield's death, which he had obtained from other Natives. They told him the canoe had been intentionally upset, and when Banfield tried to get back in, Klatsmick had pushed him off with a paddle. A Native man who had accompanied him at the time also drowned. Francis also heard a different story: that several men had waited for Banfield and had stabbed him while he was strolling down his garden path. This attack was blamed on a chief who had been disappointed at the worth of a potlatch gift given to him at a wedding.

Another of Banfield's friends, Captain Tom Pamphlet, attempted to bring the accused to justice. He hired Klatsmick's nephew in the hope of hearing something incriminating. The weeks passed, but the nephew revealed nothing, and Captain Pamphlet became disenchanted with the plan. Then one Sunday, as his ship passed Cape Beale, Pamphlet told the nephew to go down in the hold and break the sprouts off the stock of potatoes. The man went reluctantly, all the while grumbling about having to work on a Sunday.[35]

Captain Pamphlet was not a small man; he weighed about 225 pounds and had a temper that could flare with provocation. He grabbed Klatsmick's nephew by the seat of his pants and threw him into the rolling waves of the Pacific. He said afterwards, "I was going to haul him back, but he struck right out for shore and the last I ever saw of him he was on the beach running around the point of Cape Beale." Meanwhile Klatsmick continued to boast that it was he who had killed Banfield.

Nothing further was ever done about Banfield's death. His estate and effects were left to his fellow countryman, William John Mumford. In December, 1862, Captain Stamp refused an application from Francis Bell to preempt Banfield's copper claim because he thought "the transaction would likely cause trouble with the Indians as it happened to be the residence of the chief."[36]

Stamp himself prospected on both Copper and Santa Maria islands between April and July, 1862.[37] These explorations drew attention to the mineral deposits at these locations. However, within a few months, Captain Stamp's relationship with the Anderson Company soured, and he left the sawmill. Employees presented him with a $250 gold watch as a mark of their esteem.[38] Stamp returned to the mainland and established the Hastings sawmill in Vancouver.

The Anderson Company placed Gilbert Malcolm Sproat in charge of the sawmill. 1862 was eventful; not only did he accept new responsibilities for the sawmill, he also got married on December 23 to Catherine Anne Wigham. The couple would have three children: daughter Agnes Mary, and sons Alexander and Gilbert Hector. Sproat had other interests than the sawmill; he had his own importing and insurance business in Victoria and he maintained an interest in public affairs. When Governor Douglas offered him a seat in the Legislative Council, he refused stating he wanted to stay out of local politics because he believed more could be accomplished by working behind the scenes.[39]

Ships continued to load lumber at Alberni, but they became fewer and fewer. The mill faced a serious shortage of timber because all the easily accessible trees close to the canal had been felled and the mechanisation did not exist to harvest those growing up the mountainsides. The mill had made little or no profit, and Sproat faced the difficult decision to close the operation. He complained that "during the last four years (1860-1864), without any return or advantage to the proprietors," he had "paid in cash more than $800,000 to traders and laborers in this place for supplies and wages, exclusive of supplies obtained from San Francisco."[40] He was convinced the mill could not make a success because the problems were just too great. The mill closed in January, 1864.

THE WAW-WIN

Sproat, a faithful scribe, recorded all the social activities and the proceedings at the mill. He also wrote *Scenes and Studies of Savage Life,* published in 1868. In this book he told of a great deer hunt, or *waw-win*, which was organised with the help of the local hunters in February, 1864, just after the mill closed. The Native word *waw* means to speak or shout. The deer hunt would be similar to a cliff drive, a strategy used by plains Natives to take large numbers of buffalo.[41] There are sites scattered over the prairies known as buffalo jumps.

Sproat judged there were about ninety men in the forest, half of them armed with guns. By shouting they planned to drive the deer towards the canal, where they would be hemmed in and killed. Canoes would be ready to drive back the deer attempting to escape. He described the location:

> There had been a heavy fall of snow, and the Indians were certain that many deer had come down from the higher mountains, and would be found on the side of a great, rugged, wooded hill, which rose steep from Alberni inlet. A swollen torrent, rising from a source inland, flowed across the back of this hill, and, at the southern extremity of the hill, this torrent fell into the Alberni inlet. The hill itself occupied about two miles of frontage on the inlet.[42]

The evening before the great hunt, the Native hunters danced and sang, and performed traditional ceremonies designed to bring good luck. Sproat and his fellow hunters Anderson, Ker, Connell, and Gaskell cleaned their rifles and went to bed early. At about 2:00 a.m. the hunters gathered on the hill and the base line, while Sproat and three others canoed their way down the canal to the site, a journey which took them two hours. The hunters beat the bushes and pushed through clumps of young trees, all the time shouting loudly while climbing over fallen trees and sinking deep into the snow. As the hunt progressed, hunters began to collect in groups of twos, threes and fours, indicating the line was getting shorter.

Few white men could keep up with the Native hunters while they manoeuvred the deer down the hillside. Those in canoes floated about in the canal waiting patiently for the deer to emerge. Shouting and yelling could be heard on every side. As soon as a large herd of deer congregated, the hunters began firing. A few deer tried to escape to the water but they were soon turned back. "The total number killed during this *waw-win* was fifty-three, that is to say, sixteen during the chase and thirty-seven on the point of land."[43]

After the hunt the men divided the deer, giving the man who owned the hunting ground the largest share. Sproat noted, "The Indians do not much relish deer meat." They seemed to value the skins more, "except for the chance they had of selling the venison to some of the ships at Alberni."[44]

A QUESTION OF LAND

While the Anderson mill lay empty, Sproat did not give up on Alberni as a settlement site. In a letter to the Colonial Secretary he noted the district now lay in the hands of either the government or the Anderson Company, and it was the wish of the Company to form a permanent settlement at Alberni "of the right class of farmers."[45] Sproat recognised the difficulty in inducing settlers to stay in the area because of the number of Native people living along the canal and Barkley Sound area. Acting on behalf of the Anderson Company, he wrote to the Colonial Secretary on May 23, 1867, expressing concern about the hostile and unfriendly attitude by the west-coast Natives towards the traders and others stationed there.

> I have several fishing stations on Barclay Sound and the north west Coast, and much valuable property at Alberni and we have reasons to feel apprehensive for their security in consequence of this spirit manifested by the Indians. I also fear that unless this spirit is checked in time our stations may be abandoned as the persons in charge of them feel apprehensive for their own safety. Recently many articles have been stolen from our fishing station at Village Island by the Indians and although many of these articles are still in their possession we have no means to recover them.
>
> Under these circumstances we are induced to beg that a ship of war may be sent to visit Barclay Sound and Alberni at as early a period as possible as we are convinced that the presence of such a vessel besides allaying the fears of people who have

interests there, would have a most beneficial effect on the Indians.[46]

The Anderson Company may have had qualms about their investment in Alberni and may have wondered how serious the Colonial Government was about settling the Albernis. These doubts were heightened when Sproat discovered the land at Alberni had been advertised for sale in the *Gazette*, a government publication. Sproat began to search for legal title to the land, but all he could find was a land office receipt for an amount paid on account. The first payment of four hundred pounds sterling had been made in October, 1860. He claimed the Anderson Company was entitled to fifteen thousand acres.[47] He wrote to the Colonial Secretary:

No officer connected with the Government has ever visited Alberni, and the just requirements of our business, the largest and probably the only industrial enterprise of the kind that ever will exist in the Island, are therefore liable to be misunderstood. Mr. Pemberton once passed Alberni in a canoe before the settlement existed, but the labour of 150 men for nearly five years has since been employed on the place. I believe I am correct in stating that the Government is without any knowledge of the locality, the position or requirements of our business, and may therefore at any time unwittingly do us an injustice.[48]

He asked that the land in Alberni not be sold until he had read the correspondence between Stamp and Governor James Douglas in 1859 and 1860, so that the title could be verified and the company's investment protected.

In August, 1866, HMS *Scout* visited Alberni and noted how distressing it was to see the once prosperous settlement lying derelict with gardens overgrown with weeds. Two years later it was announced the sawmill machinery had been sold to the Puget Mill Company. For another ten years the mill and buildings lay empty. On September 4, 1879, HMS *Rocket* brought the news to Esquimalt that the Anderson Sawmill buildings had been accidentally burned a few days earlier, by a spark from a Native campfire.[49]

The area was eventually surveyed in 1871[50] and again in 1881 and 1886. The Anderson Company continued to hold its land investment until the settlers arrived in the mideighties when a townsite was developed.

CHARLES TAYLOR

The Anderson Company had developed a farm on the banks of the Somass River to provide fresh meat and vegetables for the small sawmill community. A man named Charles Taylor, who had worked for the Anderson Company and who remained after the mill closed in 1864, rented the farm for a dollar a year. All the cattle and horses on the farm were left under his charge. An estimated one hundred and sixty head of cattle thrived with the run of the whole district.[51] But it was not the animals alone that made the farm profitable and enticed Taylor to remain in Alberni; it was the regular trade with the Native people who had grown fond of his potatoes and turnips. In addition to the two tribes in Alberni, several of the tribes from Barkley Sound traded with him for vegetables.

Taylor was a long way from home. He had left his son Charles Taylor Jr. back in Edinburgh, Scotland. Like many other immigrants to Canada, he had been lured by the promise of striking it rich in the gold rush, first in California, then in the Cariboo, in the British Columbia interior.[52] He made his way to the coast about the time the Anderson sawmill was being built.

After the closure of the mill, life on the farm continued uninterrupted, Taylor only occasionally seeing a white man. His life revolved around work on the farm and his closest neighbours, the Tseshaht and the Opetchesaht bands. He cultivated a friendship with a young Native woman, eventually fathering several children. Still he maintained written contact with his son back in Scotland. When the farm became too much for the elderly Taylor, the company hired Dan Clarke Sr. as manager. Clarke had worked for the Anderson Company but had left when the mill closed. He returned in 1871 with his new wife Theresa and her son Dan Jr.

The problem of land ownership arose again when Taylor made his first application for preemption, on October 9, 1871. He asked permission to change the frontage with more land on the riverfront and less depth.[53] A certificate of improvement was issued on November 16, 1872. When he preempted this land, there were three large Native houses to the east of his log house. To the south lay Lupsi-kupsi, where the paper mill is located today. This had been a former Native site vacated in 1861 when the Anderson Company took over. It was this site Banfield had purchased from the Opetchesaht. Taylor seeded seven acres with grass and had pigs running there from 1872 to 1880.

His ownership of the land was called into question with a lawsuit (*David Little v. Charles Taylor*). Little was a settler who did not stay long in Alberni. Taylor won the case, which was held before Chief Justice Matthew Begbie. Little appealed the decision, but Taylor won the appeal as well. Somehow Taylor had lost his 1872 Certificate of Improvement. However, on July 20, 1884 he made a declaration before Justice of the Peace and first Government Agent John C. Mollett, and seven months later he received a Crown Grant of one hundred acres listed as Section 11, for $160.

The establishment of Native reserves by Judge Peter O'Reilly in 1882 resulted in a portion of land being taken from Taylor to complete the reserve. This portion, seventeen chains, included all his improvements and became part of the Opetchesaht reserve. The Opetchesaht chief had earlier lodged a complaint against Taylor. Indian Agent Harry Guillod wrote:

> The chief, Ka-now-ish (O-petchis-aht) complained that a man named Charles Taylor was in occupation of part of his village, and asked to have him removed. This, on subsequent inspection, I found to be correct, and have since ascertained that the land, including the Indian houses, had been recorded by Taylor on the 16 November, 1872, and that a certificate of improvements had been issued to him on the 26th May, 1875. In a conversation with Mr. Taylor on the subject, he admitted to me that the Indian houses were on the land prior to the date of his record, but were not continuously occupied by them; this I can understand from the fact that all the Barclay Sound tribes are itinerant and move to places most frequented by seal and several kinds of fish that abound in these waters at different seasons of the year. It having been established beyond a doubt, to my mind, that this land was not open to preemption by Mr.

Taylor, but was in fact a part of the Indian village before its occupation by him, I had no hesitation in declaring it to be an Indian reserve, though I much regret that within it is included the house, garden and orchard of Mr. Taylor.[54]

Taylor never complained about the removal of his land. Although the First Nations had never surrendered their land rights, government opened British Columbia to settlers, reserving only small areas for Native people. Whereas settlers could claim 320 acres and buy an additional 320 acres, Native people received reserve lands according to their needs. In 1873 these were defined by the federal government as eighty acres per family of five. The provincial government thought this was too much, that only twenty acres should be allocated. Confusion reigned for decades.[55]

In May, 1884, Taylor gave permission for the Barkley Sound Fishing Company to use two chains of his land on the Somass River and two chains on Kitsuksis Creek for salmon fishing. The fishing company, with Mr. Sweat as manager and Frank McQuillan as agent, built a store known as Sayward's store.

Taylor became friends with another Cariboo miner, Peter Merrifield, who had settled on land to the north of Taylor's property. As the years took their toll, both men wrote letters home urging family members to join them in homesteading this new land. Merrifield wrote to Australia, inviting his nephew Peter Nicholas to join him, while Taylor wrote inviting his son Charles Jr. in Edinburgh. Charles Taylor Jr. arrived in 1885 and the Nicholas family arrived a few weeks later.[56]

Charles Taylor Jr. lived on the Anderson farm for over a year before moving out to McCoy Lake where he preempted a quarter section. He worked in his trade as an engineer on Captain Huff's boat on the canal. The family moved back into town after they built a new home on River Road, in Alberni.

There have been five generations named Charles Taylor, all descendants of the Alberni Valley's first resident. Taylor Arm at Sproat Lake is named for the pioneer, as is Taylor Road, named for the Taylor family.

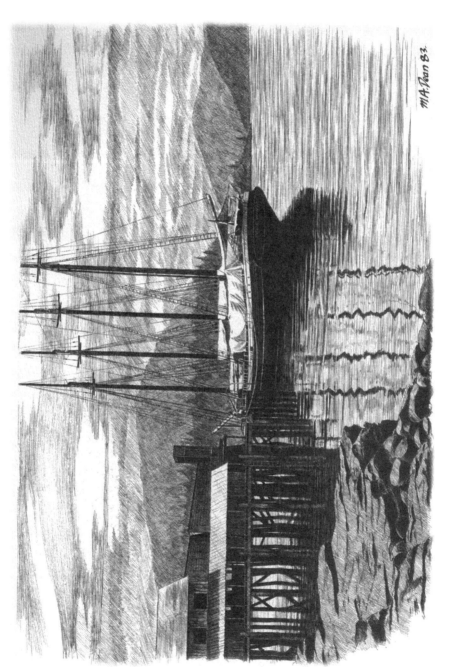

The Four Winds visited Port Alberni in June 1926

CHAPTER TWO

THE NEWCOMERS

The geographic triangle between Ucluelet, Bamfield, and Alberni remained free of settlers after the closure of the Anderson Sawmill, except for some traders who frequented the area in their small sailing vessels and made attempts to establish independent trading posts. One man who had particular success was Captain William Spring of Victoria, a trader with posts between Victoria and Quatsino. He had a store operated by a man named Georgeson at Pacheenant (Port Renfrew). Andrew Lang managed another at Copper Island (Tzartus) in the winter months and another at Dodger Cove in the summer; Peter Francis supervised the Ucluelet post and Captain Nels Moos operated one at Pachena River. Eventually there would be other traders who established posts at Ecoole, Clayoquot, Ahousat, Hesquiat, Nootka, and Kyuquot. A brisk trade in dog-fish oil had developed in connection with the sawmill industry. Traders bought the oil cheap and made a nice profit in resale, while providing the Natives with manufactured goods such as blankets, metal tools, and guns. They also purchased fish, which were sold at open market. In middens throughout the region are remnants of this active trading period, showing evidence of the rapid alteration and alienation that took place in Native life.[1]

When the Roman Catholic church decided to open a mission on the west coast, it looked to the traders for advice on location.

Captain Spring was particularly helpful, lending his sailing ship, the *Surprise*, for an exploratory visit. Captain Peter Francis, Banfield's old friend, skippered the ship. He made the journey in April, 1874, with the Bishop of Victoria, the Right Reverend C. J. Seghers, and the Reverend A. J. Brabant, a Flemish Oblate father, and Mr. John McDowell. The latter was on his way to fix the machinery at the lighthouse then being established at Cape Beale in Barkley Sound.[2]

Father Brabant kept a journal of this important voyage and encounter with the Native people. Unfortunately Captain Francis was drunk most of the time and must have given the two priests some anxious moments. They first called upon the people at Dodger Cove with introductions; however, when news of their arrival brought curious people from Keeshan (Execution Rock), the priests persuaded them to return the next morning, when they would be more prepared. The next morning, the priests said the first Roman Catholic mass in the house of storekeeper Andrew Lang. For the next few months, the two priests visited Ucluelet and other points along the coast.

 Another voyage in September, again with the inebriated Captain Francis, although the first mate managed to hide the liquor before the captain became too drunk, resulted in the *Surprise* running aground at the entrance to the Pachena River. Their plight was noticed by Captain Nels Moos who manoeuvered the ship to a safe anchor at the trading store. This was Father Brabant's introduction to life on the west coast.[3]

In 1875, Father Brabant established the mission at Hesquiat, about twenty miles south of Nootka Sound. He established another at Numukamis, near the mouth of the Sarita River; this one staffed by Father J. Nicolaye, his assistant. The priests also made regular visits to Alberni, where a small church was built on River Road at the time of settlement, in the 1880s. Other missions were opened at Kyuquot, Friendly Cove, Nuchatlitz and Dodger Cove. These missions have all but disappeared beneath a sea of salal and undergrowth. Until almost the turn of the century, Brabant's presence and missionary work dominated life on the west coast. The initial goal of the missionary may have been to save, or convert, what were perceived as lost souls. In most cases, he was received warmly. Father Brabant always seemed to have the best interests of Natives at heart. Other missionaries followed but few would have the remarkable impact of this special man.

THE COX FAMILY AT CAPE BEALE

The number of vessels wrecked along the west coast prompted government in 1873 to approve construction of the Cape Beale lighthouse on the rocky island point at the entrance to Barkley Sound. The rugged coastline was particularly dangerous for sailing ships and had earned the nickname "Graveyard of the Pacific."

There are two contenders for "who named the point." Captain Barkley reportedly named it in 1787 for John Beale, the purser on the trading ship *Imperial Eagle*. Natives killed Beale and his crew in a small river near Destruction Island the same year; an island also named for this tragic event.[4] Captain John Meares also takes credit, reporting in his log of the vessels *Felice* and *Iphigenia*, that "this headland obtained from us the name of Cape Beale."[5] He described Beale as a merchant of Canton and the agent of the expedition. Who actually named the strategic point is uncertain but it is known the two men, Barkley and Meares, held little regard for the other.

The lighthouse is situated on a rocky headland about seventy feet high. There is a fringe of rocky reefs close by. A narrow neck of water cuts off about eight acres of the headland, so that at high tide people could take a shortcut through to Keeha Bay during the summer months. Towards Pachena Point, about eight miles south, is a most formidable and dangerous coastline. The forest marches right down to the shore; hemlock and spruce trees are short and stunted. The stiff, stark and scraggly branches have been combed inland by the strong prevailing westerly winds. The trees gradually become straighter and taller farther inland. The salal is very short along the fringe of rock on the shoreline, but a few yards inland it becomes taller and thicker, making it impossible to hike on foot. Even animals find it difficult to force their way through this terrible jungle of salal stretching almost the length of Vancouver Island.[6]

When Thomas George Paterson was lightkeeper at Cape Beale (1895-1907), a bull went missing. They searched for him for five days before finding the animal standing in the salal not far back from the lighthouse. Douglas McKenzie became accustomed to salal when on survey work with Harry Brown, of Alberni. He said it grew fifteen feet high and was so thick you could lie down in it and sleep just like being in a bed.[7]

Construction of the lighthouse and related buildings was completed by 1874, and a trail was made from the head of Bamfield Inlet, three miles away, making the site accessible by land. Mr. R. Westmoreland of Nanaimo, and his assistant, Thomas Woods of Victoria, were the first to operate the lighthouse.[8] Emanuel J. Cox and his wife and family followed them.

This seemed like an unlikely place for a young Irish immigrant family to put down roots, but it was to this remote location that the Cox family, originally from Curragh, County Cork, came to take over duties at the lighthouse. Like many of their fellow countrymen, they had been lured by the California gold rush and had left home, seeking a new life in the Americas.

Cox, with his wife, the former Mary Frances Shortt, sailed to New York then travelled to Chicago by train, and by wagon to Marysville, California, where Emanuel tried his hand unsuccessfully at placer mining. This was not the lifestyle of Mary's childhood. Until her arrival in America, she had led a privileged life as a young girl pampered by her parents and "had never washed a dish."[9] She refused the titled suitor chosen by her father, deciding instead to marry Emanuel. Good fortune did not accompany the young couple; poor health and the accidental death of their first son saddened them. On the advice of a fellow countryman, they decided to come to Vancouver Island.

They boarded the paddle-wheel steamer *Prince Albert* sailing from San Francisco and arrived in Esquimalt in March 1874. Gus and his sister Frances attended Craigflower school, the first public school in British Columbia. His other sisters, Pattie and Annie, and brother Ruxton, were still under school age when in the winter of 1877-1878 their father was transferred to Cape Beale lighthouse. In his journal, Charles Augustus (Gus) Cox tells how they arrived at Cape Beale by a rather circuitous route to the remote lighthouse:

I was then 7 years of age. We lived in Victoria for a short time on View St. just above where the YMCA building is today and were well outside the main part of the city as it was then. From there we moved to the Jackson Farm at Cedar Hill, stayed there a short time then moved to the Burrows Farm at Mount Tolmie, then moved to Burnside Road near Colquitz. I can remember the late Robt. Porter peddling meat in a covered waggon [*sic*] that was before they started the shop in Victoria.

My father then secured the position as keeper of the light-house at Berns Island in Victoria Harbour in the early part of 1876. My sister Mrs. R. M. Morrison (Frances) and myself used to cross in a boat from the light-house to where Victoria West is today, then through a trail to the Craigflower school, a distance of about 5 miles. In the winter of 1877 and 78 my father was transferred as keeper of the Cape Beale light-house and left for there on the paddle-wheeled tug *Alexander*, a large two-funnelled tug, built and owned by the Morrison Bros. of New Westminster.[10]

The family landed at Sarita Bay on March 1 and secured three large canoes "with about eight Indians in each" to take them to Copper Island (Tzartus Island), to Spring's store operated by Andrew Lang. Nailed above the door of the store was the name board of the schooner *Orpheus* which had collided with the SS *Pacific* and sunk off Cape Flattery in the winter of 1876. Only a couple of people had survived this wreck.

After about two weeks, Natives transported the Cox family to Dodger Cove on Diana Island, where they waited another two weeks for the weather to clear, allowing a safe landing at Cape Beale on February 22, 1878. The landing made quite an impression on the Cox children. Pattie recalled it was Whisky Charlie who carried her ashore. It had taken two men to carry Emanuel, who weighed more than two hundred pounds. Emanuel was described as "a tall, rugged man with a beard, and a full, powerful voice that seemed to have almost the volume of a fog horn, and could not fail to attract attention."[11] Despite the surf breaking around them, they managed to land without getting wet.

Without communication to the outside world, the isolation felt by the family can only be imagined. Yet the children seemed to have thrived and they lived to tell wonderful stories about their lives at the lighthouse. Natives were the only human contacts. They also provided transportation in beautifully carved canoes which they were expert in handling. If the Cox family had to communicate with Victoria, a messenger had to travel by canoe, a journey which took from two to three days of hard paddling, and another three to return.

To signal for help, the Cox family would fly a Union Jack from the lighthouse. An elderly Native named John Mack would respond. For this, and for being available at any other time should his services be required, the government paid him five dollars a month. Mack often couriered messages from the Cox family to the marine agent in Victoria. The trip would take him two days; then he would return with the lighthouse tender *Sir James Douglas*. John Mack became a faithful friend of the Cox family and was particularly helpful when Emanuel suffered a heart attack and died several years later. In a further account of his life at Cape Beale, Cox wrote:

When we first came to the West Coast, the Indians were more numerous than they are today and I believe bigger and healthier people. It was very seldom that you ever saw them with anything other than a shirt and a blanket pinned over the shoulder. The women usually wore a loose calico shirt affair and a blanket. When it was raining they wore a cedar hat. The men usually wore a colored handkerchief around the head, or hemlock or cedar boughs made into a kind of wreath.

It was while at Cape Beale, as youngsters, we learned to speak the Indian language (*ta-tak-sup-ee*). The Indians used to go inside the light-house Island instead of going around outside, and we used to see them on the beach and ask them the names of different things, and so learned the language and the proper pronunciation. I can truthfully say that the late Father Brabant, who was missionary at Hesquiat, going there in 1874 and myself, are the only two white men who ever had the proper pronunciation. I have often spoken to blind Indians and they thought I was one of their own people and asked me what tribe I belonged to.[12]

Mrs. Cox, whose penmanship was admired, wrote the lighthouse logbook daily. She recorded weather conditions, observations of vessels inbound or outbound, landings of supplies, shipwrecks, accidents, arrivals of visitors, and various other incidentals. Visitors to the lighthouse were few; after eight years, Mrs. Sareault of Alberni was the first white woman to visit the family.

The Cox family and the Natives maintained a good relationship; only once did a crack emerge in their friendship. This happened when Emanuel became outraged when a man appeared on their doorstep clad only in a scanty shirt. He yelled at the visitor, "Hey there, you savage, be gone! Don't let my girls ever see you around here again in your shirt-tails." There were other utterances, all unfit to be repeated. The saving grace was Emanuel's good Irish sense of humour. As the man left, he looked back and there in the doorway stood Mary Frances with a smile on her face. He and other Natives soon learned that if they visited the lighthouse it was "pants on or keep out."[13]

Frances remembered one occasion during foggy weather, when she and her father were outside the lighthouse and noticed a ship close to the reef. The fog closed in and nothing more was seen of the ship. Three weeks later, when Frances was in the kitchen making a pot of tea, she thought she saw someone pass the kitchen window heading towards the front door; then again she thought she may have been mistaken. Soon a knock came to the front door and Emanuel said to see who was there, remarking it had to be a gentleman as he knew enough to go to the front door. When Frances opened the door, there stood three men who turned out to be the survivors of the ship *Glen Fruin*, which had come to grief on Danger Rock (Hornby Rock) at the entrance to Barkley Sound. The crew had gone ashore on Village Island (Effingham) across the sound where they were stranded for several days before making it to the lighthouse.[14] Captain Spring took the men to Victoria in his sealing schooner *Favourite*.

Pattie loved and respected her mother, especially for the care she gave her children. She recalled, "We children must have been a worry to her in a wild place like that. We didn't know what fear was and we used to try to take off on home-made wings. Geese could fly—why couldn't we?"[15]

The death of Pattie's father was particularly difficult. He died of a heart attack in 1885. Her mother had been tending the light and it was Pattie who discovered he had gone. The light was down, and they could not get any messages out. She remembered running up a distress signal when she saw a passing vessel, but it was either unseen or misunderstood, for the ship kept on going. She hoisted the flag and over came John Mack. Mrs. Cox gave him a letter to take to family members in Alberni. Accompanied by his father Nespus, Mack paddled to Alberni to notify Gus and his two older sisters.[16] It took some time before the family arrived, though they came as quickly as possible.[17] In the meantime, the two women grieved their loss alone. The body was transported by the *Quasar* to Alberni for burial. Mack refused to take any money for the canoe trip and was offended at being offered money for what he considered his last act for his old friend.

Mrs. Cox wanted to stay on as lightkeeper, but the position was then considered a man's job, and she was not allowed to continue. She and Pattie moved to Alberni to live with her daughter Frances (Mrs. R. M. Morrison), who then worked at the B.C. Paper Manufacturing Company mill. Pattie (Mrs. P. A. Haslam) became the government telegraph agent and operator at Alberni, serving for forty-five years. For her years of service she was awarded the King George V Diamond Jubilee medal. Emanuel's property at Bamfield was sold; it later became the location of the Bamfield Cable Station. The family had also owned Cox Lake, located a few miles south of Port Alberni on the Bamfield road. This too was sold.

Port Alberni sawmill owner George Bird remembered Mrs. Cox as an elderly woman. "Her many years residence at the lighthouse had made her quite self reliant and she was able to put her hand to almost any task. When quite advanced in years she might often be seen journeying to town on her tricycle, the only one I have seen in the district."[18] Daughter Annie married J. B. McKay, who worked on building the telephone line and life-saving trail from Victoria to Cape Beale in 1890. They became the pioneers of the Village of Bamfield. McKay built their home, named Pioneer House, and operated the first store in the village. The youngest child, Ruxton, became a telegraph agent at Hazelton.

M. V. Lady Rose

THE FIRST POLICEMAN

Son Gus Cox moved to Alberni in 1892 where he became a special constable with the B.C. Provincial Police, a position he held until 1904 when he was appointed the chief constable for the West Coast District, the first policeman on the west coast. He married Sarah L. Kirkpatrick in 1890, in Alberni, a union that produced four children; Grace, Edward, Roy, and Dora.

Gus became interested in police work when in March, 1884, George Klack-ish-kays, a step-brother of Clutesi of the Tseshaht tribe, was murdered. Klack-ish-kays had been carving a canoe on the northern end of Copper Island (Tzartus), about a mile inland, when he met his untimely death. He landed opposite Ecoole at the place known to the Natives as Ahmuckley and walked up a trail to the tree being used to make the canoe. From there, another trail led to the eastern side of the island to a place called Nu-cha-quis, opposite the Ohiaht village of Numukamis. The night of his murder there had been a light fall of snow. Three men had evidently landed at Nu-cha-quis, gone up the trail and beaten the canoe carver to death with a stone hammer. Stone hammers were used in making canoes.

Indian Agent Harry Guillod, who then resided in Ucluelet, invited Gus to join him in investigating the murder. Accompanied by two Native men, they reached Ecoole the first night. The next day they went to the scene and found the body and the partly finished canoe. The crime scene showed Klack-ish-kays had put up a good fight. Because of the snow, they could see that the trail to Nu-cha-quis had been carefully disguised to make it difficult to determine how many men had participated. The murder was never solved, although Gus maintained he knew of three men who might have been connected. Unfortunately he had no proof.

Klack-ish-kays had married an Ohiaht woman and often lived with her people at Clutus, an Ohiaht village at the western entrance to Pachena Bay. Guillod and Gus could only surmise the reason for the murder. When Klack-ish-kays' son was playing on the beach with other boys, the son of one of the suspects had a hemorrhage and died within two days. Superstition combined with gossip spread throughout the village that Klack-ish-kays' son was responsible for the other child's death, or that Klack-ish-kays himself had *min-nook-shitlle* him, which meant he had thrown something into the boy's body without him feeling it, and this had proved fatal.[19]

The case was never investigated further but it left Gus with a taste for police life. At times he did other special police work until he was permanently appointed chief constable in 1904. For many years he policed the region from the small police station on Johnston Road in Alberni.

In 1913, Gus was appointed Indian Agent for the region, a position he held until 1923. His office in Alberni held a prominent place in the community, for it was here Natives brought their concerns or made day-to-day decisions regarding life on the reserve. Alberni resident Trevor Goodall recalled the office and its contents:

> He (Cox) could talk the Native language very well and was favoured by the Indians. His house was situated in one corner of the lot, while the office occupied the other. The office was a large room with counters, shelves and a large bench for the Indians to rest on. Almost anytime you could see the old Indians heading for the office. It was very much like a museum, since everywhere weavings, carvings and totem poles filled the room. In the yard stood two totem poles, approximately twenty-four feet high, mounted on a cement stand. The Post Office was next door to the office and a usual sight would be to see his old-time friends call on him for a friendly visit. They always came out feeling good. Once a month, Mr. Cox would go up the west coast on the *Maquinna*, leaving his daughters to care for the office.[20]

In May, 1914, Cox accompanied the Royal Commission on Indian Affairs for British Columbia in its tour throughout the region investigating claims and inspecting reserves within the West Coast Agency. The Commission chartered the coastal steamer *Tees* and completed the tour in mid June.[21]

The fact that no Natives were appointed or consulted by what has become known as the McKenna-McBride Commission irritated many Natives. The Commission cut land from the Ohiaht and the Tseshaht bands. Six hundred and forty acres were cut from the Numukamis Reserve No. 1 of the Ohiaht because it was heavily forested and, as it was Department of Indian Affairs policy not to allow Natives to log their reserves, the Natives could not make proper use of the land. This same reasoning was used in cutting 242 acres from the Tseshaht Tsahaheh No. 1 reserve.[22] The Commission could have added additional reserves had it so wished; in fact there were fifty-two applications, of which only fourteen were granted and those on land the Commission considered worthless.[23] Cox played an important role in the deliberations because of his knowledge of the region and its people. The summary report noted:

> Visitations of the principal Reserves of the West Coast Agency and meetings with the Indians thereof occupied the Commission from the 6th to 23rd May, 1914, Mr. Agent Cox being examined under oath on the 19th and 23rd May. 14th August and 24th October, 1914, and on the 13th September, 1915, as to the Reserves of his Agency and conditions obtaining with respect thereto.

The summary noted that the reasons for the reserve locations were principally related to the fishing industry and Native food supply.

> The larger Reserves of the Agency present few evidences of cultivation, and the areas previously allotted in the cases of the Tsahaheh Reserve No. 1 of the Seshart Tribe and Numukamis Reserve No. 1 of the Ohiaht Tribe, being regarded by the Commission as in excess of the reasonable requirements of the Indians, their Reserves were reduced by the cutting off of 240 acres in the one instance and 600 acres in the other, 840 acres in total of Agency reductions.[24]

Throughout his life, Gus' political and religious leanings remained consistent; he was a life-long Presbyterian and a Conservative. He died in January 1938.

EDWARD J. COX

Gus' son Edward (Ed) J. also played an important role in the history of the Alberni area. Ed was born in 1896 in a little house on Margaret Street and attended the "School on the Hill" where John Howitt taught and served as principal. As a young boy, Ed's favourite pastime was watching the activities around Burke's barn, where he witnessed the comings and goings of heavy teams and wagons, livery rigs, and high-stepping horses. He absorbed Burke's love for good horses, taking his first job in the livery barn, where he washed buggies and democrats, and cleaned harness. Most thrilling were the times he was trusted to take the reins for trips over the rough roads of the district.

Ed became a member of Alberni's first fire department and, with other young men, pulled the hose reel and practised coupling and uncoupling. In 1914, he began working on the *Tees* under Captain Ed Gillam, the area's beloved mariner. The First World War was in full progress when, a year later, he joined the Canadian Army in Victoria, linking up with the trench mortar battery group for overseas service in Belgium. He was with the army at the close of the war in Germany and received the Military Medal for his service in France.

After the war, he again joined the coastal steamship service, this time as a crew member aboard the *Princess Maquinna* on her west-coast run. By 1923, he had joined the Dollar Company, an around-the-world service, as a mate aboard the *Esther Dollar*. The ship had a narrow escape in 1926 when visiting Yokohama. It had just pulled away from the dock when the great earthquake hit the city.[25]

About 1931, Ed settled in Alberni, taking the position as Customs Officer. He married school teacher Muriel Elizabeth Dixon and they had three sons, Edward (Ted) Charles, Barry Ellis, and Laurence Grant.[26] Mrs. Cox taught in the Alberni Residential School and in various other elementary schools in the Alberni Valley. She was the first principal at C. T. Hilton school.

During the Second World War, Ed commanded the twenty-five-man Alberni troop of the Pacific Coast Militia Rangers.[27] He became alderman with Alberni City Council in 1948 and served four terms. He started documenting the history of the Albernis for a radio show called "Pioneer Parade" which he hosted with Meg Trebett on radio station CJAV in Port Alberni. The scripts of the old radio broadcast, now in the archives in Port Alberni, shed light into the early development of the city. Son Ted became a professor of biology at Princeton University; Larry became an instructor at the Pacific Vocational Institute.

A small farming settlement grew in Alberni, as settlers lured by cheap agricultural land arrived to make their homes. The Anderson Company seized the opportunity and developed a townsite and sold lots. The waterfront at the junction of the Alberni Canal and the Somass River became a dropping-off point for those arriving by canoe. Captain George Albert Huff built a wharf and store to service the pioneer families. Other stores, schools, hotels, and businesses soon followed. In 1891, there were about sixty-five families living in the Alberni Valley. This same year work began on building British Columbia's first paper mill on the banks of the Somass River, a venture that lasted only four years.

In Ucluelet, in 1884, William and James Sutton operated a shingle and sawmill and opened a store. The Suttons bought timber rights as far north as Nootka Island. In the latter part of the century, settlers began moving into the Ucluelet area. Not unlike the Albernis, it was the lure of agricultural land along the Ucluelet Inlet, which drew them to the area. By 1899, there were fifteen settlers, some with families.

Bamfield settlers did not arrive until the turn of the century, but the village did garner support from traders and from fishing and shipping interests. In the early 1890s a telegraph line and rough life-saving trail were constructed from Port Renfrew to Cape Beale lighthouse, with cabins equipped with telegraphs and emergency supplies located every few miles.

The changes in the canal and sound areas were particularly disruptive within the Native communities. Traditional seasonal migration changed as bands began to remain year-round in their villages. Many left to work on Aleutian-bound sealing schooners, or in the fish canneries being established near Victoria and in the lower mainland. With their new-found wealth earned in sealing and fishing, they began building European-style homes. However,

The S.S. Tees approaching Waterhouse Wharf in 1909

without proper medical care, diseases such as smallpox considerably reduced their numbers.

HARRY GUILLOD

In 1881, the first Indian Agents for British Columbia were appointed. Harry Guillod became the choice for the West Coast Agency. In his 1882 report from Alberni he noted the Natives were "glad to see me, being no stranger to them."[28] Guillod's experience in a variety of jobs gave him an advantage over other possible candidates for the job, as he was familiar with the area and the Natives. Guillod had been a lay reader for the Anglican Church and the Reverend Jules Willemar, who tried unsuccessfully to establish a mission in Alberni during and after the Anderson settlement. The church abandoned the mission in 1871.

Guillod was born with a sense of adventure that took him from the life of aristocracy in London, England, to life on the west coast. His family tree can be traced back to a Gretna Green marriage in 1771 between Guerard Daniel Guillod of Switzerland and Jane Richardson of Durham, England.[29] Named Henry at birth on August 20, 1838, he was one of ten children born to Lord and Lady Guillod. He served an apprenticeship as a chemist before leaving for British Columbia. In May, 1862, he and his seventeen-year-old brother George, with their two sisters, sailed from Southampton to San Francisco, arriving in Esquimalt on the steamer *Oregon* on July 3, 1862.[30] One sister married Reginald Heber Pidcock in Victoria; another married Ashdown Green, who later became a Member of Parliament.

Disembarking with them was Philip Thomas Johnston, who travelled with the brothers to the gold rush in the Cariboo. Later Johnston established a horticultural business in Victoria. With a horse named "Old Moke," and some mining and camping equipment, the trio set off on the Harrison-Lillooet route to the gold mines. Guillod faithfully kept notes and sketched along the journey, recording delightful vignettes of his encounters. His brother George became ill and had to return to Victoria, leaving his partners to work the claim. Six months later, having spent all his money without getting a grain of gold, Guillod marked it up to experience and returned to Victoria. During the winter he worked at stone-breaking, then returned the next year to the Cariboo. This must have been a more profitable venture, because in 1863 he purchased a one-third interest with partners Adam Elliott and J. A. Bradshaw in a sawmill at Chemainus and preempted land known as Graham Prairie, a mile west of the mill. The sawmill was sold in 1864 to Thomas George Askew.[31]

In 1866 Guillod was appointed catechist of the Anglican Church under Bishop George Hill and was later chosen by the Bishop to accompany the Reverend Jules Willemar, a Roman Catholic priest, who was to establish a mission among the Alberni Natives. The two visited Alberni frequently, journeying from Nanaimo by canoe to Qualicum, then crossing the mountain via the Horne Lake Trail to Alberni. The two men complained they saw too little of the Natives to accomplish their goals. They were transferred from the Alberni mission to Comox in 1871. Guillod's early training as a chemist became a great asset as he helped the early settlers there by giving them medical advice. In 1877, the Reverend Willemar built St. Andrew's Church at Sandwick, and it was in this little church that Guillod married Mrs. Willemar's sister Kate in 1885. The newlyweds then moved to Ucluelet, where a house had been built for them.

In one of his first reports from Ucluelet as Indian Agent, Guillod's principal concerns were liquor and the location of the West Coast Agency office.

As far as I can judge from personal enquiry there has been no quantity of liquor brought to the west coast this year. A few bottles of gin have come by returning canoes from Victoria from time to time to Barclay Sound, Clayoquot and Pacheena. The Nitinats who were formerly the most drunken tribe on the coast told me on my visit that "some time back they went to Dr. Powell for advice and he appointed policemen amongst them, who have since watched that no liquor was brought into the camps from Victoria, but that some still came to Pacheena." The Pacheena chief acknowledged this, but promised that it should be stopped.

In conclusion, I may state that I have been well received by the Indians everywhere, and hope to spend a longer time with each tribe the ensuing year. With regard to the establishment of the Agency, I think somewhere at the mouth of Barclay Sound will be more central than Alberni, Uthulhlet (other wist Euclulet) is convenient for Nitinat, Clayoquot Sound and Barclay Sound, and a general calling place for all the schooners.[32]

Guillod's government reports of the day provided much information on the lives of the west-coast Natives. He spent his days visiting the sick, recording statistics, and reporting on economic conditions while observing living habits, traditions, and ceremonies. In many ways, he continued the work initiated by Banfield twenty years earlier. With his background in medicine, he paid particular attention to the health of the Native population.

The death rate for the past year is unusually high. In a heavy gale of wind during the sealing season 36 men were drowned at sea. Whooping-cough and measles carried off over twenty adults and fifty children at Kyakaht while whooping-cough was prevalent in all the tribes and proved fatal to many young children, especially to those whose parents called in the Indian doctor. I have been speaking everywhere against the Indian doctors and advising the Indians to take proper care of their children in case of sickness, but there is a great want of simple medical attendance in most of the tribes, as my Agency is so scattered that I cannot look after them properly in this respect.

    The actions of the provincial government appear at present to be very short sighted. I have already reported to you one case where a portion of an Indian reserve has been sold by them to a white man, and their present actions seem to indicate a total disregard to Indian rights, which must sooner or later bring trouble on the province. This is much to be regretted when we remember that the Indian population of B.C. is so much greater than that of the other provinces and that their labor might by judicious management, be made to take the place of the Chinese, the employment of whom is at present being so much cried down.[33]

Guillod's territory covered a vast area of the west coast and required a great deal of travel. For seven or eight weeks each summer he hired two experienced Natives with their large canoe to accompany him on the trip. Loaded down with supplies, he travelled from Port Renfrew to Quatsino Sound, visiting all the settlements along the coast. He took a census and recorded and investigated every incident and complaint. With a ready supply of drugs provided by the government, he ably prescribed medicine for simple disorders or injuries. In one report he states he vaccinated two hundred children and adults during a smallpox epidemic.[34]

One of Guillod's jobs was to allocate Department of Indian Affairs rations to hungry Natives. He had a reputation for giving, and sometimes canny Natives took advantage of his kindness. In April, 1887, one of the worst gales blew on the west coast. A number of Natives in the Clayoquot area of Kelsemaths were drowned at sea, leaving widows and orphans. Once a month, the storekeeper at Clayoquot, Frederick Christian Thornberg, divided out provisions for them and for the very old men. Thornberg charged the same price as the Department of Indian Affairs. The widows complained about the amount of flour, sugar, and tea they received which lasted only one week, leaving them with nothing for the remaining three weeks. Thornberg discovered why: as soon as they received their rations, other Natives from Ahousat or Clayoquot would go there and feast and all would be gone in a few days. He told the women they had to stop giving away the rations. When this did no good, he ordered them to come to the store three times a month, or every ten days, and he would give them less. They continued to complain and went to Guillod, who gave them more rations from the Ucluelet store. The Natives claimed they were given a better deal on their rations at Ucluelet. Guillod wrote to Thornberg on May 4, 1888, expressing sorrow that he had been bothered by the Kelsemaths.

> They come for the first of March and I said I would give them
> the same as you did while they were here and they asked for:
> Wa-nuch & 5 children, 1 sack flour & 75 cents sugar:
> Ohenspecasks & 4 children, 1 sack flour: Atuth & 2 children,
> pants 75 cents and sugar 50 cents: Klak-koilts, 1 sack flour.
> There was some others and all came back on the 13th and said
> you gave them every 10 days. Most of them got the same on the
> 13th and on the 24th of March.

Peter's wife, I know, took advantage of me as I found out after that two of her children was not here, but the last time she came, she said she would not ask for anymore as she was going to Ahousat. Then I gave Aquis-tahnks flour twice, she begged saying she had nothing to eat and an old man, I gave something at once. I am sorry I made trouble for you but I was busy and having my wife laid up, so I gave them pretty much what they asked for. I gave Atuth a shawl, but surely she does not expect that all the time. Several of the boys had pants. The whole bill came to about $40.00. I have made it out here, so will not trouble you to put it in A. Frank's account. I hope to see you in a month from now, when I shall be coming down the coast. You owe me $1.00 for the letter. I had to pay $2.00 to take it to Ekoll, but as I sent a letter of my own, I charged you half. I remain yours truly, Harry Guillod.[35]

Thornberg claimed this letter proved how the Natives would lie and make trouble.

During his tenure, the issue of land ownership arose on more than one occasion. No one was happy with the way Native reserves had been allocated. Indian Reserve Commissioner Peter O'Reilly took office in 1880 and began reducing some of the reserves. In 1882 he visited the west coast, calling on the Ohiaht, Toquahts, Ucluelets, Uchucklesahts, Tseshahts and Opetchesahts. Much of the land that had been set aside for reserves O'Reilly found of little value. Wherever he went, he left behind dissatisfied Natives.[36] These land allocations did nothing to satisfy the chiefs who could see the ramifications and the restrictive nature of the action. Guillod reported these issues to the Indian Reserve Commissioner Peter O'Reilly.

In the course of a long conversation with the chief, Hi-you-pa-nool, (Sesharts) and some of the leading men, in which I fully explained the object of my mission, the chief laid claim to fishing stations, extending at intervals from the entrance to Barclay Sound to the first rapids on the Somass River, at the head of Alberni Canal, a distance of 40 miles. He also stated that he wanted for his people a portion of the land owned by the Alberni Mill Company, and also the pre-emption claim, houses, and buildings belonging to Mr. George Clarke.[37]

George Clarke was the son of Dan Clarke, one of the early settlers in Alberni. The question of land on the Native reserves remained in limbo until the McKenna-McBride Commission of 1914 finalised official boundaries.

Kate Guillod was the only white women in Ucluelet. She travelled to Victoria to transact business, to visit the doctor or await the birth of a child, or to maintain a home for her children so they could attend the upper grades in school. She had three daughters: Beatrice Josephine, Kate, and Edna. Mail arrived by canoe once a month from Alberni. Any shopping expeditions to Victoria were real events—travelling to and from Victoria was no simple weekend jaunt, it was a two-day journey. "We didn't have to follow fashion's dictates. I bought few clothes and there was no such thing as keeping up with the neighbours, for there weren't any, except Indians. The Natives were a friendly lot."[38]

The Department of Indian Affairs granted special permission in 1889 to transfer the headquarters of the West Coast Agency to Alberni to enable the Guillod children to attend school there. The family lived first on the Anderson farm, then later bought one acre of land from Dan Clarke on River Road. Guillod built a small house which also served as the Indian Agent's office. His house became an attraction of sorts as it was not uncommon to see several Native women, barefoot, with shawls over their heads, waiting outside the house to see him. Among Guillod's fine collection of Native art was a beautifully crafted rope of human hair, made for whaling. The rope was extremely strong, and estimated to be three-quarters of an inch in diameter and about a hundred feet long.[39]

Guillod's musical talent was greatly appreciated in the community when he played for social events. He also trained the All Saints Church choir and occasionally played the organ when schoolteacher John Howitt was absent. He retired as Indian Agent in 1903 and died from a stroke three years later. Guillod was loved and respected by all. Many Natives joined their white neighbours at his funeral to pay their respects. Kate moved to Victoria where she became quite the dowager and continued to maintain an interest in family affairs. No family member visited the city without calling on Kate. She died in 1949 at age eighty-eight.

THE WARING MYSTERY

One of the most unusual and colourful mysteries of the west coast occurred with the wreck of the *Woodside* in 1888. The ship was returning to Alberni when a violent storm erupted. The heavy sea caused the rudder to break loose, leaving the steamer helpless as it approached Barkley Sound. When it seemed the ship was in danger of sinking, the Captain gave the order to abandon ship. The ship carried a general cargo of supplies, insured for two thousand dollars, for Henry Saunders of the Alberni Trading Company store. Aboard were crew of six: Captain Clunas, Donald Todd, William Flannery, William Knox, Joe Merritt and a Chinese cook, plus three passengers, Mrs. Mary Ann Waring, her six-month old son Albert, and a seven-year-old son. The three had been on an extended shopping trip to Victoria, which lasted several weeks. What happened next forever changed the lives of the family.

Mary Ann had been only seventeen years old in 1860 when she left Chelsea, England to travel to India, where she would join her future husband who had enlisted in the British Army. They were married on her arrival in Bengal, an historic region in the northeastern part of India. A daughter was born in Lucknow. On their return voyage to England aboard the warship HMS *Ganges*, a son was born. As the couple travelled around the world, they had four more sons, one aboard the troopship HMS *Tamar* during a storm in the English Channel; another in Dublin, one in Bermuda, and yet another in Gibraltar.

After Major Waring retired from the British Army, he brought his international family to Alberni to live. Records note the family came from Valleyfield, Quebec in 1887. Another son, Albert, was born in Beaver Creek on August 26, 1887. The first Beaver Creek School register shows four Waring children: Fred, Robert, Harry and Septimus, the last child so named because he was the seventh boy born. It was in March, 1888, when Mrs. Waring took her fateful journey with her two children aboard the *Woodside*.

At the time of the incident, the ship was only ten years old. The steamboat had been launched at Sooke on the forty-first anniversary of the coronation of Queen Victoria in June, 1878. She had been built by Muir Bros. and named after the Woodside Farmhouse, a city landmark they owned. Samuel Sea of Victoria drafted the vessel and built her with the best of materials and workmanship. Soon the *Woodside* began her life travelling between Victoria and Alberni.

The *Colonist* reported that the crew of the steamer arrived by canoe one Saturday night from Sooke with news of the loss of the vessel. All had gone well until about four o'clock in the afternoon, when, during a heavy sea and roaring wind, the rudder broke loose from the pintle and the steamer lay helpless about five miles from the Nitinat River. The vessel, being at the mercy of the waves, took on board a large quantity of water, and the captain decided to abandon her.

All hands were placed in the steamer's boat, and were landed safely on shore about three miles from Pachena, where they found some Natives living in a cabin. The Indians did all they could to make the party comfortable, giving up their beds for the night to Mrs. Waring and her children. During the night the steamer drifted ashore and became a total wreck. The party embarked in a canoe the next morning and were brought to Victoria by the chief of the Nitinats.

This version of the incident is supported by an account given by the Reverend Alex Dunn who served the Presbyterian ministry in Alberni during the years 1886 to 1889. Dunn wrote: "Tidings of the wreck of the *Woodside* have fallen upon the inhabitants of Alberni with crushing weight, for there is scarcely an individual, intending to remain on his place during the summer months but has sustained loss to a greater or less extent."[40] There had been an ongoing battle with Victoria to service Alberni with a "seaworthy boat" that had a regular schedule. Petitions had been signed and letters written, but to no avail. The loss of the *Woodside* heightened public awareness of the struggle. Dunn continued:

> The most painful case is that of the Waring family. The mother, with a babe and boy of 7 years, left here in December, and expected to be able to return in January with provisions for the family. She had been waiting in Victoria for a steamer ever since. Having become very impatient, remembering how her husband and four boys at home must be suffering, this woman actually thought of hiring a canoe and trying to reach home in that day.

When, however, Mrs. Waring heard that the *Woodside* was advertised to sail for Alberni on the 10th, although she knew that the *Woodside* was unsafe, and though she was dissuaded by her friends in Victoria, and even by the Captain of the steamer, from going on board, yet in a state of desperation she ordered her goods, to the value of upwards of $100.00, to be put on board, and she herself resolved to run all risks rather than remain longer in anxiety and misery in Victoria.

Now, think of this woman, with her babe and little boy, being obliged, along with the crew, to leave the sinking steamer, and get into a small boat in a wild and angry sea; of their boat being capsized, and their marvellous escape; of their stay in the rancherie for seven days; all her provisions and articles of clothing for her family lost; of her return to Victoria in a canoe; and of her arrival here last evening in the *Maude* (which came as usual without previous notice) to find that her husband, almost distracted, had left the day before for Victoria to enquire into their condition.[41]

Another version of the story was told by Albert Waring later in his life. According to him, his mother and the two children were put into the lifeboat, but as it was being lowered into the sea, it capsized. Natives who had witnessed the disaster from shore immediately put to sea in canoes. Mrs. Waring and her seven-year-old son were rescued and taken to a Native village. No one knew exactly what had happened to baby Albert. Mrs. Waring and her son remained at the village nearly two weeks hoping to receive word Albert had been saved. No such news came. Grieving the loss of her son, Mrs. Waring decided to return to Alberni and break the news to her family. Unfortunately there were more troubles ahead.

During his wife's absence, Major Waring became so concerned about her delay that he decided to head out on the overland journey to Victoria to discover what had happened. On his arrival there, the Major found official orders waiting for him from the military, recalling him to service in India. As he had to leave immediately for his regiment's headquarters in England, he was unable to return to Alberni to say goodbye to his family.

Immediately on landing in England, Major Waring was placed

in command of a battalion ready to leave for the Middle East. The detachment boarded a troop-carrying sailing ship and the journey began. As the ship approached the tropical South Atlantic, drinking water became polluted. The Major requested the ship's captain to anchor off St. Helena to replenish the supply. When the captain refused the request, Major Waring seized command of the ship and sent the men ashore for the water. As a consequence of his action, Major Waring was court-marshalled, but on the personal intervention of Queen Victoria, he was pardoned and allowed to continue his duties. A short time later, the Major died, never having had the opportunity of returning to his family in Alberni.

Meanwhile, back in Alberni, rumours began to surface that a white papoose had been seen in a Native village to the north of Barkley Sound. Police investigated but found no foundation to the story. But when the rumours persisted, authorities decided to send the HMS *Warspite* from Esquimalt with orders to "blast the feathers off the tribe's roosters" if the child was not delivered promptly to the captain of the warship. Albert was handed over clad in sealskins and in the best of health to his joyful mother, sisters, and brothers in Beaver Creek.

It is difficult to verify the truth; however, there is little doubt that Albert, in later life, believed the second version. Many years later, at a banquet in Victoria, a speaker was relating the story of the *Woodside*, how it had been sunk during a storm on the lonely west coast, and how a mother and her infant had been separated in the foaming waters, not to be re-united for many years. The audience was startled when a young man stood up and announced, "That lady was Mrs. Waring, my mother, and I am Albert Waring, the baby you have been mentioning."[42]

Albert Waring, a building contractor, became a respected resident of Richmond, California. In 1962, he told his version of the story to journalist James K. Nesbitt. As well, he donated a bronze plaque in the memory of the *Woodside* to the Victoria Inner Harbor Embankment project. "It is an honor for me to do this, and I do it humbly and in gratitude to my mother and the crew of the *Woodside*. This was my mother's favorite city, and it pleases me greatly to know that her name will always be here, beside the harbor into which she so often sailed."

In 1903, Mrs. Waring remarried. Her second husband Neil McFarlane died in 1909. She had a total of fourteen children by her first marriage. Who better to serve as midwife to Alberni residents? Granny McFarlane, as she was fondly named, delivered more than one hundred babies in the district. She died in 1936.[43]

CHAPTER THREE

EXPLORING RESOURCES

The Vancouver Island Exploring Expedition, 1863-1864, under the direction of Robert Brown, surveyed the Alberni Canal and reported finding possible mineral resources in the Nahmint area.

> The results of our explorations in the vicinity of the Alberni canal, and Barclay, (or as it ought to be Berkley), Sound, may be shortly summed up as follows: The discovery of gold in Franklin's river flowing into the Alberni canal, below Copper mountain, and taking its rise near the Nanaimo lakes, in quantities which as far as our Exploration permitted us to judge, from one dollar and a half to three per diem, with the rocker, with the promise of greater results in a more extended prospecting. The River is full of canons, but there is "pay dirt" for a reasonable number of men. In our opinion, the river is worthy of another prospecting.
>
> The exploration of the Nah-mint river flowing into Nah-mint bay of the charts, to its scource [*sic*] in a lake about eight miles long. The River is claimed by a tribe living in Ukl-ul-uaht arm, and we found them camping there. The soil along the banks of the River is good, but difficult to clear of fallen timber. After leaving the falls, the timber is principally maple, (*Acer Macrophylum Dougl.*) no indications of gold were found; but favorable indications of copper and ironstone. Buttle, to whom this duty was instructed, in his report to me observes:

"The Lake we named the Nah-mint Lake, it is between eight and nine miles long, with an average width of one mile; it lies north and south for about four miles and then it turns to the west and north-west, for the remainder. It lies between two large mountains, about three thousand feet above the level of the Lake. I took bearings of several high mountains to north and west. One group I named the 'Ten Spies' (in memory of the Expedition, the original number of which was ten) on account of the small rocky peaks. Below the peaks we saw large glacier banks of ice and snow, and the portion of a Lake bearing south-west. About two miles up the River at the head of canoe navigation, was found a vein of copper, which looked favorable. The same party subsequently found out-croppings of copper below Copper Mountain."[1]

FRANK C. GARRARD

The men and women who settled along the shoreline of Barkley Sound and the Alberni Canal were, on a whole, ordinary folk with dreams and aspirations of carving out a life for themselves by clearing a piece of land to grow crops, build a home, and raise a family. Frank C. Garrard was typical of these immigrants who came mostly from the United Kingdom. He was an adventurer before he settled on the west coast.

Born at Broxbourne, Hertfordshire, England on August 17, 1863, Garrard left home at age sixteen, serving as a midshipman on his first voyage to Australia. He made sixteen voyages within ten years; six around the world to Australia and back, seven times around Cape Horn, the others across the Atlantic. A trip to Australia and back took ten months. On his last voyage to the West Indies in April of 1887, he decided to come to British Columbia.

In his unpublished reminiscences, he describes life in 1888 in the coal-mining city of Nanaimo, where he purchased one hundred acres for one hundred dollars. He worked clearing land. In his spare time he was part of a "company of Nanaimo amateurs"[2] who performed in Nanaimo and Victoria. The proceeds from these performances were donated to victims of coal-mining disasters. He also played soccer for the Nanaimo team. "Victoria thought they would win easily but they did not know that Nanaimo had some top players from the Old Country." But the sea was in his blood and he was soon working on the *J.B. Brown*, a coastal ship travelling to San Francisco. He made another trip to England on his first iron ship, a large ship of 1550 tons, the largest he had ever sailed on.

On July 1, 1889, Garrard returned to England where he met and married Annie Davis, from Wandsworth, on December 10, 1889. "We had six hundred dollars, or 125 pounds between us." The young couple decided to return to Canada. They arrived in Halifax on December 30 and "spent New Years going west." Back in Nanaimo, a winter storm had dumped about five feet of snow in the area. They continued on to Comox where they purchased two acres and had a carpenter construct a small cottage for $150. When Annie got pregnant, they were shocked to learn she carried twin boys and relieved later to discover it was only one child, a girl. Lilly, or Lillian Annie Louise, was born September 19, 1890.

Garrard's seafaring experience earned him a job on the *Rainbow*, an old wooden boat built for the Gulf of Georgia service. But this job didn't last long, as the boiler in the boat was disabled. He then joined the *Cutch*, a ferry service boat running between Vancouver and Nanaimo. His next job was on the *Isabel*, a paddle wheeler running between Victoria and Comox. The young family eventually settled back in Nanaimo where Annie gave birth to a baby boy on November 9, 1891. He was christened Francis Robert Burdett. Annie and Frank had two more babies: Ethel Gertrude in May, 1893, and Noel William on Christmas Day 1894.

In the early 1890s, there was a mining boom in the Albernis, ignited perhaps by an international shortage of gold in the world and the declining economy in British Columbia. In the Nanaimo area, those who weren't working in the coal mines moved either north to Comox or west to Alberni, trying to earn a living and put food on the table for their families. With two friends, Will and Leslie Jones, Garrard first grubstaked at Englishman River, and eventually ended up at China Creek where gold had recently been discovered. The rugged terrain of the island made it very difficult for settlers and prospectors alike. Many were forced to use the Alberni Canal, the lifeline to the outside world, since the road from Alberni to Nanaimo was barely passable most of the time. Garrard had decided to settle in Nahmint.

From now on our home was to be on the west of these mountains. We, as you can judge, already knew a good many people in or near Alberni, especially amongst the prospectors that had filtered into the district, many of them were quite interested in our attempt at home making in the Nahmint Valley, our plan was to go down the canal and camp at the house or cabin belonging to Hansen, who had one on the bay at the entrance of the Nahmint Valley about 2 miles away from where we intended building our own cabin.

He arranged for Annie and the four children to travel in Jack Burke's stage coach and hired a wagon and a team of horses to transport their possessions to Alberni, where Garrard's brother Burdett had already settled. Getting all to Nahmint was not an easy task. "We bought a large sealing canoe with which I intended to convey ourselves to the cabin (at Nahmint), the bulk of the belongings were to follow with Will and Alec Ferguson in a big war canoe belonging to Serault." They left Alberni in the evening, counting on the usual prevailing westerly winds dying down. When this didn't happen and the wind picked up and darkness approached, they decided to pull in to New Alberni (later named Port Alberni), about two miles south of Alberni.

Waterhouse had a cabin close to the shore at the same time a hotel was put up fairly close, but was not yet running; having landed the canoe, we proceeded to disembark the belongings we had with us and the family. We had a tent with us and Waterhouse offered to put up the children in his cabin which they did for the night. It was rather amusing, in disembarking the belongings, when they arrived at the bow where Lilly was fast asleep, they were quite surprised to find her as they were not looking for any more children in that part of the canoe.

Early the next morning the family continued their journey. A deserted cabin, about two miles from where they wanted to settle, became a temporary home. The first night in the old cabin, the family cat caught eleven mice. Annie and Frank began building their own cabin with some help from friends.

Many of the men who had worked at the placer mine (China Creek) helped put up a cabin, making a kind of "bee" of it. We supplying the food and they doing the work. The house was about 18 feet long and 12 feet wide, chinked at first with moss, with a shake roof. We also put in a ceiling and floor underneath the roof, which was of use when we had visitors who might be stuck when prospecting or hunting, to place them up aloft to sleep, having a trapdoor and ladder leading there.

When Annie and the children were settled into their new home, Garrard went prospecting and located several claims. He also purchased a cow and calf from W. Smith of Alberni, no doubt to provide the children with readily available milk. To transport the animals, he decided he needed a type of catamaran made up of two canoes with a railed platform supported between them by struts.

I was going to have it towed down the canal by a small steam launch, owned by Mr. Huff, but just at the time we got an unusually cold spell, the launch was put out of commission as some of the pipes burst during the night. So I was for a time wondering how I would get my cow and calf down the canal to Nahmint.

I told Ferguson that if I could get anyone to come with me, I would sail the craft to Nahmint. He said he would come, so with the help of some of the Alberni people, we got the cow aboard with her calf and some feed and started off on our voyage. Luckily there was a fresh northerly breeze which gave us a fair wind as far as the entrance of Nahmint Bay, which we reached just as it was getting dark. We arrived about 9:00 p.m. and landed the cow, put it into the shed we had built and gave it a feed, after milking it and giving the calf some milk and meal.

We managed to make a living, perhaps not up to the modern standard, but between us, we were a family. We also had some chickens and hens laying eggs all winter. We killed the calf as we could not feed it with calf meal satisfactorily, and we had use for the milk from the cow. We used occasionally to go to Alberni and stay there while getting supplies, returning at night or in the evening. The prevailing winds during the day in the summer time blew up the canal and often we would start off, Annie, the family and Burdett, or perhaps Peters, and arriving at Alberni. The trip would take about 2 or 3 hours but we had to consider getting up the river at Alberni, which if the tide was falling meant considerable delay. We would then start down the canal in the evening, I would manage by disposing them (the children) in the canoe where with blankets; they would be able to sleep comfortably, more or less, while I would row quietly down the canal arriving at Nahmint early in the morning at daybreak.

Between their trips to Alberni, Captain Huff's stern-wheeler, the *Willie*, called in twice a week as it travelled the canal delivering freight and passengers. Schooling now had to be considered for the two older children, Lilly and Burdie. The family decided to move to Alberni, Garrard hoping to get work there. But first there was the cow to consider. "The first thing we decided to do was to sell the cow as she had by this time pretty well stopping giving milk. We again made a catamaran arrangement with two canoes, and Burdett and I sailed it, with the cow, to Alberni, landing it on the flats owned by Redford the butcher, to whom we were selling the cow." The flats were in the area known locally as Lupsi-kupsi, the site of the present day paper mill, near the mouth of the Somass River. As they landed the cow it fell into a slough and sank deep in the mud. With the help of friends they managed to get her out and off to the Redford slaughter house.

During this time in Alberni, Garrard worked at various jobs including survey work with George Smith. He also worked on navigational channels connecting Henderson Lake with Uchucklesit Inlet, and Kennedy Lake with Tofino Inlet. These were built to allow prospectors and miners to transport supplies to and from the mines in the area. He also worked on the telegraph line from Port Alberni to Clayoquot.

Smith surveyed two alternative telegraph lines. One went overland via Sproat Lake and Taylor River to Kennedy Lake and along the shore to its closest point to Long Beach, and from there to the settlement at Clayoquot on Stubbs Island, almost the route of the present day Pacific Rim Highway. The other route followed the shore of the Alberni Canal across the narrows near Franklin Creek to Uchucklesit, up to Silver Lake and overland to Effingham Inlet, which was crossed by an overhead span; then overland again to Pipestem Inlet, along Toquart shore to Ucluelet, and to Long Beach. The second route was chosen because of the possible difficulties with the first route during winter when there would probably be plenty of snow in the interior of the island. The government manager in charge of construction was Mr. Hovelaque. Garrard wrote:

> He and I occasionally cruising out the route ahead, at other times I was locating and spotting the trees which we were to use for poles on the construction. They were topped and barked for about two feet down. Mr. Daly was the foreman on the construction, which was undertaken by contract at so much a mile. The mileage being counted by the length of wire used. Carr was the timekeeper and general financial advisor. I remember we got $2.50 a day paying $1.00 per day for board. In view of this arrangement, it was optional for us to work on Sunday. The first Sunday I was there the men decided to work, saying that it was hardly worth while stopping work when we were out in the bush. But I noticed that the crew decided on the 2nd Sunday and following that it was worth while as the rest was appreciated, even if it did mean paying for our board that day. So that by Monday evening we would have cleared in wages for the two days, Sunday and Monday, just fifty cents.

The federal government telegraph service was part of the Vancouver Island Telegraph System. After completion of the telegraph line to Clayoquot, the contractors rebuilt the government line to Cape Beale. The telegraph service was brought to Alberni in 1895-1896 as a branch line of the Wellington Comox Line.[3] The line from Alberni to Cape Beale, via Bamfield, was completed on October 1, 1899. A government report noted:

> This new line, for which the material (No. 6 iron wire) was laid down at Alberni in the previous year, was built under contract

by Mr. T. D. Conway of Chemainus, B.C. and completed on October 1, 1899. It skirts the shore of the natural canal for most of the way and cuts across the promontories approaching Cape Beale. The total length was 57 miles. The pole line is of cedars 23 feet long, 6 inches in diameter at the top and numbered thirty-two to the mile. The line is operated by the agents who were already acting at the respective terminal offices, Miss Patterson at Cape Beale and C. T. Haslam at Alberni. A temporary arrangement has been made with Mr. G. A. Huff, proprietor of a steamboat on the route, for the keeping of the line in working order.[4]

Garrard's brother Burdett was appointed as lineman-agent at Uchucklesit. Other men who serviced the line included George Bellamy, Alex Hoskin, Bill Crowshaw, Winston Burkholder, Mike Mikalishen, Jeff Godson, Gus Orland, Frank Day, and Marvin Hansen. British Columbia Telephone took over the operation from the federal government on April 1, 1954.

Garrard worked as a lineman for a time before becoming the lighthouse keeper on Lennard Island in Clayoquot Sound. Alan W. Neill, who later became a Member of Parliament and who was a close friend, gave a personal loan to help the family move to the lighthouse. As keeper, he was paid six hundred dollars a year. This was later increased to one thousand dollars on the understanding he would employ an assistant. His wife Annie became his first assistant. He hired another assistant later. When his brother Burdett, who had moved on to Tofino as agent-operator, decided to return to Port Alberni, Garrard took over his position at Tofino. The new position paid a little more, seventy-five dollars a month plus commission on the sale of stamps and money orders.

Garrard served the west-coast telegraph service for twenty-five years. He and his wife Annie raised a total of eight children. He began life as an adventurer; as midshipman he saw most of the ports of the world, but he found his home in the rugged life on the west coast. He retired to Victoria in 1936.

MINES, MINERS AND OTHER PROSPECTS

Frank Garrard was first attracted to the region by mining prospects in the Nahmint area. Others with similar dreams of striking it rich had been mining in Barkley Sound and along the Alberni Canal years before his arrival. Copper Island (Tzartus) was the site of the first attempt at mining in the sound. The Anderson Company quickly recognised the possibilities there, perhaps buoyed by the memory of the recent gold rush on the Fraser River in 1858. Early correspondence from the Anderson Mill noted Captain Edward Stamp had staked off a piece of land opposite Santa Maria Island to work a copper claim. The Victoria *Colonist*, in 1862, reported the Barkley Sound Copper Company had shipped seven tons of copper. Banfield also staked a copper claim "about three miles down the Canal on the east side."[5] The Alberni Copper Company, located about three miles south of the Anderson sawmill, on Copper Mountain, was in operation in 1864. Little is known about this mine, but an editorial writer with the Victoria *Colonist* gave it an optimistic forecast. "This bids fair to be one of the most successful mines on the Island."[6]

The Chinese were known to be placer mining in the 1850s-1860s at Gold River, now known as China Creek. Most miners prospected, then moved on, but a few of the China Creek miners stayed, continuing to operate a small store serving other miners in the area. They continued to work the creek into the 1890s. When Father Brabant travelled to Alberni to visit the Natives, he noted in his diary he had called "at the house of the miners at China River."[7] Not much is known about the Chinese miners or where they came from, except for one man who lived to ninety-one years of age; he was Mah Bing, who claimed he had made four thousand dollars working China Creek. He moved on to the Chilcotin country where he lost all he had gained. The approximate amount collectively recovered from the creek was reported to be two hundred thousand dollars.[8] Bing arrived in the Alberni District in 1873 from the Paksa district of Canton, China. After searching for gold in California, he came to British Columbia, eventually making his home in Alberni.[9] The China Creek miners were a familiar sight in the small settlement of Alberni. "One day some Chinese miners from China Creek came into Fred

Saunders' general store to purchase some groceries. They paid for them with gold dust taken from a flavoring extract bottle, half full of precious metal."[10]

The first lode claim recorded at the Port Alberni Mining office was the Sechart quicksilver claim in 1891, located a mile from the beach at Sechart, in Barkley Sound. There were two claims, the "Lord of the Isles," and the "The Crown Prince," both located about the nine-hundred-foot level, two miles from the wharf, or about three-quarters of a mile from the nearest salt water. Here a large steep face on the mountainside had been stripped, disclosing magnetite iron ore.[11] While little is known about these early claims, the owner, Captain James Crawford Anderson, and his homestead, impressed visitors. "He was a retired English sailor named Anderson. Most people knew him as John Bull, because of his remarkable likeness to the well-known cartoon. He lived with his wife in an unusually picturesque little house constructed of lumber, doors, and windows salvaged from wrecks. Alongside the house he had an excellent flower and vegetable garden on a small patch of very good soil."[12]

H. E. Newton, a Victoria businessman interested in mining and later an owner of the Golden Eagle mine, visited Barkley Sound to obtain mining samples. In Alberni, he chartered the *Hollybank*, a small steel steam launch owned by the Reeve family of Sproat Lake, and with Reggie Reeve, the boat owner's son, and George Bird, a Port Alberni sawmill owner, he travelled to Sechart, where Anderson lived. Bird wrote about the encounter:

Anderson had claims of his own, and knew the locations of others. During the next five or six days, inspections of several prospects were made and ore samples taken, mostly on islands. Some of the claims were quicksilver. This mineral seems to occur in that neighbourhood, and at that time was much thought of by prospectors. One trip was made to the head of Pipestem Inlet. Every night we made the Anderson home our headquarters.

Mr. Newton had understood we could get anything necessary at Anderson's and had told us we need not take along any food. The Andersons informed us they had only enough on hand for their own needs. All they could spare was plenty of potatoes

85

and tea; no milk, meat, butter, sugar, bread or flour. As Mr. Newton consulted his crew at the landing, an Indian passed in his canoe and offered for sale a large, freshly-caught codfish. The crew said they could stick it if he could. So for the next five or six days the bill-of-fare was codfish, potatoes and tea. Plenty of opportunity was offered to replenish the codfish supply from Indians that came around.[13]

While Anderson's claim to riches did not materialise, in 1927, Mercury Mines Limited of Victoria operated two claims, the Sechart No. 2 and Sechart No. 3, half a mile from the beach. A government report noted, "It is claimed that this and the Kamloops showings are the only showings of cinnabar, not only in the Province, but in the British Empire, the main world supply coming principally from Spain and Italy."[14] Anderson's old mine received some interest later from Canadian Quicksilver Company, which with government help, repaired the old trail to the mine site and built a camp on the beach. Again there was great optimism—quicksilver could be produced profitably—but this too failed. Crawford Lake is named for Captain Anderson's mother, Eliza Crawford.

The first mine staked in the Alberni area was the Golden Eagle. The mining report of 1893 noted: "In the fall of 1892 some prospectors pushed up to the head of the creek in search of quartz veins; they found one, and located a claim, calling it the Golden Eagle."[15] The creek was China Creek. The prospectors were Thomas Hennessy, William Ethridge, and Archie McLaughlin. Some work had been done on the claim, the report noted, with three tunnels driven in on the lowest vein with the bottom tunnel in over seventy feet. When word spread about an English company's investment in the claim, the rumour created a "rush" on claims in China Creek the following year. A young Englishman named Baker, the son of Colonel James Baker, showed interest in the mine.[16] The Colonel was a cabinet minister who had been involved with the promotion and consolidation of the coal mines and coke ovens at Fernie.[17]

An optimistic mining report stated: "Hundreds endeavored to take up claims in the neighborhood hoping to be fortunate in making a strike. Claims have been staked out all over the mountain sides and tops, many of them on the merest chance of showing a gold-bearing vein."[18] There was more hype than substance to the reports. Other stakes adjacent to the Golden Eagle looked promising, including the King Solomon and the Consolidate-Alberni holdings, owned by James Dunsmuir, the coal baron from Nanaimo. In 1897, a trial run of fourteen tons of ore produced a gold brick worth $520.49, the only gold brick produced by a mine at China Creek.[19]

Archie McLaughlin was an old-time prospector who devoted his life to the search for wealth. After proving there was gold in the area to the east of Alberni, he decided to find out if there were prospects in other directions. While prospecting in the Elsie Lake area with his friend Dan Clarke, McLaughlin became severely ill. Miles from home and in difficult country, Clarke left his friend to find help. When he returned, McLaughlin was dead. After vain attempts to return the body for burial, it was decided to let McLaughlin rest in peace. A small wooden cross was carved to mark the spot.[20] Hennessy and Ethridge sold out their claim to Henry Saunders, the Victoria grocer whose brother ran a store in Alberni. The sale netted each five thousand dollars. Hennessy helped Matt Ward build the Arlington Hotel in Alberni.[21]

Sometimes personalities got in the way of production, as was the case when James Dunsmuir invested some money in the stamp mill at the King Solomon basin, adjacent to the Golden Eagle. He and Saunders had a difference of opinion. After tremendous effort and backbreaking work installing the mill, the two men argued. "He's a damned old pirate," Saunders thundered. "No man's going to swear at me and get away with it."[22] To get even, Dunsmuir ordered the mill dismantled. Before the argument, Dunsmuir made what was considered a "clean-up," nine ounces of gold worth $180 from one ton of rock. Saunders eventually sold his interest in the mine to Colonel Baker, whose son later became a resident agent and represented the mine on behalf of the Duke of Montrose.

Getting the Golden Eagle mine ready for production had been no easy task. It had taken two years to build the road up to the mine, which by then was fully equipped with the necessary machinery, mill and buildings. Ernest Woodward knew first hand the wagon road was badly needed when he lost several mules attempting to freight equipment over the trail which in winter was often covered with snow.[23]

By 1897, mining activity had slowed down in the area. An explosion at the Golden Eagle marked the first fatalities in the Alberni mines. The Nanaimo *Free Press* reported the incident had "cast a gloom over the community."[24] Two miners, William Dixon, of Beaver Creek, and William Sareault, of River Road, were killed when attempting to dry out two sticks of dynamite in a pan on top of the stove.

After the mine closed, Jack Congdon was hired as a caretaker. But once again, the Golden Eagle seemed burdened with misfortune. In 1914, Congdon shot himself with a rifle in front of his cabin where he had been living with two trappers. He had recently witnessed one of the trappers being nearly frozen and going mad in the snow-laden country nearby. Some considered this, combined with ill health and the lonesome life at the mine to be the contributing factors to his suicide.

The Duke of York Mine, also located on China Creek, employed about seventy-three men and gave every appearance of a small village settlement, with workers' houses, stables, an assay office, and a blacksmith shop. A disastrous fire, caused by the long hot summer of 1896, almost completely destroyed the facilities at the mine.

The Duke of York Company have lost their stables, a blacksmith shop, assay office and about 7,500 feet of lumber. They had to punch holes in the flumes and piping to save them. The women and children (and horses) had to be crowded under the piping, and their lives were only saved by the steady pour of water from the flumes. In spite of every precaution and almost superhuman effort, there were many narrow escapes. The flume is seriously scorched, and if it had gone, every person on the claims would have burned to death.[25]

The serious situation became defused when one miner found another in a crouched position practising an effective remedy against fire and smoke. The miner, on hands and knees, had his mouth placed over a small hole in the ground. His fellow miner saw the lighter side of things, and slapping him on the shoulder said, "Well, my boy, I am glad to see you saying your prayers. I have just finished mine."[26]

Workers were laid off for a time, but a year later the Duke of York reopened, if only briefly. The mine closed in 1897. The general manager, F. T. Child, had mortgaged his home in Victoria and had lost everything. The mine recovered at least enough gold to make a breast pin to present to Captain John Irving of the SS *Tees* on the ship's inaugural run to Alberni. Passenger William Wilson made the presentation:

> As a lasting expression of our esteem and friendship, we ask you to accept when made, a breast pin from the first wash-up of the Duke of York claim, the pioneer successful hydraulic mine of Vancouver Island. Your enterprise in placing such a comfortable, commodious and seaworthy vessel as the *Tees* upon the west coast route, will, we are sure, be appreciated by everybody, either directly or indirectly interested in the development of mining, agriculture and fishing interests, which it will do much to assist and advance.[27]

When mining prospects dimmed in the Alberni area, many of the miners began searching farther down the canal, at Uchucklesit Inlet, where there was a small claim-staking rush in 1897. "Over 100 locations have been received at the Alberni recording office, new finds being recorded every week, and a general rush has set in at that locality."[28] Frank McQuillan, of Alberni, is credited with the discovery. Like many other men in the area, McQuillan worked at various jobs: he farmed, he managed the Alberni post office for a time, and was the first manager at the Duke of York mine. As a prospector, he uncovered a copper deposit at Uchucklesit Inlet. It was so large one Alberni prospector noted blissfully: "We have an unlimited amount of ore in sight; we have the value; we have the greatest facilities possible, and we have, gentlemen, the prospects of the greatest mining camp in British Columbia."[29]

Once again, everyone hoped for the big strike. Many of the prospectors built cabins along the canal, near the location of exploration. Some even cultivated small gardens nearby so they would have fresh produce. One prospector from Beaver Creek,

Joseph Drinkwater, refused to pay a dollar for freight and subsequently packed a cook stove on his back the eight miles to his cabin at China Creek. The stove lids were in the oven and in one of the holes was a quart bottle of Scotch whiskey three parts full, with paper stuffed in to hold it firm. This hardy outdoorsman discovered Della Falls and later built "The Ark" at Great Central Lake. He was one of eight brothers and four sisters from the Alberni pioneer Isaac Drinkwater family.

There were over seventy mining claims staked in the area surrounding China Creek and Franklin River. Some names reflected the gambling nature of the business: Ace of Spade, Queen of Harts, Queen of Diamonds, Monte Carlo, Bonanza, Hidden Treasure, Black Jack, Last Dollar and Last Chance.

Knowledge about mining was passed down from father to son, fathers having learned by experience. Prospecting required careful scrutiny of the creeks or the hillsides. Often only an experienced miner could see what was beneath his feet. Antony Watson Sr. was such a mining prospector; he was one of the original owners of the Thistle mine located at the headwaters of Franklin River. He worked in nearly all of the mines in the area. Before his arrival in the Alberni Valley, he had worked in the Albion Iron Works in Victoria, where he gained experience as a blacksmith. He could sharpen all the drills and do most of the iron work around a mine as well as the blacksmithing. His son Antony Watson Jr., became a pharmacist and a schoolteacher, but from his early experiences trekking around the hills with his father, he learned the ways of a prospector.

In the early 1900s, the whole area was full of prospectors. After the Duke of York closed, these prospectors went all around the area, into the most inaccessible places looking for ore. Most of them would go along the shoreline 'til they would come to a creek and then they would go up the creek looking for float. Float is small pebbles or chunks of likely looking rock which had broken off and been carried down the creek. They follow up to where the float stops and then they know that it has come down into the creek from the sides of the canyon or mountain beside the creek. Then they start prospecting the mountainside until they eventually find the area where the float originated. If it turns out to be a worthwhile prospect, they usually sell it to some outfit interested in developing it at that particular time.

The difficulty in prospecting in this area is that the overburden is so heavy, in the woods—moss, salal, huckleberry and what not, you can't see the rock. But I know, and I found this from going out with my father, the early prospectors had trained themselves to see a lot more than you can see. I've been with him—now for instance one time we went down to Sarita Lake and we had a little camp there at the first fall—and we were going to spend the night there and fish in the lake the next day. The first thing he saw was a little lead off to the left. I was sitting right on it. I didn't see it or know it was there. This is the difference between a prospector and an ordinary greenhorn. You could trip over a chunk of gold and never see it.[30]

Mining activity continued at Uchucklesit, and at Sechart. Two new mining ventures were staked during 1900 at Monitor Landing, eighteen miles down the canal, and at Wreck Bay, now named Florencia Bay. The Monitor employed about twenty men and shipped its ore to the Tacoma smelter. Another ore body, discovered by Leonard Frank at Monitor, promised to surpass anything found before. It was named the Leonard Discovery. The mine reopened in 1917 but it never yielded the riches expected. This ore was shipped to the Trail smelter.

The Wreck Bay enterprise was staked by men from Ucluelet; the Ucluelet Placer Mining Company owned five claims in the black beach sands which held placer gold deposits. Captain Binns, a Ucluelet pioneer, first discovered the gold in the late 1890s. A small amount of gold was actually found; some estimate as much as twenty thousand dollars' worth over a period of a few years. Miners had to combat west-coast storms that continually wrecked sluice boxes and other workings. Eventually the enterprise was abandoned. Elsie Hillier wrote of the project: "In 1900, black gold bearing sand was discovered on Wreck Bay, so the settlers of Ucluelet formed a company. Practically everyone bought shares and staked claims on the beach. These claims were worked for two years. Since then, men have often staked claims, washed for gold, enjoyed the beach, and then gone again."[31]

Another area of Uchucklesit Inlet receiving its share of diggers was Snug Basin. Anthony Watson Sr. was one of the principals in the Lenore mine founded by Pat Sullivan. Son Anthony Jr. explained the operation:

> I remember being at Snug Basin. They took out about thirty tons of ore there and it was all in sacks. I remember tying up the sacks. I was only a youngster. I wasn't strong enough to lift the sacks. I was down there helping my father, sewing up the sacks. Then they would lift them up and put them on a line pulley and this would hold down about a hundred yards to where it was fastened to another tree and there would be a man lifting them off and piling them up. The sacked ore was moved from the mine portal to the beach by a series of five line pulley stages, each one about 100 yards in length. When they had moved them down that far they'd move the rigging and let them down another hundred yards, and so on. It took about four times handling them to get them to the water's edge about four or five hundred yards from the shaft. They would then load it onto a scow and move it up to Port Alberni. I have one of the old bills from Crolls Tug for doing this. He charged $1.00 a ton for the 30 tons to bring it up from Snug Basin.[32]

Captain J. A. Croll operated one of the major tug-boat operations on the Alberni Canal. Ore was shipped by train from Port Alberni to the smelter at Ladysmith, which was built to treat the ore from the Mount Sicker Mine.

Frank Garrard had been prospecting in the right area because a new mine emerged in 1898, a mile south of Nahmint Bay. Formerly the Three Jays copper claim, it became known as Hayes Camp, after the owner Colonel G. H. Hayes of Portland, Oregon. His Nahmint Mining Company built a small community at Hayes Landing complete with wharf, boarding-house, manager's residence, office, storeroom, stable, and other out-buildings. From the wharf a wagon road wound two miles (three kilometres) up the steep hillside to the mine. As well, the company built an aerial tramway to transfer the ore from shaft to ship. The wharf could accommodate two large ships.

The Hayes mine was one of the first large-scale mines to open in the Alberni area, and providing the lumber to construct all the buildings was quite an endeavour.

Many thousands of feet of lumber were wanted for wharves, accommodation for the miners and their families, timbers for supporting the aerial tramway cables up the mountainside and, also, for large ore bunkers. Captain Huff, of Alberni, arranged with the mining company to erect a sawmill at Franklin River to supply all that would be wanted. A complete mill with engine and boiler was taken down on a scow. Set up on the right bank of the stream near its mouth, it soon got to work. I believe the first plan was for the mill to remain there permanently. It was not found profitable and ran for only a year or so until the mine was in operation. It was then dismantled and sold.[33]

The mine eventually had 3,370 feet of tunnel and shafts and was a contender for "the best developed mine" in the region. One year later, the company had shipped three hundred tons of ore to the Tacoma smelter, and reports from Victoria noted:

There seems to be no doubt now that Hayes' mine, as it is popularly known, is one of the best properties in the province, and there are prospects that the five gentlemen who own it will reap rich harvests as the reward of their industry. Only recently a separate and distinct chute of rich ore was struck in the mine.[34]

Hayes even toyed with the idea of erecting a smelter for the treatment of island ores. In 1901, with great optimism, the company hired, in advance, a steamer to transport next year's ore shipments, estimated to be five hundred tons per trip. The move was a bit premature and perhaps too optimistic, as mining ventures were thrown a curve ball by government. The mining report for 1902 noted operations were suspended and left in charge of a caretaker. Provincial legislation had mandated an eight-hour day within the mining industry. Hayes closed the mine when workers refused to accept less than their $3.50 per ten-hour shift for the shorter work day. This may not have been the only reason for closure; it may also have been triggered by the slump in the price of copper.

After investing a quarter of a million dollars and shipping two thousand tons of ore, the Nahmint Mining Company decided the ore was too low-grade to ship and ceased operations altogether. The caretaker remained until 1910 when the buildings were salvaged and the machinery dismantled; the claim reverted back to the provincial government for unpaid taxes.

Antony Watson Sr. had worked at the mine, and he knew Colonel Hayes well. When the colonel was leaving the area, he had some financial difficulty and appealed to his friend for some money.

> Mr. Hayes when he was leaving here, he had some financial difficulty. He didn't have any money with him. He had lots of money in, I imagine Vancouver or Seattle, but he didn't have any cash with him—and my Dad gave him $100 or $200 so that he could get out of here. And so when he went to wherever he was going, he wrote back and told my Dad he could have all the buildings at the Hayes mine. It was a gesture of goodwill because the lumber was worth much more than the amount that my Dad had loaned him. So my Dad went down here and took the wharf and bunkers and buildings all apart and built a big raft and sailed it up the Canal here and then used the lumber to build the foundation to this place (his home) and the Watson block.[35]

The Watson building on Argyle Street in Port Alberni, built in 1912, was a popular hall for dancing and playing basketball, even though the ceiling was a bit low. The Watsons also operated a restaurant in the building. The family lived upstairs until they built the family home on Second Avenue. Antony Watson (Ty) Jr. continued to live there until his death in 1995. He bequeathed the family home to the Port Alberni community.

Colonel Hayes appears to have been a man of honour and to have believed every debt should be repaid. "Captain John Irving, president of the coast fleet of steamers, invested twenty thousand dollars in the Hayes mine. He sued Hayes for misrepresentation after he had shipped ore from a 'glory' hole that brought no returns. Hayes served a term in prison, but after his release, he made a fortune in 'Tonepah,' Arizona, and repaid Captain Irving every cent."[36]

In 1928, Alberni Mines Limited, incorporated with an investment of two million dollars, purchased the Hayes mine and some adjoining claims and cleared out some of the original workings. But like many of the mines before it, the venture was just another episode in frustration for the would-be miners.

During the Depression there was another flurry of excitement about mining in the region when gold was found at Zeballos, on the west coast. At Mineral Hill, twelve miles south of Port Alberni, the Vancouver Island Gold Mines Ltd. mine was reported to be making good progress with development. Life at the mining camp had drastically changed from the early days at the turn of the century.

> In addition to regular dry room, sleeping quarters and cookhouse, the camp contains a business office and complete assay office, the latter under the supervision of Pat Hurley, mining engineer. The plant is equipped with oil burning assay furnace, electric crusher and pulverizer and other necessary assay equipment. The entire camp is lighted by electricity generated on the property, has a complete water system installed and is connected to Alberni by telephone.[37]

The Vancouver Island Gold Mine was active between 1934 and 1936 and employed about a dozen men. Another gold mine active during this period was the Havilah Mine on McQuillan Creek in the King Solomon basin, less than fifteen miles south of Port Alberni. A wagon road was constructed to the site and an aerial tramway carried the ore from the tunnels to a loading station.[38] During this time, the two properties produced 1,565 tons of gold ore containing 562 ounces of gold and 1,386 ounces of silver.[39]

In all of the early mining prospects, there just never seemed to be enough of any mineral, gold or copper to make a mine productive.

BARCLAY TOWNSITE

In the 1890s Uchucklesit Inlet attracted a lot of attention, first from miners then later from fishermen. The inlet took the name from the Uchucklesaht, a Native tribe that once inhabited the area. The word, *how-chuck-les-aht* means "people who live by a spring situated on or at the end of a deep inlet." The inlet cuts deep into the island on the west side of the Alberni Canal. The Native reservation is situated at the head of the inlet, by Snug Basin. Anderson (Henderson) Lake and river, which feed into the inlet, are prime fish and wildlife habitats. Here miners discovered large copper deposits and developers dreamed of the new town of Barclay situated on the inlet.

The Barclay Sound Land & Improvement Company of Victoria had dreams of establishing a new town as a port and industrial centre. The company was incorporated with a capital stock of one hundred thousand dollars in February 1892. It proposed to "build . . . up . . . the new town of Barclay, situated on Uchucklerit [*sic*] Inlet. The harbor is three miles long and three-quarters of a mile wide, perfectly land-locked, and a natural harbor. The townsite is admirably situated on a gentle slope from the water."[40]

As an added incentive to investors and settlers, the company agreed it would put fifty per cent of all receipts from two-thirds of the townsite into improvements and would promote a railway from Barclay to Comox, fifty miles (eighty kilometres) north. Cumberland was then one of the Dunsmuirs' coal producing areas, and it seemed to the Barclay proponents that coal produced in Cumberland could be easily shipped from Barclay instead of from Union Bay. Besides, Barclay would be closer to San Francisco, one of Dunsmuir's major markets. Someone forgot to mention the fact that Henderson Lake had one of the highest rainfalls in North America. The annual rainfall is 263 inches (6680 mm). Records were kept by the superintendent of a fish hatchery, which the Department of Fisheries maintained there for twenty-five years. It closed in 1932, along with several other hatcheries.[41]

The project was doomed from the start, but that didn't stop the developers from naming two streets in the townsite Railway and Broadway; other streets were numbered. Several people in Port Alberni bought into the dream and purchased lots that never were developed. Full-page advertisements for Barclay gave glowing reports of mineral deposits, the best fisheries of the Pacific, and the "most delightful climate."

The best location on the Island, is the "NEW TOWN OF BARCLAY," situated at the head of Barclay Sound, on the finest harbor on the Pacific Coast. No towage or inland insurance. The natural terminus for the coming trans-continental line. The harbor recommended to the Imperial Government for the Naval Station and Dry Dock. It is the centre of a fine Lumbering District . . . PRICES YET AT A NOMINAL FIGURE.[42]

Maps show routes and nautical distances from Barclay to the Orient, Australia, Vancouver, and San Francisco. A large part of the townsite was slashed and burned, leaving only stumps of the large trees. The few sites where houses were built had the stumps removed. George Bird visited the area and encountered the store-keeper named Martin.

A good wharf was built (I suppose by the Government) and a general store was erected and operated by a Nova Scotian named Martin. He was about forty at the time and quite a character. When he needed to go to Victoria, he did not patron-ize the Canadian Pacific Navigation Company boat which called at the wharf beside his store. He came to Alberni by canoe and made the journey to and from Victoria on foot. Then he canoed back to his store.

I was working for the Paper Mill when the manager, Mr. Hewartson, told me to put water and firewood on board the *Lily* for a trip to Uchucklesit. Mr. Hewartson said the paper mill would need sulphuric acid which could be made from the iron pyrites which abounded in the hills around Uchucklesit. He was going to see what chances there were of obtaining a supply. We took no meals along and after prospecting along the shore on what is now the cannery side, headed across the harbour for the Barclay wharf. We were well received and Mr. Martin said he would make us comfortable for the night. After supper we had a great "telling" of experiences. I being the youngest did more listening than talking.[43]

Eventually the only customers at the store were the Natives who lived on the reserve. Martin finally closed the store and moved to Northfield, near Nanaimo, where he began work as an engineer for the Hamilton Powder Works. The Barclay townsite bubble had burst. Some years later, Frank Garrard found deserted cabins when doing survey work in the area, the only evidence remaining of the town of Barclay.[44] Today only three of the subdivided lots are owned privately, the others are owned by MacMillan Bloedel Ltd.[45] As the area has been surveyed for townsite lots, the potential for future development still remains.

THE ALBERNI COAL MINE

In 1909, there was a surge in the market value of coal due to heightened economic conditions. Coal prospecting took on new importance. The local mining office received ninety applications for licences to prospect for coal. They covered areas such as Bamfield, Hesquiat and Quatsino, where coal prospects were considered good.[46] In Alberni, one man found it in his own backyard. In June, 1910, when Roy Hanna, a local tug-boat owner, was digging a well for a new home being built in Port Alberni, he discovered a seam of coal.[47] The lot was five blocks from the waterfront and two hundred feet above sea level. The well diggers had only gone down about twelve feet when the find was made. They continued to drill and found the seam to be about four feet deep.

Hanna's find created a flurry of excitement in Port Alberni about the prospects of having a productive coal mine in town. Coal rights on the townsite belonged to the Alberni Land Company, agents for the Anderson Company in London, England, and the Esquimalt & Nanaimo Railway (CPR). Outside of town, to the south, the rights belonged to MacKenzie & Mann, principals of the Canadian Northern (Pacific) Railway.

This was not the first time coal had been discovered beneath Port Alberni. The first prospecting had been done by Archibald Muir hired by the Alberni Land Company from November 21, 1877 to September 21, 1878. Muir drilled holes to a depth of 155 feet on a lot located near Coal Creek, just south of the present day Alberni Harbour Quay. He found "seven seams of coal and shale mixed, good, marketable quality, semi-anthracite, from one-and-a-half to six feet in thickness."[48]

Drilling was suspended and nothing further heard of the coal find until Hanna's discovery years later. Six months after Hanna's find, railway graders were preparing the rail bed running between the Canadian Pacific Railway wharf and the Barclay Sound Cedar Company sawmill, when they cut into a coal seam. The Paterson Contracting Company's steam shovel exposed a seam of coal in the bluff facing the waterfront. Once again samples were collected and sent to the Alberni Land Company and also to MacKenzie & Mann, principals of the railway company.

Previous samples of finds in other parts of the townsite were compared. The burning quality of the coal was tested in the furnace of the steam shovel and proved so satisfactory the company continued to use no other fuel. The local newspaper reported, "It was only a hopeless pessimist who could not be convinced that Port Alberni stands over an enormous deposit of the best grade of coal on Vancouver Island."[49]

Following the discovery, Charles McNaughton and Thomas Rowley put in stakes and posted a notice claiming the coal mining rights on the foreshore from the wharf to the mill and under the canal for some distance. A similar application was made by George Bird and Alex Spencer for rights between New Alberni (later Port Alberni) and Alberni. The announcement came in June, 1911, that a coal mine would be developed jointly by the Alberni Land Company and the E & N Railway. Archibald Dick, a familiar figure in the Nanaimo coal fields and the former inspector of mines for the provincial government, was placed in charge. Dick believed he was on the track of "an enormous deposit of the best coal ever uncovered on Vancouver Island," and that "before long Port Alberni would have a shipping mine with a pit head right on the edge of the harbour."

Two experienced coal miners from Nanaimo were hired to do the preliminary development work. Three weeks later, after tunnelling a distance of sixty feet, they found a vein more than three feet thick. The first coal mine contained a mixture of shale, but this diminished the further in they mined. At about fifty feet they were into gas. Port Alberni residents had found a ready supply of heating fuel.

News of the Port Alberni coal mine reached Ottawa. Mining engineer for the Conservation Commission, W. J. Dick, arrived to examine the mine which now reached eighty-five feet into the hillside. Dick was the son of Archibald Dick. After carefully inspecting the coal indications, he announced the coal was suitable for "steam and house purposes and was of marketable quality."[50] There was little doubt in his mind there was an enormous body of good coal under the townsite and the land on either side and behind it. He estimated the coal field covered an area of eight square miles and recommended bringing in a diamond drill to prospect for other shaft locations. In the meantime, coal was stock-piled at the mouth of the tunnel in anticipation of having enough fuel by winter to supply the entire district and to keep the E&N Railway engines and all the steamboats on the canal running.[51]

The mine never did develop into a shipping mine, but the coal, hand-mined and brought out from the short shaft in a wheelbarrow to be loaded into horse-drawn wagons, satisfied the heating requirements of Port Alberni households during the decade 1910-1920.

Following the Great War, the Alberni Land Company had difficulty paying its taxes to the city. The company still owned large tracts of undeveloped land within the townsite. Herbert Carmichael, representative for the company, appeared before Port Alberni City Council in 1919, suggesting the city investigate securing the mineral rights on land sold for delinquent taxes. Carmichael warned the city that if it didn't act, the coal under the townsite might pass into the hands of various individuals, making it difficult to develop a coal field.

His suggestion was met by a cynical council unsure whether or not the Land Company was trying to put something over on them. Carmichael tried to assure council that he held no ulterior motives, but that the city might in future plan to develop the mine.[52] If the mineral rights, which had been reserved by the company when the first conveyances were issued, were not held intact, they would be of no use to anyone. The right would pass with the property when it was sold for taxes. Legal opinion showed the mineral rights were registered in the name of the CPR, or the Alberni Land Company, therefore, the owner of the surface was not the owner of the minerals. The city retained ownership of mineral rights covering only three hundred acres, making coal mining almost impossible.[53]

The dissolution in 1922 of the Alberni Land Company, which then owned twenty-five per cent of property in Port Alberni, only muddied the legal battle regarding mineral rights. Under the original Anderson grant, only the gold and silver rights were reserved. During the Great Depression in 1932, a group of unemployed men wanted to open the old tunnel with the hope of mining sufficient coal to keep themselves employed during the winter. When Port Alberni City Council wrote to the CPR for permission, the CPR refused to give consent because it "laid claim to the coal rights in most, if not all the area concerned."[54] A portion of the tunnel the men wished to reopen just happened to be on the railway right-of-way. The railway also noted it was illegal to sink a shaft in proximity to a railway. The legal wrangling left even the most optimistic miner disillusioned. There would be no coal mining in Port Alberni.

CHAPTER FOUR

TRADITIONAL FISHING AND WHALING

SALMON PEOPLE

Natives were harvesters of the sea. Archaeological information indicates they fished the west coast for salmon for at least nine thousand years. Many varieties of fish flourished in the ocean and rivers, namely halibut, cod, herring, and salmon. Natives made good use of each, but salmon provided the largest portion of food. Explorers were denied access to rivers for washing or sanitation. Natives made every effort to keep the water absolutely clean, for fear the salmon would not return. The people never went into the actual spawning grounds. No bailing out of boats was allowed, and women were forbidden to bathe in the rivers during their menstrual period.[1] As the Natives were totally reliant on fish for food, so too were the settlers. This relationship between the settlers and the Natives produced the first fishing resource economy in British Columbia.

There were several methods of harvesting the salmon, by net or spear, or the most common, by use of a weir, or trap, a fence-like structure positioned across a river. These were normally placed where the water was shallow or slow moving, which made it easier to catch the salmon. Large numbers of salmon could be caught in this way. Early reports mention as many as seven hundred fish being caught in less than fifteen minutes.[2] Eventually the weirs were banned, much to the dismay of the Natives who argued their point before the Royal Commission of Indian Affairs in 1914.

> Only the Chiefs had traps—there were 15 traps, and what fish we caught they were distributed amongst the Tribe. We only used the traps for a couple of weeks and when there was a freshet we put our traps away and allowed the fish to go up. The traps were only in use for two weeks. The whites came in here and stopped them fishing with traps and ran the river with their laws and also ran the fish—they thought they would run the place better and thought they would have more fish by having the Indians not use traps. The purse seine came and began fishing at the mouth of the river, and sometimes they caught 10 and 15,000 salmon and they caught the salmon before they got up to the spawning grounds. Even the small fish were caught in the seine.[3]

The Natives were also expert at spearing salmon. During the salmon run in early summer and autumn, Natives used their skill to harvest their winter supply of fish from shore, or from canoes. Often this was done by torchlight.

> The Indians made torches by tying finely split pitchwood into bundles. These they lit and fastened at the prow of their canoes. One man paddled in the stern. The other, standing in the bow with spear poised ready, watched for the salmon to be attracted to the surface by the bright flickering lights. Once the salmon came in sight, the spear left the thrower's hand. A few seconds afterwards, the slapping of the unlucky fish was heard against the bottom of the canoe. Seldom was the aim not true. A dozen or more of these canoes moving slowly on the water, the torch-light glowing against the dark, made a most unusual and im-pressive spectacle.[4]

Preparation for curing salmon required removing the heads, tails and fins, and splitting the fish down the back. The heads and tails were boiled or steamed and eaten fresh, while the bodies and roe were hung on poles to dry in the smoke of the fires.

The Anderson Company employees were quick to capitalise on

the abundance of salmon. A letter dated August 23, 1861, from Barkley Sound noted:

> The Colonial schooner *Surprise*, McKay master, is laying in the sound trading furs; also the yacht *Templer*, Francis master, the *Meg Merrilies*, Pamphlet master, has been carrying lumber, salt barrels and merchandise to Craftary Island, at the mouth of Barclay Sound, from Alberni settlement, where Captain Stamp has established a fishing station and a sort of pilot house for directing vessels and affording information to such proceeding to Alberni.[5]

The Anderson Company established a fishing station at Effingham Island (Village Island), the first such commercial venture in Barkley Sound. They began salting down salmon in large quantities around 1866. During the 1880s, Captain Frances established small salteries for salmon at his trading posts in Barkley Sound for the Honolulu salt fish trade.

The run of salmon from the Somass River must have been spectacular. A letter dated August 16, 1861, noted: "The salmon are much more plentiful this year than the year previous. The water is literally alive with them. Quite a common thing in the evening to see young Indians shooting them with bow and arrows as they leap out of the water."[6]

All along the coast, Native villages processed and preserved enormous numbers of salmon of all varieties by either drying or smoking. They were in every respect the first fish processors.

SEAL HUNTING

Natives were also adept at hunting seals. Not only were the seals used for food, but the skins were particularly prized for trading purposes. With the consequence of famine uppermost in their minds, the use of all available resources ensured an adequate supply during the winter months. Thomas Mowat, Superintendent of Fisheries for British Columbia (1886-1891), reported to authorities on a trip he took to Ucluelet in 1886, when he met Fishing Guardian and Indian Agent Harry Guillod and the Reverend Father Brabant. He learned the Natives were doing more sealing than fishing. Sealing was so lucrative that a man could make enough to support a family all winter.[7]

Seal meat was highly prized by the Natives and used often in feasts. They took great care after harpooning to prevent the seal from swimming through kelp or seaweed and entangling the line which could break or be pulled loose. Hunters usually knew where the seals could be found asleep. As the seals dove into the water, the harpooner made his thrust before they could escape. Gradually rifles and shotguns replaced the harpoon. Sealskins were made into oil containers, or into floats to be used in whaling. The stomachs made ideal fishing floats.

When sealing was at its height, schooners were outfitted from the Ucluelet reservation and other Native communities every year with crews of thirty each. Hunting for fur seals was hazardous and difficult. Native canoe experts familiar with hunting techniques could expect to earn an average wage of three dollars per pelt, or between one hundred and two hundred dollars for the season. Records show that in 1894 fifty sealing vessels employed a total of 518 Native crewmen.[8]

> The sealing season began in January and lasted until the latter part of June. For the remainder of the year, the Natives fished for dog fish, extracting the oil from the livers and trading it to the storekeepers. In return, they received a stick marked in gallons at 25 cents a gallon. They then traded the stick back for goods.[9]

Traders purchased sealskins at Ucluelet, Tofino, and Clayoquot. In 1928, Ucluelet trader Edwin Lee received a visit from the Governor General of Canada, Lord Willingdon. The Queen's representative and his wife were on the inaugural trip of the *Princess Norah*. Gala events were planned at each port of call. Lee proudly displayed his sealskins before the important visitor. As these were the first skins Lord Willingdon had ever seen, he listened intently as the trader described the process involved in processing the furs for shipment. He even climbed into the bins for a closer look.[10] Lee operated a general store in Ucluelet and was also postmaster and Justice of the Peace.

Bamfield resident Irma Cashin described the early days of sealing and her family's involvement:

> They fished, and in the spring they'd all go sealing. They'd go out in their canoes to spear the seals and get the fur, but I don't know when that was stopped here in Canada, and the Russian and American government have some sort of treaty where they can go up and get so many each year, up in the Triple O Island, up where the seals go to have their young, so there are no Indians doing it like they had before. And before that, they used to be like Babe's grandfather who had a big schooner, two or three of them, and they used to go up the coast to go sealing, get the Indians for a crew from around here and then go up there and salt the furs down and the men would come back after the end of summer.[11]

Irma explained the process of salting the furs. Her father was a furrier who sold furs to various companies, such as the Hudson's Bay Company. Before shipping, they had to be preserved.

> So we used to have to salt these things down. Tough on your hands if you had any cuts, you know, rubbing the salt in the damn things. It would be in the shed on the float, you know, it used to be the ice house in the fishing time. We'd go in there and it would look like the graveyard with all these mounds in there. The skins, you had to lay them down and rub the fine salt into the fat side. Then you put the next skin with the fur side down on top of that, then you put the rock salts in as well. Then you rub the fine salt into the next one, then you rub some more salt on the top of that, so you had a pile this high. Then when they were done, we used to roll them up and put them in sacks and ship them out on the *Maquinna*.[12]

Sealing was a thriving business with Victoria serving as the home port for the sealing fleet. For forty years, beginning in 1870, Natives worked on the British Columbia coast sealers. The first pelagic sealing vessels were the *Reserve* and the *Wanderer*. The *Wanderer*, from Nanaimo, took on a crew of Ohiaht hunters.

A newspaper report of 1912 noted:

The Indians have already commenced their sealing offshore, but it is many years since they started so early in April. At the present they have been fairly successful, getting five pelts last Saturday the 13th (1912). They are forbidden by the new treaty to use firearms and they now have to fall back to their old system of spears, and probably they will do fairly well.[13]

American, Russian, and British sealers participated in the annual hunt in Alaskan waters. There were so many vessels, estimated to be over one hundred, that the seal colony was almost decimated. In 1911, Canada ratified an international sealing convention banning commercial sealing in the North Pacific. Only Natives continued to hunt by use of spears. In 1916, 290 seals were killed on Vancouver Island.[14]

DOGFISH INDUSTRY

The dogfish is a small shark about five feet in length and found in abundance off the west coast. The fish range from southern California to north-western Alaska. Dogfish oil became an important trade item in the Native fishery. Oil taken from the fish livers became one of the earliest products of the fishing industry in British Columbia. Natives extracted the clear oil from the fatty livers by heat and pressure, mainly for domestic use. A more primitive method of extracting the oil from carcasses produced an inferior oil used mostly for skin dressings and greasing skidways on logging roads.[15] The fish were cleaned, cut into pieces, then boiled in vats before being placed in large tubs where women trampled the oil out with their feet.

One of the main dogfish oil manufacturing curing plants was first established at Ecoole in 1889. Ecoole had always been a trading post from the time white men ventured into Barkley Sound. It was in this location, on the south side of Seddall Island facing Rainy Bay, in 1860, that the Anderson Company established a fish curing plant. Large rings were once visible where visiting sailing ships had tied up in the harbour. And it was here, in 1916, that Butterfield & Mackie built a fish packing plant to handle dog fish on a large scale, processing fish oil and fertiliser.[16]

Dogfish oil production employed many people and opened up a valuable industry. Sawmills of the province and coal mines at Nanaimo required large quantities of the oil for lubricating and lighting, as did steamers and sailing vessels.[17] Two lighthouses burned dogfish oil exclusively. The oil was claimed to give a luminous and brilliant light and was cheaper than any other oil that could be imported.

The first large commercial plant for the production of dogfish oil in British Columbia opened in the Queen Charlotte Islands during the spring of 1877.[18] A heavy duty was placed on the highly prized oil, which almost prevented its export to the United States. This resulted in the decline of commercial fishing for the dogfish. When they were no longer economically viable, the fish were regarded as a nuisance and a great annoyance to fishermen in other branches of the industry. It was said the dogfish would cut through fish lines and eat fish from the hooks, leaving only the heads.[19] In 1908, the Dominion Fisheries Commission of British Columbia recommended the dogfish carcasses be marketed as fresh fish. This they considered would help alleviate complaints from fishermen. The dogfish was marketed, mostly to the United States, at various times as "whitefish," "ocean whitefish," "flake," "greyfish," and "salmon shark." After the end of the First World War the market for the dogfish declined.

HERRING

Herring roe was always a favourite food of the Native people, who called it *quock-a-mis*. The fish eggs could be gathered in great quantities simply by placing cedar or hemlock brush in shallow water on the shore of the canal where the fish came to spawn. The branches would soon be covered so thickly with herring spawn that the green foliage would be completely hidden. The eggs were dried in the sun.

The Natives used a "herring rake" to catch the small fish. The rake was a piece of wood, several feet long, and nearly three inches wide. A row of wire nails about an inch apart and filed to sharp points lined one edge of the rake. The water was so packed with fish that a quick strong sweep alongside the canoe impaled one or more on the spikes at nearly every stroke.[20] When the canoes returned with the catch, the women cut the heads off, opened and washed the fish, then hung them to dry in smoke by the fire. Few were used as food; most were used for barter with the tribes of the interior. No one complained about the harvest until the herring industry developed; then there were moves to curtail the activity.[21]

Schools of herring were so prolific that whales plunged through their solid masses; seals herded them into giant balls to be devoured at their convenience; dogfish harried their enormous schools from below until they rose to the surface to be further harassed by seagulls.

Seining for herring started early but little of the catch was used for human consumption. Instead, the fish were used as halibut bait. The year 1902 saw attempts to market salted herring in Australia, and four years later Japanese fishermen founded the dry salt herring industry. Thousands of barrels of salt herring left Nanaimo and white fishermen decided to take up the trade. The Dominion Government brought in an expert from Europe to instruct local fishermen in the art of Scotch-curing herring, adding kippers and bloaters to the list of herring products.[22]

One timber cruiser in 1909 experienced quite a sight while "down the canal" and wrote a letter to the editor:

From our tent door, half a thousand feet above the sea, one could toss a biscuit well into the blue waters of the Alberni Canal. The blue is flecked with white where the good north wind meets the tide and the air below us is thronged with seagulls floating and eddying like great flakes of snow in a March breeze. Their beauty of form and grace of movement appear to unusual advantage as seen from above, and one seldom has the opportunity of viewing a larger number than are now visible, seeking safety from an off-shore wind, perhaps, and certainly filling themselves to gluttony with little fishes. So too, are the porpoises who just rolled by, cooling their curved spines, if they have any, on top of the water. Just at the closing in of dusk, we rowed among them, barely discernible as they rippled the surface of the sea but as the night grew quickly dark, the water proved to be extremely phosphorescent, and for more than two miles every stroke of our four oared boat was full of interest.[23]

In 1915, Barkley Sound fishermen complained the herring were so thick in some harbours, that they were interfering with the spring salmon fishing, as the salmon could not be tempted with artificial bait.[24]

TRADITIONAL WHALING

Like a seasonal clock marking the passing of time, hundreds of whales of many species migrated through the waters of the west coast of Vancouver Island on their way to their breeding grounds in Alaskan waters. Natives celebrated their arrival with ceremony. Only a couple of the tribes took part in early whaling, which was mainly for food. Although other tribes did not participate in the hunt, they did make use of whales stranded on the beach.

While the whaling season began in early summer or late spring, preparations for the hunt started months before. Those taking part in the hunt separated from their families and abstained from eating their usual food. They prepared their bodies by washing, morning, noon, and night, and by rubbing their flesh with ferns, or twigs. Personal cleanliness was essential for the hunt to be successful. Should an accident occur, a crew member could be blamed and punished for not carrying out the proper cleansing ritual.[25]

Each year they set out in canoes to do battle with the giants who had all the advantages of the sea on their side. The harpooner headed the whaling expedition. He chose a crew of eight or nine men and was in supreme command of the hunt. This prestigious position was often handed down from father to son, as were the careful instructions of the hunt. When they reached the hunting grounds, the canoes were spaced a short distance apart, each having a particular area to cover. The harpoon was generally a very crude affair made from a piece of hoop iron off a barrel, with two horn barbs bound or gummed to it. Next to the harpoon, a line made of deer sinew was attached to the main line, about the size of a three-inch rope, made of cedar twigs bound together, and coiled at the bottom of the canoe.

Twelve feet from the harpoon a number of seal-skin floats were tied to the line. These were inflated like balloons and served to wear the whale down by making it difficult to dive; they also kept him from going too deep or staying under the water too long. The harpoon was tied lightly to a ten-foot piece of wood which would fall away, leaving the whale on the line. When the whale surfaced, hunters in nearby canoes fired their harpoons. Soon there were so many buoys attached to the whale that he could no longer dive. As he thrashed around on the surface of the ocean, the hunters moved in for the kill with their short spears.

Now began the difficult task of towing the whale's carcass to the shore. Everyone sang, their paddles keeping time with the song. The whale meat was distributed among the tribe. Almost the entire animal was consumed or used. The black skin was eaten, the sinews were used for ropes, and the digestive organs became containers for oil. The bones and waste portions of the flesh were left on the beach for scavengers. The "ceremonial hump," a wide piece of choice meat taken off the back near the fin, was presented to the chief.[26] Considered taboo for eating, the blubber was hung on a rack outside the chief's house and decorated with eagle feathers and down. The chief also received a piece of the tail for eating purposes.

John Jewitt wrote of the whale hunt led by Chief Maquinna and the joyous celebration in the village afterwards:

Great was the joy throughout the village as soon as it was known that the king had secured the whale. All the canoes were immediately launched and furnished with harpoons and seal skin floats, hastened to assist in buoying it up and towing it in. The bringing in of this fish exhibited a scene of universal festivity. As soon as the canoes appeared at the mouth of the cove, those on board of them singing a song of triumph to a slow air, to which they kept time with their paddles, all who were on shore, men, women and children, mounted the roofs of their houses to congratulate the king on his success, drumming most furiously on the planks and exclaiming *Wocash—wocash Tyee*. The whale, on being drawn on shore, was immediately cut up and a great feast of the blubber given at Maquinna's house to which all the village were invited.[27]

The Ohiaht tribe from the Bamfield area were particularly skilled in hunting whales. George Bird, a pioneer sawmill owner in Port Alberni, recalled going into the Coleman blacksmith shop in Alberni and finding Ephraim Coleman busy trying to make a harpoon for some Ohiaht Natives. "They wanted it made just so and Ephraim always had an idea that he knew a little better than the customer, what was wanted. The Indians did not know much English, but with their wooden pattern to work to, I think in the end, they were able to get just what they required."[28]

Traditional whaling declined when sealing became more lucrative.

SECHART WHALING STATION

Commercial whaling began in 1905 when the Pacific Whaling Company, formed in Victoria, built the first whaling station at Sechart, near the entrance to Pipestem Inlet in Barkley Sound. Three sealing skippers are credited with starting the first British Columbia whaling fleet. They were Captains Reuben and Sprott Balcom, and Captain William Grant. The Balcom brothers were from Nova Scotia; Captain Grant lived in Victoria.[29] When it appeared the seals were reaching extinction, the men invested in the whaling industry. Sprott was familiar with the whaling industry in Newfoundland, then a separate colony, where whaling companies paid an annual licence of fifteen hundred dollars to operate, and new shore stations were prohibited within fifty miles of any existing plant.[30]

In Canada, there were no such rules or regulations governing whaling on the Pacific Ocean, and the federal government showed reluctance to legislate policy. When licence applications appeared on the desk of Joseph-Raymond Fournier Prefontaine, the Minister of Marine and Fisheries, the government made amendments to the Fisheries Act to regulate whaling. One of the first applications received came from the Balcom brothers and Captain Grant. As in Newfoundland, there would be a fifty-mile separation rule restricting shore-station sites. The four sites chosen by the applicants were Fitzhugh Sound, Rose Harbour, Ucluelet Arm and one north of Nanaimo.

SECHART STATION - WHALES CAUGHT BY MONTH/YEAR

MONTH	1908	1909	1910	1911	1912	1913	1914	1917	TOTAL
JANUARY			5						5
FEBRUARY	3								3
MARCH	7	4	26	18	2				57
APRIL	40	34	44	92	27	10	3		250
MAY	24	44	70	75	68	45	11	11	348
JUNE	61	63	84	60	66	72	22	29	457
JULY	42	54	102	71	44	74	19	28	434
AUGUST	23	73	60	84	38	44	14	11	347
SEPTEMBER	34	48	26	70	37	29	17	11	272
OCTOBER	16	34	10	4	2				66
NOVEMBER		2							2
DECEMBER		3							3
TOTAL	250	359	427	474	284	274	86	90	2,244

SECHART STATION - WHALES CAUGHT BY SPECIES/YEAR

SPECIES	1908	1909	1910	1911	1912	1913	1914	1917	TOTAL
SPERM	1			1	5	4	4		15
BLUE/SULPHUR	32	14	15	23	12	5	8		109
FIN	16	10	23	46	43	30	40	12	220
HUMPBACK	201	335	389	403	224	235	34	48	1,869
SEI								29	29
BLUENOSE				1					1
CALIFORNIA GRAY								1	1
TOTAL	250	359	427	474	284	274	86	90	2,244

Whaling licence No. 1 was issued May, 1905. It was for a maximum term of nine years, renewable annually on payment of a fee of twelve hundred dollars, and whales had to be completely and thoroughly processed within twenty-four hours, without the dumping of "noxious or deleterious matter" into the waterways. A new enterprise, the Pacific Whaling Company, spent about $260,000 developing the Sechart station, and began operations September 1, 1905. The company had raised two hundred thousand through the issuance of preference and common stock shares. The biggest problem was finding a suitable steamer for whaling. No Canadian shipbuilder would contract to build such a unique vessel without specifications. The company looked to a shipbuilding yard in Norway to build the proper chaser boat. The *Orion*, under the command of Reuben Balcom,[31] was the first steam chaser boat in British Columbia.

The Norwegian crew who brought the ship to the west coast elected to stay with the Pacific Whaling Company. Canadians objected to signing a foreign crew. James Clarke of New Alberni (Port Alberni) thought this was unfair competition and petitioned unsuccessfully to the Department of Labour for changes to the employment practice.[32]

It was not always easy adhering to the new rules and regulations. The government insistence that whale carcasses be processed and disposed of within twenty-four hours proved difficult to follow, as no machinery existed in Canada to undertake the task. Sprott Balcom looked to Germany, where an engineer, Dr. Ludwig Rissmuller, had developed machinery capable of the task. The Rissmuller machinery was installed for the start-up at Sechart. As payment, the German engineer became a major shareholder in the company.[33]

The Pacific Whaling Company had a silent partner in Alberni—Captain George Albert Huff. Captain Huff had a reputation of being an entrepreneur and operated various boats on the Alberni Canal. In September, 1907, Huff applied for a licence to operate a whaling station at the entrance to Skidegate Channel on the west coast of the Queen Charlotte Islands.[34] His application referred to the Rissmuller reduction methods "now in use by the Pacific Whaling Company" and implied that the engineer was affiliated with the new project. Huff eventually located his proposed station at Rose Harbour on Moresby Island. This site was granted in March, 1908. In 1909, Huff incorporated the Queen Charlotte Whaling Company Limited and issued 5,500 shares of stock at fifty dollars each.

The Alberni newspaper reported on his movements in 1908. "Capt. George A. Huff returned on Monday from the Queen Charlotte Islands where he selected a site for the new whaling station which is to be established by a company of which he is the head. Capt. Huff left on Wednesday for the Sechart Whaling station where he will continue some experiments he has been making."[35]

Initially, the Sechart venture was quite successful. No sooner had it reached full steam, than construction began of a second plant at Kyuquot Sound. A third station was built at Page's Lagoon, north of Nanaimo, where the company owned 132 acres of waterfront property. This station planned to hunt whales in the inside passage. The first shipment of oil from Page's Lagoon, four hundred barrels, was shipped via the CPR steamship *Otter* for delivery in Vancouver. There were a few prosperous weeks of whaling then suddenly the operation at Nanaimo ceased on January 25, 1908. No one knew precisely why, although there had been complaints lodged against hunting whales in the Strait of Georgia, mainly from the Terminal Steamship Company which operated whale-watching boats.[36] The whale catcher, the *St. Lawrence*, which had been brought out from eastern Canada to begin operations at Nanaimo, was diverted to the Sechart station. "Within a few years, the company converted to a fertiliser plant. The [Nanaimo] plant closed in 1912."[37]

The Victoria *Colonist* reported in 1908 that the Pacific Whaling Company, with two of its stations, the other being Kyuquot, together with winter quarters in Nanaimo, had brought in three to five whales per day during the season, taking a total of five hundred between April and August. The oil was shipped to Glasgow and the fertiliser to Honolulu.[38] Whales were valued between four hundred and eight hundred dollars each. Approximately thirty-five barrels of oil were pumped from the head of each whale. Oil shipped to the United States had to pay duty.

William Roff, of England, visiting his daughter Jenny Spencer in Alberni, toured the whaling station at Sechart in 1907.

There are two or three whaling stations on the island. The one I visited was at Sechart and I saw a whale which measured 85 ft. or 95 ft. being cut up on the stocks. Indians are principally employed and they eat the flesh with avidity. The Japanese being the principal purchasers. The whale bone is used for stiffening purposes in dress. I spent about nine hours at the station. I found the stench arising from the guano was terrible.[39]

One of the largest whales ever captured measured eighty-seven feet (26.5 m) in length. It was harpooned in 1909 in Barkley Sound and landed at the Sechart station.[40] Fishery reports note a total of 581 whales were captured in 1913 with the Sechart and Kyuquot Sound stations in full operation.[41] The first whalers were the *St. Lawrence*, the *Orion*, the *Sebastian*, and the *Germania*.

They were small fast vessels, in the neighbourhood of seventy feet long and very sea worthy. They could do about twelve knots. The original whalers came from Norway, and were manned by Norwegians, who stayed on them for some years after their arrival. I myself have sailed with a lot of whalers and they were, as a rule, a fine bunch of men and very good seamen.[42]

Since the original whalers were so successful, the company ordered a whole fleet of them from Norway. This fleet of steam whalers became well known on the coast as the "rainbow fleet." They were the *Blue*, *Black*, *White*, *Brown*, and *Green*.[43] Why the whalers were given such colourful names is an interesting story. When the time came to launch the vessels, the Norwegian builders began searching for names. The German engineer, Dr. Ludwig Rissmuller, wanted to name them after the rivers in Germany. When a Vancouver shareholder, a Scot named MacMillan, heard about the proposal, he flew into a terrible rage and demanded the vessels be named after rivers in Scotland. The international debate almost resulted in the whalers being launched without any names at all, a very unlucky omen for ocean-going vessels. Directors of the company reached a compromise by naming each a colour.[44] The whaling tender *Grey* was formerly the old *Petriana*, which once transported powder and supplies to contractors building the railroad into Alberni.

The whalers became a familiar sight around the sound and in Alberni. Ed Cox was there when the *Orion* made an emergency run to Alberni.

> I remember once when I was working in the Waterhouse store, when it was down at the foot of Argyle Street, on the old wharf (Port Alberni), the *Orion* made a record run up the canal from the Sechart whaling station with a Japanese that had fallen into a tank of boiling oil. He was treated here and lived, although very severely burned. The crew of the whaler told me that the funnel was red hot, and I do know that she was blowing off steam for quite some time after her arrival.[45]

The whaling station at Sechart left many with not-so-poignant memories, particularly regarding the smell that radiated from the plant. One Port Alberni resident compared the smell to the pulp-and-paper mill there. "The pulp mill here is a rank amateur, as far as smell is concerned. A whaling station really hums, in fact you can almost lean against the smell, when they are really going good."[46]

The coastal steamers *Tees, Queen City, Otter,* and *Amur* used to tie up at Sechart to load whale oil and fertiliser for transportation to Victoria.

> The passengers would, if they could stand the smell, go ashore and watch Chinese, Indian, and white men tearing the blubber from carcasses hauled up on the slipway or ramp. In the evening, whale meat would appear on the menu of the steamers. No attempt was made to disguise it, and there was nothing in the taste or texture of the flesh to discourage the diners. The meat, which was a shade darker than beef, was said to have tasted like pork although a little on the dry side. On the whole, it made a palatable meal.[47]

A small recipe booklet, published by the Victoria Whaling Company, is one of the few reminders of the once prosperous whaling station. Entitled "Whale Meat As Food," it contained twenty recipes "tried and true." The Sechart salad ingredients included: "3 cups cold roast whale, chopped coarsely: $2/3$-1 cup cooked green peas: 4 radishes (sliced). Moisten with salad dressing, mix lightly with a silver fork, serve on a crisp lettuce leaf, and garnish with slices of hard-boiled egg or tomatoes."[48]

In the summer of 1915, Mary Wood spent a two-week vacation at Sechart with her family. Her father, James Wood, was then the Fishery Officer for the district.

> Arriving at the Sechart Whaling station dock, we walked along the dock and passed vats, or tanks, full of whale oil. The door was indescribable—we, literally, gagged. Just prior to our arrival a party of four was touring the closed plant, when one member, a Miss Kendall, I believe, slipped at the top of the slimy whale chute and slid down the chute into the water. We were privileged to live in the manager's house, on the hill, and nearby there was a small classroom where the children played school each day and swam. We roamed along the beach and found Captain Anderson and his wife. We were quite intrigued by their home as we could see it was made of material from shipwrecks. The panels varied in colour and the windows varied in size.[49]

In a series of manoeuvres, Sprott Balcom handily created a monopoly within the west-coast whaling industry by buying up or merging with existing licences. This was the case with Captain Huff's licence in the Queen Charlottes. In August, 1910, The Queen Charlotte Whaling Company and the Prince Rupert Whaling Company were sold to the Pacific Whaling Company. By Christmas 1910, the new corporation, the Canadian North Pacific Fisheries Limited, held ten permits to operate whaling stations.[50] Huff's original site at the south end of Moresby Island was changed to Rose Harbour, and it was here the machinery from the Nanaimo operation found a new home.

The decline in stock was inevitable considering the number of whales harvested each year. No stock could sustain such a slaughter. Sprott Balcom retired in 1913 and returned to Nova Scotia; perhaps he had seen the writing on the wall. It was a subject no one wanted to address. In 1914, the Canadian North Pacific Fisheries Limited went into receivership. Between 1915 and 1918, the industry came under the control of William Schupp, a German-

American, who operated the Victoria Whaling Company.[51] In 1917, Schupp petitioned Ottawa for the cancellation of the licence at Sechart. The cancellation became effective February 20, 1918. The buildings at Sechart were leased to Vancouver Island Fisheries for use as a herring packing plant.

Bill McDermid, of Bamfield, remembered the early whaling industry:

> Whale wise, there were a lot more bigger whales, like sperm whales and humpback. Years ago, I remember, not nearly as many grey whales; there's way more grey whales, and they're just little dinky little toys compared to a big humpback. They were all over the place. They'd be in and out, all around. But they were hunting whales up until, I think, the late fifties, early sixties. They used to have to harpoon them, and then they'd fill them full of air and then they'd flag them and put a radio beacon on them and away they'd go and get another one. Then they'd catch them, a processor would come around and pick them up. They'd take them aboard the ship and process them. And the next time you saw them, they were in your ice-cream.[52]

In February, 1926, the old whaling station at Sechart was sold to Millerd Fish Packing Company and converted into a fish reduction plant, where oil and fish meal were manufactured from pilchards and dog fish.[53] Whaling continued for another two decades but the number taken was considerably reduced. Annual catches were reduced to two hundred whales. The Second World War further curtailed the catch by destroying the Japanese market for oil and whale meat. In 1946, measures were taken to protect the remaining herds. An International Whaling Convention established the species and minimum lengths which could be taken, set closed seasons, and restricted the taking of females accompanied by calves. Factory ships were limited to the Antarctic. Canada signed the Convention.

When stock in the Antarctic declined, whalers headed back to the Pacific Northwest. Attempts were made to enforce the terms of the Convention, but Fisheries had no power outside territorial waters. For a brief time whaling resumed in British Columbia. B.C. Packers, Nelson Brothers, and the Gibson Brothers, under Western Whaling Corporation, revived the old steam whalers and outfitted them under experienced Norwegian skippers. Gordon Gibson tells of his family's involvement:

> In September of 1947 Clarke telephoned me at Tahsis to tell me that the Consolidated Whaling Company of Victoria had four or five old whaling ships that were going to be sold at public auction. He wanted our company to put a bid on them since we were always interested in acquiring more ships to assist our fishing and towing operations. I suggested to Clarke that he should bid no more than $5,000 to $10,000 a ship, which was a hell of a lot of money but far less than it would take to build a hull from scratch.[54]

The company, however, was not interested in selling the individual ships, so Clarke tendered five thousand dollars for the complete package, which happened to include two whaling plants, four whaling ships, tanks, wharves, guns, ropes and cables. "Who in the hell wanted whaling plants in 1947?" The Gibsons had also acquired the whaling rights for British Columbia granted sixty years before to Consolidated Whaling Company. "We had bought the right to lose money and were more than pleased with ourselves." The family had never considered going into the whaling business, but after talking with the Nelson Brothers and B.C. Packers, they decided to join forces and set up a new company called Western Whaling Corporation. Clarke Gibson became the new president.

The Gibsons' involvement in the whaling industry did not last long, mainly because whales caught in British Columbia waters were worth half those caught in Japanese waters. The Gibson and Nelson Brothers sold to B.C. Packers, who immediately brought in whaling ships from Japan and went into freezing whale meat for export.[55] The old whaling ships, the rainbow fleet, were sold to a junk dealer in Victoria.

In 1948, after a lapse of four years, three killer boats were equipped with standard harpoon guns. The operation covered an area from Cape Cook to Cape Scott and up to fifty miles off shore.[56] The junior biologist at the Pacific Biological Station in Nanaimo, Gordon C. Pike, noted that during the 1948 season only one of the prized blue whales had been seen.[57] The blue whale at one time had formed a substantial part of the catch.

Meanwhile, Japanese and Russian factory ships continued to operate offshore, leaving local operations with little profit. In 1964, an estimated eighteen thousand whales were taken by foreign vessels. Fisheries received a complaint about a Russian factory ship slaughtering whales of all sizes. A Fisheries plane flying over the operation confirmed this, but nothing could prevent the slaughter. It was the last big herd of sperm whales seen in the area.[58] The lucrative and adventurous days of commercial whaling ended in the sixties.

Today, a new resort is being developed at the site of the old whaling station. Sechart Lodge is the former administration building of the Alberni Pulp and Paper Division of MacMillan Bloedel Ltd. The building was barged down the canal and now serves as a lodge facility for kayakers and canoeists during the summer months.

ONE OLD WHALER

Some of the early crew who manned the whaling ships settled in the Ucluelet area. One old whaler, August Jansen, from Sweden, arrived with the sailing ships and first stayed with the Sutton family. He became a good friend of George Grant, a young man from Scotland. The two bachelors lived together for a time. Jansen was short, with blue eyes and fair hair, and had a good nature, showing kindness to everyone. This sometimes got him into trouble, especially when he looked after the store in the Suttons' absence, as he often gave customers credit. Many would-be settlers left Ucluelet deeply in his debt. One man who owed money repaid the debt with two old steers named Barney and Sandy. Jansen turned the animals loose on the beach for the winter. Sandy was brought home in worse shape than when left to roam; only skin and bones remained; Barney was never found.

A round pot-belly stove occupied pride of place in the Sutton store and attracted customers on cold wintry nights. Many fishermen and settlers would gather to hear Jansen tell stories of his seafaring ventures whaling on the coast. Often, on stormy nights, six boats and some of the whaling fleet would be tied up at his wharf. All the sea captains knew each other and would gather to swap stories. Captain Vic Jacobson, Captain Christen, the two Captain Healers, and others called in to visit the old salt.

Jansen operated a small fishing enterprise, where he bought salmon and cod from the Natives, then smoked them in a big smokehouse at the back of the wharf. The fish product was then shipped in case lots to Victoria. The store, sheds, and wharf were once located at East Ucluelet.

Jansen had a reputation as being a good cook, having served in that capacity on the whaling ships. Elsie Hillier remembered his hot cakes which were eaten with honey and served with thick cream from his Jersey cow. "He also liked to cook halibut heads. They were nice, but he refused to remove the eyes first. I once saw him eat one. 'That's fine,' he said, as he smacked his lips in enjoyment."[59] The old whaler loved to sing, and often he would give a good rendition of "Sweet Flora Belle," a particular favourite of his.

Jansen owned Shelter Island, at the mouth of Ucluelet harbour, and had cattle grazing on it. This island was later renamed Fraser's Island in honour of George Fraser. The island was a favourite place for picnics.

CHAPTER FIVE

JOURNEYS

With Christianity, they have adopted civilisation. The people under my charge are now, as a whole, docile and law abiding. They have used their earnings to improve their material conditions. They have built neat and clean dwelling houses; they dress well, both men and women, after the fashion of civilised people; they are regular at church and at the Sacraments.

—Reverend A. J. Brabant, Hesquiat, October 1899

A MISSIONARY'S JOURNEY

Father Brabant brought the white man's religion to the Natives of the west coast. From his arrival in 1875, and the establishment of the mission at Hesquiat, he set out to bring change to the Native way of life and to instil a set of western values and beliefs garnered over hundreds of years of European culture. To a people whose own systems of belief, religion, and ceremony were based on thousands of years of living close to nature, the newcomers with a new message appeared foreign, yet intriguing. Particularly appealing was the music and ritual of the church, since most of the traditional Native social activities had been suppressed.[1] Brabant learned their language and gained their trust. Other missionaries, including the Presbyterians and the Methodists, followed.

Ucluelet was the centre of the first Presbyterian mission which opened in Ucluelet in 1890 under the Reverend J. A. MacDonald, who also started the first school for Natives near the Tseshaht reserve in Alberni. This became the Alberni Residential School. Alexander McKee, who had taught "the rudiments of farming and building"[2] at the school in 1892, also moved to work in Ucluelet in 1894.[3] These two men were succeeded by the Reverend Melvin Swartout, who arrived with his wife and their two children Nina and Viola in February, 1895. Swartout became proficient in the "Aht" language, the Native language of the west coast, and communicated easily. They in turn called him by a Native word meaning "The Indian." This may have prompted him to open another mission at Dodger Cove, among the Ohiaht tribe. Early in 1895 he opened a day school and began teaching children in the community. He relinquished this chore to school teacher Mr. J. W. Russell. Swartout maintained the mission at Dodger Cove until another missionary arrived to relieve him enabling him to continue his work elsewhere.[4]

Emily Carr described the Presbyterian mission and missionaries when she visited Ucluelet in 1898.[5] Although she never mentioned them by name, the time period would suggest the missionaries would have been the Reverend Swartout and Mrs. Swartout. The Mission House stood above high-tide. "The house was of wood, unpainted. There were no blinds or curtains. It looked, as we paddled up to it, as if it were stuffed with black."[6] Toxis, the Native name for the Mission House, was about a mile from the Native village. The school house which lay half-way between also served as a church on Sundays "and looked as Presbyterian as it could under the circumstances."[7] Carr dramatised the description of the missionaries: "The Greater Missionary had the most dignity; the Lesser Missionary was fussy. They had long pale faces. Their hair was licked from their foreheads back to buns on the scruffs of their necks. They had long noses straddled by spectacles, thin lips, mild eyes, and wore straight, dark dresses buttoned to the chin."[8]

From her written sketch of the encounter, she observed the stark life and meagre existence of the missionaries; the Natives, she described with warmth and humour. Their affection for her is noted in the name they called her: Klee Wyck, meaning Laughing One. "Her laughter in Ucluelet went out to meet the Indians, taking the place of words, forming a bond between them. They felt at once that the young girl staying in the missionaries' house understood them and they accepted her."[9] Impressed by the surroundings, she wrote:

> On the point at either end of the bay crouched a huddle of houses—large, squat houses made of thick, hand-hewn cedar planks, pegged and slotted together. They had flat, square fronts. The side walls were made of driftwood. Bark and shakes, weighted with stones against the wind, were used for roofs. Every house stood separate from the next. Wind roared through narrow spaces between. Houses and people were alike. Wind, rain, forest and sea had done the same things to both—both were soaked through and through with sunshine, too.[10]
>
> The great forest hugs its silence. The sea and the air hug the spilled cries of sea-birds. The forest hugs only silence; its birds and even its beasts are mute. When night came down upon Ucluelet the Indian people folded themselves into their houses and slept.[11]

On May 28, 1896, Alfred Carmichael, a close friend of Reverend Melvin Swartout who chronicled much of the early life in Alberni and on the west coast, accompanied the Swartouts and teacher Russell and his wife on a journey from Ucluelet to Village Island (Effingham), a distance of approximately fourteen miles. The destination was O-mo-oh, situated on the northeast side of the island in a sheltered bay, where the Tseshaht tribe from Alberni spent the spring and early summer hunting and fishing. Swartout arranged for the party to travel in two canoes, one manned by Charlie Hy-use and the Russells, the other by the Swartouts and Carmichael. "A race was also agreed upon between Charlie Hy-use's canoe and Mr. Swartout's—Charlie being sure his was the fastest canoe, which he proved by winning easily. Charlie was anxious to visit his *Lillicucus* on Village Island and being a 'Tyee' in his tribe in Ucluelet, he knew he would be well received among the Indians over the water."[12] Swartout made a point of taking along blankets and pillows to ensure the comfort of his wife.

Swartout dropped off a sack of potatoes at Soquah Village to encourage Natives to plant seeds and cultivate the soil. A similar experiment earlier at Ucluelet had left the Natives totally discouraged because the crop had been eaten by caterpillars. The Natives were convinced it was the *chehahs*, not the caterpillars, that had caused the destruction. *Chehahs* spirits took many forms and caused all manner of woes, even entering the body and causing sickness. Native medicine men were supposed to have the power to pull out the *chehahs*, enabling the patient to get well. Natives were convinced the *chehahs* were in the potatoes. When Swartout delivered the potatoes, the men of the village were away sealing. A frightened delegation representing the women accused the missionary of planning to murder the whole tribe. Swartout tried to explain the caterpillars were eating the crop and advised them to kill the insects. They brought him the larvae in big shells, expecting all manner of evil to befall him if he crushed them. Swartout had dedicated himself to educating and calming these fears.

At Soquah, two Natives in another canoe joined the excursion. The small armada set off in brilliant sunshine. At first there was only a slight swell on the sea instead of the gigantic rollers so familiar on the west coast. Each canoe took turns leading the small flotilla. About four miles from shore, when the waves became choppy, the canoes were separated. The Swartouts' canoe plunged into a huge wave and the occupants lost sight of the others. Carmichael handed over the paddle to the more experienced Reverend Swartout. As they passed between two islands, they found the other canoeists waiting by a sheltered bay. Another four miles lay between them and Village Island. Hoisting the sails this time, they skimmed across the water and within the hour were within sight of their destination.

The Native village lay nestled in a bay bordered by forest, with rocks on either side and a sandy beach in between. Surf pounding the shore made the landing difficult. Fortunately there were many willing hands on shore to help pull the canoes up the beach. Native men were busy on the beach doing various chores; one carving out a wooden bailer, another skinning a deer. The travellers explained they wished to stay one night and were pointed to a house. Of Siwash architecture, the building was forty by thirty feet wide, with two windows and a door facing the sea. Inside, on two sides, were sleeping benches raised about two feet from the ground, and a table. Russell lit the fire on the earthen floor beneath a hole in the roof.

Chief Shewish of the Tseshaht tribe occupied a house so large it could accommodate all his people with ample space to feast and dance.[13] The Shewish family used the section of the building furthest from the door. The Coat of Arms of the family hung on the wall and told in graphic form how the name of Shewish was famed among the whale hunters. A Native there named Ka-koop-et, or Mr. Bill, was known to the Tseshaht tribe as the "Keeper of the Songs." He was a twelve-year-old boy at the time of the Anderson Sawmill in Alberni and had been a favourite of Captain Stamp.[14] During Swartout's visit to O-mo-oh, he acted as interpreter between Swartout and Chief Shewish.

After dinner, Reverend Swartout held a church meeting in one of the Siwash houses. This was the first time the gospel had been preached on Village Island, although many of the Natives had encountered religion before in Alberni. First Chief Shewish voiced his thoughts on the subject of being a Christian:

Missionary, we are glad to have you with us. We are glad because you help us. You do things for us. Your medicine is good; your schools are good; we are pleased to have our children learn the English language. We do not want you to go away. We want you to stay and help us. But, Missionary, we do not understand what 'Christian' is. You are always talking about being a Christian. You want my people to become Christians. Yes, Missionary, I do not know what a Christian is. The Haidahs are Christian, and the Tsimsheans and some other tribes. A Christian is a man who never eats with his friends, but always sits down alone with his wife to eat. He never invites the other Indians to eat with him. He never gives a potlatch. That is a Christian, and Missionary, I do not want you to try to make Christians of my people. I do not want you to use the name 'Christian'. Do you hear me, Missionary?

I also want you to be very careful not to say anything about potlatching. You know this is our law and we do not want to give it up. Our fathers before us have potlatched and we want to do as they did. It is good to call our friends together and give them presents. I want all my people to do this. I do not want them to sit down, every man in his own house, and eat their meals alone with their wives. Missionary, do you hear? You must not teach my people to quit potlatching.[15]

Swartout chose his words carefully, acknowledging he had heard the Chief's words but wondering who had said he preached against the potlatch. Chief Shewish replied that Christians objected to their customs and wanted to make white men of them. The missionary admitted he did not understand the potlatch, but if the Natives worshipped birds and animals and placed them beside the Creator, then he had to speak against the ceremonies. He had no objection, however, if the custom was simply a social act. As for the term Christian, Swartout could think of no other name for a true follower of the Lord Jesus Christ, the Son of the Great Chief above. Chief Shewish laughed. After discussing the conversation with Ka-koop-et, the Chief concluded Swartout had no alternative but to use the word Christian. Afterwards everyone joined in singing all the well-known hymns. As the party bedded down for the night, an elder brought sacks and a piece of sail cloth to cover the windows and door.

Swartout described the scene at dawn:

At the earliest dawn there was a movement among the Indians. One by one they rose from their couches, wrapped blankets closely round them and silently passed outside. Standing for a moment at the threshold, each gave an anxious look towards the Eastern sky and then quietly sat down on the shore. Not a sound was made. The careless passerby might have been unaware of their presence, or, had he noticed, would easily have mistaken them for protruding stumps or rocks; but the morning light revealed the curious sight of a beach dotted with motionless watchers. It was the matins of the sun-worshipers.[16]

The visitors were presented with a quarter of venison, which they cooked in slices on spits in front of the fire. A storm battered the coast that day, making the journey back to Ucluelet impossible. Part of the afternoon was passed singing hymns. In the evening, some of the men practised singing for a grand potlatch Chief Shewish planned to give in the future. Russell and Carmichael joined them; Carmichael tried to imitate them, which caused some laughter. "Pronounced Yah-an, there is only one word in this song and they sing it over and over again, the big drum keeping time, and the singers going into all manner of attitudes, decked in paint and feathers. It is a weird sight, and very interesting."

Swartout organised another church meeting in the next house. Not everyone came, as some of the Natives continued with their potlatch practice. Those who did talked to Swartout afterwards. They wanted to know the full truth, but also wanted to show how "the old Indian law was the same as Jesus Law." They also expressed concern about the ban on potlatches and the old traditions. Carmichael questioned, "But can we forbid a tribe to whom the Christian faith has never been revealed to stop their otherwise innocent enjoyments?"

The return journey to Ucluelet was difficult; rough seas churned the Loudoun Channel with swells fourteen feet high. The canoes only saw each other when one or the other canoe topped the rollers. The wind blew from the southeast and they were heading west. The swell came from the southwest and the tide came in from the other direction. "We were very glad to get into the shelter of the islands and as the wind was favourable we encountered no more danger and we got home in time for a late breakfast."

The missionary continued to spread the gospel, admitting the Natives' greatest evil was drunkenness. White men visiting the area were more than willing to make a dollar by selling or trading alcohol. Swartout called his congregation together to advise of his new policy in dealing with this evil. "I am not going to watch you. I am going to trust you. If you want to get drunk, I will not inform against you or in any way seek to get you into trouble. Nor do I want to bring a white policeman here. We are men and we ought to know what is good and what is evil. If it is good to drink whiskey, then let us all drink, but if it is evil let us put the evil thing away from us."[17] The policy appeared to work. There were no loud drunken brawls; only an occasional bottle of liquor found its way onto the reservation.

IN AN OPEN BOAT FROM ALBERNI TO UCLUELET

One spring, Alfred Carmichael and Reverend Melvin Swartout rowed in an open boat from Alberni to Ucluelet. Swartout had been visiting the Tseshaht and Opetchesaht tribes whose villages lay on either side of the Somass River in Alberni. Now he was returning to the mission in Ucluelet. They made the journey in Carmichael's flat-bottomed boat purchased in 1891 when he worked at the Aberdeen cannery on the Skeena River. The boat was about fourteen feet (4.3 m) long and heavy to pull, but this did not deter the two men from making this historic trip to Ucluelet. The following is Carmichael's report of their journey.

We did not get away until late in the afternoon. It looked like rain. There was no wind—we had to row. We soon reached the mouth of the Somass River and the head of the wonderful deep sea inlet, the Alberni Canal. As we were anxious to get as far as possible before night, we kept rowing on. At every stream we passed, we said: "Let us go on to the next creek." At last it got so dark, and we were so tired rowing the heavy boat, we were forced to pull for the shore. There was no beach. The rocky side of the inlet was steep, and slippery, and wet also from the rain. We selected the flattest place whereon to spend the night. With difficulty, we found dry wood with which to make a fire, as by then it was black night, and there was no beachwood.

After eating supper, we crawled into our blankets, and drawing the canvas sheet over our heads, as it had begun to rain again, we thought of sleep. Our couch was hard, as we camped too late to make a bed of hemlock boughs. The rain increased, and soon little streams of water were running under our ground sheet. We did not budge. I do not think we slept very much that night. We were up at the streak of day. The morning was fine, and we soon forgot the troubles of the night. This was my first trip to Barclay Sound, and my friend was anxious for me to see some of the lovely spots among the islands and inlets of the Sound.

We rowed through Hell's Gate, passed the mouth of Uchucklesit Harbour and entered Imperial Eagle Channel of Barclay Sound. Here I had my first taste of the ocean swell, as there was quite a little sea coming in from the open Pacific Ocean. It made rowing quite awkward, as we were taking the sea on our beam. Bird Islets, now named Beerie Rooks, in Imperial Channel, were covered with nesting seagulls. We landed for a few minutes and climbed the rocks, finding numerous nests with eggs. The gulls flying around in clouds loudly protesting the intrusion.

Having safely crossed the troubled waters of Imperial Channel, we entered one of the most charming bits of inland water. It was called Boat Passage, or Canoe Pass. This passage lay between the twin Alma Russell Islands and the Sechart Peninsula. It is absolutely protected from every wind that blows. Never to be forgotten, was the idea of rest after storm which it suggested, as we passed through the very narrow entrance into that haven of tranquility. There was not a suggestion of a ripple on the water. The reflection of the over-hanging trees, and the barnacle-covered snags and rocks, still lives in memory.

Passing out through the southern end of Boat Passage, we crossed the Sechart Channel to that archipelago which lies between Imperial and Louden [sic] Channels. Hundreds of islands and islets in this one group cover an area of water of not more than two miles by four. What intricate waterways, what entrancing passage ways to explore! No wonder we spent some hours among the islands before emerging from behind the shelter of Turret Island to make the last dash across the seven miles of open, reef-strewn water, to Ucluelet Harbour.

It was our intention to delay crossing the open water until late in the afternoon, as the wind, if any, generally moderated towards evening. It must have been 4:00 p.m. before we left the shelter of the islands. There was a heavy ground swell, but no wind. We made good progress for about half the distance, then suddenly, with little warning, a strong, westerly breeze sprang up, which developed into a gale before we had made another mile, and almost in the time it takes to tell it, a heavy sea was running. As it was dead in our teeth, we soon found progress slow—indeed, it was all we could do to keep our boat straight pointed in the direction we wanted to go. The wind and waves caught our bow and swung us around. Even if we desired to turn and run for shelter, we dared not, as we were liable to be swamped in the act of turning. All we could do was to keep the nose of our boat straight for Ucluelet.

Darkness fell before we reached Shelter Islands, which lie about a mile from the entrance to Ucluelet Harbour. These islands consist of a few small islets surrounded by numerous reefs over which the sea was breaking heavily. There was no shelter for us there. A tremendous sea was now running. It was so dark, we could not see the shore, but marked quite clearly against the jet background, masses of white spray leapt [sic] up as the sea swept over the rocks. Every now and then a comber broke over our bow, and one of us would have to bail while the other kept the boat straight to the waves. We were absolutely done. We had been rowing, with few intermissions, since early dawn. It was only with the greatest effort that we made any progress whatever.

At last we saw the lighthouse on Amphitrite Point. Inch by inch, we worked our way across the entrance of the harbour to the sheltered side. Here, a cruel surprise awaited us. We had thought our difficulties over on reaching calm water. Instead of this, not only was there a strong wind blowing out of the harbour, but there was an ebb tide and the current was running swiftly out to sea. This was about the last straw to break the camel's back.

The house of the Indian Agent, in which the Swartout family lives, was some way up the harbour. We made up our minds to reach it before collapsing. Following the rocky shore as near as we dared, we kept rowing. It was very ragged rowing, and whose would not be after seventeen hours at the oars. At last we reached a point where we felt it safe to cross to the northern side of the harbour. With one last supreme effort, we just did that and beached our boat within one hundred yards of Swartout's house. It was just midnight. We had planned to be in by 6:00 p.m. It had taken eight hours to make as many miles. My companion was too weak to move, and just lay down for a few minutes before he recovered strength to walk up to his house. It was not long before Mrs. Swartout had a midnight supper ready, and did we not enjoy it! After a good night's sleep, we were in fine shape again.

Carmichael dates this adventure in the spring of 1898, but he may have been mistaken as he does claim this was his first trip to Barkley Sound. His previous journey from Ucluelet to Village Island took place in May 1896. The narrative was probably written later in his life, as he also mentions the lighthouse at Amphitrite Point. It was not until 1906 that a wooden tower was built and the point illuminated by a Wigham lamp.[18] Whatever the date, his description of the journey shows the incredible effort made by both men.

Swartout had been an excellent sailor and knew the sea well, having travelled widely on missionary trips to Native villages. Then came a fateful day on July 11, 1904, when he set out in his sailboat to visit the Reverend James R. Motion in Alberni. On his return to Ucluelet he was accompanied by a settler who lived ten miles out of the village. When the man landed at his farm, he stood and watched the receding sailboat and its sole occupant until they disappeared around a point of land. This was the last time the missionary was seen alive.[19] The weather had been stormy, and it was at first thought Swartout might have sought shelter on a small island at the entrance to Ucluelet Inlet. Searchers failed to find any trace of the missionary or his boat until a piece of the boat washed ashore on a beach near Toquart. His body eventually was recovered at Florencia Bay (Wreck Bay), five miles west of Ucluelet.[20]

Mrs. Swartout continued with the mission in Ucluelet for several years. After she left, the Presbyterians were served by laymen until Joseph Samuel was appointed in 1910 and Thomas Shewish in 1912. In 1920, Ucluelet became part of the West Coast Marine Mission which serviced all of Barkley Sound.

While the Presbyterians were establishing their mission centre in Ucluelet, the Methodists appointed the Reverend W. John Stone, in 1894, to serve Clo-oose and Nitinat, south of Bamfield. During the Stones' first year there, their second son died. Despite this tragic loss, the Stones continued their mission. There was a large population of Nitinat Natives receiving Stone's indoctrination. In 1902, Stone reported that the moral quality of life in Nitinat was improving. Drunkenness on the reserve was absent but he felt a need for a spiritual awakening.[21] The Stones remained there until 1904 when they moved to Ucluelet and went into the transportation business, operating a small boat, the *Tofino*, between Ucluelet and Port Alberni. The Methodists continued to fill the position until Church Union in 1925, when they joined with the Presbyterians to become the United Church of Canada.

Natives felt no hostility towards the Roman Catholic, Presbyterian, or Methodist missionaries; some even welcomed their presence, perhaps for motives other than religion. However, churches have since recognised and regretted the role they played in diminishing Native traditions and culture. "The missionaries were helpful, in a way, because they taught English to the Indians. Although some people seem to think they would know more of their culture without the Church being present."[22]

> Whiteman's religion we believe in, as we had our own religion that we believed in. We prayed the same way as the same religions of today. Our religion was done in private homes when help was needed. The people practised this religion very strongly. Churches ask us to do the same thing today, to help each other to go to church and say in your own way of life and your own way of praying. Physical way of life meant peace of mind, get up early in the morning, go to bed early.[23]

A JOURNEY TO ALBERNI

First traders, then missionaries, and then settlers began taking up land along the shorelines, bays and inlets of the Alberni Canal. The largest settlement was Alberni, where businessmen and farmers looked to a new industry to supplement their growth. They came up with a project to build the first paper mill in the province. Victoria and Vancouver were benefiting from the influx of business and industry, why not Alberni? Great things were forecast for this central island community.

George Hubert Bird heard about these glowing reports of Alberni in Nanaimo, where he worked for the firm Foreman and Campbell of Nanaimo Boat House. "On Vancouver Island, the name of Alberni was on many people's tongues, though so far not many outsiders had ever visited it. It was before the days of photographic cuts in the newspapers, so the magic name was a sort of Shangri-la, to be pictured only in one's mind."[24] He answered a newspaper advertisement for a steam engineer for the new paper mill being constructed there and got the job.

Bird was born in 1866 at Ampthill, England; he spent his early childhood on a farm near Peterborough, England. Following a grammar school education, he apprenticed as a machinist for Kitson and Company of Leeds. In 1886, the company sent him to Australia to oversee their exhibition at the Melbourne Exposition. He liked the country so well he promised himself he would return one day.

On his return to England, he married Florence Amelia Longly. They sailed for Australia with the intention of only visiting Vancouver, but plans changed when he fell in love with the west coast and decided to stay in Canada. Bird first worked with the Canadian Pacific Railway as an engine wiper, tending locomotives after their cross-Canada run. He moved on to Harrison Hot Springs Hotel where he was put in charge of the engines which pumped the water from the springs to the swimming pool. There was a short stint in Port Angeles, Washington, before moving to Nanaimo.

At the time, there were only about sixty-five families living in Alberni, a relatively small agricultural community compared to Nanaimo which thrived on coal production. In Alberni, however, there were numerous opportunities for growth with the building of the British Columbia Paper Manufacturing Co. plant. This was the first paper mill built in British Columbia and there were great expectations for its success. The company had purchased a boat for use between Alberni and the paper mill, which was located two miles upstream on the Somass River. Bird's first job was to deliver the *Lily* to Alberni, not an easy task considering the boat.

This boat, the *Lily*, had been owned previously by Robert Dunsmuir and used in the construction of the first Esquimalt Drydock. It was then turned over to a Mr. Foster of Departure Bay, who used it to carry fresh water to sailing ships loading coal. She was about forty feet long and very wide of beam. Her boiler was set in brick work. The steering wheel was so arranged one could fasten it, step down into the fire hole, throw on a few shovels of coal or sticks of wood, and hop back again. Usually if one had moved quickly, it was found that the boat was not very much off its course. Although she was slow and sure on the Somass River and Alberni Canal, she was not the boat one would choose for travel out at sea. Foster was to deliver her to Victoria and I was to go along to help and to learn.[25]

William Sutton, of the Sutton sawmill in Ucluelet, would have accompanied Bird on the journey around the island, but after he saw the boat, he changed his mind. When no pilot could be found, the small steamer *T. W. Carter*, owned and skippered by Captain Foote, was chartered to make the trip. With the *Lily* in tow, the *T. W. Carter* left Victoria in calm seas and arrived at Port Renfrew the next morning without incident. The sea turned rough so they waited there for better weather; on the third day Captain Foote decided to continue the voyage. There were heavy swells and fog, as is common on the coast. They had not gone far when the fire-bars in the *T. W. Carter* boiler fell down. The *Lily* continued on although it now received little assistance from the other boat which could barely gather up enough steam. They rounded Cape Beale in high winds often losing sight of each other, but arrived in Bamfield safely.

Bird noted, "We reached Banfield [*sic*] which then showed no sign of any development." The next morning he continued on to Alberni without escort, but with a good chart. On the way up the canal, Bird passed the old Pocahontas '62' sign painted on the rock at Hell's Gate thirty years before. The old ship's name had been repainted but the date was no longer visible. Also, clearly visible, on a mountainside opposite Copper Mountain, he saw two huge black bears facing each other. Later he learned they were painted on wide hand-made boards, which at a distance had looked very real. The boards were set up one-third of the way up the mountain to mark a bear hunter's last resting place.[26]

He stopped at Green Cove in Uchucklesit Inlet to eat dinner and noted that, as at Banfield, there were no settlers except Natives. Meanwhile, those Alberni residents expecting Bird's arrival, including his wife Florence, who had arrived two days earlier by stagecoach with their son George, thought the worst when the steamer *Maude*, having steamed up the canal, reported no sign of seeing Bird or his boat. Before long, Bird put their anxiety to rest when he docked the *Lily* at Captain Huff's wharf, in the present location of Victoria Quay. Because he had handled the boat by himself, he earned the Native title, Tse-wees-tah, meaning "One man in a boat." It was the first week of August 1892. Bird's first impressions of Alberni were duly recorded:

> On the left corner, facing the wharf, was Fred Saunders' general store, owned by his brother Henry of Victoria. Saunders' store seemed to be the chief gathering place of the many miners then prospecting in the neighbouring hills. Saunders bought furs when offered. I remember seeing him buy a very good mink skin for seventy-five cents and coon skins for fifty cents. Next to Saunders' store, facing opposite the Kitsuksis Creek bridge, was the building containing the post-office. Mrs. Erickson, the post-mistress, owned it. Beyond the post-office was the Alberni Hotel, also newly constructed—the largest building in the settlement. It was the first and only place on the West Coast where intoxicants could be purchased. This was owned by Mike Sareault. Another building in sight on the river front was Archie McLaughlin's small board and batten house. Shoemaker Parkinson's little house beyond was hidden in the trees.[27]

The village settlement had a recently completed Presbyterian Church, a courthouse, and a small log cabin which housed the jail, as well as a number of residences. Beyond Alberni and across the Roger Creek bridge, a trail wound its way south towards the mines on China Creek. At the former site of the Anderson Sawmill settlement, only the old piles of the mill wharves remained standing, blackened by fire. Little else remained except the cribs filled with large stones on which the mill buildings had stood. The road to Nanaimo was "not wide enough and straight enough to be seen all the way to the top of the hill. On its way it disappeared in the trees."

The family settled down in a place rented from Thomas Paterson, a local landowner who also operated a stable where locals could hire a horse, buggy or sulky, and who later became lightkeeper at Cape Beale. Bird worked in the small sawmill that provided the lumber to build the paper mill. A home was built in

"Mill Town" in 1901. The family quickly assimilated into the social life of the community. Bird was also firmly committed and worked diligently for All Saint's Anglican church in Alberni. Even after he moved to New Alberni, he continued to support his church. Many Sundays, he and his wife walked through the forest to attend services there.

Bird was still a young man, only twenty-six years old, who enjoyed sporting activities. In January 1893, he overheard Dr. Robinson, a young Nanaimo doctor visiting Alberni, say he planned to be the first to ride across Vancouver Island on a bicycle. Bird decided to beat the doctor for the record. He had never been over the road so did not know what to expect, but he thrilled at the adventure and the challenge. He met no one, either coming or going, on the whole twenty-eight miles from the Cherry Creek junction to the Half-way house near Parksville, but there were a few settlers between there and Nanaimo.

Wellington was a considerable town of several hundred people. Coal trains chugged through the streets on their way to the ships at Departure Bay. The town had the name of being the best of its size for business in the Dominion. There were churches, one with a spire, and a large colliery close on its outskirts. No one would look at a coin of less value than ten cents in either Wellington or Nanaimo. The road between the two towns was alive with horse-drawn vehicular traffic. I called in at the *Free Press* office on my arrival. The next day I was surprised to see a short account of my journey, headed "The First Bicycle across Vancouver Island."[28]

While Bird continued working in the mill, Florence gave birth to three more children, Charlotte, Doris, and Flossie. The paper mill closed in 1895. The first paper had been produced in 1894 from old rags, clothing and ropes, but it was not of sufficiently high quality to become a saleable product. "Getting an adequate supply of rags in a country where the population had trouble clothing itself was difficult. Coast towns were searched for material, but by the time it reached Alberni, the cost was prohibitive. Everything from ships' sails to construction overalls was used; ferns, manila rope and wood were all tried."[29]

After the paper mill enterprise failed, Bird continued operating the sawmill providing lumber for the local market. The arrival of Arthur E. Waterhouse in 1896 to the old Anderson mill site changed the future business development pattern, when he opened a wharf and a store in Stamp Harbour, eager to cater to the needs of the miners. It was closer for the miners to frequent the Waterhouse's store than to travel to Huff's or Saunders' store in Alberni. Bird decided to move his sawmill to the foot of Argyle Street, near the Waterhouse enterprise. "I have often thought that in a small way I gave an impetus to the start of our city, for I recall the building of eleven houses as soon as I was able to supply the lumber." Bird supplied the lumber and George Forrest the construction expertise for the new Waterhouse store on the waterfront. It faced down the canal and adjoined the approach to the warehouse on the wharf. There were now two communities growing, Alberni and New Alberni, separated by a two-mile wagon road.

The Bird family continued to grow; two more children, Tom and Esther, were born in New Alberni. George and Florence now had six children. As the two towns grew, so too did Bird's business. He supplied lumber for the Somass Hotel, the King Edward Hotel, Grandy's Livery Stables, and the Kildonan cannery. When New Alberni incorporated, changing its name to Port Alberni, on March 15, 1912, Bird became one of the first aldermen under Mayor Waterhouse. Alberni incorporated in 1913. Bird closed his sawmill when he enlisted in the Great War. He returned to England to work in a munitions factory. Son George also enlisted; he had worked for the Royal Bank of Canada. Florence received news in October, 1916, that her son had been wounded. Confirmation came the following spring—he had died in France.

Bird was very much a family man, his wife and children were the centre of his life. He must have missed them terribly when he returned to England to serve and protect the land of his birth. His daughter Florence recalled her father's return:

At times father amazed us. In a sense, the following incident illustrates his character. Upon returning from England after the war, he found upon arrival in Nanaimo that he had missed the stage coach for Alberni. Not wishing to wait a few days for the next stage, he set out on foot and walked home, a long and lonely journey of about fifty-five miles through the woods.[30]

Bird sold the sawmill, which was converted into a shingle mill, and it operated continuously until 1952. Meanwhile, Bird worked in the construction business spending most of his time on administration. In 1941 he began writing and documenting the early history of the Albernis. In 1947, he was made an honorary life member of the Alberni District Board of Trade for his contribution to the community.

GEORGE FRASER

As the new century approached, a few settlers began taking up land at Ucluelet, at the western entrance to Barkley Sound. In 1899, there were only fifteen whites and two hundred Natives living there.[31] The name of the village means "People with a safe landing place," and the harbour was that to many of the fishing and trading vessels finding safe anchorage there. This influx of Native money and trade was good news for Ucluelet and it encouraged some entrepreneurs to open businesses.

When Herbert J. Hillier left Victoria for Ucluelet, he was told that it was a good move, that the road was going that way, and that there were years of work ahead. On arriving in Ucluelet, April 9, 1899, aboard the CPR steamship *Willapa*, which sailed from Victoria four times a month, he met James Sutton, with wife and family, owner of the store and also part owner of larger tracts of timber and land. He also met George Fraser, a botanist, who had started his gardens about 1895.[32] William and James Sutton began a shingle-and-sawmill operation in 1884 and opened Ucluelet's first store. The Suttons had purchased large tracts of forest along the Estevan coastal plain, as far north as Nootka Island. Hillier found work as a lineman; he lived at Curvin Beach on Barkley Sound and travelled by canoe from Ucluelet to Effingham Inlet to check on the line which ran along the beach.

The reputation and name of George Fraser is known throughout the world in horticultural circles. As spring arrives each year, you might be fortunate enough to have a rhododendron *R. Fraseri* growing in your garden. If so, then you are perpetuating the legend of Fraser who, in his lifetime, became known as a landscape artist and expert horticulturist. The Village of Ucluelet has recognised this remarkable man by dedicating a memorial garden in his name. The garden contains rhododendron plants which he originally hybridised. From Lossiemouth, on the shore of the North Sea in Scotland, to Ucluelet on the west coast of Canada, George Fraser travelled far to become one of Canada's prominent horticulturists.

Fraser was born on October 25, 1854, to John and Eliza Fraser, servants at the Drainie Manse in the parish of Drainie, near Lossiemouth. Scotland was studded with large estates, some with magnificent gardens maintained by servants who lived in estate cottages. When he grew up, it was inevitable he would follow in his father's footsteps and take a position on a nearby estate. At the age of seventeen, he served as an apprentice gardener at Gordon Castle, in Fochabers, a few miles from his birthplace. Over the next few years, he worked on various estates, including Millance, in Kirkcudbrightshire, and Hartfield House, on the Clyde, near Glasgow. In 1877 he was foreman at Craigflower, in Fyfe, and later became head gardener at Auchmore, in Perthshire.[33]

One wonders why he would decide to emigrate to Canada after having attained a position that gave him a certain amount of prestige and security. Possibly he wanted to own his own property where he could develop a nursery and be his own boss, or like many of his generation, he was attracted to the lure of the new world. In 1883 he arrived in Canada, settling first in Winnipeg, where he worked for the Canadian Pacific Railway and in his spare time operated a greenhouse. The bitter cold winters of Winnipeg were not to his liking, so in 1888 he moved to Victoria where he and some partners landscaped what is now known as Beacon Hill Park. Some rhododendrons planted by Fraser, near Fountain Lake, or Goodaire Lake, in the park, are still thriving today.

Still he was dissatisfied, he wanted some land of his own to develop. The perfect location seemed to be Sproat Lake, near Alberni, where in 1889 he purchased 136 acres on Kleecoot Bay, on the north side of the lake.[34] But the land was heavily timbered and he soon discovered it would have been a monumental task to develop a nursery business in that location. In 1894 he moved to Ucluelet, where two years earlier, on October 5, 1892, he had purchased Lot 21, consisting of 236 acres, just north of the entrance to Barkley Sound. Today this covers half of the Village of Ucluelet. His two brothers James and William later joined him.

Fraser, by this time forty years of age, began clearing his land of cedar, hemlock and fir trees and the dense undergrowth of salal. It was back-breaking work completing over four acres on which he planted his first nursery and built his home. The heavy rains on the west coast depleted the soil of nutrients, requiring Fraser to install a drainage system of split cedar wooden drains. He supplemented the soil by adding seaweed, fish refuse and cow manure which he hauled in a flat scow behind his skiff from further up the inlet. He then carried the fertiliser up the bank to his clearing and spread it on the land.

The ingenuity of the Scottish gardener was remarkable. In a lean-to behind his house he constructed a small rooting frame, providing bottom heat for the beds by installing a wood-burning stove in a hole at a lower elevation and conducting the warm smoke through clay tiles buried beneath the seed beds, which vented into the atmosphere. It took Fraser seven years from the time he began the hybridisation process until he could see the results. Gradually the garden bloomed with displays of heathers, roses, azaleas, rhododendrons, fruit trees, holly and maple trees, berries of different varieties and ornamental shrubs.

Fraser used the earth's natural landforms, including outcroppings of rock, where he designed small and secluded areas for special plants. "There were beds of pansies, ferns and violets growing unobtrusively at the foot of a tree or behind a pile of stones. He used a ridge of rocks along the west side of the lower footpath to incorporate into a rock garden."[35] A small wooden bridge crossed the end of a pool, and on the south side there was a bench where visitors liked to have their photographs taken. Given the location of Fraser's nursery, most of his business had to be done by mail. George Fagerberg, foreman at the Layritz nursery in Victoria, recalled that when they received shipments of plants from Fraser's nursery, the plants would be carefully packed in sphagnum moss in wooden crates which appeared to have been constructed of pieces of driftwood.[36]

During the summer months when the *Princess Maquinna* and

Princess Maquinna

later the *Princess Nora* stopped in Ucluelet, Captain Gillam tied up for several hours to allow passengers time to visit the garden. From all reports, Fraser enjoyed these visits and was always willing to share his knowledge. One traveller wrote a glowing report of the village and Fraser's garden.

Ucluelet, a pretty little settlement, well sheltered from the winds of the west, is situated at the end of the run (CPR steamer, Tofino). Evidence of the mildness of the climate is obtained when the splendid gardens of George Fraser are seen. Even in February there is a greenness about the place generally that gives a slight indication of what the splendid mass of rhododendrons will look like when they are in fall foliage and bloom. Mr. Fraser, who supplies the CPR with shrubs for the various large gardens on the Company's system, is in a position to cater to the horticulturist, with almost every variety of shrub.[37]

Fraser maintained some ties with Alberni; in 1922, he returned as a judge for a daffodil flower show organised by the newly formed Alberni District Horticultural Society.[38]

Since his arrival in Ucluelet, Fraser tried rhododendron breeding but his most important rhododendron hybrid came about almost by chance. In a shipment of cranberry plants sent to him from Nova Scotia in 1897, which he intended to cross with the local wild variety, he recognised a weed as *Rhododendron canadense*, the wild rhododendron of eastern Canada and the United States. He planted it separately, and fifteen years later, when it bloomed, promptly crossed it with *R. japonicum*. This cross bloomed in 1919, and later that year, he sent a budded plant to the Arnold Arboretum in Boston. When they failed to acknowledge receiving the plant, he sent another budded plant to William Watson, curator at Kew Gardens in England, who in 1920 named it *R. Fraseri*. The same year and quite independently, the Arnold Arboretum also named it *R. Fraseri*. In 1920, Watson wrote in the Gardeners' Chronicle, "I believe that this is the first hybrid of *Rhododendron canadense* recorded."[39]

Fraser was especially interested in developing new strains of plants by crossing local native varieties with selected domestic

Captain Edward Stamp. PN 502

Harry Guillod. PN 101

Gilbert Malcolm Sproat. PN 538

Captain Edward Hammond King.
COURTESY ALBERNI VALLEY MUSEUM.

*Kate Guillod
with daughters
Caroline & Kate*
PN 41

Gus Cox with Native family AVM PN 9078

Petroglyphs at Sproat Lake near Port Alberni. PN 1918

George Bird family. Back row: George H. Bird, wife Florence; Centre: Eldest son George and youngest son Thomas on knee. Standing left to right; daughters Charlotte, Doris and Florence. Another daughter Ester was born in 1907. PN 106

Native homestead with Mabel Taylor. PN 469

Bamfield Cable Station. PN 478

Schooner loading lumber in 1860 at the Anderson sawmill. PN 497

Ralph family picnic scene down the Alberni Canal. Identified in front row are Everett, Janet and Leonard Ralph: Left and right, Mrs. Ralph and Mr. Ralph. Extreme top right, A. E. Waterhouse. This photo was used in a Centennial movie produced in Ottawa. The scene was considered typical of Vancouver Island in the period up to 1914. Leonard Frank photo. PN 567

Falling with power saw. PN 775

Identified aboard the Quadra *are Mayor C. Frederick Bishop, Mayor Dick Burde, and Cory Wood an employee. Circa 1912.* LEONARD FRANK PHOTO. PN 912

Emanuel J. Cox with daughters Patty (Mrs. Haslam) and Frances (Mrs. Morrison).
PN 1007

Watson saltery at Port Alberni, 1912. PN 1159

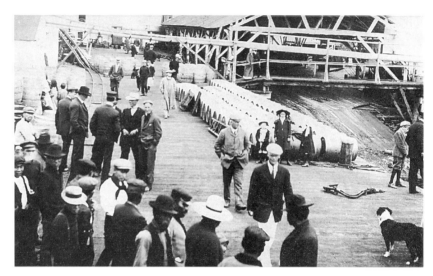

Excursion of the Vancouver Island Development League at Sechart Whaling Station July 17, 1910. WRIGHT PORRITT PHOTO. PN 1411

The gentlemen of the British Empire. Staff of Bamfield Cable Station. PN 1399

Sarita Pole on reserve.
PN 1824

Indian Village, Uchucklesit Harbour. PN 1773

Harpoon gun on board whaling vessel. PN 2369

Capt. Binns and Wm. Sutton, left, panning for gold at Wreck Bay. PN 2704

Entrance to Port Alberni Coal Mine, 1910-1920. Businessman second from left is Alfred Carmichael; third from left is Archibald Dick. PN 149

Ore concentrator - Toquart Bay. PN 3006

Antony Watson, right, with a two day food supply for approximately 100 men working on the road from Underwood to the Thistle Mine. PN 3009

Section of water flume for Duke of York mine on China Creek in 1896. The trestle-work was 60 feet high and suspended from the cliff by chains of 5/8 iron, the flume was 6 feet wide by 3 feet high and one and one-quarter miles long. PN 3021

Above left: A giant cedar at Franklin River. Harold Bronson, foreman, holding hard hat. BCRSA 82050. PN 3038 ***Above right:*** *Topping a spar tree at Franklin River.* PN3045

Franklin Camp B, 1939. BCRSA 82048. PN 3047

*APL Co.1931 Camp 4 Underwood Cove. Identified are L. L. Brown, Labor
Commissioner for British Columbia, Ross Pendleton, manager, Martin Allerdale
Grainger, chairman, Jack McMillan, sales manager, John Lofer and Nuta Wright.*
BCRSA 52266. PN 3051

Sarita Bay 1976. Harry Dyler photo. PN 3337

Ecoole fishing dock. Mabel Taylor photo. PN 3385

Captain George Albert Huff's stern-wheeler Willie *docking at the Thistle mine wharf at Underwood Cove.* PN 3752

Mabel Taylor
in 1975 at Polly Point.
PN 4160

Agnes Dick

Vanlene *wreck.*   PN 5248

ones. He created a popular hybrid rose by crossing the local *Rosa Nutkana* with the hybrid tea *Richmond*. The local honeysuckle, which lacked fragrance, was crossed with a European species to produce a rampant grower that produced fragrant blooms in spring and again in autumn, and whose bright coral berries remain ornamental into the winter.

In 1919, Joseph Gable of Stewartstown, Pennsylvania, the dean of all American rhododendron hybridizers and the first recipient of the Pioneer Medal, the American Rhododendron Society's most prestigious honour, was put in touch with Fraser. The two men became firm friends; although they never met, they would correspond for the rest of Fraser's life.[40] This connection between Ucluelet and Stewartstown, Pennsylvania, had a considerable influence on rhododendron hybridising. Fraser urged Gable to try his hand at breeding and sent him a letter of introduction to E. J. P. Magor of Lamellen, Cornwall, England, who also exchanged seed, pollen, plants and correspondence. From these letters emerges of picture of a kind and gentle man who lived life frugally and enjoyed his plate of porridge every morning because it was easy to make and he liked it.

In 1935, on the occasion of Fraser's eighty-third birthday, the community held a social in his honour at the Ucluelet Athletic Hall. The whole community showed up to show their appreciation to their "oldest settler." Fraser not only danced but played his violin with the orchestra. After supper everyone joined in a sing-song accompanied by the guest and his violin.

> During the evening, he was persuaded to sing several familiar Scottish airs which were enjoyed greatly by the eager audience. Mr. Fritz Bonnetti sang a Swiss yodelling song; Mr. Burbridge amused everyone by singing the Jolly Old Miller, during which everyone joined in the chorus. Mr. Henrico Bonnetti gave several accordion selections. The evening was brought to a close by the singing of Auld Lang Syne. Then everyone joined in giving three cheers for Mr. Fraser.[41]

Although he was getting on in years, Fraser continued to keep an active interest in the affairs of the Vancouver Island Horticultural Association. In 1936, he was elected a life member of the association, the first to be so honoured. He also received a special gold medal from the association for his work in the interests of horticulture on Vancouver Island.[42]

Fraser was not above voicing his opinion in public if something bothered him. In one case, it was a logged-off area at the entrance to the canal. In a letter to the editor of the *West Coast Advocate* in Port Alberni in 1937, he offered some professional advice to anyone who would listen.

> One of the first stands of Douglas fir cut down and logged off in Barkley Sound was on what is now a rather steep hill-side above Kildonan cannery and Green Cove saltery, near the entrance to the Alberni Canal. It is very conspicuous to visitors as no young trees have grown up to take the place of those logged off. If evergreen trees are expected to be grown there again, it is time the matter of replanting was being considered as Douglas firs or any other evergreen conifer will take at least a hundred years to come to maturity.
>
> If a hard-wooded deciduous tree such as the silver-barked birch was contemplated, its seed could be sown now and the trees would be full grown in 30 years. The European silver birch is particularly adapted for just such situations as this. This European tree would be almost sure to do well on that bare hillside or anywhere in Barkley Sound. A number of trees of it have been growing in Ucluelet for the last 25 years, where the climatic conditions are almost similar.[43]

In the late thirties it became evident Fraser's physical strength was waning. An editorial pointed out what a loss his passing would be to British Columbia. "His greatest passion, his lovely flowers and his garden, must not be neglected; the creative genius of this famous plant specialist is soon to be lost, and to those who know him and who have visited his garden when it was at its best, this is a real catastrophe to Canada and British Columbia."[44]

After Fraser's death in 1944, the contents of his shack were thrown out and burned and the shack he called home was torn down to make way for a housing development. All his records were destroyed. Fortunately Gable saved his correspondence and in 1960 sent the letters to the British Columbia archives in Victoria.

Fraser was buried in Ucluelet Cemetery but no marker was placed on his grave. In 1990, the Army, Navy, and Air Force veterans, the Lions Club, and the Ucluelet Historical Society placed a marble stone on his grave. During his lifetime in Ucluelet, Fraser endeared himself to children who came to picnic in his garden around his lily pond where he would teach them about growing plants. He never forgot his Scottish friends in Winnipeg and Victoria, sending them boxes of heather in January for their Burns night celebrations.

He was a charter member of the Ucluelet Athletic Club and donated the eleven acres of land on which their hall was built. The hall still stands today and is used for all types of community activity. Most of this land was later given to the Ucluelet school board and is the site of the elementary and secondary schools as well as their playing fields.

Fifty years after his death, Fraser was honoured for his contribution towards the growing of rhododendrons on the North American continent. He was awarded posthumously the Pioneer Award by the American Rhododendron Society, the fourth such person to receive such an honour.[45] His friend Gable was the first.

BAMFIELD BEGINNINGS

Bamfield would undoubtedly have become a community, with or without the Bamfield Cable Station, because of its strategic position at the entrance to Barkley Sound on the south shore. However, the emergence of this international institution created credibility and position on the west coast by bringing staff and services that would not otherwise have arrived until much later in the decade. The location was chosen because it was the nearest point in Canada to Australia.

In 1902, the Trans-Pacific Cable arrived in Bamfield. The round-the-world communication system was designed to touch only the British Empire so that it could be defended in time of war. At a cost of $1,795,000, the stretch of cable between Bamfield and Australia was seven thousand miles long, with sub-stations at Fanning Island, Suva, Fiji and Norfolk Island. In places the cable lay three thousand fathoms deep on the bottom of the ocean.

Building the longest cable in the world was considered by many experts to be unworkable, ill-considered, and ill-conceived. Halifax was already the terminus of the first Trans-Atlantic cable laid in the 1860s. Initially the cable proved unreliable as it broke several times before a new type of cable was introduced. Credit for forgoing all the naysayers lay with Sir Sandford Fleming, the chief engineer of the Canadian Pacific Railway (CPR), who persisted and, against all odds, brought the successful project to fruition. Sandford Island and Fleming Island in Barkley Sound were named after Sir Sandford Fleming. From Britain to Australia the cable laid around the world provided a world-class telegraphic communications system. The task of laying the cable required a special ship, the *Colonia*. George Bird recalled seeing the ship:

> On October 6, 1902, I was taking a small steam launch, the *Vladimir*, to Port Renfrew. As we neared Cape Beale, this great ship (the *Colonia*) came into view—the cable had been successfully laid and with the cable storage tanks empty, she floated high in the water. That day the end of the cable was put ashore and test messages were sent. It was officially opened October 31, 1902.[46]

The *Colonia* proved too large a ship for maintenance so two smaller vessels were built for this purpose, one being the *Iris*, a twin-screw steamer, 295 feet in length. Built in Scotland, specifically for servicing submarine cables, the *Iris* went into commission in 1902 and continued her service at Suva and Fanning Island. Some time later a submarine cable was laid down the canal from Bamfield to Port Alberni, because the land telegraph line, worked on by Garrard and others, proved too unreliable.

The CPR's western division architect, Francis Mawson Rattenbury, designed and supervised the building of an accommodation block in Queen Anne style to house as many as twenty operators and staff, as well as a separate place for the chief telegrapher.

> A verandah with Roman Doric columns distinguished the residential block. Arched windows in the side projections and a gabled roof were included for a cost of $25,000. The interior of the main building was finished to help reduce any feeling of

148

isolation for people at the cable station. A billiard room overlooked Barkley Sound; there was a library with more than 3,000 volumes on hand; and a music room. Married quarters were also provided.[47]

A large concrete building housed the generating engine for electricity and pumping water, and a wood-frame shingled building housed the operating and maintenance personnel. The building stood on a strategic point on a hillside between Grappler Inlet and Bamfield Inlet. The sight of this beautiful building caused many to pause and reflect on its surroundings.

> The cable station at Bamfield, which is the next stopping place, is ideally located amid surroundings that ought to appeal to the most indifferent. Situated high up on a commanding bluff, a magnificent view of the surrounding scenery is obtained. Islands, sea and mountains, stretch as far as the eye can see, making a picture that only a Turner could hold, in some small measure to reproduce. Amid these pleasant surroundings, a large staff of telegraphists is employed for it is here that the news from Australia is received, relayed all over the continent and to the British Isles. Some sixteen men are employed in shifts, to ensure an uninterrupted service. Astern is Bamfield, looking prettier than ever in the distance, and on the right, the gleaming snow capped peaks of the Saw Tooth range, rearing their lofty heads all along the coast.[48]

The Pacific Cable Board operators were highly trained and among the best in the world. "Some men could handle half a million words in a year without making a single error. Errors could cost an operator his increment for the year."[49] Twenty-four of the forty-five people employed at the station were operators. Most senior staff were either Australians or New Zealanders recruited from the system's headquarters in Sydney. They were rotated from one station to another.

The *Iris* returned to Barkley Sound when a second cable was laid in 1914. "After the *Iris* has completed coaling at Ladysmith, she will survey the proposed route with a view to discovering the nature of the bottom on which the cable will rest. Owing to the rocky nature of this coast, it is expected that a heavier cable than usual will have to be used."[50]

Originally the cable landed in Port Alberni near the oil tanks, but when the forest industry prospered, the landing site was moved south to the present area, above the former plywood plant and north of Polly Point, to avoid the cable being sliced by ships' anchors. The Pacific Cable Board further extended services by building a trench cable from Port Alberni to Parksville, and a submarine cable from Parksville to Nanaimo, which connected with cables from Nanaimo to Vancouver. This provided a link directly to Vancouver and Montreal without manual transmission.

In 1907, the Albernis were abuzz with William Roff's suggestion that the Cable Station be moved to Port Alberni. He had written to several English weeklies advocating the move. Roff gave his hypothesis:

> While it would be a great advantage to the staff to get away from the isolation of Bamfield into the genial atmosphere of social life in Alberni, it appears to me to be a step of far greater import to Alberni itself. The cable is the connecting link between England, Canada, Australia and New Zealand, and the immediate point where continent is joined to continent must, of necessity, be of world-wide reputation. I do not think the advocacy of the removal of the station is a wild goose scheme but a very practical and probable one, and likely to be put into execution. Alberni should be the ocean port of the western coast and one of the necessities it would require is telegraphic communication with all parts of the world. With the cable established here that requirement would be accomplished and its existence would be a powerful advocate and inducement for the realization of that object.[51]

His letter received the endorsement of prominent Alberni citizen James Thomson, who added a further suggestion: If the Cable Station should come to Port Alberni, the building in Bamfield could be used for "life saving and fisheries."[52] The editor of the *Alberni Pioneer News*, Dick Burde, an advocate for anything that would further the prosperity of New Alberni, got in on the fray by supporting the idea of contacting the Member of Parliament

William Sloan "in order that he may have some time to work on it during the present session of parliament."[53] Only one voice questioned the financial ramifications of the move. New Alberni businessman Wright Porritt reasoned, "The cost of removal would be approximately seventy-five thousand dollars. Would the removal to Alberni increase their revenue to this extent? The benefit to Alberni is, of course, self evident."[54]

A petition to relocate the Cable Station began circulating in the twin cities of Alberni and New Alberni. One month later, in January 1908, Porritt congratulated Roff on how skilfully he had avoided the financial question of the move.

> Unless it can be demonstrated to the cable board that a removal to Alberni will enable them to lessen expenses, it is my firm conviction that petitions will be useless. I return to Bamfield on this boat and will make enquiries there, and try to help the thing along. I am just as anxious as Mr. Roff to see the station here, and I think we shall find that we of Alberni, and not the cable board, will have to prove the benefits of removal before the matter will receive due consideration at headquarters.[55]

Porritt's dose of reality seemed to put a damper on any further enthusiasm to relocate the station. The subject died a sure death. If there was one ingredient the residents of the Albernis had in abundance, it was optimism. They always had high hopes and dreams for their city, which they thought one day would be "the metropolis of Vancouver Island."[56]

Bamfield Inlet had been the home for thousands of years of the Ohiaht tribe. At the time of construction of the Cable Station, only a few Native shacks remained of the ancient village. It was here the whale would be brought after the hunt for distribution among the tribe. Whale bones and clam shells were everywhere. Natives continued their migratory lifestyle. "Each spring we would see a gas boat towing a long line of canoes, Indian canoes, about ten of them ladened with people, and furniture, going to summer encampment on Village Island, and in the fall, they proceeded with the reverse, and they were heading back to Sarita."[57]

The Ohiahts' main winter village was at Sarita. Their other village sites were situated at Grappler Creek and Dodger Cove and

Effingham Island (Village Island). They inhabited both sides of the inlet including Burlo Isle and the No. 9 reserve. At the time of Banfield's arrival, Cli-shin was the ruling chief. Elders tell the story of a smallpox epidemic that hit the band in the mid-1870s; the exact date is unknown.

A ship arrived in Bamfield waters but failed to anchor and just drifted around. The curiosity of the Ohiaht people led them to investigate. One young man lived to tell what happened on the ship: "John and his friends climbed aboard ship and to his horror saw men completely undressed, their bodies covered with some kind of disease and they were twisting in pain."[58] The disease was smallpox. He hurried back to his friends to warn them not to eat the food but it was too late. Several people contracted the disease, and before long villagers were dying. John and his family quickly moved away to Keeh-k-k-in, a bay past Long Beach. Chief Cli-shin's family moved to a lake behind Grappler Inlet. Very few Ohiahts escaped the disease.

George Bird confirms the story of the smallpox epidemic: "I believe it was about 1875 that the worst epidemic of smallpox raged amongst them, all along the coast. It was said there was scarcely a bay or inlet where their bodies could not be seen floating about. Many tribes lost half their numbers. They feared even to approach the stricken ones."[59]

In the latter part of the 1800s, Chief Cli-shin died. His daughter Ginny married John and they had three children, Annie, Mary (Moses), and John Jr. Ginny related this history to her children. Mary remembered that when she was twelve years old, white people started to explore Bamfield. One summer they were told to leave the area as the white men were establishing a Life Saving Station there. Others were told to move as someone wanted to establish businesses. About this time, the Ohiaht people began moving into the Grappler Creek area and the No. 9 reserve.

With the arrival of the Cable Station people began settling in Bamfield. Anne Cox, daughter of Emanuel Cox, of the Cape Beale lighthouse, married James B. McKay, who had worked on building the telegraph line. They settled in Bamfield and built a home on the western side of Bamfield Inlet, which they named "Pioneer House." The McKays opened the first store in the settlement. They were joined by fishermen and others who worked in support businesses for the Cable Station, or for the Life Station that was established there following the wrecks of the *Valencia* in January, 1906, and the *Coloma* in December the same year. These two incidents resulted in the establishment of the West Coast Lifesaving Trail in 1907. A lighthouse was built at Pachena Point near the site of the wreck of the *Valencia,* and a lifeboat station was established at Bamfield. The Bamfield trail had improvements made. The Paterson family were then the lightkeepers at Cape Beale, and Minnie Paterson's heroic effort in attempting to save the lives of the passengers is well documented. Only thirty-eight of the 164 passengers and crew of the *Valencia* survived; fifty-nine bodies were recovered. All aboard the *Coloma* were saved, although the vessel was a total loss. The infamous stretch of water appropriately named "the Graveyard of the Pacific" had claimed two more ships.

Building the trail, lighthouse, and keeper's house at Pachena Point provided much needed work for Alberni residents, who were hired to work on the trail. The lumber for the lighthouse came from George Bird's sawmill in Port Alberni. Bird considered this a large order for his small sawmill. Alberni builder George Forrest managed all the construction work. The government lighthouse tender, the *Quadra*, then anchored off Bamfield Inlet, transported the lumber.[60]

The first lifeboat stationed at Bamfield, purchased for fifteen thousand dollars, met an untimely end after it drifted from its moorings at Bamfield to the rocks off Robbers Island in Barkley Sound, where one side was completely destroyed. The boat was salvaged and brought to Victoria, where an Esquimalt resident purchased it for fifty dollars. "The motor lifeboat was built at Bayonne, New Jersey for the Dominion Government, which sent Chief Engineer Anderson, of the marine department, to watch its trials in New Jersey before being shipped by train to Victoria and established at Banfield Creek with a crew of life savers."[61] A second lifeboat, built by the same company, the Electric Launch Company, replaced the original one.[62]

Since there were now enough residents in Bamfield to start a school, a meeting was held on Thursday, December 17, 1908, in the Pioneer House. Elected trustees were James McKay, Alexander McKee, and Captain Gillen. Votes of thanks were given to Alan

W. Neill for his offer of two lots for a school site, and to the Barclay Sound Cedar Company sawmill in Port Alberni, for a discount on the price of lumber.[63]

Like many of the other points on the west coast, Bamfield residents took their claims for consideration into the public forum. Regardless of having an excellent harbour with shipping facilities, there was still no local boat service on the Alberni Canal to bring mail and passengers to the community, nor was there a road connecting Bamfield to the outside world. Ucluelet had already demanded a boat service to Alberni for mail and passengers, and there seemed no reason why the same boat could not service Bamfield as well. "It is up to the people who live along the Alberni Canal and the Barclay Sound District to get busy with the matter and insist on better facilities for both mail and other business."[64]

The transportation needs of both communities would soon be met by local entrepreneurs: the Ucluelet Transportation Company with the *Merry Widow*, and W. J. Stone and his two sons, Stuart and Chet, with the *Tofino* and the *Roche Point*.

BENSON ISLAND (HAWKINS ISLAND)

Captain G. H. Richards' 1861 nautical chart of Barkley Sound shows Hawkins Island situated about seven miles (11.2 km) from Ucluelet, in the Broken Group Islands, the same area explored by Swartout and his excursion party, an area known for its strong tides, hidden reefs and fog. The name of the island was changed in 1934 to reflect its first owner, John Webb Benson. Natives originally had two summer villages on the island, the larger was Ts'ishaa, from which the tribal name Tseshaht is derived. They were not included in the reserve system in the early 1880s, indicating a decline in use.

Benson arrived on the coast during the mining boom of the 1890s. He was a resourceful man, able to put his hand to almost anything. Born in 1850, in Maine, USA, "he was a tall man who had to stoop when going through a doorway. He had long white hair, a flowing white beard, and must have looked rather like a prophet—a prophet with a broadaxe slung over his shoulder. Wherever he went, he carried that axe."[65]

He put the axe to good use clearing the land, and with the help of oxen, managed to turn several acres of forest into agricultural land suitable for growing hay to feed the oxen. He planted the remainder with fruit trees and vegetable crops. The grove of deciduous European ornamental trees, chestnut, sycamore, poplar and beech, continue to grow on the island today.[66] Benson could see this location would make an ideal retreat location for tourists and set about building a hotel on the eastern side of the island where people could come to fish, boat, bathe on the beach, or just to enjoy the scenery.

> The hotel was two stories high, shaped like an L, and faced the ocean. The top storey contained eight bedrooms, and on the ground floor were living room, kitchen, two more bedrooms, and at the foot of the L, a storeroom. There was also a bathroom equipped with bathtub, although there was no running water. The living room was large, and part of it was used as the dining area. Each bedroom was furnished with bed, dresser, washstand, and a matching porcelain set consisting of basin, pitcher, toothbrush holder, and chamber pot. From the hotel windows was a wonderful view of sea, islands, and mountains. This was his home and hotel.[67]

Today Benson would be considered an eccentric because of his unconventional ways of doing things. His unique method of travelling in Barkley Sound and the Alberni Canal involved hitching his oxen to an old boat. He would drive them into the water where they would swim, towing him to the next island. After the animals had rested, he would continue on to the next destination. This mode of travel may have been slow but it allowed him to travel for miles.

Benson advertised his resort in the *Port Alberni News:* "Barclay House, Hawkins Island, Barclay Sound. An ideal spot for the tourist, good fishing, boating, bathing and beach. A quiet, homelike resort." Deciding he needed help running the hotel, he sought out a marriage broker. The first woman to arrive did not stay long but left on the next boat. Whether it was the remote location, or the man that changed her mind, no one knows. For a time there was considerable traffic back and forth as Benson searched for the right woman. One potential wife was discovered on the beach, frantically trying to flag down a passing boat. The woman wore few clothes, as Benson had hidden all her belongings, not wanting her to leave. His search netted eight would-be wives. Later in life, at the age of sixty-one, he did manage to marry one, Ella Matilda Benson, in 1912.

He even tried his hand at logging. In 1907, Benson operated a logging camp at the north end of Tzartus Island (Copper Island). During that summer, he logged about one million board feet of logs but could find no ready buyer. His only customers were the Sutton sawmill in Ucluelet and the George Bird sawmill in Alberni. However, his little logging operation provided work for Captain George Huff's towing vessel, the *Tasmanian*. It was no easy task finding a market for logs when so few people populated the sound, leaving little opportunity for house building. Benson tried further afield.

> Mr. Benson recently made a trip to Victoria with a view to finding a market for his logs, but he found the lumbermen there unwilling to take the risk of bringing them through. He expects that next summer there will be enough demand on the west coast to keep him busy all the time. Mr. Benson owns some of the finest timber in British Columbia. He took over 300,000 feet off two acres.[68]

George Bird remembered Benson as a man who believed the beauty of Barkley Sound rivalled that of Alaska. "This old man was very industrious and ranged around all over the sound. He brought up two or three booms of saw-logs for me from Copper Island and took some lumber in exchange." As canny as Benson may have appeared, he did miss out on one opportunity, much to his chagrin.

> On one of his travels he was startled to see, looming up in front of him, a large steamer, with no sign of life on board. He climbed on deck and considering the situation, let go one of the anchors. At the time the vessel happened to be lying in a place very suitable for safe anchorage. Now this is where he missed a great opportunity. He left the ship, no doubt with the idea of

finding and getting in touch with the owners, and his place was taken by a number of Indians from Sarita and elsewhere. They looted everything, the ship's stores, a lot of the cargo and even the curtains, carpets and other fittings of the vessel. There was also a supply of liquor on board which was not neglected.

After some days the news got to Alberni. Mr. Guillod, the Indian Agent, and Constable Gus Cox left for the scene and, catching many in the act of carrying off ship's property, arrested several. It was only natural for the Indians to think that to what no one else laid claim, might easily become theirs. In those days they did not know quite as much of the white man's ways. I do not think that any further action was taken against them beyond giving them a good scare. The owners, I have no doubt, or at any rate the insurance companies would be well satisfied at getting their vessel back safely, without any legal action or claims for salvage. If, after anchoring the vessel, Benson had stayed on board and kept all the ship's property from loss or damage, he would have been able to have claimed a large sum of money for salvage. Such golden opportunities did not often come his way.[69]

This may have been the schooner *Amethyst* abandoned by its crew in April, 1902, and found adrift in the sound.[70]

Barclay House continued to be a busy resort during the summer months and to thrive on American tourists. During the winter months, Benson invited friends to join him hunting. They arrived with dogs who drove the deer into the ocean, making them easy marks for shooting.

He had only been married a year when he became ill. Mrs. Benson flagged a passing boat for assistance, but it was too late. Benson died on his island February 10, 1913. He was buried in Alberni by local undertaker, George Forrest. Mrs. Benson continued to operate the resort for a few years and received her share of tourist trade from Port Alberni residents looking for a day's outing.

Enjoyable excursion to Hawkins Island was held on Sunday, when twenty-six residents of Port Alberni journeyed on the *Maid of Ecoole* to the picturesque little island by the sea. The hospitality shown by Mrs. Benson was highly appreciated by the

157

party and as a mark of esteem a contribution was made to her by the crowd. Mrs. Benson handed this over as a donation to the local Red Cross.[1]

The hotel was sold in 1919 to Vancouver businessman Jens Peter Petersen for fifteen hundred dollars. Petersen hoped to continue the operation and made improvements for transporting visitors from Port Alberni to the island. He had the Port Alberni Boat and Launch Works fit the island's twenty-seven-foot launch, the *Lacota*, with a new Frisbie engine. A trial run held with the new engine reached the highest speed of eleven knots. Painter & Bacon, owners of the Boat Works, were pleased with the success of the run and the installation of the first Frisbie engine in the city.[2]

Petersen made a few headlines of his own because of the size of fish caught off his island. On April 21, 1920, he caught an eight-foot-long halibut, which weighed 170 pounds.[3] The fish was the largest ever seen in Port Alberni, where it was sold to the Port Alberni Meat and Fish market. It weighed 140 pounds dressed.

A year later, Petersen sold the hotel to Alfred Henry Clarke, a judge from Calgary, for the grand sum of fifteen hundred dollars. Benson had originally purchased the island for thirty-three dollars, then had sold it to his wife for six hundred dollars, a year before he died. Over the years there were a number of owners until the island was ultimately reclaimed by the Crown in 1975 for ninety-five thousand to become part of Pacific Rim National Park. Today nothing remains of the once prosperous hotel, the island name being the only reminder of the colourful character who once inhabited it.

CHAPTER SIX

WHAT HAPPENED TO THE FISH?

FISH, FISHING AND FISHING CAMPS

For decades, there was a fishing bonanza in Barkley Sound and the Alberni Canal that could almost be compared to the gold rush. Sockeye, chinook, coho, chum, and steelhead could be fished with relative ease; salmon spawned in most of the rivers and creeks; fishing camps, canneries, salteries, reduction plants, and cold storage facilities dotted the waterway, as fishermen cashed in on the lucrative industry. Cannery boats returned to camp loaded with salmon, herring, or pilchards for processing. Herring were scooped up in huge baskets and quickly conveyed into cold storage, some to await the halibut season when they were required for bait. Kildonan, Ecoole, Nitinat Lake, Green Cove, Ritherdon Bay, McCallum Bay, San Mateo Bay, Sarita, Sechart, Toquart, Port Albion, Ucluelet, Bamfield, and the Albernis all benefited from the good fortune.

Centuries before, Natives had used the fishing resource extensively. There had been enough food to accommodate an estimated ten thousand Natives who once occupied the sound, an area with the greatest west-coast concentration of non-agricultural people north of Mexico before the arrival of the white man. Early settlers tried farming but discovered the soil unproductive, and before long the would-be farmers turned their attention to fishing and forestry. For the first time, there was competition for fishing. Natives believed their fishing rights had been secured by treaty, an argument still being made today. They responded by joining the commercial fishery; some bought larger fish boats, others worked in the canneries and fishing camps.

Ucluelet resident Arthur Baird witnessed the huge herring run and the over-fishing that almost depleted the stock.

> When I was a kid they used to come in the bay, just so, the bay was so full of herring that when the tide went out at the head of the inlet, there'd be herring all along the beach, and we'd just go and rake them in and make kippers or whatever; but they took so many out of the bay, that it just finished it. The sea lions used to come in by the hundreds in the bay here too. I talked to a lot of the old-time fishermen, Scotchmen mostly, that fished at Kildonan; they fished this inlet here, and they claimed they took twenty-six thousand tons out of this little bay alone (Ucluelet Inlet), and there hasn't been any back since.[1]

The fishing bonanza brought its own set of problems as the industry modernised, making it easier to scoop up larger and larger quantities of fish. Soon alarm bells rang as fishermen realised their resource was in trouble. Inquiries were held and subsequent restrictions enforced by fisheries officers whose territory was too large to police successfully. Bamfield fisherman Bill McDermid remembered the early days of fishing in the sound and how it changed:

> When we started, we used piano wire, or a braided nylon leader. Your lure was all wooden plugs and brass spoons. It's changed now, with really sophisticated lures, the fish don't have a chance. You know, it's like dangling a marshmallow in front of you, you're going to grab it anyhow. The boat has every conceivable instrument there is: radar, sonar, sounders, lorans, GPSs—you can go on forever, its like an airplane cockpit. It's technology of navigation that is really, really superior. They can position themselves about eight or ten feet from anywhere on

the ocean floor. They can go back to exactly where you were, where the fish are.

At one time, you drifted off with the wind or tide; you didn't know where you were. You were just guessing, a quarter of a mile was good. You had to allow for your tide drift, so you knew which way the tide was running because your gear lies in the water, everything changes angles, so you'd guess it, and actually you were pretty accurate. You turn around to come home after four or five days out there and you can find the lighthouse, you were within a half mile of it. That is not bad. And then in the same industry, we went from pulling the seine by hand onto a flat table, and had seven or eight guys pull it by hand. Therefore small boats, small nets, light gear, up to a power block, which was a big power block in the rigging that came up and down.

So the boats got bigger because they had a bigger net and became more efficient. Then you come into the eighty- or ninety-foot seine boats instead of the little thirty-, forty-, or fifty-foot boats. Then it went to a drum seiner, the table increased it up to about eight sets a day; now they can make a set every twenty minutes. Now you get one drum seiner can out-fish the whole fleet. They're that efficient, so that's why they get maybe a week here, two days there, or eight-hour fishery, that one time they got a whole year, now they get an eight-hour fishery. And the biggest boat, it doesn't matter, the size, the table, everything, is just a machine. It's highly efficient.[2]

The technological change in the industry had a tremendous impact on the communities on the coast. Where harbours once were filled with fishing camps and boats, now only a few are busy.

In the fifties, there were thirty or forty boats fished regularly out of Bamfield, all year round, and in the summer it would build up into fifty or sixty or eighty or a hundred boats. Ucluelet would have a fleet of a couple of hundred, but then as the gulf got shut down, all around Vancouver and Sidney, the boats came out to the west coast, and Bamfield never did grow any further on account of the ice plant situation and that, but Ucluelet and Tofino grew into six or eight hundred boats at the peak of the season. So the harbour would be right full of boats.

This harbour here, you would see ten, twelve, fourteen abreast at every dock in the harbour on a stormy day. Now you'd be lucky to see six or eight. So there's nothing here. They don't even fish this end of the island anymore; they've got to go above it because there is no reason to come in here anymore.[3]

Not only the salmon stocks suffered; basking sharks were almost depleted. The increase in fishing boats drastically reduced the numbers of sharks as they got caught up in fishing nets.

Oh, there were hundreds of them around, hundreds of basking sharks. You could look out in the harbour here [Bamfield], in August, and you could see two or three on any given day cruising up and down the harbour. You'd go out, and you'd see forty, fifty, sixty, just going up to Sarita and back. There were way too many, now there's way too few. So, they eliminated them, but what was left over? I would say, I've caught seven or eight I've had to destroy, like in my gillnet to get my net back. They wind themselves all up in it and drown themselves. So, if you put in 150 gillnetters in here and everyone gets one or two, that finishes off the few that are left. And, I guess naturally, they move so god damn slow, they wouldn't find each other to mate anyhow. They're not that aggressive, so they are a slow, poky thing.[4]

Attempts were made in 1921 to establish a shark-fishing industry under Sidney Ruck, head of Consolidated Whaling Company.[5] Huge sun sharks, some weighing over two thousand pounds, could be found in schools of thousands. Sun sharks are the second largest fish in the ocean. In one incident on the canal, a school of sharks packed against the side and bow of one of the coastal steamers, which stopped her completely.

Sharks were fished in much the same way as whales, with harpoons shot from guns. When caught they were taken to Toquart to have the oil extracted. Shark livers were prized for their oil, which was used for lubricating medical equipment; teeth were in great demand for jewellery; the fins, being almost pure gelatine, were cured and sold to Chinese, who used them in cooking. The shark skin was sought after for its toughness and used in leather work.

Fishermen complained there were too many sharks interfering with their nets, something had to be done. As a child, Joe Garcia of Bamfield remembered chasing them with hand-made harpoons and running over them with small boats.

> They used to destroy the nets of the fishermen so badly, there were so many of them. I mean, it was nothing to see ten or twelve of them right in the mouth of the harbour, maybe twenty or thirty in the sound at one time, you know, in sight at one time. But they put a big knife on the bow of the *Comox Post* and just cut them in half. And I guess they went a little bit too far, because now there are very few left.[6]

Hinged like a clasp knife, the blade could be lowered into position at will. It had a razor-sharp cutting edge at the top and a sharp point at the bottom. Very little skill was required in hunting the slow docile sharks, which were usually found floating on the surface of the ocean straining plankton through their gillrakers. Soon pieces of shark floated in the waters and rotted on the beaches of Barkley Sound as the giant knife effectively sliced them in half. In 1955, sixty-five basking sharks were butchered; eighteen were killed in a single day.[7]

The slaughter had been carried out with the best of intentions: the protection of salmon fishery. Those attempts to start a shark fishing industry in Barkley Sound failed. Today, Norway has a thriving shark fishing industry, with markets around the world.

Perhaps the biggest fishing mystery of the coast was the arrival of the pilchards. Johnny Williams Sr. remembers catching pilchards, and the Native community's participation in the fishing bonanza:

> I bought my own boat in 1914 for four hundred dollars. It was a twelve horse-power, thirty-six foot Japanese built. I bought it from Steveston. I named the boat the *City of Clinton*. I was the first man to go seining with Harry Masso, on the whole west coast. We'd mend our own seines and splice ropes, etc. One year I was paid $1,500 for the season of pilchards, herring and dog salmon. The biggest catch for herring was 1,300 tons in Queens Cove. In the year 1917, we caught 106,000 dog salmon one

season. In 1918, we'd start pilchards 1st of May, and August and September would be dog salmon, 1st of November we'd start herring fishing, the season would end in March. There would be two months' holiday out of the whole fishing season. Pilchards in those days were four dollars a ton, herring $3.75 a ton, dog salmon were three cents apiece in 1918. We used a boat named *Nakomis*. The last time I went pilchard fishing was in 1946.[8]

There were no pilchards when the white settlers first arrived on the coast; then for some unknown reason, they began crowding the waters around 1916 in ever-increasing numbers which peaked in the late twenties. Pilchard reduction plants were built to capitalise on the profitable catch; fifteen were built within eighteen months, from 1925 to 1927. There were eventually twenty-five plants processing a hundred thousand tons of pilchards annually. About forty-five gallons of oil were extracted from one ton of pilchards. Twenty years later there was barely a glimmer of the tiny fish.

A comprehensive study and tagging experiment conducted both in California and British Columbia indicated pilchards were essentially a California stock at the northern extremity of their coastal migration. Only the large fish seemed to reach British Columbia. In the early forties, possibly as a result of heavy spawning in northern California waters, young pilchards were abundant off the west coast, and they influenced the fishery for a few years. By the late forties they had almost disappeared, and scientists speculated oceanographic conditions may have contributed to their decline by altering migratory paths.[9]

Pilchard oil was used in the food industry for margarine and salad oil; it was also used as a base in some high-grade paints and cosmetic products. The remaining pilchard meal went into animal food. Ask west-coast fishermen what happened to the pilchards and you will get a variety of answers.

No, the pilchards have a bad habit of up and disappearing. They can come at any given time or go out at any given time. The south coast of Africa had pilchards, now they're moving from there. South America had pilchards, they moved. You know they move on and on, they're not constant, they seem to move in a big body and then stop. You don't fish them out, they just move, they pick up their bags and they're gone.[10]

The small canneries disappeared when the big companies in Vancouver and Steveston took over. The same happened with the salteries that were built mainly for the herring and dog salmon, as easier and faster ways of processing were introduced. The reduction plants closed when the pilchards left and the herring were depleted. At Dodger Cove there were three fish camps, B. Gregory Fishing Company, Western Chemicals, and Nelson Brothers.

At that time the boats had very small engines and the extra run from Dodger Cove to here (Bamfield), meant an hour each way for the fishermen, so they'd meet the fishermen out there and then they'd buy the fish there. And they were all floating camps, and there were no ice plants or anything. They were day fish, and they were sold, and the packer would take them in almost every day into Alberni. And the seine fish, well the Nelson Brothers and others would collect that and take it into Vancouver. Then as the boats started to get bigger, they packed ice, and there were price differences. In the forties, there were bigger boats like the forty and forty-two footers; they would pick up ice in Vancouver or Victoria, fish for twelve to fourteen days, then go back in.

So it was just strictly the day boats out here, and that sort of just petered out. There were two or three fish companies, like Kildonan, going full bore at that time. They had a big ice plant, and the B.C. Packer boats could get their ice there, or at Victoria, or Vancouver. Kildonan was going great guns as a reduction plant and a canner, but then labour costs started to get too high, and it was cheaper for them to have the plant in Vancouver, or Steveston, and take the fish down rather than bring the people up. Kildonan was quite a community; they'd bring these cannery girls and Japanese people up there to work, but they only paid them for the hours they worked. Some people were getting fed up with that and it all moved down. The boats got bigger and they kept the ice plant there for quite a few years until the crew decided they should get union wages, and if they were cold storage workers, they didn't fix the dock, so they just shut the plant down.[11]

165

The floating fishing camps were a way of life for many of the early settlers in Barkley Sound. They moved from one location to another, depending on the fishing season. Fishing camp families made a modest living but forged bonds with local fishermen and Natives who sold them fish and purchased groceries. The Tuttle family were typical; their company, the Pachena Fish Co. Ltd., began operations in two buildings built on a cedar log float. In one building they operated a general store, in the other, they bought and sold fish. The family lived at the rear of the store. A tug was hired to tow the float around to different locations to accommodate fishermen and Natives.

> Business was first started in a place called Effingham Inlet, a sheltered cove, on the south side of Village Island, the summer home of the Alberni tribe of Indians; other tribes used the island also during the summer. Most of the Indians owned trolling boats and used the cove. After a day's fishing, they would first sell us their fish and then buy from us meat they needed, groceries and fishing spoons, etc. Our float was anchored to the shore and had a sidewalk leading off it so Indians could come and go to their village after shopping. Little wood mice often came aboard at night. They raided our peanut bin and carried rice and beans back to their dens in the woods. We called them our unpaying guests. We set traps and caught many of them. In late August our float was towed up to a place called Nahmint and anchored near another Indian village, the fall and winter home of many tribes who live there. Business was brisk and my husband had to hire an Indian girl to clerk in the store and a man to help him in the fishing department.[12]

The Tuttle family float anchored in various locations up and down the coast, until the children needed schooling, then the family settled in Alberni. Grace Tuttle noted in her journal that fish camps dotted every little inlet and harbour, buying fish "because it was all-day fishing" and there was no ice. These camps disappeared when ice became available. With hydro and road access, fish buying centralized in Ucluelet and Tofino, and the smaller camps disappeared.[13]
Fishermen developed a sense of camaraderie on non-fishing

days, or picnic days, as they came to be known to residents of the sound.

> Impromptu picnics happened on non-fishing days—windy days when there was a big westerly and the boats couldn't go out. As the boats didn't carry ice, they came in every night. At these times someone would get the idea, Let's have a picnic. People brought from their larders whatever they had. Bottles of home-made brew came out in wooden milk boxes. They would go out to one of the islands to have a community picnic. There was no planning, no tickets sold, no arrangements made. It was won-derful.[14]

Older fishermen and their families lament the passing of a way of life, a time in history with its own share of dreamers and char-acters who romanticised the industry, leaving lasting impressions that are difficult to extinguish.

SEA SERPENT STORIES

Periodically sea monsters were reported along the west coast, some dating back to before the turn of the century when an un-known sea creature made its appearance off Cape Beale.[15] There were many things in the sea which might have led observers to think they had seen a serpent. During the thirties and forties there were many sightings, causing speculation there really was a sea monster swimming in Barkley Sound. Fishermen have been known to tell big fish stories, some believable, others not so cred-ible. Those who believed made the link to Victoria's famous Cadborosaurus, or Caddy. Perhaps the sound had its own sea monster, maybe a twin of Caddy. In April 1935, this was a chief topic of conversation among west-coast salmon fishermen and there appeared little doubt about its authenticity. The sea serpent had been seen on three different occasions by different fishermen, all of whom claimed to have had a close-up view, and all said they were sober at the time. Who would not believe such a claim?

Jack Patterson had been trolling in the middle channel near Nettle Island when he first saw the creature. He thought at first it

167

was a cedar tree with its wide butt showing high above the water, but when it dove suddenly and re-appeared closer to his boat, he saw a horse-like head. Patterson immediately pulled in his lines and left the area. He said nothing about the incident, fearing ridicule from other fishermen.[16]

A Native fisherman next saw the serpent as it frolicked in the water near his boat, but it remained for a Swedish fisherman to give the best description of the strange sea creature. He chased it for half an hour with his troller. At times it was so close, he was able to make a sketch of the head, which resembled that of a horse with a long, under-curled upper lip like that of a camel. The body was similar to a huge snake with the addition of rather large flapper fins, and it wriggled under the water much as a snake does when swimming. He judged its total length to be about thirty feet. For the greater part of the time, the serpent was submerged about two feet below the water and it swam ahead of the boat, at times lifting its head clear to the surface and breaking the water with its fins. The Swede described it as slate grey in colour.

A Ucluelet troller, Thomas Taylor, next saw the sea serpent in May, 1935, as he returned from the fishing banks just a few miles from shore. At first he thought it was a huge whale asleep on the surface of the water, but being an old whaler, Taylor knew it could not be a whale. He slowed his boat to half-speed and drew closer to the creature, which appeared oblivious to his inspection and continued to splash its tail. Taylor described the sea monster in boating terms as being "one hundred feet long, about six feet in circumference amidships and tapered toward bow and stern. The head appeared to be twice the size of a large sea lion and was dull grey in colour, with stripes near the head."[17] As he approached the creature to investigate further, it suddenly arched its back and raised its head, as a snake might do. This movement alone convinced him this was no sea animal he had ever known. He quickly left the area leaving the sea creature swimming slowly about in the water.

Taylor was a credible witness to the strange occurrence as he had a reputation for being very familiar with creatures of the sea. He was born in Newfoundland, and after many years spent on the Atlantic fishing banks, he came to Vancouver Island, where he whaled, sealed, and fished. He knew the practical side of getting swordfish, sharks, and other sea life, but never in his seafaring career had he ever believed stories about sea serpents. After this brief encounter, he changed his mind.

This same year, the public's fascination with sea monsters was considerably heightened when the fossilized remains of an ichthyosaur, an extinct genus of huge fish-lizards that roamed the seas some thirty million years ago, was believed discovered near Ahousat. The large fossil had been salvaged from the lower Cretaceous formations encased in the rocks in front of the home of Mr. G. J. Smith.[18] A Geological Survey team, headed by Professor M. F. Bancroft, cut the fossils from the rock with cold chisels and sampling moils. Bancroft was convinced it was part of an ichthyosaur.

The next sighting of the sea serpent occurred off Cape Cook on the Brooks Peninsula in October, 1936. The seine boat *Marmae*, skippered by E. Clark, was cruising in search of pilchard, when Sig Trelvik, who was on the lookout, spotted what he thought was a log floating on the water. The boat changed course and ran within twenty-five feet of the serpent, when suddenly a long thick neck raised itself six feet above the water. "The neck was surmounted by a small head with large protruding eyes, something like those of a dragonfly but on a much larger scale. The body was light brown and appeared to be of tremendous size and covered with fur or hair."[19] Before the crew could mount a camera or gun, the monster quickly sank to the depths. For two hours the *Marmae* cruised the area but saw no further sign of the serpent. Four men had witnessed the incident; all were experienced fishermen who made a living from the sea. They were Sig Trelvik, J. McPherson, Collie Hill, and E. Clark. There was undoubtedly some strange sea serpent in the waters off the west coast.

No further sightings were reported for the next decade until the long-standing secret of the sea serpent appeared to have been solved. In November, 1947, a group of Alberni fishermen found a skeleton, more than forty feet in length, unlike anything they had ever seen before. The remains were made up of more than 150 vertebrae, with a flat-skulled head "like a sheep's head."[20] The skeleton was discovered at Vernon Bay, between Ecoole and Effingham Inlet, by Harry Schwarz and his fishing companions, Jim McCullough, Paul Hertel, and George Anderson, owner of the

Dana. They kept the discovery a secret until December, not wishing the remains to be tampered with.

The sea creature appeared to have been dead for about six months or more. When found it was lying partly upon rocks. The fishermen could immediately see the public interest in such a creature and planned to put their find on exhibition, donating a portion of the money to charity and splitting the remainder between the fishing partners. They brought the skeleton to Alberni and housed it in a shed at the foot of Heaslip Street.

News of the find reached across the American continent. Vancouver newspapers carried headline stories of the Alberni Sea Serpent. The Biological Station in Nanaimo was contacted, and Dr. Albert L. Tester headed an investigative team to the site of the discovery. After several hours searching at low tide, the team found gillrakers and two teeth plus the rest of the skeleton, including six more vertebrae. Dr. Tester concluded the skeleton was that of a gigantic basking shark, the largest ever found in British Columbia to date.[21] The previous record length for basking sharks was forty feet. This one was at least forty-five feet long, and the skeleton contained more than 160 vertebrae. The lower jaw and parts of the skull were never found.

The Alberni Community Hotel Company Limited, with Harry Schwarz as secretary-treasurer and Jean Cardinal as president, were not convinced the scientist was correct, and Schwarz wrote Dr. Tester asking him to consider several points.

I found the skeleton on the other side of the reefs; no whole skeleton could float in there. There was still some meat on the skeleton and before I put the lime on, it was Cohoe Red. The vertebrae taper considerably towards the head. The eye sockets are very large. Your own books states, "The teeth of a basking shark are conical." The teeth you showed me are absolutely different to any shark's teeth I have ever seen. I am rigging up a small boat to fish in the same locality on the same bottom where years ago I caught a very repulsive small specimen "about five feet" that resembled what I have and I hope I will be able to prove to you that what I have is no shark. Cludecy, an educated Indian, states what I have is the animal he has seen alive. He talks about large protruding eyes and a fold above the nose.

Another party states about the same thing but says his was far larger. If we have anything of the kind here I cannot see anything gained by trying to disprove it, and I am seeking your support as soon as I am able to furnish more evidence.[22]

Dr. Tester could not be swayed from his original identification and advised Schwarz, "With regard to the sea serpent. It still seems to be a good newspaper story. I still feel that the identification was correct and that a high tide washed the main part of the skeleton from the spot where we found the gillrakers and several other spare parts to the spot where you found the remains."

A similar basking shark skeleton had been found at Prince Rupert several years before, and it too had been subject to speculation that it was a sea serpent. The vertebrae were similar to those found at Vernon Bay. The meat had also been reddish in colour. But Tester left the door open for further investigation. He noted: "While I am at present convinced that the monster is a basking shark, I am always willing to admit the possibility of being wrong. Sea serpents other than basking sharks may still exist for all we know." He was pleased Schwarz was planning to investigate further.

The publicity surrounding the find was far-reaching. The Pacific Biological Station had inquiries from individuals and institutions throughout the continent asking for information about the Alberni Sea Serpent. William Douglas, in Courtenay, who had "chased sea serpents" for forty years wanted to know what had been found. Ronald Willis, of Missouri, inquired about the alleged sea serpent discovered off the west coast. *Fate Magazine* in Chicago was interested in publishing photographs and text about the find. A radio broadcast from the University of California with stations in Los Angeles, San Francisco, Palm Springs, Fresno, and Sacramento did a program on "The Mysterious Monster."

Dr. Tester's insistence that it was only a basking shark appeared to dampen enthusiasm. Schwarz wrote to Dr. Robert C. Miller, director of the California Academy of Science, asking if his group would be interested in buying the remains sight unseen. Miller in turn contacted Dr. Tester, asking what the excitement and enthusiasm over the so-called sea serpent was all about. Dr. R. E. Foerster, director of the PBS, replied to Miller explaining the proper identification. Regarding the skeleton, he noted, "We had hoped that the finder of the skeleton, Mr. N. H. Schwarz, would donate the skeleton or at least some of the important parts to this station for future use but to date no such succession has been made. Apparently if Mr. Schwarz is trying to sell the skeleton, he will not be disposed to turn it over to us unless he finds no one else interested."

Dr. Tester's identification did not get the same publicity as the recovery of the skeleton had. Some of the news items appeared to castigate him for destroying the sea serpent myth. No one was anxious to follow up and give the scientist credit for the proper identification. Several sharks had been observed off the west coast that summer and it seemed possible that the skeleton at Vernon Bay had been one of those. A fisherman had captured one, removed its liver, and towed the carcass away from Bamfield, allowing it to drift in the open sea. Could this have explained the skeletal remains? No one knows for sure. The legend of the Alberni Sea Serpent ranks among world reports of sea monsters. There is even speculation the Loch Ness monster was nothing more than a basking shark. A twenty-four-foot dead basking shark was found on the shore of Loch Ness in June, 1942.

Sea serpents were part of west-coast lore even before the arrival of settlers. A Native legend relates a story of a sighting by the Tseshaht tribe in the Alberni Canal. The sight of the monster as it raised its head from the water so alarmed the Natives that they vowed to kill it. Armed with whaling harpoons in their canoes, they paddled to the place where the sea creature had been sighted. As they approached, with harpoons raised, the creature spoke to them pleading for his life:

I will not harm you. I have been sent by the Great Spirit on a special mission and therefore am worthy of your protection. All that I desire is to be allowed to swim up the river so that I may lay my eggs in the warm shallow reaches of the river. Permit me to do this and great blessings shall befall your tribe.[23]

The creature was allowed to swim up the river where she laid six eggs. Before she swam away, she told the people she would return in six moons, and warned them not to touch the eggs for any reason. If they were damaged, she would return and punish the offender. The Natives attached great importance to the eggs and watched them faithfully to ensure their safety. Over the course of time, the eggs grew to an enormous size and in six moons to the day, the sea creature returned. She saw her eggs were undisturbed and lay down beside them until they hatched.

The legend tells of six different monsters that emerged: one with horns like a deer, another with legs, and another with wings; each creature different from the other. The Natives were horrified to see the birth of these monsters, but the sea creature reassured them that they were harmless and that she would take them away to the ocean. Before she left she promised the people a wonderful era would follow. There would be freedom from war and strife; pestilence would not touch them, although it might other tribes; and there would be plenty of food. With these promises, she swam away to sea taking her family with her.

According to legend, the promises all came true. The Tseshaht tribe was unharmed by war or pestilence, and food was plentiful. Today the sea serpent is depicted on Native basketry.

Prehistoric petroglyphs are a common sight on exposed rocky shorelines around Vancouver Island. They consist of rock drawings representing a variety of figures, including a zoologically unknown animal with features reminiscent of the descriptions of the Cadborosaurus.[24] Petroglyphs at Nanaimo and Gabriola show a creature similar to the sea serpent.

SCOTTISH CROFTER FISHERMEN SCHEME

In 1926 a group of twenty-five families of Scottish Hebridean fishermen was brought to the west coast by the provincial government. The Minister of Lands in charge of the project was the Honourable T. D. Pattullo. The project was called the Scottish Crofter Fishermen Scheme. The Chief Inspector of Fisheries, Major Motherwell, announced in September, 1924, that fifty of the five hundred Scottish families who were to emigrate to British Columbia and work in the fishing industry on the west coast were on their way to Canada.[25] As if heightening expectations, a week later Pattullo stated the Hebrideans who would arrive during the next twelve months would settle in Port Alberni "if arrangements for home sites can be made with the council."[26]

The Ministry of Lands wanted to open immediate negotiations with the city. The settlers would pay for the land, but the government would make the arrangements. It was expected they would purchase those properties that had reverted to the city for non-payment of taxes. Port Alberni seemed a desirable place to locate the immigrants if a suitable deal could be made:

> The Hebrideans prefer Port Alberni to any other point on Barclay Sound because it already possesses all the facilities of a modern community. They are particularly anxious to be near up-to-date schools so that their children may receive the best possible education. A representative party of Hebrideans, composed of Canon A. MacDougall, Dean of the Outer Isles, Angus MacDonald, Lachlan MacLeod, Neil MacMillan, and Lachland Nicholson, under the guidance of Reverend Father R. A. MacDonnell, of Victoria, who is well known throughout the Dominion for his successful efforts in the establishment of colonies of these hardy Islanders in the prairie provinces, was in Port Alberni last week. Father MacDonnell said the party were fishermen first and crofters afterwards.
>
> Each new settler would require to be given a small piece of land, besides the fishing rights, to allow him to keep one or two cows and some sheep. In the party was one Presbyterian, the others being Catholics. He said he did not propose to have any religious distinction. What he wanted was the happy settlement of these people who he claimed to be among the best citizens in the world. Their devotion to work would be the asset they would put up to the government for the repayment of advances. He expected several hundred families to locate in Barclay Sound.[27]

There is every indication the City of Port Alberni looked warmly on the prospect of these new emigrants from Scotland and welcomed the Pattullo scheme, but there appeared to be some wariness that this was not a signed deal and that the emigrants might settle elsewhere. This apprehension was precipitated by a letter from the Reverend Father Andrew MacDonnell disclaiming some of the information that appeared the week before in the local newspaper. He wrote:

I see in a paper today that I am bringing Hebridean fishermen to Port Alberni. That is news to me. There is a possibility of such a thing if there is the possibility of securing lots, or blocks of land, at a reasonable price. I am not going to recommend our folk to pay fanciful prices for land. There is no good starting life in a new country with a millstone of debt on one's neck. I do believe if public men, like yourself, would get busy something could be done in getting public opinion formed as to land prices in a place like Port Alberni. There is no good in getting people into a place and then taxing them out of existence. It would pay the City of Port Alberni to make a present of some of their town lots to get a bigger population. I am looking for a good bargain for my folk and I intend getting it, if not in one place then in another.[28]

The sitting member of the legislature and also the newspaper publisher, Major Richard J. Burde, who happened to be running for mayor of the city, said he had spoken with the Honourable T. D. Pattullo on the subject and had received assurances the province would do everything it could to encourage settlement in Port Alberni. Mayor Alexander D. MacIntyre, with full support of council, proclaimed the city was ready to do business with the Hebrideans. The city clerk was instructed to write to Father MacDonnell advising him of that fact.

A few weeks later, the Vancouver *Daily Province* reported on a special delegation of Hebrideans who had visited settlements and issued a report. Of the fishing opportunities on Vancouver Island, they stated:

The harbors in the Alberni Canal and Barclay Sound are safe and excellent in every way for fishing boats. Reasoning from what we observed in inside waters and learned from others, we should be inclined to think that the outside fishing would be the more lucrative. Furthermore, from the evidence we could collect, we have formed the opinion that the very finest herring can be caught off this coast, and if the necessary means were used to that end, Scottish cured herring would become a valuable industry on the island. In regard to the making of a fishing settlement, or community, we would not advise that the at-

175

tempt be made on any isolated beach or island on the canal or sound. As the beginning, on the western coast of Vancouver Island, we suggest the neighborhood of the cities of Port Alberni and Alberni. The fishing will shift from time to time along the coast and the fisherman must follow. He will do so with a contented mind if his wife and family are where church, school and doctor are easily available.[29]

Among the Pattullo papers, now in the British Columbia archives, is a confidential report, dated February 23, 1925, from Mr. D. T. Jones, chairman of the Fishery Board for Scotland, regarding the emigration scheme. Jones visited Vancouver the previous December and found the province had appropriated four thousand dollars for "assisting the settlement of Hebrideans and Salvation Army schemes of settlement." His stay in Vancouver lasted four weeks because of "abnormal wintry conditions."[30]

Since the war, the crofter fisherman has shown a preference for farming, rather than fishing—and on that account recent settlement schemes in Canada have been confined solely to the former—and this fact emphasizes the view that the financial terms offered for settlement there will require to compare not unfavourably with those for settlement on the prairies.[31]

There had been previous schemes to settle Hebrideans in Alberta, where they were successful in establishing farms. Most of those emigrants were married with children, a fact that was considered important to the program's success. Jones recommended the British Columbia plan be implemented on a more modest scale with not more than twenty-five families—twenty to Alberni and five to the Queen Charlotte Islands.

The families would have to be carefully selected and should preferably be composed of parents with some children of a working age, say, over fourteen or fifteen years old. They should, if possible, possess a certain amount of capital of their own, receive passages to British Columbia, and be met at the port of debarkation by a responsible official and conducted to their destination. Plots of one or two acres of cleared land

176

should be purchased for them and wooden houses of at least three rooms should be ready for their reception—the furniture to be provided by themselves.[32]

The Honourable T. D. Pattullo announced in August, 1925, that negotiations and arrangements were completed for twenty-five families of Hebridean fishermen to settle on Vancouver Island. They were expected to arrive the next spring and would be located near Port Alberni.[33]

There were a number of Scottish women who worked in the canneries, but it is unknown if these were members of the same Hebrideans who were brought over on the Crofter Fisherman Scheme. Nicknamed "herring chokers," the women were quite familiar on the Port Alberni waterfront where they assembled for transportation to the canneries on the canal each morning. Many of these women spoke Gaelic, which would indicate they were from the Highlands of Scotland or from the Outer Hebrides. Some went to Kildonan where they Scotch-cured the fish. Two fishermen, Pete Gregory and Stan Littleton, remembered the Scottish emigrants: "They sent over to the Orkney Islands and brought a bunch over. They couldn't speak English, they spoke Gaelic. All they ate was dry salt herring and potatoes with their jackets on."[34]

The new immigrants were a welcome addition to the fishing industry on the west coast. As in Alberta, they set down roots and became part of the growing communities of Alberni and Port Alberni.

THE PROCESSORS

One of the largest fishing camps to develop on the Alberni Canal was at Kildonan. Undoubtedly this was the finest fishery location in the area; Uchucklesit Inlet had one of the best salmon-producing rivers, the Henderson, that was second only to the Somass River in Alberni. This was a natural location for one of the largest fish canning operations to develop. From 1903 to 1910, a small company named the Alberni Packing Company operated under Captain Dan MacDonald and Chalmer Ternan. Ternan, who came from Ontario in 1886, was already experienced in the cannery business when he joined friend Captain MacDonald in the new cannery venture at Uchucklesit.[35] They sold the business to the Wallace brothers, Peter and John, who renamed the company the Wallace Brothers Packing Company. This became Wallace Fisheries Limited after the company reorganised. The brothers changed the original site name of Uchucklesit to Kildonan after their Scottish hometown.[36] The largest shareholder in the company was General Alexander McRae, who by the early twenties had made a fortune in the forestry and fishing industry in the province.

A cold storage and ice plant, wharves, and buildings designed by architect J. H. Mason were built over the water on pilings. Government fishery officers were impressed by the investment being made and said so in their annual report of the year. "A new cold storage plant with a capacity of three million pounds has been erected by the Wallace Fisheries at Uchucklesit harbour, Barclay Sound. It is modern in every respect, and will be of great value to the fishing industry."[37] Various other buildings dotted the small community: the herring building, where the small fish were prepared; a small general store, several bunkhouses and residences for the employees of the plant, and a school for the children of plant employees. The community had its own electric light, water, and sewage system.[38] At the time the cold storage plant at Kildonan began operating, the herring were so thick in some harbours that they could be caught in large quantities just by dipping a net in the water. These were dry-salted for shipment to Japan for sale to the Chinese.

News about the small community developing along the canal began appearing in the Port Alberni newspaper. Sporting events between the two communities were duly reported, and the cannery boats occasionally tied up at the wharf were a welcome sight to local businessmen. Kildonan had every convenience of a small town—it even had a yacht club. "The Kildonan Motor Yacht Club announced it intends to build a float house and landing place large enough to accommodate all motor launches. The latest addition to the fleet, the newly fitted launch *Vanity*, owned by Charley Clarke made her trial run Sunday."[39]

To feed the cannery, Wallace Fisheries spread its influence far out along the west coast. In 1913, the company established a fish buying post in Ucluelet.[40] The company steamer also cruised the west coast buying halibut and salmon in Barkley Sound, Clayoquot and Kyuquot Sounds, Esperanza Inlet, Nootka Sound and Hesquiat Harbour.[41]

Fishermen sometimes had to slaughter predators to protect the industry. In 1912, Thomas Horne and W. E. Miller of the Ucluelet fishing post, H. J. Hillier of Ucluelet, Sid Toy of Alberni, and timber cruiser George Galley from Chehalis, Washington had an encounter with a herd of sea lions as they crossed the middle channel of Barkley Sound *en route* to Alberni. Their clash with the sea lions turned the water red in the bloodbath that followed. "There must have been a thousand of them. We each had a rifle and there were over two hundred rounds of ammunition in the launch. We used it all. The lions were bold and as the shooting commenced they became furious. A number of them ventured within fifteen yards of the launch. They were all such big fellows, and such easy marks, that I don't think one of us missed a shot."[42]

Fishermen considered sea lions and whales a threat to fish life. A large number of sea lions were killed annually as a conservation measure for the salmon fishery.[43] Even loons were enemies to be watched. One man at Sarita, a Mr. J. Davie, estimated loons caused almost as much depletion of the resource as sea lions did. He had observed hundreds of loons fishing in the Sarita River preying on young trout.[44]

By the twenties, the fishing industry in British Columbia had become a million-dollar industry, about one-third of the total for the whole of Canada. "Eat Fish" was the slogan promoting greater use of fish as a diet food. The province's fishing fleet numbered four large trawlers, ten steamers, 247 gas and sail vessels and more than six thousand small boats. Their value was estimated at five million dollars. Approximately twenty thousand people were directly engaged in the fishing industry. And as more importance was placed on the science of fishing, the Biological Station in Nanaimo was enlarged and improved.[45]

Kildonan cannery was the first large processor, but others followed. A cold storage plant opened in Port Alberni (New Alberni) in 1912 under Captain John Kendall and employed fifty men. Kendall was one of the more colourful characters in the early fishing industry on the canal. He came from Newfoundland in 1901 and earned the title Captain from his business as a fish boat owner.

I went to sea when I was twelve years of age on a sailing ship. Although I left school early I always had a great desire to learn, and as a boy always wanted to get at the bottom of things, and would never rest until I was satisfied that no one had had the better of any argument when I knew I was right. I have always believed that a spade is a spade and not a shovel, and it has always been useless for anyone to try to make me believe differently. I have always been in the 'wars' simply because I have always believed I am in the right.

It has not always been smooth sailing for me on sea or land. Once I was nearly shipwrecked on a sailing ship in a severe storm in Newfoundland waters. All the canvas was blown off the ship and we barely got home. On one occasion I was in an iceberg area and fully expected to be shipwrecked. It was the first time I had ever heard a sailor pray, and this was his prayer; "Ere I fall in a lump, body and bones all in a crump; if I should die before I wake, it would puzzle the devil to make me straight." I really thought my days were numbered on this trip. I simply closed my eyes and trusted to luck. I always think it a miracle I am alive today to tell the story.[46]

Kendall gained a reputation as a fighter, mainly because of his running battles with the local Fisheries Officer, James B. Wood. The two often locked horns; Kendall believed he was being persecuted by Wood, who had to defend his actions in court on several occasions. The conflict between the two men made good front-page copy for the local newspaper, also placing the editor, Dick Burde, in an adversary position with Kendall.

Among the principals involved in the early fishing industry were Butterfield, Mackie & Co. Ltd, wholesale fish merchants and curers, who first established a plant in Port Alberni in 1913, then later moved to Ecoole Bay to operate a fish reduction plant.

In 1918, Watson Bros. Fishing and Packing Company opened a plant in Port Alberni for salting, curing and packing herring.[47] Trevor Goodall recalled the herring plant:

At the foot of Argyle Street was the packing plant, or fish wharf. There were large salting sheds, on pilings, with about a dozen large bins, each holding forty to sixty tons of herring every day.

The herring were brought up to the bins on a conveyor belt. Several men, up to their waists in fresh fish, shovelled coarse salt on them. In a few days, after turning almost red and hard, the herring were packed in four-hundred-pound boxes and loaded on a freighter to Japan. A portion of the catch was cleaned by Scottish fish girls, put into casks, or tubs, of two hundred pounds each, salted or mildly cured, and shipped all over by rail. I have seen the lower part of town covered with barrels, ready to ship. You could smell the herring for miles, and at night herring scales glistened in the light. The farmers would haul the waste onto the fields for fertilizer.[48]

In 1925, the Somerville Cannery Company headed by Francis Millerd, one of the partners in Gosse Millerd Packing Company, took over the operation. Nelson Bros. of the Nootka Packing Company operated a reduction plant at Toquart and at Ecoole. Their subsidiary company, the Bamfield Packing Company, had a large reduction plant in Ucluelet.[49] Bamfield Fisheries built a cannery at Bamfield in 1919 and Marine Products Company established a fish buying post. Also in Ucluelet, "about 1910, a small saltery was started for herring. These were for the Japanese trade. Two small boats with seines caught the fish inside Ucluelet and Toquart Harbours. They were the *Ucluelet No. 1* and *Tofino*. Dan, Billie, and Johnny Bain and Jim Barnes, four Scotch fishermen straight from Scotland—did the fishing."[50] A Japanese saltery was built at Sarita in 1917.[51] There would eventually be eleven salmon salteries owned by the Japanese on the west coast. Gosse Millerd Fish Packing Co. had a cannery at San Mateo Bay.

In the late twenties and early thirties, amalgamation of the fishing industry in the area was underway and would change the way fish were processed and distributed. Kildonan cannery merged with B.C. Fish and Packing Company, who in turn merged with Gosse Millerd, and B.C. Packers Ltd. was born.[52] B.C. Packers remained a dominant influence in fishing on the west coast. There were many, many other owners of small fishing plants who added their name to historical records.

A MILLION FISH A YEAR

Ucluelet fisherman August Lyche once processed over a million dog salmon a year in Barkley Sound. Lyche held the dog salmon licence in the sound for the year 1904. The licence cost him fifty dollars. At a later date, he leased the Kildonan cannery, plus a large building at the Hayes Mine; he had a plant at Toquart and also a large shed at Ucluelet for salting the fish. The Toquart plant alone employed forty Japanese and Chinese splitting and salting. Five seine boats were employed. "These were not the type of seine boats familiar today. There were no diesel or gas engines; there was a crew of eight, each man to an oar, plus the seine boss who steered the boat and was in charge of the net."[53]

American crews from Bellingham manned these vessels, as it was difficult to get men skilled in this type of fishing in Canada. The crews were paid fifty-five dollars per month with the seine boss receiving an extra twenty dollars. The season lasted about three months. No fishing limits were observed as the closest fishery officer lived in Nanaimo. James Wood, of Port Alberni, became the first fishery officer for the West Coast district in 1912.

Salt used in the process came from Mexico and was delivered to plants in Barkley Sound at six dollars per ton. Boxes for shipping the fish were made at Sutton's mill in Ucluelet. Lyche recalled that was about all the business the mill did that year. Over a million fish were processed in dry salt that first year. The largest haul made in Ucluelet was ten thousand fish. Much larger hauls were made at Nahmint, but there is no accurate record. The fish were shipped directly to China in sailing ships from Seattle, the business broker being a Mr. Bostock in Vancouver.

In 1905, Lyche affiliated with the A. R. Johnston Fishing Company of Nanaimo. This firm held the licence for the east coast of the island. This partnership lasted only a couple of years, as the bottom gradually fell out of the market and trade died away, only to be revived in later years by others. As the plants for salting the dog salmon were used only a small portion of the year, Lyche began looking around for another method of fishing that would ensure him employment for a longer time. He knew of a group of Germans, from Hamburg, who fished the Sacramento River for salmon for mild cure. They had not been successful there, so they

Seine boat harvesting salmon.

moved to the Columbia River. Being still dissatisfied, they were induced to lease the Lyche plants in Barkley Sound where they started to mild cure in 1906 with fish taken at Nootka and Barkley Sound. The German company representative, Mr. Weiser, brought a gang of splitters from Anacortes to work in the plants here. Weiser later worked for Peter Wallace at Kildonan, when that plant started to mild cure.

Lyche believed the failure of mild curing at this time was in the method of fishing. "Spring salmon do not school up as do other species. If there had been another method involved at that time other than seining, the mild curing of the British Columbia spring salmon would have been a major industry at that time." The loss of markets for any length of time in any business made it nearly impossible to build them up again with any measure of success. "The trouble affecting this fishery could not be solved until trolling became a commercial possibility." He said the product was of the highest quality.

Lyche watched the old days of brutal back-breaking work disappear as the industry evolved from the days of the old-style seine boats with oars, to the diesel and gas engines. He watched the introduction of brailling winches, wire purse lines, and all the paraphernalia of present-day fishing boats, together with reduction plants, cold storage plants, refrigeration cars, and fish shipped to all parts of the world from British Columbia. He witnessed all this change and still had great faith in the fisheries of the west coast.

THE POLITICS OF FISHING

Where one could fish and who could fish, were always difficult decisions for the fisheries officer. Inquiries into declining fishing stocks and restricted licensing were held at various times; the most raucous occurred when the Judge D. M. Eberts Commission of Inquiry opened in Port Alberni on February 5, 1919. It debated declining fish stocks, returning soldiers looking for work, increased fishing by the Japanese, and perceived pandering by fisheries officers to the Wallace Fisheries at Kildonan. At the height of the debate, Theodore Magneson of Vancouver was refused a licence to build a salmon cannery at Sarita because it would have been too close to the Wallace Fisheries plant. Magneson then decided to build his plant in Port Alberni, if he could secure a licence. This application was also denied, despite recommendations from Port Alberni City Council.[54]

This caused an uproar between city council and the Department of Fisheries. Fisheries claimed that fishing limits were set according to the available stock and the Kildonan cannery could more than take care of all the available fish. Council argued Kildonan must have been unable to process the catch, since Magneson had shipped large quantities of fish to foreign canneries the previous year. The city threatened to put the matter before the House of Commons if Fisheries put more obstacles or delays in the way.

There was a growing feeling of resentment against the Department's apparent policy of pandering to the Wallace interests. On May 11, 1918, a special meeting was held in the Fisheries Office at New Westminster to investigate Port Alberni's claim that a salmon-canning licence should be granted Magneson. At the meeting were representatives of various fishing industries on the coast, including Wallace, who gave their opinion that Barkley Sound was not fished out and thus could accommodate more seine fishing. Magneson claimed his previous hearing had not been impartial. The Chief Fisheries Inspector argued that if he granted the licence to Magneson, he would prejudice the interests of Wallace Fisheries.[55] Powell Chandler, speaking for Port Alberni City Council, pointed out the obvious. "There seems to us to be something radically wrong when a man is told to go and find whether his potential competitor is of the opinion he should be granted permission to go into business."[56] Magneson never did receive his licence.

One fisherman from Ucluelet, Christian Olsen, applied in 1916 for a dog seine licence, which he was promised on the condition he would cooperate with Wallace Fisheries. When he refused, the licence was refused. He tried again in 1918, this time for a gill-net licence for the Ucluelet harbour. After some difficulty he succeeded in getting one, but with a reservation and a note attached by Fishery Inspector Woods— Olsen could not use the licence in Ucluelet Harbour.[57]

John Kendall applied for a floating trap licence for use in

Sechart Channel and Effingham Island. He was promised it in 1918, but Fisheries Inspector Edward Taylor, from Nanaimo, intervened and asked Indian Agent Gus Cox to protest against the granting of the licence.[58] The licence was refused; the reasons given were that Wallace Fisheries did not want Kendall, an independent buyer, operating there, and that Kendall was antagonistic towards the fisheries officers. Wallace Fisheries itself operated a trap near Cape Beale without a licence, but it was eventually destroyed in a storm.

The Judge D. M. Eberts Royal Commission of Inquiry opened in Port Alberni on February 5, 1919. There were many claims and accusations made against the fisheries officers by independent fishermen who had been refused licences. Taylor and Wood denied all the allegations, and denied ever pandering to Wallace Fisheries.

The fishing inquiry continued in Vancouver, Nanaimo, and Duncan amidst a growing controversy about increased Japanese fishing on the west coast. The Board of Trade of Vancouver Island urged the government to take measures to restrict the activities of "alien fishermen off the West Coast . . . who were worming their way into the fishing industry."[59] There were so many bad feelings towards the canneries and the Department of Fisheries that fishermen began taking steps to protect their interests. They formed the Deep Sea Fishermen's Union of the Pacific Coast.[60]

The fisheries officers were exonerated of any wrongdoing by the inquiry, which prompted a tongue-in-cheek editorial in the *Cowichan Leader*. "All the complaints made by reputable citizens or organisations, at great cost in time and expense, are groundless. The administration of the fisheries is admirable and the officers of the department are pearls beyond price. Mr. Justice Eberts' discernment is beyond the ordinary man's understanding. That the report has been made at all is a small crumb of satisfaction. It may now be properly pigeonholed and more money of the people of Canada sent to pay for it."[61]

The annual report of the Fisheries for 1919 briefly noted the inquiry: "Charges of all kinds were filed against the officers and his Honour Judge Eberts was appointed by the Government to investigate the same. All evidence was taken under oath and it is satisfactory from the investigation in so far as it set at rest in the public mind wild rumours of graft and maladministration of the fisheries in this province generally."[62]

The Japanese continued to fish despite growing hostility from white fishermen. Many Japanese settled in Ucluelet and Tofino, where they built homes for their wives and families. The peak of Japanese employment in the industry was reached in 1919 when they received 3,267 licences, nearly one-half the total issued in that year.[63] But the growing agitation and complaints resulted in a Fisheries policy to reduce Japanese licences. In 1922, salmon trolling licences were reduced by thirty-three per cent. In each succeeding year, licences continued to be reduced until it was feared, in 1926, the Japanese would be driven out of the industry completely. The Amalgamated Association of Japanese Fishermen took their case to the courts. On May 1, 1928, the Supreme Court of Canada delivered judgement in their favour. The government appealed, but in 1929 the appeal was dismissed on the grounds the federal minister could not withhold a licence to a duly naturalised Canadian citizen. By 1934, Japanese owned eleven salmon salteries on the west coast, employing 298 white and 395 Japanese workers.[64]

It is difficult to assess the result of the policy. No doubt it drove many Japanese fishermen away from the industry. Many probably returned to Japan, but the majority remained in Canada and found their way into other industries. On the west coast, they were drawn to forestry, where many found work during the off-season. Like forestry, the commercial fishing industry has been cursed by cycles of boom and bust. Every crisis faced the same dilemma: how to maintain stock while protecting the industry and the small communities who relied on the trade.

The Pacific salmon fishery had been Canada's principal fishery. The government paid very little attention to the intensity of fishing until the late forties, when it did some tagging, mainly to study fish migration to and from the ocean, and put some regulations into place to guarantee adequate spawning escapement. However, the main focus of attention was the fresh-water phase of the fish cycle which could be controlled to produce more young.[65] Authorities recognised fishing practices were highly developed and fishing intensity was at a peak, but few believed the fish resource was in danger of depletion.

CHAPTER SEVEN

SEA PATROLS AND ROAD PROMISES

THE *THIEPVAL*, THE *ARMENTIERES* AND THE *GIVENCHY*

Patrolling Barkley Sound and engaging in lifesaving services on the west coast was not easy, but the minesweepers *Armentieres*, *Givenchy*, and *Thiepval* were up to the task. These vessels were often stationed at Bamfield for the winter months to co-ordinate with the Bamfield Lifeboat and to assist ships in distress. Month after month they were required to stand by day and night, ready to proceed to any call from a ship in distress. On two occasions the *Armentieres* and the *Thiepval* had to rescue each other.

At high tide, on September 2, 1925, the *Armentieres*, commanded by Captain C. D. Donald, was passing between Refuge and Bazett Islands at the entrance to Pipestem Inlet, when she hit a rock. Until this time, the only navigational chart available was that surveyed by Captain Richards in 1861. The rock did not appear on Richards' chart. The ship's hull had almost passed over the rock before her stern became lodged while her bow floated free. Captain Donald tried everything to dislodge her. He soon realised the ship would sink by the bow as the tide ebbed. To stop this, heavy cables were attached to trees on shore. But the trees snapped and the cables flew as the weight of the vessel proved too much. The captain called for help when the bow began to sink.

Water poured into the ship as it listed on its port side in fifty feet of water. The next morning, the *Thiepval* and the tug *Salvage King* came to the rescue. They refloated the *Armentieres* and towed it to Victoria to be recommissioned.

Five years later, it was the turn of the *Armentieres* to come to the rescue of the *Thiepval*. On February 27, 1930, the *Thiepval*, under the Command of Lt. H. R. Tingley, was travelling through an unnamed channel north of Turret Island in the Broken Group Islands when she too hit an uncharted rock. She grounded at ebb tide, and fearing she would turn over, the crew of twenty-two men and officers abandoned the ship in lifeboats. The *Armentieres* and the *Salvage King* tried to refloat her on the next high tide, but all efforts failed and the ship sank to her resting place.

The *Thiepval* had had a twelve-year career with the Royal Canadian Navy. She was built in 1917 by Canadian Vickers Ltd., and commissioned into the navy in 1918. In March, 1920, she was transferred to the federal department of Marine and Fisheries to be used as a patrol vessel. Three years later she returned to the Royal Canadian Navy for service on the west coast.[1]

In 1924, when Major Stuart MacLaren began planning his round-the-world flight, *Thiepval* had been sent across the North Pacific to Hakodate, Japan, to provide assistance. Her job: to deposit fuel and lubricant caches for MacLaren's long flight. During this operation, *Thiepval* travelled over ten thousand miles and eventually was involved in salvaging the wreckage of MacLaren's ill-fated airplane. This mission had been *Thiepval's* last before she crashed against the rock in Barkley Sound.

After these incidents Captain Pariseau of the Canadian Hydrographic Services aboard the survey ship, the *William J. Stewart*, resurveyed Barkley Sound. Many of the old names were changed at this time to avoid confusion. The channel where the *Thiepval* had sunk was named Thiepval Channel in her honour. With the introduction of radio direction finding installations at Pachena, Estevan, and other lighthouses, the service of the patrol ships was subsequently withdrawn.

In 1962, Ucluelet Scuba Diving Club salvaged the three-inch naval gun from the wreck of the *Thiepval*.[2] Those divers involved in the recovery were Ray Vose, Jim Hill, Malcolm Miller, Lou Klock, Loslio Hillier and George Hillier. It took three dives to prepare the gun for its raise. When unbolted, the gun was lashed to the *Hillier Queen* and towed to Ucluelet.

The *Givenchy* had served as a minesweeper during the First World War, then as a Fisheries patrol vessel on the Atlantic coast before being brought to the west coast to be used in the same capacity here. The Fisheries annual report of 1919 noted:

> I wish to refer to the good work done by the Fisheries patrol steamer *Givenchy*, commanded by Captain Laird. This boat was one of the trawlers brought from the Atlantic coast and utilized in the Fisheries patrol service of this province. She is a most seaworthy boat and eminently suitable for work on this coast, and replaced the Fisheries patrol launch *Fispa*, which was transferred for service in District No. 3, under Inspector E. G. Taylor, replacing the *Alcedo*, sold by public auction.[3]

Like the other two patrol vessels, the *Givenchy's* major roles were patrol, prevention of poaching, and enforcement of fishing regulations. Perhaps the biggest headache for the ships was the enforcement of the three-mile limit which forbade fishing by foreign vessels. The *Givenchy* was a coal-burning vessel, and while her officers would have preferred burning oil, Ottawa insisted on coal because of the pressure brought to politicians to protect Vancouver Island's coal mining industry. As a result, her smoke could be seen for miles, permitting any poacher time to pick up his gear and escape.[4]

MP Alan Webster Neill, an Independent in the Alberni Comox riding, also used the services of the *Givenchy* on his trips around the riding, which included the west coast of Vancouver Island.

RUMRUNNERS

Prohibition during the twenties and thirties gave the patrol vessels another headache: being on the lookout for rumrunners. The birth of rumrunning can be traced to a simple response to a highly rewarding market south of the border. When the United States Congress passed the Volstead Act, it was the final touch in a thirty-year campaign by the suffragettes, church groups, politicians, and others to outlaw liquor. Although a portion of the country was already under prohibition, the Volstead Act made it national. Some Canadian businessmen seized the lucrative opportunity and came to the rescue of the "alcohol impoverished" people south of the border. The Dominion government tacitly condoned the trade and took full advantage of the exercise by creating a twenty-dollar-per-case export duty on liquor cleared to American ports. It was easy for rumrunners to slip around this tax by claiming their shipments were going elsewhere, perhaps to Mexico. A few years later, a general tax of ten dollars per gallon was added to all liquor exported from Canada. These additional taxes had little effect and were easily absorbed into operating costs.[5]

At no time was rumrunning illegal in British Columbia. The only offence was evading the duty. The west coast was alive with small vessels intent on evading customs with loads of contraband liquor illegally consigned to the large ocean-going vessels lying out at sea, out of reach of the United States and Canadian officials. Customs officers were always on the alert for suspicious boats running in darkness or in foggy conditions; they frequently caught owners red-handed and seized the liquor. In 1925, Customs officer William Fraser, brother of George Fraser, discovered a cache of 575 sacks of liquor hidden on Amphitrite Point, near Ucluelet Inlet. Not surprisingly, no one claimed ownership, but it was suspected the liquor was part of a larger shipment of 1,125 cases previously found aboard the *Chakawana*, which had been taken to Victoria. The value was estimated at fifty-one thousand dollars.[6]

Hunting down rumrunners was never something the crew of the *Givenchy* enjoyed, "but when several hundred cases, packed in gunnysacks, of good Scotch whisky was confiscated, many hands made light work bringing it aboard."[7]

The *Malahat* was well known on the coast for her days as the mother ship of the rum fleet sailing the coast from British Columbia to California. It was not unusual for the ship to carry sixty thousand cases of liquor on board. During prohibition she became a floating warehouse, receiving shipments from small fast boats scattered along the coast. They unloaded their burlap sacks then disappeared into small inlets, coves and beaches, impossible to catch. No law was broken unless the ship was caught within the three-mile limit.

The five-masted wooden sailing ship was built in Victoria and launched on August 11, 1917. After loading lumber there, she was towed to Port Alberni, arriving September 21, where another shipment of lumber lay ready for shipping to Australia. The Australians were not too happy that another shipment had been loaded before theirs, and they sought a court injunction to stop further loading. It was finally agreed the remainder of the space would be filled with the Australian order. The *Malahat* set sail without her engines on October 13, 1917. Every space taken, the deck load stood ten feet high. As the ship was towed away from the Port Alberni dock, her sails were unfurled and she was on her way. The journey took sixty days. The Bolinder engines were installed when she returned.[8]

Captain Stuart Stanley Stone became master of the *Malahat* on March 16, 1929. He had already experienced several encounters with United States authorities when he captained the *Federalship*, which was also involved in rumrunning.[9] The son of Methodist minister Reverend Stone, he married Emmie May (Beal) of Ucluelet, whose father Captain C. C. Binns operated a trading post in the village. Emmie May's growing-up years in Ucluelet were fairly uneventful; she attended Girls Central School in Victoria then went to work for B.C. Telephone in Vancouver. Five years later she married Stuart Stone. The *Malahat* was then rumrunning to California and Mexico. Emmie May remembered spending Christmas off the coast of Mexico at a place called Rum Row. The crew at first resented her presence aboard the ship but soon changed their minds after she proved her seamanship—she could and did climb the rigging in rolling seas. Crews from around the world were welcomed aboard to visit "Mrs. Capt." "It was an excuse for them to wear a white shirt."[10]

During this time, the Gibson Bros. were propositioned to make some fast money by chartering their two vessels, the *Otter* and the *Maid of Orleans*.

We could have made $100,000 a year, but our father gave us sound advice which we have stuck to: "Stay out of the liquor business, boys—drink whatever you want in front of the bar, but never be sober standing behind it. I don't want our family ever to make a dollar out of the liquor business."[11]

The *Malahat* had been built for the lumber trade, and her combination of wind and engine power made her an ideal rum supply ship. She was elusive; she evaded capture time after time, and she left the US Coast Guard looking foolish and feeling frustrated. For nine years of her life on Rum Row she became one of the most wanted ships on the California coast. The coast guard won in the end. When her rum running days were over, the old ship dropped anchor and returned to her original trade. Stone, who had skippered the ship through many rough seas, died tragically from appendicitis before a doctor could reach him. Emmie May returned to Ucluelet. The *Malahat* was sold in 1934 and for a brief period returned to carrying lumber. On April 14, 1934, she was back in Port Alberni loading a cargo of aspen logs destined for China. It seemed like old times. A few days later, she was stranded in dense fog on a reef south of Prince Rupert. Following a period in dry dock, with debts mounting, she was seized by the courts and put up for sale.[12] The *Malahat* was then purchased by the Gibson Bros. family and converted into a log carrier running from the Queen Charlotte Islands to the pulp mills at Powell River and Ocean Falls. The Gibson Bros. paid $2,500 for the ship that had cost three-quarters of a million dollars to build. Now she was considered a white elephant: too big for a pleasure yacht and too slow for a cargo ship. Gordon Gibson remembered the first time he inspected the family purchase:

> She was a schooner in the grand old style, with a coal burning fireplace in the owner's quarters and two full-size bathtubs, one for the owner and one aft for the captain and crew. The officers' quarters were excellent, too, with heat in each stateroom, which was a luxury in those days. Aft there was a stateroom for the captain and a stateroom for the mates, chief engineer and cook.[13]

The ship was converted to carry logs, and served the Gibson family well until 1944 when, unable to run under her own power, she was turned into a log barge to be towed by the *James Carruthers*. Death came to the *Malahat* while she carried a cargo of spruce logs. "Schooner *Malahat*, famous old rumrunner, which foiled coast guarders more often than they were successful, is now reported a 'constructive total loss' by surveyors, who flew last week to Green Bay, Barkley Sound, to inspect the log-carrying barge. She has been pounded to pieces by Pacific waves and B.C. logs."[14] The barge had been caught in a gale off Cape Beale and towed to shelter at Uchucklesit Inlet, but her cargo broke free and pounded the hull of the vessel. Insurance underwriters declared her a total loss.[15]

The *Malahat* had been the only self-powered, self-loading and unloading barge until MacMillan Bloedel built the *Haida Brave* in 1978 at a cost of fifteen million dollars. It cost six thousand times as much as the *Malahat* and carried only four times as much cargo at twice the speed.[16]

The old lighthouse tender, the SS *Quadra*, also became a rumrunner. She had been the pride of the west coast and was a friend to lighthouse keepers, delivering mail, supplies, fuel, and even mail-order brides. She was also a law enforcement vessel. It was the *Quadra* that enabled the rescue of all hands aboard the *Coloma* shortly after it wrecked near Cape Beale. The ship's contribution as a patrol vessel ended when on February 26, 1917, it collided in fog with the Canadian Pacific Railway steamer *Charmer* at the entrance to Nanaimo harbour. The ship was beached to prevent her from sinking in deep water. Only a portion of her funnel and masts were visible at high tide. This ended her career as a lighthouse tender. She was refloated and sold to Britannia Mines, who used her to carry ore concentrates from Howe Sound to the Tacoma Smelter.

In 1924, a rumrunning company chartered the *Quadra*. After making several very successful trips, she was seized by the U.S. Coast Guard cutter *Shawnee* on October 24, 1924, while unloading liquor to a speed boat off the coast of California. The ship and her cargo valued at one million dollars were confiscated and her captain fined one thousand dollars and given two years in jail. The *Quadra*'s owners retained the entire crew on full salary for eight months following the seizure. The crew spent their seemingly endless shore leave enjoying the glories of San Francisco. During the period of litigation, the ship deteriorated to such an extent she was eventually sold for $1,625 and was broken up for scrap.[17]

The successful delivery of liquor to the United States became increasingly difficult due to the presence of a large Coast Guard detachment off the coast in 1927. Then came the Depression when it was more important to put food on the table than liquor in the stomach. Rumrunning faded months before the repeal of Prohibition on December 5, 1933.[18]

This was a colourful time in British Columbia history; tales of search and seizure, of clandestine meetings far out at sea, hidden caches and unexpected finds, all added to the fascination with this period of time on the west coast.

PROMISES FOR UCLUELET

Early settlers in Ucluelet had roads on their mind when they settled on the west coast. They were told Ucluelet would be a good place to settle as the road from Alberni would go through and there would be years of work ahead. Herbert J. Hillier, of Victoria, attracted to Ucluelet by the gold fever, arrived in 1898 and worked as cook at the Wreck Bay mining camp. Later he helped construct the telegraph line down the west coast and for fifty years was linesman and agent at Ucluelet. His brother Jack Hillier also worked as a telegraph operator and linesman at Toquart Bay.

Ucluelet first asked the provincial government for a road to connect to Clayoquot, a request that was endorsed by the Alberni Board of Trade in 1908.[19] A wagon road of sorts connecting to Tofino was pushed through in 1911.[20] Hillier worked on the wagon road construction, using wheelbarrows, picks, shovels and crosscut saws, the only equipment affordable from the paltry government grants. Then in 1912, Premier Sir Richard McBride announced there would be a trunk line road along the west coast. With those promises of a road connection, Ucluelet started a branch of the Vancouver Island Development League, hoping to attract new settlers and investment possibilities. First president was Herbert J. Hillier with George William Grant as secretary-treasurer.[21] Grant, a bachelor, originally from Aberdeen, Scotland,[22] wore a kilt and played the bagpipes. He tried farming but gave that up to become the lightkeeper at Amphitrite Point. Later he became Ucluelet's postmaster.

The lighthouse at Amphitrite Point was built following the wreck of several ships in 1906. Ucluelet residents forwarded a petition to government requesting a lifeboat. At first all the government could muster was a rowboat. The volunteer crew was under the command of Captain August Lyche. Years later, a motor boat captained by W. L. Thompson replaced the rowboat. The point was named by Captain Richards after HM frigate *Amphitrite*, which had sailed the coast in the 1850s.

In 1909, E. McGaffey, the general secretary of the Vancouver Island Development League, toured Ucluelet. While impressed with George Fraser's rhododendrons, he also praised the efforts of other small farmers. He glowed with praise over a farm owned by John H. Kvarno, "where the growth of grass was really remarkable and where gooseberries were so big I dare to give their dimensions. I also visited Mr. Lyche's farm, James Fraser's and G. W. Grant's places, all of which are thriving. Ucluelet district is another part of the country which will forge ahead rapidly when transportation is provided and a district bound to be benefited by the railroad to the Alberni District."[23] Kvarno, a Norwegian, supplied dairy and vegetables to the community from his farm. He became Ucluelet's first policeman.[24]

In 1912 the Mile 0 post had just been planted in Alberni by the Canadian Highway Association; the next leg of the road was planned to link to the west coast. Canada would have a coast-to-coast highway, though it would not be completed until 1959. Who would not be optimistic about the future? The Rural Telephone Company was formed with all settlers buying shares and owning telephones. This became the first charter telephone system of its kind in British Columbia. The line replaced one that had connected only three homes around the harbour.[25]

In 1922, the road from Ucluelet to Tofino was allocated a ten-thousand-dollar grant. Two small gangs of men under James Fraser of Ucluelet, a brother of George Fraser, and J. P. Cooper of Long Beach worked at clearing and grubbing the part of the road already logged. An eight-mile stretch of the road had already been built; additional men were hired to make further improvements.[26] The road came out on the beach north of Sand Hill Creek and travelled along the beach for six miles to Paul's Landing, then through the bush again to Tofino, nine miles further to join the last two-mile stretch which had already been built.

The 1923 Arthur Lineham ten-million dollar scheme to build a series of roads, one to Long Beach on the west coast, another north to Campbell River, and another road from Victoria to Port Renfrew, had tourism in mind, not the interests of islanders hoping to see their communities develop.[27] The project did reach the ear of Premier John Oliver, but it was an idea ahead of its time. Ucluelet still hoped. Today those same roads carry thousands of tourists visiting Vancouver Island.

The land from Ucluelet to Tofino opened for pre-emption when the road linking the two communities was completed. Settlers took up every section between the two villages, some coming from as far away as England. There were families on every quarter section between Wreck Bay, Long Beach on the west and Kennedy Lake on the east.

> A quarter section, 160 acres for nothing, looked pretty big to people in the old country, who couldn't own any land. And they had the road promised then too. The road was promised before my father came in, and when he came he had to row up the bay, and then just go through a trail, pack everything on his back the five miles up into his pre-emption. And there was no sign of the road. Well, he didn't even see the road. Mother lived to be 94 and she saw the road. She went over part of it, but Father never saw it, even.[28]

The building of the road meant some ready work for the men in both communities. The road was cleared and partly corduroyed.[29] Without a road link to Alberni, settlers were still forced to use water transportation. Many would-be settlers left the area having found it difficult to support a family. Others like pioneers Chris Fletcher, Charles Hughes, Fritz Bonnetti, Walter Saggers, and W. Karn moved to the Ucluelet waterfront. Karn was the first carpenter.

The first school was a one-room school under teacher Mrs. Lyche, wife of August Lyche and sister to Edwin Lee, the fur buyer. She taught in her own home when there were only three or four children that needed schooling, until the population increased and a school was built.[30] In 1928 there were thirty students attending Ucluelet school under Douglas W. J. Noble. Many of the students were Japanese.[31]

The head of Ucluelet arm at this time became a separate community called Stapleby, with its own post office and store operated by C. Grant. The Stapleby school opened with more students than the Ucluelet school. They walked for miles along plank walks. The shifting of population also took place south of Ucluelet where settlers like customs officer William Fraser, Mr. Jacobs, Mr. Soderlund, and Mr. Whipp had taken up land along the shore of Barkley Sound with the hope the Alberni Highway would partly follow the coast.[32] Eventually they too moved into Ucluelet.

It was fishing, not road access, that increased the population of Ucluelet. Japanese fishermen arrived and settled in the village. Their arrival caused alarm in what had been predominantly a white or Native fishing industry. There were estimates of five hundred fishing boats owned and operated by Japanese between Ucluelet and Clayoquot.[33] Stories began appearing in a local newspaper about "Japanese supremacy and insolence unbearable for white subjects."[34] Slowly white fishermen recognised the expertise of their Japanese counterparts, some even entered working partnerships to hold fishing licences. The hundreds of boats docking in Ucluelet harbour were good news for local businesses, especially the Ucluelet Engineering Works operated by J. L. Thompson from 1925 to 1946. During stormy weather it was not an unusual sight to see twenty or more large seiners tied up at the Ucluelet dock, each worth over forty thousand dollars.

At Port Albion, on the east side of Ucluelet harbour, a cannery and reduction plant brought months of employment to many in the area. The *Princess Maquinna* and *Princess Norah* visited both Ucluelet and Port Albion carrying passengers and freight, while the *Uchuck* brought in the mail from Port Alberni. The arrival of the steamers was a special day in town as residents gathered to pick up freight, or just to visit with neighbours.

Sheila Mead-Miller remembered the old hotel her father operated in 1929 when the family moved to Ucluelet. The building had belonged to August Lyche. However, neither of her parents knew anything about operating a hotel and it never was a "moneymaking concern. Because they hated to give anyone their bill. Someone would stay there for a week, and they'd think, 'Gee, that's too much to charge, shouldn't charge him that much,' and they'd take a little bit off."[35]

The hotel, "with ten rooms, a few bathrooms, also a large living room and big kitchen," provided accommodation for visiting doctors, lawyers, businessmen, or vacationers. When the family wanted to go on a picnic for the day, they just closed up leaving a note on the door. "We are away for the day. Come in and help yourselves. Play the record player and have something to eat if you can find it. We should be home this evening." Once, when the family returned in the evening there was a note left for them from a Billy Lord, who later "became a well-known judge in Vancouver." He had been up to Ceepeecee, to the Canadian Fishing Company, and he and two other men had stopped in at the hotel. Seeing the note, they did as it suggested, went in and helped themselves. Lord's note stated, "We did as you said. We helped ourselves, we had bacon and eggs, and we played the record player, and we read the paper. Thank you very much." The visitors left the family some money and cleaned up all the dishes.

There were good and bad times for Ucluelet during the Second World War. There was sadness when all the Japanese residents were rounded up and sent to the interior of British Columbia for internment. Many had become friends and neighbours. Mr. Kvarno's land became a sea plane base for the military. The seaplane base was later transported to Tofino to become the Wayside Chapel.[36] Hundreds of men trained there until a larger landbased airport was built in Tofino. With a need for easy transportation between the two military airports, the road between Ucluelet and Tofino was finally completed and kept in good condition.[37] Hillier's front lawn, with a commanding view of the mouth of the harbour, became an artillery site. Soldiers practising firing shots with the large guns at rocks outside the harbour unnerved everyone.

After the war, logging became a factor of everyday life in Ucluelet. The Thornton brothers, who had taken up land in 1910, leased a portion of their land to Harry C. McQuillan to start the North Coast Timber Company. McQuillan became a member of parliament for Comox Alberni in the 1958 election.[38] The truck logging operation employed up to 150 men.[39] MacMillan Bloedel Ltd. later purchased the timber holdings of the company thus establishing the Kennedy Lake Division. The company also purchased the timber leases of the Sutton Lumber and Trading Company.

B.C. Forest Products Ltd. with no timber holdings in the area, made an application for a tree farm licence, inviting both Ucluelet and Tofino for their support, promising if the application was accepted, the road to Alberni would finally be constructed. Despite some opposition from C & B Logging Ltd., logging in the Ucluelet area, the application was granted.[40]

In 1952, Ucluelet attained the status of village municipality. Letters Patent incorporated the village Municipality of Ucluelet. Five temporary commissioners, R. Matterson, E. Edwards, G. Gudbranson, J. Watters, and F. Rhodes were sworn in, with Matterson elected chairman. The first item on the agenda was the question of street lighting. The B.C. Power Commission was asked to install twenty-five lights at strategic points on village streets.[41]

Not until the Social Credit government came to power in 1952 did it appear the years of lobbying for a road would finally end. Philip Gaglardi, or Flying Phil as he affectionately was named, became Minister of Highways and announced in 1954 there was a possibility of the road being built with financial assistance from the lands and forests department. The good news came in 1955; the road to the west coast would finally go ahead.[42] On August 22, 1959 a caravan of seventy-five cars with four hundred people in Volkswagens, Cadillacs, war surplus trucks, jeeps, and pickup trucks set out from the west coast. Ucluelet and Tofino finally had road access to Alberni and the east coast of Vancouver Island.

Ucluelet now had street lights. The fishing industry still thrived and logging had been incorporated into the wealth of the community. Miles of roads had been built. The dream which had led many to settle here in the first place had finally become reality: a road connected to the Albernis.

PORT ALBION - UCLUELET EAST

From the time of earliest settlement, Port Albion lay on the east side of Ucluelet harbour. The Native village lay on this side, as well as the mission and church. It would have been Port Albion that Emily Carr visited in 1898. As the west side of Ucluelet developed, the village became known as Ucluelet East and was incorporated into the Municipality of Ucluelet. In 1937, utilising the old shingle mill, Nootka Packing Company and its subsidiary the Bamfield Packing Company built a reduction plant for processing herring and pilchards. Mr. D. Wilson became manager of the new plant, which became known as the Bamfield Packing Company.[43] Joe Lysness, one of the shareholders, constructed the plant. The company owned eight boats, seiners and packers; the seiners were named *Pacific Sunrise, Pacific Queen, Pacific Sunset* and *Midnight Sun*. Skippers were Johnny Dale, Martin Brevice, and Olaf Anderson.[44] During the Second World War, a cannery was built to supply the military with canned herring.

The Canadian Fishing Company purchased the Port Albion fish processing facilities in 1942 and added their own fleet to the existing one. These fish boats included the *Cape Perry, Cape Batherst, Cape Mark* and *Canfisco*. The small fishing community now included a cookhouse, sixteen family homes, two bunkhouses for single women, one large two-storey house for Chinese workers, a store, and a recreation hall for social activities.

Port Albion also had its own school. A few of the earliest teachers included C. H. Lewis, R. T. Pollock, Charles Leys, Mell Edwards, Myrtle E. Paylove, and P. A. Murphy. In 1946 there were eleven students registered.[45] The school eventually became incorporated into the Ucluelet School.

The community began to decline as people moved across the harbour. In 1951, Herman Hedman operated a refrigeration unit during the summer and a reduction plant in the winter. By 1967 all that remained were a fish buying camp and a refrigeration unit. In 1980, B.C. Packers purchased the facilities and wharf, the remainder was demolished.

CHAPTER EIGHT

THE LOGGING INDUSTRY

LOGGERS AND LOGGING CAMPS

The logging industry has evolved through many phases, from A-frame shows, high-lead "swinging" set-ups, railroads, and large-scale clear-cut logging to helicopter logging. The shores of the canal have been logged since the turn of the century, from Bamfield to Port Alberni on along the east side and from Toquart Bay to Nahmint River along the west side. Traditionally, logging took place as close to the water as possible for easy access; today logging shows are further inland. Booming grounds and log dumps are a familiar sight on the waterway.

The parade of players in the last hundred years is as large as the huge Douglas-fir, cedar, and hemlock trees they processed. Following the Anderson Company enterprise in 1860 were the Wood brothers' Barclay Sound Cedar Company; Carlin, Meredith and Gibson; Canadian Pacific Lumber Company; Howard A. Dent; Denny, Mott and Dickson Ltd; Bloedel, Stewart & Welch; H. R. MacMillan Export Company; MacMillan Bloedel Limited; Coulson Forest Products; and the Gibson Brothers. Many other smaller pioneer logging and sawmill operators added their name to the players list, including Wiest Logging Company, George Bird at Port Alberni and William Sutton at Ucluelet, sawmill owners; and Thomas Winger at Ucluelet shingle mill. Captain George Vancouver once viewed the primeval rain forest as being totally unfit for human habitation. He could not have forecast how valuable this resource would be to the province in the future. Those who made their living cutting down trees look back wistfully to the Glory Days of logging.

The list of logging camps in the vicinity of Port Alberni and farther along the canal read like alphabet or number soup. The Franklin River logging operation was first developed to serve Bloedel, Stewart & Welch's Somass Sawmill in Port Alberni. Camp A was located on the canal at the mouth of the Franklin River. Logging started in the river's drainage area; a railway extended along the river for four miles then turned south along Corrigan Creek to Camp B. This camp operated in the area until 1940, when it was moved south to Parsons Creek, where the old Canadian National Railway (CNR) railway bed was used to haul the logs to the boom grounds at Camp A. In 1914 the CNR had abandoned plans to construct a railway into Port Alberni from Victoria. In 1945, Camp B moved to Coleman Creek.

In 1926, Camp 4 was located at Underwood Cove, just south of China Creek Park; in 1934 it was moved to Nahmint Bay and renamed Camp 5. Camp 6 was on the south side of China Creek for logging around Lizard Lake, now part of the City of Port Alberni's watershed. This camp lasted only eighteen months; the buildings and equipment were moved to Grassy Mountain in 1936. Logging there only lasted a year before closing. These were all railroad camps with log dumps on the canal at Alberni Pacific mill, Underwood Cove, and Nahmint Bay.

Sarita River Camp was located just south of Sarita River, in 1945, to harvest an area which had become infested by the Hemlock Looper. Bloedel, Stewart & Welch built the camp and logged there until 1959, when Sarita River merged with Camp B and became part of the Cameron-Franklin River Division of MacMillan Bloedel Ltd. In 1974, the camp was reestablished at Christie Bay.

FRANKLIN RIVER CAMP

The logging camp at Franklin River, which opened in October 1934, became the largest railway logging show on Vancouver Island and had the distinction of being the first in North America to use power saws and hard hats and the first in the Alberni Valley to use logging trucks. The combined truck and railway logging show covered a total area of about fifty square miles from the Beaufort Range to the Pacific Ocean and contained some of the finest timber found on the west coast. One memorable stand of three-hundred- to five-hundred-year-old Douglas-fir measured up to ten feet in diameter at the butt and scaled out at more than 25,000 FBM. "One tree this size produced enough plywood to cover both the playing field and the stands at Empire Stadium."[1]

The first thirty fallers arrived at Franklin Creek in September 1934.[2] By October, there were 125 fallers. Twenty-two camp buildings had been constructed, including a cookhouse, a dining room and a storehouse, an office with commissary attached, numerous bunkhouses, and other buildings. In addition, a long railway pier was constructed along the edge of the booming ground, and railway sidings had been laid to accommodate the rolling stock needed for the operation.[3] The first booms of logs, towed by Victory Navigation, arrived at the mill site ready for the start-up of the new sawmill.[4]

Hard hats, or "skull guards," also affectionately nick-named "widow makers," were introduced in the camp in June 1939. These were so heavy loggers felt they could break their necks by wearing them. Although heavy, they did save lives. The safety director Ted Parkinson reported a record of twenty days accident free, soon after the hats were introduced.[5]

By 1946, there were ninety miles of railway in operation; however, truck logging gradually reduced railway logging until finally railway logging was abandoned. Camp A became known as the "beach camp" because of its location at the mouth of Franklin River on the Alberni Canal. Several families lived at this camp, while others commuted from the Albernis. The larger camp was Camp B, where several hundred people lived year round, including approximately seventy children. There were several bunkhouses for the two hundred single men. This was considered the most modern logging camp in all of Canada. It had the latest in construction design; amenities including sewage, plumbing, electric light; and a planned housing development with a central heating system.[6] A two-room school was built, along with a large recreation field and a specially designed recreation hall for holding indoor and outdoor activities. A gas speeder, which could carry forty passengers, provided transportation between the two camps, and a daily boat service connected Franklin River and Port Alberni. Harold Brownson was resident camp foreman, and Jack Bell assistant foreman.

Fishing was an obvious pastime in nearby lakes and rivers such as Coleman Creek, upper Nitinat River and Lake, Sarita Lake, and the Alberni Canal. Residents also took great pride in their gardens where they grew fresh vegetables. Movies were shown twice a week in the recreation hall where other community events such as dances and stage shows were held. There was also a small library supervised by Mrs. Bernice Poole. The small two-teacher school operated under School District 70 from Port Alberni. Until a road was built connecting to Port Alberni, food was delivered by truck to Camp A and shipped to Camp B by rail speeder. This was considered a minor inconvenience and just part of living at camp. The social life was much like that of a small community; there was a Social Club, the Franklin River Rod and Gun Club, and a Drama Club. Sports activities were also an important part of community life. Money raised at dances and other events was ploughed back into the Social Club coffers to buy sports equipment and other necessities.

In 1948, a giant tree from Franklin River became the flagpole for the Tower of London, in England. The pole, a gift from Prentice Bloedel, president of Bloedel, Stewart & Welch, was sent as a token from the Boy Scouts of Canada to the City of London.[7] The pole, eighty-two feet long, had been made from a 158-foot tree that was 389 years old and had started to grow during the reign of Queen Elizabeth. The flagpole was ceremoniously transported through the streets of London to its final destination and was received by Lord Wavell, Constable of the Tower. The original flagpole had been damaged in the air raids during World War II.

SARITA RIVER CAMP

One little worm is credited as being the founder of Sarita River camp. The Hemlock Looper played a major part in the decision to start logging operations there in 1948. The bug infestation killed large tracts of timber in the low-lying areas before the insects could be brought under control by aerial spraying. Operations began immediately to log the dead timber while it was still in prime condition. A Japanese company, the Trans-Pacific Company, had previously logged some of the area, but all activity ceased when the Japanese were rounded up and shipped to detention camps in 1941. The logging had ceased so abruptly that rigger Frank Walker left with a spar tree partially rigged for the opening of a new site. Walker was a little satisfied when eight years later, working for Bloedel, Stewart & Welch, he completed the rigging of the same tree.[8]

The job of salvaging the 11,900 acres of timber, bearing between 350 and 400 million feet, fell to Bloedel, Stewart & Welch, because they had the biggest stake in the infected area, and also because they had the men and equipment necessary for a high-ball salvage job. Veteran logger Robert S. Banks became superintendent. Company forester John Mottishaw was charged with researching what happened to infected timber and preparing for the loggers' take-over. His studies concluded that standing trees deteriorate more rapidly than those which had been felled. For this reason, the company judged it important to get the timber down as quickly as possible.[9]

Early in 1948, Banks moved his 350-man crew into the Sarita River site. This was a major undertaking, considering there was no regular transportation system on the canal with equipment heavy enough to handle the trucks, bulldozers and other logging equipment. Almost everything had to be barged to the site. After rough living quarters were established and a wharf was built for landing supplies, the top of a nearby hill was bulldozed as a site for the camp. It consisted of bunkhouses for the single men, cookhouses, warehouses, offices, first-aid and other buildings. Even a central heating plant was installed. The machine shop, equipped with everything necessary for major repairs, was built on the main road, near the wharf.

There were married quarters, a school, and a recreation hall to the north of the camp, away from the main section. The school had twelve pupils and was maintained by the Department of Education, with the company supplying the building. The cookhouse

Uchuck III

looked like the letter H, the crossbar being the section where the serving was done and the arms being the dining rooms. At one point, there were 275 people living there year-round.[10]

In January, 1949, a fire almost destroyed the camp. The machine shop and warehouse were totally incinerated in the blaze. Darwin Bjarnson was severely burned when fire exploded in the welding shop early in the morning. The speed boat *Jane Banks* transported the burned man to West Coast General Hospital in Port Alberni, where he was treated for first degree burns under the care of Dr. A. P. Miller.[11]

As in the Franklin River area, some giant trees also grew in the Sarita River area. The saws at the mill in Port Alberni carved up one spruce log that could produce enough lumber to build a five-room house. Thirty-six feet in length, it measured eleven feet, six inches at the butt and nine feet, two inches at the smaller end. Before its journey up the jack ladder, it was quartered down its length by the eleven-foot splitter saw operated by Mike Sopiwnyk. Each cut required two hours of time. George Dunbar, of the company's head office, estimated the log contained 20,180 board feet.[12]

Sarita Logging Camp, more isolated than Franklin, had the same community spirit and social life. There were concerts, clubs, service groups, and a Community Social Club. The Hospital Committee looked after the needs of camp residents who were in West Coast General Hospital in Port Alberni. Each Monday and Thursday evening, falling and bucking supervisor Fred Espley showed movies in the community hall. The Anniversary dance held every May was a gala affair, complete with orchestra. The Social Club sponsored a thriving library under Mrs. Velma Wright, who claimed the men in the bunkhouses kept her busy with their requests for more books.

Boat Day was a big day for everyone when the *Uchuck* arrived with mail Tuesdays, Thursdays, and Saturdays. Often the ship made a round trip from Port Alberni to accommodate the loggers. It also carried store supplies for the coffee shop run by Mr. and Mrs. Spooner. School teacher Miss Madeleine Poole, who taught grades one to six, did not mind life at "Box X," the Canada Post box designation for Sarita at the post office in Port Alberni.

The negative impact of the Sarita River Camp was the displacement of the Ohiaht Natives from their reserve at the mouth of the river. There were approximately three hundred Natives living on the reserve at the time logging commenced. Logging practices damaged the excellent fishery; now the Ohiahts are embarking on a restoration program to return the river to its former fishing status.[13]

THE LIFE OF A LOGGER

Logging has always been a dangerous occupation. From the turn of the century, deaths from logging accidents appeared regularly in newspaper obituaries. "Alex MacVickers killed instantly when huge log crushed him to death."[14] The logger was thirty-one years of age when a log slipped and pinned him beneath it. There was no inquest, the coroner considered it unnecessary. Logging accidents happened all the time. "Arthur Soderland an employee at APL logging camp was fatally injured while at work."[15] He was a hook tender and had been manipulating a large log attached to a cable. The cable caught a small tree nearby and bent it to the ground. The tree slipped from under the cable and in its rebound struck Soderland on the side of the head, smashing his skull. The Fraser Logging Company, Soderland's employer, closed for the day and Alberni Pacific Lumber Company gave a half holiday to allow workers to attend his funeral. Soderland, a Swede, had been in Canada only a year and was thirty years old.

Every tree provided a slightly different problem for the logger; there were no hard and fast rules. He had to be ready to meet every new situation as it arrived and to deal with it. "The occupation bred men of brain as well as brawn, but it also carried with it the penalty of hazard to life and limb."[16]

When the Anderson Company first logged in the area, Rogers and his crew dropped the trees right into the Alberni Canal. When the shoreline had been cleared they cut further back into the woods. Natives were hired to roll the logs into the water. The farther back they got, the more power they needed; the use of oxen and skid roads was a major step in British Columbia logging.[17] The team of oxen hauled the logs from the woods along greased skid roads. The bull puncher, or man in charge of the oxen, was the highest paid of the crew. Only the best trees were taken; those most accessible to water were harvested first because they could be floated easily to the sawmill.

Life seemed so much simpler then; our natural resources were endless and loggers could take whatever they wanted. No one thought about "old growth forests" or "sustainable forests." After the Anderson mill closed, those who worked in the woods were early settlers who took time off from their other work to supplement their income. The logs taken were processed and used to build houses for the settlers.

The age of steam changed the way trees were logged. Gradually the skid roads were phased out, as they were no longer necessary with the newfangled rig, the steam donkey. Railway lines were laid deep into the forest as loggers worked further away from the canal. The logged trees were loaded on flatcars for transportation to the sawmills. The 2-Spot Shay engine, and other engines of similar design, pulled the enormous log trains, chugged over trestle bridges and wound their way through deep canyons to deposit their loads at the dumping ground where the boom men took over the task of sorting. The boom men were pretty athletic and nimble on their feet, leaping from log to log with their pikepole pushing or pulling the logs through the water.

Still, logging was slow and tedious; logs were constantly hung up behind stumps or boulders. Someone came up with the idea of hanging two lead blocks high in a topped tree, providing the lift element, allowing the logs to clear the stumps. High-riggers were adventurous men. Not everyone was daring enough to decapitate a standing fir standing over 150 feet above the ground. When the top dropped, the motion sent the tree whipping back and forth. As daring as it was, before long this method was in general use on the west coast.

Jack Bell was a high rigger for the first ten years of his long career in the woods. "It wasn't all that risky if you knew what you were doing and were careful. I got careless once, fell ninety feet out of a tree and broke my leg. It's the only accident I've ever had in the woods and I went right back to high rigging after the leg mended."[18]

The "age of steam," as it was known, lasted until the Second World War when the Franklin River Camp converted to truck logging in 1946. The sounds of the old locie whistles still echo in Port Alberni, only these are now the sounds from restored railway engines. Locomotive whistles screeched while rail cars loaded with logs barrelled over tracks between wood operations and dumps. Those who manned the trains became experts in surviving derailments. Many jumped and lived; but some died in the wreckage. The first logging trucks, with their open cabs and hard rubber tires, gradually replaced the trains. They could go places trains could not and they did not require rails. Franklin River Camp pioneered the use of the power saw, which to some was not much of a break because those early chainsaws were enormous and cumbersome, and required two people to work them.

Logging camps such as Franklin and Sarita were considered large-scale, but there were also the smaller camps, the gyppo outfits. They were a different breed of men. Their territory included the entire canal, up the steep slopes, in the inlets and bays, and among the islands of Barkley Sound. Usually there were a couple of partners slugging it out, with the base of operations near the water for the sake of mobility. In many ways they resembled mountain goats, logging up the mountainside because all the level ground had been taken by the big operators. They usually logged using an A-frame. Guftason Bros. logged in the MacTush Creek and Headquarters area from 1924-1928 and Phil Welch logged in Nahmint Bay from 1928-1931. Other loggers along the canal included Earl O'Brien with his nephews the Creelman brothers, and Chinese logger Frank Sing. There was also a Japanese logging outfit in the Sarita area in the late twenties. Hand-logger Johnston was a big man who salvaged drift logs and floated them down the canal to Alberni Pacific Sawmill. A number of small operators worked in the Bamfield area, at Port Desire and Grappler Creek and at the head of Bamfield Inlet.

Joe Lamb, Johnny Born, Massey, they all logged, different logging companies. It was just a way of life, you had to make a living, so you did it. When they were logging in here they used A-frame, donkeys, like winches, and then spar trees. They would haul it to a central spar, from one to another and then A frame it into the water. So they could swing it two or three times along before it got into the water. When you're logging first growth, its all rotten and dead anyhow, like its over mature, its all dead top cedars and hemlocks that are ready to fall over. And, if you logged it and you left one here and one there, there's wind storms that would blow it over, there's nothing to support what's there, there's nothing around it. In this country here, it only takes eight to ten years after they have logged it. It looks like a carpet anyhow, like a big lawn from a distance. It doesn't take any time. They've logged (in Bamfield) since I can remember. Joe Lamb did the most of it; Johnny Born did some of it, and Massey did all the cat logging, like at Kelp Bay, the lagoon there, and out at Brady's Beach.[19]

In Ucluelet, in the fall of 1924, the Gibsons of Tofino took over the assets of the Ucluelet Sawmill, the water-powered mill owned by the Sutton Lumber Company, a subsidiary of the Seattle Cedar Company. The Gibsons were able to increase the number of salt herring boxes manufactured.[20] The North Coast Logging Camp employing up to 150 men was the first large-scale logging operation in Ucluelet. "The logs are brought down by trucks and dumped into the water. Small tugs sort and tow them to the loading works where they are loaded onto flat booms. Tugs from town came in and tow these out to sea every few days. This is a long way from 1904 when Herbert J. Hillier and William L. Thompson had logged two booms of logs of a hundred thousand feet each and sold them to the Ucluelet mill for six dollars a thousand feet, which was the price then."[21]

The old logging camps like Franklin and Sarita have disappeared, although some are operated by small contractors. Loggers now live in cities and villages and are transported to the logging site by water taxi or by crummy, the logging camp bus. Still, the logging industry retains some of the romance from its earlier days. There are fewer accidents in the woods now and safety regulations are strictly enforced. When a tree crashes to the forest floor, the sound heard is familiar, like an echo from the past.

A JOURNEY TO FRANKLIN RIVER CAMP IN 1945

On May 17, 1945, Prentice Bloedel, the young president of

Bloedel, Stewart & Welch Ltd., escorted a group of visitors to Franklin River Camp to show them where the trees were logged, bucked, and sent to the sawmill in Port Alberni. Along for the trip were Sid Smith, Bruce Farris, Charles Robson, Bob Laird, and Roy Olsen. Included also were Miller Freeman, shipbuilder Kemper Freeman, his son from Seattle, banker Pat Hunter, and trade commissioner Gerald Selous, from Vancouver. They were transported to Franklin by the motor launch *Commodore III*, skippered by Dorothy Blackmore.

Before viewing the camp, they had to wait while a train consisting of twenty-five flatcars loaded with gigantic logs rolled past *en route* to the waters of the booming grounds. The log train was followed by a motor-driven caboose of unusual shape, constructed to the company's special design in their base-camp workshops for service on the line. The trade commissioner christened this vehicle a "Bloecab," short for "Bloedel-Caboose," in honour of Prentice.

> Out of this Bloecab stepped three mothers and their children, families of loggers at the camp in the interior which the rubber- necking party was about to inspect. Bound on a visit to the outer world, they were nicely prinked up and, had it been a Sunday morning, they might have given the impression they were on their way from the "Big House" to the village church for morning song. This chance evidence that a logger's life need be neither a lonely nor an egocentric one was illuminating, indicative as it was of a great improvement of conditions in what must perforce be somewhat of a solitary life.[22]

At the workshops, a "skidder" undergoing overhaul was an awe- inspiring sight to the visitors. Considered the monster of the log- ging grounds, "it belched steam at one end while at the other end lifted gigantic logs by means of its crane, then laid them down gentle as if they were matchsticks." The visitors piled into the Bloecab and were driven along the canal and eastwards into the interior, to a "logged off" area where another skidder was in full operation. Next they were taken to a spot in the forest to witness the topping of a Douglas-fir. The "high-rigger" was already up the tree removing branches, while two fallers were preparing for the fall with the help of a man-handled power chain saw.

Soon the high-rigger reached the point selected for topping and with deft and doughty blows quickly whittled his way through the trunk till the thrilling moment came when the head of thirty foot or more broke away from the bole and plunged silently towards the ground far away below whilst the high-rigger swayed terrifyingly (to us) to and fro through the air at the top of his new headless Fir as the tree whipped back and forth in slow gigantic motion, a natural though unexpected reaction to the final snapping away of the heavy head. An unforgettable sight. In twenty minutes and twenty-one seconds to be precise, the warning cry of "Timber-r-r-r" echoed weirdly through the silent forest depths and at first almost imperceptibly, then with slowly gathering momentum, the mighty untopped tree fell crashing towards its duly selected bed with quite uncanny precision.

The visitors mounted a little sweepstake to decide who could guess the age of the tree. Gerald Selous first calculated the tree to be 363 years old, a sapling in 1583. Roy Olsen won the sweepstake by estimating 370 years; Prentice Bloedel guessed 375 and Pat Hunter, 347. With their sight-seeing excursion completed, they ate lunch in the Camp 1 dining hall.

After the party returned to Port Alberni they were entertained at the homes of Mr. and Mrs. Bruce Farris and Charlie and Katharine Robson of Redford Heights. Later Prentice Bloedel escorted them to Klitsa Lodge on Sproat Lake for dinner.

CHAPTER NINE

SHIP TRANSPORTATION

SHIPS AND SHIPPING

From the 1860s, when sailing ships quietly dropped anchor in Stamp Harbour in Port Alberni to load lumber for markets around the world, to the present day and its motor boats, freighters, fishing boats, private yachts, mail boats, and all manner of ships, this waterway, a ribbon of glittering silver, accommodated all. Those who lived in Ucluelet or Bamfield, or in any of the other small settlements along the shoreline, found a boat to be essential; it came before a car or other luxuries. Former Bamfield resident Mary Rockingham Hughes noted, "The children know the local boats by their engines and can say who is passing without getting up to look."[1]

Before the road from Alberni to Ucluelet and Tofino opened in 1959, or the road to Bamfield opened in 1964, coastal residents relied on all manner of vessels to bring in mail, groceries, and household items, or to transport passengers to and from Port Alberni. The ship's arrival on "boat day" was a day of celebration because it brought news from the outside world and provided an opportunity to meet and discuss the affairs of the day.

The history of transportation by water began with the Native canoe and a few rowboats. The Ohiahts were known for their expertise in building canoes designed for hunting whales. Larger canoes built for war could carry fourteen or more warriors. Native canoes were a familiar sight in the early days of the canal. "It was a pretty sight to see, on a breezy summer day, three or four canoes sailing up the canal. Often they carried two sails, which were sometimes nothing more than blankets. When paddled they moved with the least human effort."[2]

Many of the early settlers were experts in paddling a canoe, though more often they hired Natives to get them to their destination. A trip to Victoria by canoe was not a unique event. Early prospectors also used canoes or rowboats. The area's first appointed coroner, John McGregor Thomson, founder of Thomson's General Store in Alberni, travelled to many far-flung places, including "virgin forest and barren pathways"[3] to conduct his business. He and his son John rowed the entire laborious journey from Alberni to Tofino in a small ordinary rowboat.

The first gasoline-driven boat to arrive in Alberni, the *Royal Oak*, caused a great deal of interest in the small community. Sid Saunders was walking down the street the morning after it came in, when he met one of the local Irish characters, Mike Comerford, who stopped him and said, "We never know what will come next—a boat just came around from Victoria and it runs on Vaseline."[4] Of course, he meant gasoline. The boat, owned by Mr. Reeves of Sproat Lake, was operated at his summer resort on the lake.

Captain George Albert Huff's stern-wheeler steamer, the *Willie*, or *Weary Willie* as it was sometimes called, was familiar on the canal during the early days of mining. The steamer was available for charter trips, "even out into open water"; she also made regular trips to the Hayes and Monitor mines.

The small sidewheeler, the SS *Maude*, operated by the Canadian Pacific Navigation Company, generated some not-so-happy memories from early pioneers and regular travellers to Victoria. Many were stricken by "*Maude* fever,"[5] an illness induced by the odours of food cooking and the smell from the hot oily engine room combined with the motion from the ocean swells. There were many victims. "The old *Maude* carried many pioneers and their gold, mail, fish, furs, tools, machinery, vehicles and all manner of goods."[6]

The *Rainbow*, a cabin power boat, was first brought to the area by J. W. Stroud, an agent for a Pennsylvania lumber company, who was interested in securing forest rights at Nahmint. Stroud built a large house at Nahmint in 1909 and used the *Rainbow* on his trips up and down the canal. When the *Maude* was out of service, the *Rainbow* replaced her.

The SS *Tees* also dipped her bow deep into west-coast memories, carrying all manner of freight and passengers. Captain Adam Smith who brought the little vessel from England via the Strait of Magellan into Victoria in August, 1896, remarked, "She rides the water like a duck."[7] She made her inaugural run to Alberni on August 22, 1896. "The *Tees*, fully lighted up, lying at the wharf on the Alberni waterfront, looked quite a brilliant spectacle to us."[8] The steamer ran four times a month.

Out of Ucluelet, Fred Ferguson and H. Walthew formed a partnership known as the Ucluelet Transportation Company in 1910. Their first vessel, the *Merry Widow*, was described as "a stout craft." The ship carried west-coast delegates to the Vancouver Island Development League convention held in Alberni in July, 1910. It could carry ten tons of freight and was also available for charter.[9] The following spring, Captain Ferguson brought a cargo of halibut and other fish for the local market in Alberni, then announced he planned to make weekly trips with fresh fish for the city.[10]

Another service which originated from Ucluelet, but operated out of Port Alberni, was provided by W. John Stone, with sons Stuart and Chet, the same Stone who had been the Methodist minister in Clo-oose and Nitinat before the turn of the century. In October 1913, the family began a mail, freight, and passenger service with the "gasoline cruiser" *Tofino*.[11] Promotional advertisements read: "The mail launch *Tofino* leaves Bird's wharf every Tuesday and Friday for Ucluelet, touching at Kildonan, Hawkins Island, Sechart and Bamfield, returning on the same day."[12] The Stones also operated the *Roche Point*, which fish buyers sometimes chartered for the salmon season.

A small ship-building enterprise in Port Alberni found a ready niche in a growing transportation market. In July 1911, Stone, Blandy & Wise were busy constructing a power craft for the Dominion government to be used on Anderson Lake (Henderson Lake) in connection with a fish hatchery there.[13] Stone had no relationship to W. John Stone. This would have been the ship-yard's first contract as E. Douglas Stone only arrived in Port Alberni on May 23, 1911. Stone brought with him years of experience from working with his grandfather and father, who had a large barge-building yard on the River Thames, in London, England.

Stone had been lured to the area by glowing reports from his cousin, Robert Blandy. The two pooled their resources and began the Stone & Blandy Shipyard. Blandy, and Clifford Wise, who managed a hotel, may initially have had money in the enterprise, but had no further association with the company.

Stone took a keen interest in speed-boat racing; it was a sport he enjoyed most of his life. In 1912, he organised the first out-board regatta in British Columbia on the Somass River, an event he won himself with a three HP Waterman.[14] For the next several decades he raced his hydroplanes *Golden Arrow I, II,* and *III* to victory in Nanaimo, Courtenay and Esquimalt, always adding to his trophy collection.

> Alderman D. Stone added to his laurels as a speed boat racer last week with his hydroplane "Golden Arrow 11" and brought home with him the Nanaimo Regatta cup and Courtenay Fall Fair cup to add to his numerous collection. He also holds the Victoria Native Sons' 30 mile marathon trophy which he won at Esquimalt on July 7th. On May 24 he competed at Esquimalt and came second in the 40 mile marathon.[15]

One of the first passenger ships constructed at the yard was the *Somass Queen*, which served for many years as a passenger vessel for the west coast. When the shipyard closed during the Great War, Stone returned to England to work in a munitions factory. Blandy, who became the City of Port Alberni's first city clerk, moved on to Victoria. Douglas Stone reestablished his business with his brother Percy after he returned from war. They renamed the busi-ness Stone Bros., and the shipyard became the Port Alberni Ship-yard.

The shipyard was a fair size and garnered some early business by installing gasoline engines on Native fish boats. "The partners began a water scow business operating from the west side of the canal to the sawmill, as there was no other source of water at the time. Marshall Bros. tugs also used to tow water scows. The boats were all wood burners. Heaps of logs were piled up on the canal beaches so the skippers could run in and fuel up."[16] Residents of Port Alberni did get their water supply in 1912, when a timber crib dam was built downstream from the Duke of York mine dam to supply water to the city.

One of Stone's first contracts was to transport supplies to the men working on the Canadian National Railway (CNR) grade along the canal from Headquarters to Port Alberni. The CNR had every intention of completing a railway from Lake Cowichan to the Alberni Canal, but the First World War intervened. The railway construction crew at Headquarters meant lots of business directed towards Port Alberni. In 1912 there were an estimated 750 men at work blasting heavy rock for the railway grade and living in camps situated about twelve miles south of Port Alberni.[17] This same year Stone's shipyard received additional business from John Kendall to build three boats for his fish business: the *Mayflower*, the *May Queen* and the *May Fly*. Stone also purchased the *Oh Mi Mi*, a small charter vessel. The *Oh Mi Mi* was so named because the previous owner always ended his sentences with, "Oh mi mi."

The company moved from shipbuilding to concentrating on towing, freight, and passenger services and began the famous *Victory* fleet in January 1921 with the *Victory I*. Stone had obtained the mail contract of the mail boat *Rainbow* before he went to war. "The *Oh Mi Mi* became the first *Victory* boat. When he came back, he sold Victory bonds in order to pay off debts, so he renamed the boat the *Victory*."[18] The brothers operated the Barkley Sound mail service contract for sixteen years. The ship visited Franklin River, Sarita, Kildonan, Green Cove, San Mateo, Ritherdon Bay, Bamfield, Sechart, Port Albion, Ucluelet, Toquart, and Ecoole, all villages, camps, or fish processing plants. In 1921, as the service grew, a bigger ship was required, so the *Victory II* was put in service.[19]

Five years later, with increased passenger and freight commitments, the brothers purchased the Howe Sound Express No. 1, and renamed it *Victory V*.[20] It could accommodate eighty-five passengers. Between the *Victory II* and *V*, they were able to provide service to fourteen ports of call three times a week. The *Victory III* was a converted U.S. seine boat.[21] The *Victory IV* was a pilot boat; the later *Victory VII* and *VIII* were camp tenders.

Fire destroyed the shipyard in August of 1925. Stone Bros. carried no insurance. There was speculation the fire had been caused by sparks from the open burner at the sawmill. Five months later Stone Bros. leased the Port Alberni Shipyard to Jack Greene and Teddy Smith of Vancouver, both experienced boat builders and machinists.[22]

> My grandfather, who was fairly wealthy, had Stone & James
> Bros. in England. When he heard about the fire, he came out
> and financed a big new shop here. But Dad was too busy to be
> bothered with the shop; he was busy with towing, freight, and
> passengers. Teddy Smith and Jack Green were working at
> LaPages Shipyard (in Vancouver) where business was slow and
> they were afraid they would be laid off. Dad hired them and
> arranged for them to lease the shop.[23]

The shipyard was rebuilt to almost twice the size of the original, and Greene and Smith were back in business. In 1927, the first tug boat was added to the fleet. The *Victory VI* was designed by Douglas Stone and built in 1927 at San Mateo by Japanese shipwright Tami Nakamoto. Douglas Stone Jr. related how his father got into the towing business.

> With the *Victory III*, Dad put Chris Johannsen and Fred
> Fredrickson in charge and told them to go into Barkley Sound
> and catch some herring. But they didn't go there, instead they
> went around to Nanoose, and loaded to the gills with herring,
> took them to Vancouver. They made three trips and came back
> with about twelve thousand dollars. Chris had heard the herring
> were coming up the coast. All this time Dad was wondering
> where the boat was. But they came back up the canal, drunk as
> lords, and took all these cheques up to the office. Percy grabbed
> them and paid them off and still had enough money left over to
> build a little tug boat. And that's how they got into the tug boat
> business.[24]

The Marine Towing Service, a branch of Stone Bros., operated

Victory III

from 1927 to 1974 when it was sold to Pacific Towing Services of Vancouver.[25] Another branch of the business was the Port Alberni Ice Company purchased from John Kendall in 1929; it operated until 1935.

In 1934 passengers aboard Stone's mail boat witnessed an unusual sight: thousands of Portuguese men-of-war covering the waters of the middle channel. These are small rounded marine creatures, bluish in colour and almost like jellyfish except that each has a "sail" that projects above its back and propels it along with the wind. Percy Stone said afterwards he had never seen the tiny animals in the waters before, although others had reported seeing them. He stopped the mail boat and scooped up a few for his passengers. Pilchards feed on these creatures; their appearance means pilchards are surely in abundance.[26] A patch of Portuguese men-of-war will sometimes cover several square miles of the water's surface.

Stone Bros. reached a business milestone in July, 1934, when they made their two-thousandth round trip to the west coast. The average distance covered each trip was around 120 miles. When the mail contract expired in July of 1936, Stone Bros. had completed 2209 mail trips down the canal, all of which had been made without injury, loss of life, or mishap. The company had covered a grand total of 235,000 miles in the course of eighteen years of service.[27] In 1936 Douglas Stone moved to Vancouver, where he continued to operate a fleet of boats out of Vancouver harbour under the Anglo Canadian Towing Company.

Over the years a succession of tugs came and went. Early in 1937, the brothers built a powerful new diesel tug boat which became *Victory IX*. Within a few months the company operations were working to capacity handling scows for the H. R. MacMillan Alberni Pacific Sawmill and Bloedel, Stewart & Welch mills, plus a regular three-times-weekly passenger service to Bamfield and a daily service to various logging camps. The west-coast service operated Mondays, Wednesdays, and Fridays. On Friday it also made a trip over to Ucluelet. In 1940, they added the *Victory XI* to the fleet of seven vessels. She was built in Vancouver from a plan drawn up by Douglas Stone, and was christened in Vancouver by his daughter Ruby.[28]

As the years passed, the tug-boat fleet increased in size and power to thirty-one vessels operating with a payroll of forty-five employees. Douglas' son Douglas E. Jr., who had apprenticed as a diesel engineer, began working in the business. From 1937-1947, he worked at the Vivian Engine Works, on False Creek, Vancouver, before returning to Port Alberni to become part of the family business.

The brothers purchased the old George Bird sawmill property across from Alberni Engineering. They dismantled the old shingle mill and salvaged some of the material. They then built two sets of slipways; welding, machine, and chandlery shops; and a shipbuilding shop.[29] In April 1959, Douglas Sr. announced the operations of the old company would continue under a new company, Port Alberni Marine Industries Ltd. Douglas Jr. became marine superintendent of the new yard with manager J. D. Stuart and shipwright foreman Russ Ettinger.[30]

In 1967, another powerful new tug was added to the fleet, designed again by Douglas Sr. The *Anglo Canadian VIII*, built at the John Manly's shipyard in New Westminster, was designed for tending the ever-larger freighters that were now entering Stamp Harbour.[31]

Throughout his lifetime, Douglas Sr. remained interested in speed-boat racing. Percy remained active with the company, acting as a pilot for the various boats of the fleet. Percy died in 1950 and Douglas in 1972. Douglas Stone Jr. has since retired and his son, also Douglas, still works in the industry.

Yet another fleet of ships, named the *Uchuck I, II,* and *III,* left their mark with coastal residents. When the Stone Bros. relinquished the mail service in 1936, one of their captains, Captain Richard Porritt, took over the business with a B.C. Packers cannery tender which he named the *Uchuck*, an Indian name meaning "quiet waters." This was a ship Reese Riley knew well, having installed her engines and operated her since she was built for B.C. Packers at Kildonan. His wife, Alice Riley, had fond memories of Kildonan and the *Uchuck*:

Those months were some of the happiest of my life. The small community of 12 to 14 families made their own fun. They held weekly dances in the school house and there was no shortage of male dancing partners as the fishing fleet was tied up for week-ends. The *Uchuck* was a smart little boat of about 40 feet and being the manager's boat it was always kept trim and clean.[32]

Captain Porritt continued servicing logging camps, fishing camps, and canneries as well as the communities of Bamfield, Ucluelet and Tofino. In 1941, he launched a new vessel, the *Uchuck I* in Vancouver and brought it into service. It could carry seventy passengers.

In 1946, two veterans of naval service in World War II, Essen Young and George McCandless, decided to purchase the *Uchuck* business from Captain Porritt and put their wartime and marine experience into a new business, the Barkley Sound Transportation Company. They hired Captain Richard McMinn as a skipper.

I got a letter from them, down in Victoria, saying "How would you like to bring your Master's ticket, which I had then, up to Port Alberni and work for us?" I thought, "Boy, that's a long way round. I start here as a paperboy and finally come back to Port Alberni." I thought this would be a wonderful thing, because I liked this country. So I came back, and they ran the *Uchuck I* for two or three years.

Then one day Essen and I went off to Vancouver and picked up the old West Vancouver ferry. There was no more horrible ship on the west coast, in the state she was in, there in Vancouver. You could stand in the wheelhouse then—not the way she was reconstructed here—and you couldn't find the bow of your ship. It was two storeys below you, with just a little wedge sticking up. With this great high wall of housework, you can just imagine what would happen to it in a south-east gale. But we bought this old girl. She was a good ship, really; strongly built. She had only two hundred horsepower. I remember coming in with that ship. We met the *Princess Maquinna* at Cape Beale. I could almost see the *Princess Maquinna*, my old ship, stagger at seeing this old ferry approaching Cape Beale.[33]

The *West Vancouver No. 6* ferry was renamed the *Uchuck II* after reconstruction in Port Alberni. The old ferry may have appeared more graceful, but there were some practical realities in the modifications, such as adding a bow, a cargo space, and room for freight. McMinn and McCandless axed part of the ship, then McMinn pulled the parts across the canal with a rowboat and burned them.[34] "She very often put her nose under a sea and took out a few tons of water. She occasionally worried us. All the time I've run out there, she is the only ship we ever turned around and brought home again because of weather. She was the wrong type for that kind of sea."[35]

The *Uchuck II* was put on the Ucluelet and Port Albion run, while the *Uchuck I* serviced Bamfield with stops at Franklin River and Sarita River logging camps. The logging camps were good business for the company. Each Friday night loggers were picked up heading to town for some recreation and entertainment. Many were returned on Sunday night feeling a little under the weather from over-indulgence.

> The "booze runs" were always on Sunday night, taking the loggers back to Sarita for another week's work. A load of inebriates. Very often we were punished further, when "Daddy" Banks, the old-time logger and woods boss of Sarita, would fire some of the drunks, put them back aboard, and we had to return them to Port Alberni—but at least their liquor-locker had run dry.[36]

Groceries, tractor parts, and huge logging truck tires were all part of the regular freight the ship was required to carry. Refrigerators for Sarita families were not unusual. Once the ship carried a small sleeping trailer straddled across the foredeck. Two cars at a time were carried on one trip.[37] The run from Bamfield to Ucluelet was not an easy crossing, especially in winter.

> In the winter some of these crossings were "hairy" to say the least. The cargo hold was small, good for about five tons. We carried bread on deck, lashed down with a tarpaulin in front of the wheelhouse, and very often many other cartons in the midship, upper-cabin passenger space. We carried fresh milk, in those days, in large twenty-gallon metal containers which were lashed to the forward bulwarks. On many a trip when the heavy seas lifted a lid, the entire foredeck was awash in milk and cream. This run made no passenger happy.[38]

The first two *Uchucks* did not have radar. McMinn remembered the days before radar, when it was a "by guess and by God" operation, when navigators relied on whistle echoes.

The process of coming in—well, I can remember one night bringing the *Uchuck III* in. We ran into fog at Franklin River. We had no radar. The *Uchuck III* was a nasty ship in some respects. None of us liked her wheelhouse because she had little port-holes, and they were high portholes. The result was you didn't have good visibility in front on you. You looked through this porthole, you could see there. Then you had to whip across to this one to see anything over there. It partially blocked your whistle echoes. We were approaching Lone Tree Point, black night, thick fog. We heard a tug give two short blasts, which meant he had a boom of logs behind him. Unknown to us, Alex MacKenzie was coming in from his camp with a steel boat with his crew aboard, and had run ashore in the Cous Creek flats, just across the way. He was staying there until the tide came up to get off. It turned out later, that the first deep-water ship had gone between a boom and its tug, and had cut the tow-line. Having done so, she went astern. On those ships the propeller goes one way, when you go astern you turn your ship, you can't help it, you thrash astern.

So she was sideways, pointed at Lone Tree Point. Behind her was a ship coming out, which hearing her go astern, also had to stop. Somewhere behind her, there was a boom of logs, and somewhere, a tug looking for it. So help me, I don't think I ever got into such pandemonium in my life! Every time we ran slow ahead, we found the great bow of a deep-water ship beside us. We would stop. You would clear that slowly, and there was a tug boat. You would just get started again, and there was a boom of logs in front of you. Anyway, that's the sort of thing you run into without the technology of radar, which has certainly been a great boon to ships.[39]

The company added to its fleet another boat, a former U.S. Navy minesweeper, the YMS *123*, which after conversion was re-named the *Uchuck III*. She was put into service July 23, 1955, on the Ucluelet run, while the *Uchuck II* served Bamfield. The services of the *Uchuck I* were no longer needed so was sold to Harbour Navigation of Vancouver for the Horseshoe Bay to Bowen Island run.

John Monrufet remembered towing the old minesweeper to Port Alberni from Vancouver:

> The YMS was a minesweeper. They designed it to be lifted. They detonated the mines right under the ship. They called it a hammer on the bow stem; it had a vibrating mechanism that would set a mine off when it would come to the surface. The ship was 135 feet long and a twenty-five-foot beam, and the explosion would blow it right out of the water and it would come back intact. No trouble. We towed one of these; they sold it as a war asset, we towed it with the *Uchuck I* from Vancouver right to Port Alberni. We stripped it all down and changed the housework construction. We put two diesel engines in. It's still operating up there in Nootka Sound, the *Uchuck III*.[40]

For years the residents of Ucluelet, Tofino, and Alberni had pressed the government for a road linking the three communities. On September 4, 1959, the highway finally opened, and while it greatly improved communications to the west coast, it had a detrimental effect on the Barkley Sound Transportation Company. A road was also pushed through to Sarita, and with planes operating out of Port Alberni, the company's passenger and freight business decreased to the point where it had to look around for other potential runs. Many communities up the coast were still without service, and opportunities still existed. By March 1960, the company pulled the *Uchuck II* out of the Ucluelet service and put her on a new schedule linking Gold River, Tahsis, and Zeballos. The *Uchuck III* was chartered to Captain Eric Murray of Alert Bay. The community of Ucluelet had been well served over the years and its residents were sorry to see the end of the run. Many were on hand to witness the final sailing on Friday, June 10, 1960.[41]

The *Uchuck III* was recalled in 1961 and placed on the run from Port Alberni to Nootka Sound. There were now two *Uchucks* operating on the west coast, their schedule determined by the amount of business. In 1966, after eighteen years of service on the west coast, the *Uchuck II* was sold to the provincial Department of Highways to operate as a marine school bus, transporting students from Sointula and Alert Bay to a new school built at Port McNeill,[42] leaving the *Uchuck III* to carry on the service which still operates today under the Nootka Sound Service Limited. The company is owned by ship's captain Fred Mather, his son Sean, and Alberto Girotto. The three men had worked together on the *Lady Rose* and purchased the *Uchuck III* in 1994.[43]

When Essen Young and George McCandless decided to pull out of the Ucluelet run, it was not long before McMinn realised an opportunity was there for him to start his own business.

> George figured this wasn't the place for them. Their ships were fairly expensive to operate; they were running two crews, and they didn't think there was enough business to support them. My present partner (Johnny Monrufet) and I were up in Zeballos, in Nootka Sound, operating the *Uchuck II* for them, when we heard they were pulling out of Barkley Sound. We sat down in Zeballos that night and said, "You know, there's a lot of business in Barkley Sound yet." Neither of us was very taken with Nootka Sound because, well, you never get outside. You're locked in between the hills. It's a beautiful country, mind you, it really is, but it's a different country. We have the biggest sound on Vancouver Island right here on Barkley Sound. We have an expanse of water, and you occasionally catch sight of a horizon, which makes you feel more as if you're going to sea.[44]

McMinn and Monrufet left the *Uchucks* and began their own company, the Alberni Marine Transportation Ltd. McMinn and Monrufet had years of experience behind them; McMinn had worked on twelve different Canadian Pacific vessels, including the *Princess Maquinna*; Monrufet had been an engineer on the *Uchuck II* and on the MV *Machigonne* (owned by the Gibson Brothers), had served various stints on tow boats and fishing vessels, and had worked for Alberni Engineering in Port Alberni. They were well qualified in the shipping business.

> So Johnny and I took off for Vancouver with no money— practically nothing—and talked for quite awhile, and left with the little *Uchuck I*, the original one that was here. After the little *Uchuck I* had almost broken our hearts for two or three months,

228

we went back and got the *Lady Rose*. Rather, Johnny went to get the *Lady Rose*. I was taking the *Uchuck I* out of Bamfield when the *Lady Rose* came around Cape Beale. When we first looked at her we thought, "My God! What have we got? She looks so big beside this one!" But she turned out to be a very fine little Scotch ship. They don't build them very beautiful, but they build them strong.[45]

The two men had only two hundred dollars between them when they went to Vancouver to negotiate a deal for their first vessel. Although the *Uchuck I* was the first for the new company, it was with the *Lady Rose* the company would make its name.

The *Lady Rose* began her life as the *Lady Sylvia*. She was designed by W. D. McLaren of Vancouver, under the supervision of the Coaster Construction Company (1928) Limited of Montrose, Scotland. The ship was built with a proud Clydeside shipbuilding reputation behind her by A. & J. Inglis Limited, of Pointhouse Shipyard, Glasgow, for service under the flag of the Union Steamships Limited. She was launched on March 17, 1937, by Sylvia Jupp, daughter of J. H. Welsford, a major shareholder in the Union Steamship Company. With her saloon windows and rails protected by heavy planking for the voyage, *Lady Sylvia* left Glasgow on May 7, 1937, under the command of Captain W. S. Smales of Leeds.[46]

This sturdy little vessel made the formidable journey to Vancouver becoming the first single propulsion vessel to cross the Atlantic. The final entry in the engineer's log says much about the rough journey experienced by the crew: "Sunday, 11th July, 5:30 a.m., Vancouver—Thank God!"

The *Lady Sylvia,* renamed *Lady Rose* after her arrival in Vancouver because of a duplication in the name registry, was designed for the sheltered waters of British Columbia and had travelled 9,800 miles with three stops for fuel and food. The ship had been threatened with mountainous seas, unbelievable heat, lightening, tropical storms and strong winds; moreover the crashing and pounding of waves had almost driven the crew to complete exhaustion. "No man, unless he has made such a voyage in such a ship, can have the remotest idea of the work and preparation involved."[47]

What is amazing is that the ship is still working today, carrying freight, passengers, and all manner of goods to remote locations along the Alberni Canal, Bamfield, and Ucluelet. She has become part of British Columbia marine history, a pioneer excursion boat, lifeline to many, and a major tourist attraction. Dick McMinn first saw the *Lady Rose* in 1937, little realising then how his future would be intertwined with the small ship.

> I happened to be leaving Vancouver northbound to Alaska in 1937, and we met the brand new *Lady Rose* inbound to her owners in Vancouver. We were only four thousand tons, but we looked very large beside the *Lady*'s two hundred tons, and she had just come from Scotland. After twenty years of operating her all year 'round in Barkley Sound, I cannot remember how many times I have touched her steel deck and said, "Well done old girl!" We tend to personify our ships.[48]

The *Lady Rose* worked the short runs to the Gulf Islands and Howe Sound until the emergence of the Second World War brought all the Union Steamships into wartime service. In 1942, she was painted battleship grey and assigned to Barkley Sound where under the command of the Royal Canadian Army Service Corps she carried army and air force personnel and supplies between Port Alberni and Ucluelet.[49] The ship normally carried seventy passengers, but there were times when she carried up to two hundred soldiers with full gear on board. "Over three years she carried 53,000 service personnel through Barkley Sound. She ranged from this usual route as far as Prince Rupert, where she picked up troops for their return to Vancouver after the Japanese threat had passed. Towards the end of the war she carried members of the Pacific Coast Militia Rangers."[50]

After the war, the ship returned to the West Howe Sound route.[51] In 1951, Harbour Navigation Company purchased her for the passenger-freight run between Vancouver and Port Mellon, where a new pulp mill had just been built. In 1954, she was chartered by Coast Ferries for a run out of Steveston, and for a time the *Lady Rose* serviced the Gulf Islands including Gabriola and Galiano Islands. She returned to Harbour Navigation until she was first leased, then later purchased, by Alberni Marine Transportation, finding a permanent home in Port Alberni. The only modification made to the ship was the replacement of the old National diesel 380 HP Caterpillar diesel, which was half the weight of the original diesel. The *Lady Rose* began her long career servicing Ucluelet and Bamfield and all points in between. During her colourful history she encountered all manner of weather, missing only one trip because log booms had broken loose in a storm, making it impossible to get out of the Stamp Harbour.

Eventually McMinn and Monrufet retired, leaving the *Lady* in capable hands. Diversified Holdings Ltd., of Victoria purchased the company in 1979, and operated it until 1982 when it was purchased by the present owners, Brooke George, Larry Barclay, and Ken Toby.[52] The new owners painted the ship the colours of the Union Steamship fleet, red funnel with black band around the top, black hull, white topsides.[53] Year round, the *Lady Rose* travels to Bamfield Tuesdays, Thursdays, and Saturdays, breaking the routine in the summer with runs Mondays, Wednesdays, and Fridays to Ucluelet through the Broken Group Islands. Each morning, to the sounds of the forklift bustling about loading freight, the wooden benches of the old ship fill up with tourists jostling with regular passengers and hikers heading out to the West Coast Trail, or canoeists and kayakers gathering for a group adventure in the Broken Group Islands. People from around the world rub shoulders with residents and exchange conversation, while sipping coffee in the galley below as the shoreline widens out into the canal in calm and deep green water. The *Lady Rose* is at home.

Another ship has been added to the run; the Alberni Marine Transportation Company purchased the *Frances Barkley* in August, 1990, and named her after the first European woman to see the west coast. The ship began life November 7, 1958, in Stavanger, Norway as the *Rennesoy*. She was commissioned by the Norwegian Ferry fleet and renamed the *Hidle*, operating out of Stavanger. A company crew travelled to Norway and sailed the vessel across the Atlantic, arriving in Port Alberni August 11, 1990. In many ways, the *Frances Barkley* almost retraced the 1937 voyage of the *Lady Sylvia*, crossing the Atlantic in forty-one days. The *Lady Sylvia* had taken sixty-five days.

The *Frances Barkley* helps relieve the *Lady Rose* during the busy summer season and has taken several excursion trips along the west coast and to Victoria. The new ship begins a long tradition of service established first by the Stones' *Victory* fleet, followed by the *Uchuck* fleet, and the *Lady Rose*, all gallant vessels who have provided a valuable link for the communities along the canal and Barkley Sound.

THE GOOD SHIP MAQUINNA

Back when coastal steamships were plying the waters of the west coast, a radio broadcaster named Kelly of Vancouver's radio station CJOR announced the location of the *Princess Maquinna* each night during his broadcast. Islanders relied on this announcement to inform them when to expect supplies, visitors, and mail. Kelly referred to her as the "Good Ship" and ended each broadcast with "Good night, Good Ship—wherever you are."[54]

There are few residents of the west coast who do not have fond memories of the *Princess Maquinna*, who made her maiden voyage to Port Alberni in July, 1913. The Brass Band played and the whistles of the Canadian Pacific Lumber Company and the Wiest Logging Company blew on her arrival. Boats of all descriptions and anything else that floated gathered around the big ship as she steamed into Stamp Harbour.[55] The captain of the *Maquinna* was Edward Gillam, who knew every inch of the west coast from his days as captain of the *Tees*. The ship was built at Bullen's yard, in Esquimalt, and was the largest steel vessel then built in British Columbia. She was launched December 24, 1912, by Mrs. W. Fitzherbert Bullen, granddaughter of Sir James Douglas and wife of the owner of the shipyard that later became Yarrows Limited. She was christened *Princess Maquinna* in honour of the daughter of Chief Maquinna of the Nootka tribe. After her first run to Port Alberni, in August, she was sent on a voyage to Alaska with seventy delegates to the International Geological Congress. On this trip the new ship struck an uncharted rock in Yakutat Bay, Alaska.[56] This was one of the few mishaps in her long career.

The *Princess Maquinna* had accommodation for four hundred day passengers and sleeping facilities for one hundred. She made three round trips per month from her Belleville Street, Victoria, berth on her way to visit west-coast ports of call. "The ship's timetable had 'special arrangement only' stops, some of which were hardly more than lonely cabins, or floating rafts along the canal or in the sound. Messages had to be sent several days ahead to notify the *Maquinna* where and when to stop. But the kindly *Maquinna* was always ready to tie up to any rickety dock and go alongside a floating logging camp to give cheerful service when needed."[57]

The *Maquinna* had what was termed a "boat landing" off Clo-oose (Nitinat Lake), where Natives paddled out in canoes to receive supplies passed out of the side port doors. In heavy seas, a seaman wearing a body harness stood on the ship's guard rail and exercised a good deal of skill as he landed cargo items in a canoe as it passed the doors during its vertical ascents and descents. There were many occasions when Clo-oose had to be bypassed due to heavy sea conditions.

Bamfield pioneer Irma Cashin, a new emigrant from England, arrived at Clo-oose via the *Maquinna;* it was a memorable landing for the five-year-old. Her parents, among others, had been lured to the remote west-coast location with promises of a major development. A large number of lots were sold by the West Coast Development Company, which planned a three-hundred-room hotel, a golf course, and mineral baths. The whole project depended on a road being constructed between Port Renfrew and Bamfield. The company and its investors soon discovered there were other problems associated with the development, and the project died. Those who had arrived at Clo-oose did not stay long and moved on to Victoria and Port Renfrew and other points along the coast. Irma's family moved to Bamfield, where her father had worked at the Cable Station in the early days, from 1904 to 1908. He had returned to England and after the First World War had decided to return to Canada because "it appeared to be a better living here." As the ship could not come close to shore at Clo-oose, passengers and their possessions were loaded into canoes.

They put them into these canoes, and took them to shore. You had to wait for fine weather or else you couldn't land. Cause I know when we left there, it was rough, we couldn't take trunks and stuff, they were all left there until they could get them out and send them down to Victoria.[58]

Irma's father started a general store in Bamfield where he also bought fish and seal furs from the Natives. He eventually sold out in 1940 to B.C. Packers.

The *Maquinna* carried all manner of goods and products, from fish to building supplies. The ship brought lumber from Port Alberni for Bruce Scott's new house in Bamfield.

> To get the material from Port Alberni, I arranged for it to come down on the coastal steamer, *Maquinna*, at a time that coincided with high tides so I could take it around immediately and pull it up as close to the shore as possible. However, the *Maquinna* was delayed about twelve hours and it didn't come until the middle of the night and we had to unload this lumber on to a raft from the ship by the glare of the floodlights on the ship.[59]

Generally passengers loaded at Port Alberni sometime after midnight and proceeded to Ucluelet and Port Albion, then onwards up the coast. Passengers often included loggers destined for remote logging camps to the north. "People from Vancouver could save a day's journey by short-cutting by ferry to Nanaimo and bussing to Alberni." The *Princess Maquinna*'s ports of call blended a mixture of Native, British, and Spanish names such as Toquart, Sarita River, Kildonan, Franklin River, Ucluelet, Tofino, Ahousat, Clayoquot, Sasvedra Island, Kakawis, Refuge Cove, Zeballos, Esperanza, Winter Harbour, Holberg, Quatsino, and Port Alice, the last port of call.[60] There she unloaded the last of her outbound cargo then loaded baled pulp from the mill to be transported to Vancouver. On her way south, she only called in at major population locations.

> I can remember the *Maquinna* stopping in mid-stream on a lonely inlet while some logger in a rowboat rowed out to her to pick up some supplies and to get his mail. She would often pull into a small float camp or a booming ground and unload the logger's cargo out the side hatches. With all our modern styles of shipping, I don't think the coast has ever seen the style or service given by the *Maquinna* in those days.[61]

During the days of the fishing bonanza, Natives found ready

work in the industry. Early each summer on her way north, the ship picked up a few hundred men at various stops along the way and delivered them to canneries at Rivers Inlet on the northern mainland. The Natives would be gathered together on deck and below, sleeping where they could and providing their own meals. When the ship reached dock, they caught some fish to cook in their big iron pot. The trip to Rivers Inlet took several days.

Captain Gillam endeared himself to many residents of the west coast. He was always willing to go that extra distance to help someone in need, even if it meant getting off schedule. Many times the captain rushed the *Maquinna* to the nearest hospital, at Port Alberni, Tofino or Port Alice, to save a life or help a birth. The ship also had to contend with the usual bevy of travelling salesmen as they made their calls to stores and logging camps along the route.

The arrival of the *Maquinna* in Port Alberni was always a time of social significance for the young people in the community. Captain Gillam had a reputation for enjoying life, and when in port he and his passengers joined in community dances and social events. When the steamer arrived in Bamfield, passengers were entertained at the Cable Station.

I was one of the bachelors in the Cable Station and every time the coastal steamer called in at Bamfield in the summertime, it was filled with tourists, and the bachelors used to put on their flannels and blazers and go down to eye the human freight, and if possible . . . well the best way to get to know a person or say, a young lady, was to ask them if they wished to see over the Cable Station. Of course everyone wanted to do that, so you had your foot in to a good start. So you saw them over the Cable Station and saw them on board and said well, when you come back they usually hold a dance in the hall at the Cable Station and I'll see you then. So the boat came in on its return journey about five days later, came into Bamfield about midnight and stayed until about four or five o'clock in the morning and the bachelors entertained the passengers to a dance in their hall. We had our own orchestra, a five-piece orchestra, and it was an affair which was much looked forward to by the passengers and much enjoyed by the bachelors too.[62]

The *Princess Maquinna* made headlines in 1919 when Captain Gillam attempted to rescue a ship in distress off Long Beach. While the Chilean vessel *Carelmapu* awaited a tow to Puget Sound, strong winds and rough seas pulled her closer to shore. Her anchors were released in an attempt to prevent her crashing to shore. Captain Gillam took the *Maquinna* as close as he could and anchored, hoping to hold her while the *Carelmapu* crew in two boats rowed out to her. But both were swamped by heavy seas and all aboard were lost.

Still a few men were seen aboard the *Carelmapu* as the *Maquinna* edged even closer. Then suddenly a huge wave hit the ship, and Captain Gillam, not wishing to endanger his ship further ordered the anchor chains cut free. He considered the situation hopeless. The Captain is quoted as saying, "Never in all my long experience in the west-coast service have I been called upon to nurse a ship through such terrible seas."[63] The *Maquinna* headed for Ucluelet and advised the Tofino lifeboat. Several hours later the *Carelmapu* split in half, leaving her stern firmly trapped on the rocks. Five men survived: Captain Desolmes, three seamen, and a nineteen-year-old Chilean student on his way to school in Seattle, and a dog. The survivors were taken to the Clayoquot Hotel by the Tofino lifeboat to await the next southbound trip of the *Maquinna*. The dog lived out its days as companion to a couple at Long Beach.

Starting in 1930, the *Princess Norah*, a sister ship in the CPR fleet, joined the *Princess Maquinna* for a double run on the west coast during the summer months.[64] She became a regular visitor on the coast, sharing the load of passengers and freight. On the *Princess Norah's* second trip, Captain Gillam died of a heart attack while climbing the stairs and fell on the deck below. He died doing what he loved. The "Good Ship" and the good captain had earned their place in west-coast history.

The *Norah* was built at the shipyards in Glasgow in 1928 and designed for west-coast service. It was her first captain, Martin McKinn, who found Captain Gillam after his fatal heart attack. The ship had an observation room, smoking room and social hall and spacious promenade decks. The staterooms were furnished, and each had hot and cold running water. There were a number of rooms on the upper, or promenade deck, with separate toilet and shower bath.[65]

During July and August the *Princess Norah* called in at the Cable Station in Bamfield and at various ports in Clayoquot and Nootka Sounds, Esperanza Inlet, Kyuquot and Quatsino Sounds, terminating at Port Alice. The round trip from Victoria took five days. The *Norah* later became known as the *Queen of the North* and the *Canadian Prince*. When the vessel ended her life on the coast, friends and admirers were happy to learn she would become the "Beachcomber Hotel," a cabaret at Kodiak, Alaska, replacing property destroyed in the 1964 Alaska earthquake.

The years eventually took a toll on the *Princess Maquinna*, but it was not age alone that sealed her fate. Road, truck traffic, aircraft, tug and barge service all reduced the volume of passengers and freight. In 1952, the *Maquinna* limped into Victoria harbour, her boilers leaking so badly CPR officials announced the old vessel had probably completed her final run.[66]

It was difficult to replace the *Princess Maquinna* in the hearts and minds of people on the west coast, but a number of smaller vessels tried to take her place. First was the *Veta C.* then the *Princess of Alberni*. These were followed by the *Nootka Prince, Tahsis Prince,* and *Northern Prince* of the Northland Navigation Company.[67]

The *Princess Maquinna* had served the area faithfully for thirty-nine years and it was not without a whimper the old lady was retired. Amidst public protest on September 24, 1952, she was sold to Union Steamship Company of Vancouver, who stripped her down to become the ore carrier *Taku*, a barge destined to carry ore from Alaska to the Trail smelters.

ONE MEMORABLE BOAT LANDING

In March, 1934, John Evans of Port Alberni sailed aboard the *Princess Maquinna* to Carmanah Point Lighthouse, south of Nitinat and Clo-oose on the west coast. This is an account of his first trip aboard the ship and his arrival on the west coast. Not yet seventeen years of age, he had left his home at Westholme, near Duncan, to go to his first real job as helper at the lighthouse. His fare from Victoria to Carmanah Point was $3.60 and he was to receive a mere fifteen dollars a month with room and board.

I sat up on the bench on which I had been more or less sleeping since boarding the *Princess Maquinna* around 11 o'clock the night before. The ship had been pitching severely as we headed through the Juan De Fuca Straits. I soon realized this was mild compared to what was to come. We had altered our course, turning broadside to the waves as we headed out along the west coast of the island, our first stop being Port Renfrew.

After letting off passengers and supplies we got into heavier waves. Now, instead of pitching like a bucking bronco, the *Maquinna* was rolling and pitching. I used to think the water on the east coast of the Island could get rough, but this! I couldn't believe it. I knew that morning had come when I smelled coffee and bacon. I was hungry as a bear by this time and it sure smelled good, but not for long, because this was when I got seasick. Boy, did I get seasick. Then, as if that wasn't enough rough treatment, one of the crew came around and asked us to stand up, so he could tie everything down. I'm afraid I would never have made a good sailor. My sea-legs just wouldn't hold me steady. In my seasick stupor, I watched the crewman fasten down the furniture. Even the piano was hooked down. By this time I was beginning to wonder what I had gotten myself into.

Yes, it was a scary experience all right. I remember someone telling me that I would probably have to continue on up to Bamfield instead of to Carmanah Point as planned, since it was doubtful that anyone would be out to meet the *Maquinna* due to the stormy weather. They told me that I would be taken back to the Carmanah Point Lighthouse by lifeboat. This new arrangement didn't appeal to me very much either, but there was little I could do about it.

By this time I was so miserably seasick that I decided to go out and get some fresh air. I managed to stagger my way to the door, congratulating myself for not falling flat on my face. The angle at which I had to walk was first up, then down, at which time I fell against the door. I waited until the ship righted herself again, then opened the door. The sight that met my eyes was terrifying. All I could see was a mountain of water! I'm sure it must have been fifty feet high. Luckily one of the crewmen came and grabbed me or I would probably have been washed overboard. He warned me not to open the door again. I didn't eat breakfast that morning. What's more, I lost my supper from the night before, along with what felt like half of my guts.

I don't know how they spotted it but one of the crew informed me that there was a canoe out from Clo-oose to meet me. Clo-oose had a better beach to land on, I learned later. The canoe had gone out to meet the boat, which had to wait about a mile and a half from the beach, for fear of getting washed up on the rocks. They tried to hold the ship steady so they could unload myself and about six other people, along with supplies, baggage and the mailbag. We had to go down to the cargo-hold where they opened only half of the door, and threw a rope ladder over the side. Looking out, not knowing what to expect next, I could only see that mile and a half of white rollers between ship and shore. I remember thinking, "My God, do I have to get out into that?"

I turned around, sicker than hell and sat down. I guess Captain Red Thompson must have felt sorry for me because he came over and put his arm across my shoulder. He tried to console me by telling me that he had been on the sea for 47 years and he still got seasick when it got really rough. I wondered how much rougher it could get. The question now was, how to get into that doggoned canoe. I tried to watch from a safe distance from the edge as the other passengers got off. It seemed to take an awful long time. Then it was my turn on the ladder. I crawled over the edge, hanging on for dear life. I looked down and there was no canoe. It was sitting on top of a wave, thirty feet away. The ship rolled and I found myself lying on her side. The canoe was close in now, so I climbed down a little but the next thing I knew that ship had rolled back and I was up to my armpits in water, and I didn't even know how to swim. I started to climb back up the ladder, and some of the old-timers were getting quite a kick out of my misery. Two of the crew were standing on each side of the cargo hold door. They hollered at me, telling me to jump when they said "jump." Well, I finally got up enough nerve and was kind of surprised when I landed in the canoe.

I know now that timing was all-important. The canoe was manned by a Native from Clo-oose and a man named David Logan, whose father, also David Logan, ran the store and Post Office there. It's odd, but as soon as I got into the canoe I was no longer seasick. It could be that I was experiencing the calm that hits a guy when he realizes the end is near, as I just couldn't see us making it to shore through the towering seas. More likely, it was the change of motion, as we were now crossing the waves and the land ahead sure looked good to me.

We did make it to shore and I was soon on my way to Carmanah Point in the company of one of the linesmen. It was a seven-mile hike along the West Coast Trail, but I didn't mind. It was a good feeling to get my feet on solid ground. We reached the lighthouse and it was there that I met my new boss, Captain Seymour-Biggs, who was an ex-British Navy Captain. I remember promising myself that no matter what, there was no way I would ever set foot on the *Princess Maquinna* again, and I wondered how I would get back home.

I didn't think it could ever happen, but I learned how to launch a lifeboat from Carmanah, also a canoe from Clo-oose. It was tough to get in during rough weather, but it was even tougher to get out. We had to time it just right. Coming in, if I remember right, there would be three small waves, then two large ones in quick succession. We would ride in on top of the first small wave, then pull the boat in before the next two big sons-of-guns hit us. I guess this succession of waves could have varied, depending on the underwater shelf.

One thing I was warned about was the fog. I watched it many times, a black massive cloud rolling in toward shore very quickly. At times like this we had to turn off the light and turn on the foghorn. At one time we had to blow it for 110 hours straight, which was by no means a record. It sure got to me. Even when I slept, it penetrated my brain. It was sure monotonous.

Going out to meet the *Maquinna* was a real experience. As soon as we heard her whistle blow as she came up the coast, we would push off from the lighthouse. It was a pretty peculiar feeling to push off into a mile and a half of fog with nothing but the foghorn and boat whistle to guide us. Even though we could hear the *Maquinna*'s whistle, it was always a surprise to see her come looming out of the fog above us. We made a point of holding back a little for fear that she might run us down. Getting back to shore was equally difficult. We would angle back, keeping the foghorn always to our left. It seemed rather stupid to be out there, but we hated to miss her, knowing that she wouldn't be back for a couple of weeks. Getting that mail from home was mighty important.[68]

John remained at the lighthouse for nearly a year, exploring parts of the West Coast Trail and promising himself one day he would hike its entire length, from Port Renfrew to Bamfield.

The night before he left, he stayed with the Logan family at Clo-oose. The following day they packed the canoes and waited for the familiar whistle before they pushed off to meet the *Princess Maquinna*, now a welcome sight to John. It was a calm day so he could paddle the canoe alone. He felt pretty good about that. He laughs now when he recalls that he gave the purser a cheque for his fare. The purser informed him that they didn't accept cheques. John said, "Well, what are you going to do about me?" The purser, quite amused, told him they would throw him overboard. John never returned to Carmanah Point but the memories will always be with him.

MV MACHIGONNE

Memories of the *Maquinna* are still fresh in the minds of many residents of the coast; so too, are those of the MV *Machigonne*. Although her stint serving communities between Zeballos to Port Alberni was a short one, the old submarine chaser disposed of by the Canadian War Assets Board to the Gibson Brothers in 1946, made every trip one never to be forgotten. The press noted the company had decided to include Port Alberni in its service, owing to the demand by Ucluelet residents. The maiden voyage, after conversion at Vancouver, was made in January, 1947.

The *Machigonne* made two trips a week under Captains Bill Olsen and Dan Backie and engineer John Monrufet. Both captains had skippered the *Malahat*. Mrs. Backie also accompanied her husband. The ship had a coffee bar, lounges, and seats that could be converted into bunkbeds; she could carry seventy-two passengers and freight.[69] The Gibsons had noted the increased interest in the Albernis as a shopping centre. Freight included four hundred gallons of milk, plus ice cream and eggs. Fast service made the transportation of ice cream possible. Items such as flowers were now going out of Port Alberni to west-coast points, and the demand for logging equipment had increased.

The first passengers to travel the route were a family from the prairies who had never been to sea. It would be one they would never forget and the worst the skipper could remember. The ship cleared the Alberni Canal about eight o'clock on a calm, sunny morning, and after sailing past Ucluelet, headed north to Tofino. Here the seas became rough but nothing compared to those encountered on the four-hour run between Tofino and Estevan Point at fifteen knots with a stout westerly blowing. No storm in the Pacific deterred the skippers who were on a tight schedule. Even an experienced seaman would have been queasy as the converted submarine crested a big wave and rolled, twisted and dove in one single sickening movement. For four hours the passengers endured the punishment, hanging on in terror to anything bolted down, as the *Machigonne* plunged and cork-screwed through thirty-foot waves.

There were occasions when workers hired in Vancouver made the trip to Tahsis. Usually they had been drinking before boarding the ship, "but after twelve hours on the *Machigonne* they were sick but very sober men. Rarely would any of them feel strong enough to work the next day." As Gordon Gibson related in his book *Bull of the Woods*, "The only virtue I could see in bringing workers up on that ship was that most of them were scared to death to make a return trip and were willing to put in a few months' hard work before going through the same misery to get back to Vancouver." Most passengers preferred to fly back to civilisation.

The Gibsons maintained the service for about a year while their Tahsis mill was being built and until the gold rush to Zeballos subsided. They then decided the ship could be put to better use elsewhere, on the Horseshoe Bay to Bowen Island to Gibsons Landing route, where their two other boats were too small to handle the growing traffic. The *Machigonne* provided excellent service on the inland quiet waters of the Sechelt Peninsula, until a car ferry replaced her.

PILOT BOATS

In the history of the canal and of the sound, few women were involved in day-to-day shipping operations. Men were normally at the helm of the industry in the early days, so to have two women participating directly was quite unusual. Dorothy Blackmore, of Port Alberni, became the first woman in Canada to receive a Master Mariner certificate, while Alice Riley took over the Riley Boat Service when her husband died accidentally. Both women were involved in the pilot boat service assisting deep-sea vessels through the waters of Barkley Sound and the Alberni Canal. Neither gained public recognition for their efforts but they were rewarded by doing the job well and gaining the respect of their peers.

Dorothy came from a pioneer Alberni family. Her father Captain George Wortham Blackmore, a veteran of the Boer War, had arrived with his wife Clarice in 1918 and had founded the Blackmore Marine Service, operating speed boats and tug boats as well as the pilot boat service. Their boats the *Blue Swallow*, the *Skidoo,* and the *Moon Dawn* were familiar sights on the busy canal. Captain Dorothy Blackmore was only twenty-three years of age in 1937 when she received admission into the master mariner ranks.

Ten years before, Mrs. J. Hay had tried to obtain a Master certificate, but the Department of Justice ruled that a woman could not hold a Master Mariner certificate in Canada. The issue of female mariners arose later and was supported by R. K. Smith, director of nautical services for the Dominion Government. In January of 1937, the government finally relented and approved admission of women. Mrs. Hay and her husband later drowned when their cruiser was wrecked.[70]

Depending on weather conditions, pilots boarded or disembarked at Bamfield, or off Cape Beale, and assisted freighters with the journey through Barkley Sound and the Alberni Canal waterway. Occasionally the pilot boat acted like a sub post office delivering mail for crews aboard the freighters. The life of a pilot often had dangerous moments. Climbing the rope ladder onto the deck of a freighter from a small boat bobbing in heavy seas required as much skill as it took manoeuvring the pilot boat.

Pilots were dispatched from Nanaimo, Vancouver, Victoria, or New Westminster by the B.C. Pilotage Authority. Their estimated time of arrival was often amended several times, and telephones were kept busy until the pilot actually arrived in the harbour. Crew, pilot, and dispatcher were on twenty-four-hour call when on duty, and many times they had to make the trip down the canal at night.[71] Dorothy Blackmore and her father operated the pilot service until 1950 when it was taken over by Riley's Boat Service.

Alice (Clegg) Riley was also born into a pioneer Alberni family. Her father Joseph Clegg and his wife Clara came from Manchester, England, in 1912. Joseph had been in the painting and decorating business and he continued in this business in his new country. An amateur photographer whose work had won many awards in international competitions, Clegg owned and operated a commercial studio in Port Alberni for thirty-two years.[72] His daughter Alice married a young Tofino man, Reese Riley, in 1927 and began her long association with west-coast waters.

Reese had worked on various boats including those in the *Uchuck* and *Victory* fleets when the Rileys bought their first boat in 1935. They named her the *Maureen R.* after their daughter and used it as a water taxi, visiting logging camps and canneries. They purchased another boat, the *Black Hawk*, which was a little faster than the *Maureen R.*, and between the two, the Rileys had a successful water taxi service: "Riley's Speed Boat Service, Port Alberni. The two fastest boats on the coast, *Maureen R.* and *Black Hawk.*"[73] The water taxi service carried out a variety of tasks, including rushing maternity cases to hospital in Port Alberni. Only once did "the stork beat the boat to it."[74]

The *Black Hawk* was sold to B.C. Packers in 1945, and in 1950 Riley purchased a new boat from the Alberni Shipyard, the *RE Riley*. Reese Riley was on his way to Port Alice to deliver the *Maureen R.* to a prospective buyer when he drowned at sea. The wreckage of his boat washed ashore north of Tofino. Alice Riley had to decide whether or not to continue with Riley's Boat Service. A visit from the superintendent of pilots convinced her to carry on. Her son Doug was only fourteen years old and still too young to manage the company, but in 1964 Doug received his captain's papers. The company purchased another boat in the early 1960s, the *RE Riley II*. This vessel had better accommodation for the pilots, who now had night runs and often had to wait at Bamfield for delayed shipping.

The company prospered under Alice's direction. In 1970 she retired, leaving the company with her son Doug and his wife Mickey. In 1975, they signed a contract with the Pacific Pilotage Authority to have a pilot boat built similar to those the government had in service. They named it the *RD Riley*. Doug continues today with the Riley pilot boat service, the only private pilot boat company in Canada.

THE LONGSHOREMEN

Port Alberni was one of the first ports in British Columbia to export forest products, and it was the first to hire stevedores, or longshoremen, to load the ships. Ships from around the world, docking to take on lumber, were small by today's standards, and all were built of wood. Masts worn, or broken, were replaced by spars made from trees logged in the area. The cargo was loaded over the stern, coming aboard on roller carts, or over greased planks. Loading the ships required careful thought and procedure, especially with the stacking. A team of oxen moved the lumber into position at the boat's stern, while longshoremen pulled it aboard with block and tackle, stacking it carefully. Any shift in the cargo while at sea could result in the ship keeling over, losing cargo and possibly ship and crew.[75]

Initially longshoremen's equipment consisted of a team of oxen, a peevee, an axe and an extremely strong body. Men remained on the job until the work was completed. Someone might bring food as needed and an open bucket of water was available for refreshment. There were no toilet facilities, but with the sea near at hand, no one thought it necessary. Without first-aid facilities or compensation for the sick and their families, longshoremen worked through illness or injury or else found other jobs. They worked hard loading the ships. When their wages were spent, society viewed them as shiftless, or as drunkards. The longshoreman image became firmly entrenched, one difficult to shake.[76] Trevor Goodall noted local farmers made a few dollars helping longshoremen load a ship.

Approximately 1913, all loading was done by local help. I can remember when a freighter came in, the loaders would all rush to Port. They didn't have any special gangs of longshoremen. The men were hired on the spot, first come, first served. The better workers became well known and were always sure of a job. The hours were long and the work hard, hand labour, many times working steady for twenty hours or more. The pay was high, eighty cents per hour, later one dollar per hour, compared to the mill worker who only made forty cents per hour. Accidents were plentiful and there was no compensation, but in all it gave small farmers a chance to make a few extra dollars. Horses were used to pull the small two-wheeled carriers with a load of about five hundred board feet. Long square timbers were on rollers and pushed by hand. In later years, it was a steady job, as a Union was formed and gangs were organized who worked together.[77]

When the First World War broke out, longshoremen and other British Columbians enlisted *en masse*. Some died, others returned wounded. Those who stayed behind because of age or other reasons, felt they were doing their part loading lumber for the war effort in Europe. They worked tirelessly with little recognition for their services.

After the war, those who survived returned to the docks and found ships had changed little. "They were still nasty, filthy old scows of about 8,000 tons. They had no refrigeration and most carried live animals for butchering. The odor was unbelievable."[78] Loading had not changed. The lumber was lowered into the middle of the hatches by longshoremen wearing protective leather aprons. They stacked each board individually, hour after hour, day after day, until all the cargo was aboard. Wages were better than in the sawmills and they had more time off, but they also had more broken fingers and sprained backs.

With three new sawmills operating in the Alberni area, the port operation ran full steam ahead. "In July, 1926, lumber shipments from Port Alberni amounted to ten million board feet, the greatest amount for any one month since the opening of the port."[79]

Hughie Watts worked forty-five years as a longshoreman in Port Alberni. He started longshoring in 1923 when there was only one

Port Alberni Terminals. Newsprint being moved dockside.

dock. Lumber was brought to the wharf by a team of horses driven by Sammy Archer. There were four gangs and wages were eighty-five cents an hour.

> I can remember back in 1923 when the APD (Alberni Pacific Division) used to haul the logs sideways, using horses, onto the boats. Judge Patterson was a side runner with me in those days. There were wooden sidewalks and we all drove to work on bicycles, since nobody had a car. I worked down in the holds for twenty-two years, and was a hatch tender for the next twenty-three years. In the old days we would sometimes work fourteen and twenty hours a day. We had a form of union then, but it wasn't much good.[80]

One of the first "motor ships" to load lumber from Port Alberni was the Norwegian *Fernglen,* which travelled from New York via the Panama Canal in less than twenty days. It arrived in February, 1931, and loaded over one million board feet of lumber.[81] It arrived at the start of the Depression, just as lumber shipments began to trickle to a standstill.

With few markets for wood products, and shipping down, longshoremen were out of work. In 1934, they banded together in face of this situation to form their first union, the Alberni District Waterfront Workers' Association. The general economy of the region was jeopardised by a forest workers strike. Striking loggers walked from Parksville to Great Central Lake sawmill calling for an increase in wages, establishment of unions, and improvements in working conditions in the logging camps. The strike spread throughout the island, involving four thousand men.[82] Loggers appealed to the longshoremen to refuse to handle lumber produced by the logging camps using "scab" labour.[83]

Management tolerated the ADWW union because it had little power and was strictly a local brotherhood. The union had no say in hiring or firing, but it could discuss better wages and working conditions even though these were of no real importance at the time. Longshoremen still made twice what sawmill workers made, so if they dared complain about their wages or working conditions, they found themselves out of a job.

Despite this, there were some improvements. Foremen were

trained in first aid, but they also worked and got dirty, and sanitation problems marred what results there might have been. The men worked hard and eventually a wobbling weak recognition of seniority rights became established. Union meetings were unlike those of today. Only strong and dedicated men ran for office— "the equivalent of a Japanese admiral standing on the bow of his burning ship contemplating hari-kari. The companies tolerated the unions as long as they did not hear or see them. Any member of the work force who leaned toward the union was as good as fired if he said a word and as good as blacklisted if he said two."[84] The old back-breaking hard-working ways continued.

Perhaps it was an American who brought changes to the union and gave a wake-up call in Canada. When Harry Bridges led American longshoremen in a strike, defying management and the police, Canadian owners got the message and declared war on the Canadian Stevedoring Union. By 1935, the union, prostrate but not dead, held secret meetings and continued work behind closed doors. Companies, oblivious to the underground movement, finally considered the union nonsense over and done with and longshoremen continued to work, with little or no change.

When the Second World War broke out, once more longshoremen responded to the call to enlist. At the beginning of the war, those left behind had difficulty getting work on the docks. Despite huge orders placed to sawmills from the Timber Control Board of Great Britain, there was a shortage of ships to transport the lumber.[85] When a ship carrying lumber was torpedoed off the California coast, almost all shipping was brought to a standstill. To fill the void, the Canadian Transport Company purchased the *Vigilant*, renamed her the *City of Alberni*, and put her to work transporting lumber to Australia. She was the last of the old sailing ships, and she made an impressive sight with full sails blowing or when tied up at the docks in Port Alberni. The five-masted sixteen-hundred-ton schooner loaded with 1.6 million feet of lumber, sailed to Sydney, Australia, managing to dodge enemy raiders and even a hurricane to deliver her cargo.[86] On her third and final trip in 1941 she stopped into Valparaiso for repairs and was sold there. The last sailing ship in the forest industry was eventually lost on a reef.

Longshoremen who were not working on the docks managed

to find jobs in other industries until conditions improved on the waterfront. After the war, enlisted men returned to join in the development of their community, and helped build a stronger union.

During the Second World War, Hughie Watts travelled along the coast of the entire island, loading and unloading ships. The most regular run was from Nanoose to Chemainus and down to Victoria and back. Sometimes they unloaded nitro at James Island. When shipping was slack, Watts went fishing for a few weeks to make ends meet. The *Alberni* and the *Malahat* were pressed into service during the war to load lumber in Port Alberni. These were the days when logs were loaded from booms in the harbour. Sometimes gangs were dispatched to load salt fish and fish meal at San Mateo and Green Cove in Uchucklesit Harbour, not considered the most pleasant job by longshoremen.[87]

Port Alberni, in 1947, now had a pulp-and-paper mill, two sawmills and a plywood mill. The loading docks in Stamp Harbour were busy with increased shipping, and there were improvements in the way cargo was handled. Now hand carts replaced the back-breaking grab-it-and-lift-it work of the past. Soon dumping carts were used for newsprint. In 1959, the slow sleepy change accelerated with the introduction of packaged lumber, which was first loaded aboard the *Marten*. A whole new world of shipping technology emerged. Gone was the back-breaking work in the holds; now a crane replaced the winches; eight men in the hold became three, one to drive the forklift and two to stow the lumber. Longshoremen became tradesmen and specialists capable of handling all sorts of equipment: mechanics, electricians and radio technicians.

Some new inventions were successful, others were not. The dumping carts for newsprint, in particular, had a bad habit of either dumping the longshoreman with them or lurching backwards against a man's legs with a force capable of breaking them. The carts were quickly abandoned.

Loading docks could be a very dangerous place as some longshoremen found out on Friday, March 31, 1966, in Port Alberni.[88] There were seventy men in five gangs on board the MV *Archangel* loading packaged lumber and 12 x 12 timbers. The timbers were going to be the last cargo loaded. There had been problems with the vessel listing and the men had left the ship while the crew shifted ballast to correct the list. The timbers were being loaded in the No. 4 hatch on the offshore side, when suddenly there was a sound of snapping and popping. The ship's tie-up line parted and the ship took a violent shift to port, dumping a considerable amount of cargo into the water on the port side.

> The 12 x 12s were rolling out from under our feet. We ran to mid-ship as fast as our legs would carry us, then jumped down in between the winches. The ship's rigging was shipping around with derricks crashing into the Sampson posts. There were sling men on a scow on the port side and 12 x 12s were hailing down all around them like arrows. Fortunately no sling men were hit. When the ship heeled back to starboard, the cargo was thrown onto the dock and between ship and dock. Brother Art Dube went down between ship and dock and was killed. Brother John Egresits was standing on top of the deck load on the starboard side 20 feet above the dock and landed on the dock with timbers spread out behind him. To this day its almost unbelievable how someone well over 200 lbs. could survive and be standing on the dock still on his feet.[89]

Longshoreman Harold Fuller, who was on the port side deck load, was thrown into the water with packs of lumber and timbers raining down around him. When the *Archangel* threw its cargo to the dock and then heeled back to port, the railing of the ship came down to water level and Harold grabbed the rail and was pulled out of the water. He proceeded to climb straight up the remaining deck load where he hollered for help as he came over the top. He was grabbed and taken to safety before the ship listed back to port and dumped again.

Another longshoreman, Andy Poirier, who was working on the starboard side aft was trapped when his foot became pinned between the timbers as the deck load opened and then closed. Men nearby grabbed peevees and pried his foot loose, pulling him out before that part of the deck load discharged to the dock. Jim Hamilton, also working on the starboard side, fell into a crack in the deck load but managed to pull himself out before the crack closed again. Gill Carrier, hatch tender, injured his hip when he fell as the cargo shifted on the starboard side.

There were many other close calls. Longshoremen working the *Archangel* have not forgotten the incident or those who helped save fellow workers. An inquest into the death of Art Dube ruled human error. The chief engineer had pumped out eighteen hundred tons of ballast, which created instability.

Today there are ships that require no longshoremen in the holds and side loading ships that need only a foreman and a few drivers to load an entire ship. There are fewer vessels calling in at Stamp Harbour, but the tonnage loaded has not changed significantly due to the large-size ships and the more sophisticated loading methods they employ. In 1972, longshoremen were blessed with many call-ups as 221 vessels visited the port and loaded eighty-five thousand tons of cargo. The year 1979 was the biggest shipping year ever when 135 ships much larger in size loaded 937,000 tons.

While ships continue to call in at Port Alberni, the International Longshoremen's and Warehousemen's Union, Local 503, has watched the waterfront work force become drastically reduced.[90] In 1973, there were about 195 full-time longshoremen and about sixty-five casual workers who made a good living on the docks in Port Alberni. By 1983 the number had been reduced to just over one hundred, with ten casuals. The work force shrank with the arrival of large bulk lumber carriers with cranes that can lift large forty-ton modular packaged units of lumber at a time. The men who worked, and still work on the docks, have witnessed the evolution of shipping. Their efforts, diligence, and work have made changes in shipping possible.

CHAPTER TEN

CHALLENGES

MARINE MISSIONS

Many remote settlements up and down the west coast were without any regular religious service, so the United Church decided to establish the West Coast Marine Mission. In 1925, the Reverend C. E. Motte served the coast from Barkley Sound to Kyuquot Sound aboard the vessel *Broadcaster*, whose home base was Bamfield. With only an engineer aboard, Motte made calls to settlers, fishing camps and villages, often fighting heavy seas and the treacherous coastline, and sometimes-endless fog. The mission boat was a welcome sight. One man reportedly said, "Although we cannot get to church, it is a great satisfaction to us to know that you are around."[1]

There were no churches or organized congregations to work with, and Motte agonised that the work with the Natives was not being adequately done and that they were drifting back to primitive ways after coming out of the residential schools. He felt his little mission boat was not enough to serve the vast region. After only four years, Motte left the mission and was succeeded by the Reverend A. R. Wiseman. The *Broadcaster* was an ageing vessel and considered unsuitable for the work it was required to do and was withdrawn from service, leaving Wiseman to find his own way around the coast by passenger ship or fish boat. The church commissioned another vessel, the *Melvin Swartout*, which was named in honour of the early missionary lost at sea. Wiseman left the mission during the Depression, and left the ship tied up.

In July, 1934, the West Coast Marine Mission was reactivated under the Reverend R. G. B. Kinney who stayed only two years. A Newfoundlander, Reverend Uriah Laite, took over the post, and with the *Melvin Swartout* established a church presence in many of the coastal communities. His log book of Thanksgiving weekend in 1938 notes a busy schedule:

> October 7: . . . visited among the one hundred men . . . in the evening went seven miles into the "woods" on a speeder and spent the night visiting twelve families and amongst the two hundred men. October 10: . . . Sunday school at 11:00 a.m. After a hurried lunch went to Kildonan for a Thanksgiving service at 3.30 and 4.30. Left again for Bamfield. Arrived at 6.30 and conducted worship in the Cable Hall decorated with vegetables, fruit and flowers for Thanksgiving service. There were fifty persons present, which is a record in the history of Bamfield's twenty-five years. October 11: Placed the motor vessel at the disposal of our day school, and at 10:00 a.m. Mrs. Laite and I accompanied twenty children to Copper and Roberts Islands beach.[2]

Laite left to become a chaplain during the Second World War and was in Hong Kong with the Winnipeg Grenadiers in 1942 when the Japanese captured the city. He was taken prisoner and spent the remainder of the war as a Japanese prisoner of war. The Bamfield Marine Mission was closed temporarily after Laite left in 1941 until a new missionary could be found. Twelve years passed before that person arrived. In the interim, the *Melvin Swartout* served the navy.

When the Reverend Roy Rodgers took over the mission in 1953, accommodation at Bamfield was not exactly what Rodgers and his family had expected. There was no church and hardly any sign of a manse. They had to borrow space to tie up the *Melvin Swartout* and then begin to look for the mission house, which they found hidden under a growth of morning-glory vines gone wild. It had been rented out for a few years after Laite had left, but had since been unoccupied and was badly in need of repair. With the help of J. J. Jones, a retired minister from Alberni with building skills, Rodgers began renovating the old house. Meanwhile the family lived aboard the *Melvin Swartout*, still tied up in Bamfield.

The mission house was on the east side of Bamfield, the same side as the Pacific Cable Station. Local fishermen and businesses were on the west side. Rodgers established a church presence in the community by holding services on alternate Sundays on the east side and on the west side. He also visited Sarita River and Kildonan, as well as isolated families in Barkley Sound.

He began services in Ucluelet where a large number of Newfoundlanders had settled. They made him feel quite at home. The Anglican Church minister, the Reverend John Leighton, offered Rodgers the use of his church because it had been built by the community and United Church people.

After three years at sea, Rodgers felt his children needed schooling, something they could not get in Bamfield, and he was ready to come ashore. In July, 1956, he turned over the marine mission and the *Melvin Swartout* to the Reverend William L. Howie, and he and his family moved to Alberni. Howie met entirely different conditions at Bamfield and was amazed at the fine condition of the old house. He began visiting all the population centres on the coast and developed a good relationship with Reverend Leighton. Sometimes Howie would take over a service for the older minister who now found rigorous travel difficult.

The *Melvin Swartout* had become almost an institution on the coast and to all the small communities who relied on the mission ship for guidance. The ship, because of its size and availability, sometimes served as ambulance for the Bamfield area, transporting patients to West Coast General Hospital in Port Alberni. Technically, Franklin River Camp was within Howie's pastoral charge, but when he found he could not reach the main camp except by going into Alberni and borrowing a car to drive back to camp, he left it to the Alberni ministers.

In 1958, the *Melvin Swartout* became the first ship in the mission fleet to be equipped with radar. This same year, the Reverend John Romeril took over the marine mission. He was a young minister from Scotland with some navy experience. During his ministry, a community church was built at Bamfield. "A logger cut ten miles of 'cat road' to get his tractor on the new church site to prepare it for building. Most of the work was volunteer, often with equipment rented from Port Alberni. Material was barged out from Port Alberni and carried from salt water to site by hand. One carpenter was hired to co-ordinate and supervise the work."

Romeril served six other communities; he had three services one week and four the next. He made his rounds aboard the *Melvin Swartout*, had two cars and a motor bicycle which he carried aboard the ship. Statistics show he gave services to three thousand people spread over three thousand square miles. In 1962, Romeril left the marine mission to settle his family in a more normal setting. When the first marine mission was established there had been no roads linking communities, now logging and access roads provided links to larger centres. The Reverend W. O. Mackenzie was the last appointee to the mission before the decision was made to sell the *Melvin Swartout* in 1963, bringing to a close the United Church Marine service.

THE SHANTYMEN

Percy Wills and the Shantymen's Christian Association are also remembered for their marine ministry in the region. Wills, a veteran of the First World War, returned home to Victoria scarred by war in body and spirit, and after hearing a man preach, decided his future lay in mission work and spreading the gospel. For ten years he preached in northern Canadian communities, receiving little pay and living in inadequate conditions. During those years he married Margaret and they had two children, Frank and Jean.

Wills was the only Shantyman missionary to be appointed to Vancouver Island. He was young and strong and travelled miles with Phillip Mack, a Ucluelet Native, in a dugout canoe over treacherous open waters, and with a pack on his back to logging camps, fishing villages, lighthouses, and communities where there were new settlers. In 1924, Wills approached Port Alberni City Council with an idea to provide a home for men in "unfortunate circumstances."[3] There were about nine hundred city lots sitting empty due to unpaid taxes. The city was now selling these for the value of the taxes.[4] The councillors looked kindly on Wills' request and granted one lot and ten dollars to buy lumber to build the home. Soon work began on what would be known as "Strangers' Rest." The house was located on Second Avenue and offered accommodation for about twenty men, as well as a residence for the managers Mr. and Mrs. Felis J. Bourdignon.

A small report giving statistics of the home and its activities was published in April 16, 1936, under the headline "Make Good use of Strangers' Rest."

> A large number of men stayed at the Strangers' Rest during March, the total number of beds provided amounting to 264 and total meals to 177. Income for the month was $19.46 and expenditure $16.70. In addition several donations of food and fuel were received. The prayer meeting was held on Monday evening, with Mrs. Lammonth giving a paper on prayer. After the meeting refreshments were served by Lieut. Frewing.[5]

Prior to the Second World War, Strangers' Rest was a haven for the needy, a place where they could find accommodation for the night and a good meal. As many as thirteen hundred men passed through in one year. The rooms were kept spotlessly clean and maintained by the Bourdignons, who themselves were pensioners and received no payment for their services, other than donations. Despite difficult economic circumstances during the Depression, the Rest managed to remain free of debt.

During the war years, the building became a recreational centre for soldiers and airmen who were stationed in the district. In 1946 it reverted back to its original function and again provided accommodation for unfortunate men.

Meanwhile Wills continued with his mission work, visiting logging camps and sawmills. Gwen Howe, once a resident of Great Central Lake, remembered his visits to the small sawmill community:

> Percy Wills, a Shantyman's Missionary, called many times through the years and was much loved and respected by the entire community. Percy always visited the bunkhouses where he talked to the single men. If the young lads of the Townsite

happened to be playing marbles when Percy came along, he would immediately get down on his knees and join their game. To this day he is a good and dear friend to these people.[6]

Due to his intervention, a doctor was found for the Nootka Sound area. "The area was breathtakingly beautiful yet the people were overwhelmed with sickness, despair, and severely limited public transportation, and no medical help."[7] Dr. H. A. McLean arrived in 1937 to begin his practice at Esperanza, on the west coast. But a hospital under the Shantymen's Christian Association was not to be, for it was not within the association's mandate to own or build a hospital. The Toronto-based mission owned no land, established no churches, and settled in no specific spot. Its ministry was to preach the Gospel in all the isolated communities of Canada. Wills, undeterred, gathered friends in Victoria and formed "The Nootka Mission Association." He and McLean shouldered the entire responsibility for the development of the hospital.

Like the *Melvin Swartout*, the *Messenger II*, manned by Percy Wills, Harold Peters and Earl Johnson, plied the waters of the west coast, calling on islands, inlet villages, settlements, and fishing camps. The greatest thrill to the McLean family was looking out and seeing the *Messenger II* nearing the dock.

There were shouts of joy in the household and a "whoopie" as everyone climbed into boots and coats hurrying to be the first to be enfolded in the strong welcoming arms of Percy Wills and his rugged shipmate-skipper, Harold Peters. The McLeans and staff also knew they had better have hot water for the Messenger crew so they could bathe and have their clothes laundered. A visit from these two was like a spring day after a cold dark winter. Their zest for life was contagious and their stories knew no bounds. It was like a constant celebration during their stay and it was a sad day when they had to depart.[8]

The Tofino hospital which opened in 1944 became an extension of the Nootka Mission. It was destroyed by fire in 1952 and subsequently the Village of Tofino formed its own board of governors and constructed a new building which opened in August 1954.

In Ucluelet, in 1952, Andy and Hilda Ritersgaard donated two lots to the Nootka Mission Association. A building was purchased from the Ucluelet Military seaplane base and moved to the lots to become the Ucluelet Evangelical Church, now known as Christ Community Church.

A NATIVE PERSPECTIVE

Missionaries got to know many of the Native families within their mission. Some became friends and developed an understanding of Native issues and the problems associated with living on a reserve. "The missionaries were helpful, in a way, because they taught English to the Indians."[9] Natives learned the English language and also participated in the general economy of the region by logging, fishing, and hunting. The work was seasonal and allowed time for traditional pursuits. While the men and boys fished, many Native women worked in the canneries strung out along the canal. Mabel Taylor worked in a cannery salting eggs. "It was the hardest we'd worked, even to one o'clock in the morning, and sometimes 3 days and 3 nights, didn't even get to sleep day in and day off. If you didn't work everyday, you would be fired."[10] Historian Jean Barman noted, "Indian women were vital to the survival of families and communities."[11] When times were difficult, making baskets and weaving became another way of earning money for their families. West-coast Natives were the only Canadian Natives to develop the art of weaving.[12]

Mabel Taylor was an extraordinary woman. She became one of the area's most noted basket weavers; she travelled thousands of miles translating legends for anthropologists and was an inspiration to many young Natives. She was born Mabel Hayes in Ditidaht territory in 1900. Her father was from the Tseshaht tribe, her mother was Ditidaht. Her father, Joe Hayes (Chimsky Joe), was related to Jimmy Santo, the Chief of the Hikwuulhsath group, a sept of the Tseshaht tribe. Mabel spent her childhood amongst her mother's people.[13] When she was fifteen years of age, she moved to Port Alberni. In 1918, she married Jack Cook, an Opetchesaht, and about one year after his death, she married Roy Taylor, a prominent Tseshaht. Roy Taylor also was Hikwuulhsath through his relationship with Santo. For most of their long married life, they moved about the Tseshaht territory using its richness much as their people had done for centuries.

There were a total of twenty-three reserves within the Barkley Sound-Alberni Canal area during the 1880s. Many were just small tracts of land; eighteen were less than fifty acres in size, set aside for use by the various bands. The Tseshaht had six reserves, the Ucluelet four, the Ohiaht eight, and the Toquaht five.[14]

At various times Mabel and her husband lived in their houses at the Somass River Reserve, Polly Point, Keith, Nettle, and Village Islands. They had no children of their own but they played an important role in the raising of Adam Shewish, who became Chief of the Tseshaht. Adam's mother died when he was twelve and Mabel, his aunt, assumed her role teaching him traditional values: to love people, to show generosity, and to share with his fellow man. She told him to have patience with others who lacked it and to take pride in whatever he achieved.[15] Anthropologist Susan Golla wrote of Mabel:

> In the years I knew her, I never heard her raise her voice in anger to speak harshly to anyone. She preferred to teach in the Indian way, by showing and doing, and if someone needed correction, she was most likely to do so with a humorous remark. She had the respect for other people that encompassed the willingness to let them make their own mistakes and enough self-respect to make her tolerant of other people's ways. She found humor in everything. Her laughter was hearty but gentle and embracing. Mabel possessed a deep and wide knowledge of Tseshaht life generations ago.[16]

Mabel travelled thousands of miles with Susan Golla translating stories that made up the legendary history of the Tseshaht. What brought her fame, however, was neither history nor humanitarianism but basket weaving, a skill she learned as a child from an aunt. For most of her married life she worked at the craft only occasionally. After the 1960s she wove almost constantly. She said, "Can't stop making baskets." Like other basket weavers, "I make baskets to make my living . . . to buy clothes and food." As her skill became known, she gave demonstrations at the University of British Columbia Anthropology Museum and was sought after by the National Museum in Ottawa.

She also shared her skill with local people, teaching basket weaving through the Port Alberni Friendship Centre. She gathered the reeds for her baskets from the swamp near the summit on the Old Nanaimo Highway and from Shoemaker Bay; or she stripped and softened cedar bark. The special grass she called "three-cornered grass" because of the triangular shape of the stocks, had to be picked, cleaned, and dried in the open air. Her senior years were spent at Polly Point, south of Port Alberni, where she died in 1983. Her baskets are proudly displayed in the Alberni Valley Museum with other notable weavers from the Nuu-chah-nulth.

Many basket weavers were Ohiaht from the Sarita reserve and learned their craft from mothers and aunts. Annie Clappis was born in 1922 at Dodger Cove, the summer home of the tribe. Her father Dan Williams was a fisherman and boat builder; her mother May, a basket weaver. Annie's earliest memories were of her mother making baskets. "She was always weaving—always working. She wove while she cooked, while she talked. She always cleaned up from meals quickly so she could get back to work."[17] Annie learned by example, by watching her mother. She started by weaving a small mat and when she got stuck, her mother was there for advice.

For many years she did not weave, but concentrated instead on raising her children. While they attended the Alberni Residential School, she wove a little, but not as frequently as her mother. Then illness struck in 1965; Annie was confined to the "Indian hospital in Nanaimo for a spot on her lungs." During a long period of recuperation, almost eighteen months, she occupied time in hospital doing various crafts, such as making "picture frames with plastic covers with flowers or verses. That was my work for quite a few years." These were sold for a dollar. She also learned leatherwork and began making wallets until she could not get leather. Having little else to do, she started basketry again.

Released from the Nanaimo hospital, she stayed in that community for a year before moving to Bamfield in 1967. When she finally returned to her home at Sarita she found that everyone had moved away. Still she stayed, finding life difficult; living day to day but never starving as there was always fish and other seafood readily available. Now she made baskets for a living. "It was so cheap in those days." With no ready market for her baskets and few buyers, the prices she did get were low. There was not much money coming in.

> For many years I was like that, I struggled. I had nothing else to make money with so I guess I had to turn to my basketry. But it's such slow work, needs lots of patience, needs coloured straws. Ella Jackson used to sell straws, and Jennie Cootes. I remembered how to start it. I didn't ask. Auntie taught the open work. I'm a forgetful person but I remembered. I know a lot of things women don't know how to do. I had nobody to show me. Mother died in 1957. If I got stuck I had to do it myself. I have patience to back up if I make a mistake. Some say people won't notice [a mistake] but they do notice. Because I'm selling for money I want to do it right. You've got to have patience to do this work. I used to watch my mother, pulling the toh toh—you learn to feel the size.

In 1971 Annie moved to the Anacla Reserve at Pachena Bay, leaving everything behind at Sarita because she did not want to live there alone any longer. Annie raised six daughters; only one does not know how to weave. The skill has been passed on.

Two other Sarita women have carried on traditional weaving: Mary Moses was once called the finest basket weaver in North America, and Dora Frank dyed and sold grasses to other weavers. Lucy Bill was known for making Maquinna hats and claimed to be related to Chief Maquinna. Born in 1875 at Pachena, she first married an Ohiaht, Chief Willy from Sarita, who mistreated her. "He was very cruel to her; he would drag her down the beach by her hair," according to her second husband Tommie Bill who witnessed her being dragged before he rescued her. Lucy refused to speak English and it took Bill several years to learn her language, a Nuu-chah-nulth dialect. Lucy and Tommie lived on the Tseshaht reserve. Her baskets and hats were sold to an agent who resold them in the United States.[18]

Angie Joe lived most of her life at Sarita. She attended residential school in Port Alberni from 1950 to 1959, then A. W. Neill Junior Secondary and Alberni District Secondary School. This was at the time when the residential school was closing and Native children were being placed in public schools. Her mother was Della Watts, her father was Wilson Joe from Sarita. There were nine children in the family, including Angie.

Growing up in Sarita, surrounded by family, was a wonderful way of life. There were many children to play with, and fruit and berries to pick; and the hunting and fishing were good. Her father had been a fisherman all his life, but like many west-coast men, he was able to turn his hand to any job that came his way. He built houses and his own boat, the *Saucy Jane*.[19] There were about fourteen houses on the Sarita Reserve and a large hall used as a community centre where most of the parties and celebrations were held. Many of the homes have disappeared along with the hall, only the trails remain and the beach.

> We used to play. My Mom used to teach us. We learned math through cards, playing cards. We used to play around outside and used to help with the work, packing wood and water. We used to do a lot of swimming. Things like the berry picking were all day sessions, lots of walking and picking and we used to picnic while we were at it, in between picking. That was fun. We never used to be bored. It's not boring. Some people they think you have nothing, but there's always things to occupy yourself. Nowadays we do basket weaving, we know how to bead and crochet, and it occupies our time.

Angie's home was without running water or electricity, but it had propane lights, and a kerosene lamp was used in the bedroom. Outside the deer were plentiful. One day about a dozen grazed in front of their house. Since venison was part of their diet, her father picked one out. "We didn't bother them unless we needed it for food." Bears came around in the fall hunting for the fish going up the river, and in the summer they raided the apple and plum trees. The salmonberries, salal berries and thimbleberries didn't escape the bear's search for food. Wolves also came around, possibly lured by the swans in the estuary. Most years there were around sixty swans that over-wintered, arriving around the end of October and staying until the end of February or March. It was an almost idyllic location.

Angie used to fish with her father in the *Saucy Jane* at San Mateo, and she had caught fish as large as seventy-six pounds. These were brought home and canned. Fish, vegetables, berries, fish and deer; all were canned. "That was our way of having food, keeping our food for the winter." Trips to Bamfield by boat took about an hour, and it was a three-hour trip to Port Alberni. "I remember getting ready to go to Port, we'd have to take our mattresses and blankets and everything to sleep in the boat. It really used to make it seem like it was a real trip."

Schooling was important in Angie's life. She was seven years old when she first went to the Alberni Residential School. "There was probably around five hundred of us. They used to have girls' side and boys' side, and we used to have our classes, elementary like one to grade seven. We used to have four grades in one building and four in the other." Angie stayed for nine years. After that she boarded with her sister when she attended A. W. Neill school. She remembered the brand new school where students sat on the floor for the first week because there were not enough desks for everyone. "But it was neat, it was a new school and everybody seemed to get along really good there; the kids, like in the afternoon games, sports days, just everybody got along so well. There was really lots of school spirit there too."

After she left school she found work as a chamber-maid in Port Alberni. She had a son, Tommy, and when he was old enough to attend school she took him to Bamfield where they rented a house. She found work in the Bamfield Marine Station helping in the kitchen; it was a job she enjoyed because she met people from all around the world. But she didn't like being away from home, so she moved back to Sarita and taught her son by correspondence until he had completed grade seven. "I just kept coming back here and it's where I relax the most. I guess I'm comfortable. And I don't know, it just seems too fast in town. Life is moving fast and it's getting more and more hard to even grocery shop." Angie was proud when Tommy received his high school graduation certificate.

Until the sixties, the government regarded schooling as a tool to assimilate Natives into white society. A fishing-based culture had to be transformed into an agricultural one. Officials reasoned that removing children from their parents would cause the parents to lose influence. All children were required to be in school from September to June; however, some students never did return home and were kept in school over the entire year. While some parents sent their children off to school willingly, others rebelled.

Many stories have surfaced of beatings, abuse, and unhappiness suffered by children within the residential school system. By far the greatest crime was forbidding children their Native language and forcing them to speak English. This shattered their personal links with their traditions. It is little wonder, therefore, that when the residential schools began to close in the sixties and Native students were placed in public schools, there were many drop-outs. But something positive had happened in the residential schools; there had been successes, some Native students began graduating from university. These young people would become future leaders. Historian Paul Tennant noted that students who were thrown together at school with Natives from a wide area of the province developed an awareness of Native issues and a wider knowledge of their culture.[20] These young graduates had new skills that were useful both on and off the reserve and which led to a political resurgence of Native issues, especially the land claims.

Agnes Dick, a respected elder of the Tseshaht in Port Alberni, spent a lifetime working to improve health, education, and living conditions for her people. She graduated from Civil Defence as a home nurse in January, 1959, and continued training in the Nanaimo Indian Hospital. In September, 1970, she received a diploma in home nursing in Sardis, B.C. The diploma gave her authority over health issues on the reserve.[21] Working with federal and provincial authorities, she often acted as foster parent and directed juveniles in trouble. She knew and recognised the triumphs and tragedies of her people and was frustrated when she was unable to find a solution to a problem. "What could I do, for instance, when they called me to tell me that a baby, nine months old, had died in a fire at Tofino? It happened when a one-bedroom house, twenty-eight feet by twenty feet, was burned."[22] Agnes knew that inadequate housing conditions were common and that they affected the health of her people. In 1976 she pleaded for change:

We cannot expect to go back to the old ways of life, not after a taste of the way things are now; electric stoves, cars, central heating for those of us fortunate enough to live in areas that have plenty of jobs. These amenities we can never give up. So we must go on. We are gradually being absorbed into the white society. This too cannot be stopped, but let us make an effort to slow that process as much as possible and maintain our identity and never forget our heritage.

The struggle of the Indian has been a long hard one and will continue to go on much longer than we can now imagine. All our future hopes are with our children, the vast majority now being taught in white schools. Though we cannot or do not wish to deny them an education which is so essential if they are to get along in later life in the same white society, this same education contributes to a break down in the Indian identity and culture. It is you older folks, you the "grass roots" that hold the responsibility of teaching the Indian language, the stories, the legends to the children.[23]

Agnes became president of the Native Awareness Society formed in 1976, a society which recognised the need for Native students to feel they were a part of the learning population. This at a time when Native students were dropping out of school at Grade Eight level. She also became an integral voice within the Indian Homemakers Association of British Columbia and travelled across Canada speaking out on Native issues affecting home life on the reserves.

Agnes Dick became an advocate of the provincial education system and recognised the danger in segregating Native students. She encouraged parents to go into the schools and see what their children were doing. Her strong beliefs in education were garnered over the years, from the time when she too had attended the Alberni Residential School. She remembered how things used to be:

I remember as a girl of eleven, we had senior elderly women come into the house, they would counsel us on how to preserve our culture. They told us never to borrow. We were taught how to weave baskets and table mats. The world is changing fast. As a teenager I spent two months at home learning the traditions, then ten months at Alberni Residential School. There I was punished for using my Native language. I was put in a dark room for twelve hours and I learned to be disciplined.[24]

Agnes recalled the time when noted Native elder and author, George Clutesi, as a teenager, was ill at school and "everyone had to walk around very quietly for fear of disturbing him."

> We lived in a long house which means a "loving house that is loved by the people inside." In the long house we learned to share everything including fish and deer. Now everything is polluted, all the forests and rivers. We now have problems of alcoholism among our people.

Education for Native students has improved considerably. Many Native councils administer their own schools on reserves where they are taught and learn in their own language; students regularly graduate from university. Agnes once reminded fellow Natives, "In these times of changes that we now live in, we must be more aware of the trends, of what is happening. We must contribute to things that affect Indian lives. We have a heritage no one else in this country can claim."[25]

Still, life was not easy for Natives trying to make a living in a white society. The skills needed to enter the outside world were not taught in school. But the Natives were a practical people; while never abandoning or forgetting traditional ways, they reconciled to a new way of life and did what had to be done to earn a living.

Cecil Mack was a man of distinction and Chief of the Toquaht Band, a hereditary chieftainship since passed down to his son Bert. He became chief through a family connection. The first chief of the Toquaht Band had no sons, but had a niece. The chief did not want his niece to marry out of the band so he arranged a marriage for her with the second chief's son. These were Cecil's grandparents. Cecil married Jessie, a daughter of the Chief of Ucluelet. Both were initiated into the Wolf Clan at a very early age. To celebrate the initiation, a feast was given for ten days during the winter, then a smaller version was held the following year.

Cecil and Jessie both attended the Alberni Residential School. Cecil was eleven years old when he first went to Alberni, where he remained until he was eighteen. Their parents arranged the match while they were still in school, but the couple did not marry until Cecil was twenty-one and Jessie twenty. As part of the dowry they received an island with good fishing grounds. Jessie never did see the island because she was afraid to go out on the open ocean.

Only a few months after Cecil had finished his schooling his father died. To help support his family, Cecil began working on his father's boat, an old sail boat converted into a trolling boat. Later he purchased a small boat of his own plus another larger one. At the close of the fishing season in the fall, he worked for a fish packing company for the winter months.

When there was no work during the Depression, Cecil and Jessie found work in the hop fields at Yakima. Many Vancouver Island Natives found work picking hops in Washington. A steamer left from Victoria on a regular basis but many paddled down in their canoes where they were met by the field bosses and directed to the farms.[26] Cecil first worked at pruning, which paid twenty-five cents an hour. Later he drove a large sprinkler truck between the vines, a job considered a promotion, but for the same wages. Their stay in Yakima was an unpleasant experience, for the house they rented had bed bugs that were impossible to get rid of. They were happy to return to the west coast and continue fishing as before.

The Macks lived in Port Albion during the Second World War, where Jessie became a forelady at the local cannery. The Japanese evacuation from the west coast resulted in the Toquaht Band acquiring the Stuart Bay reserve. The Department of Indian Affairs purchased this land which had previously belonged to Japanese people. After the war, the couple lived on the Stuart Bay reserve and Cecil continued fishing. In 1954 their house burned down and they decided to move to Port Alberni where Cecil found work on the log booms.

Through a Winter Works project, Cecil got a job as a carpenter in Victoria. He helped build the Lord Simcoe Apartment building and was proud of the fact that when there was work to be done near the edge, he was the only one who could do it. He worked on other construction projects, such as Redford School in Port Alberni and the pulp-and-paper mill at Gold River. In their senior years, the Macks settled comfortably in Ucluelet, having lived a full and rewarding life.

The Toquaht tribe used to be one of the largest tribes on the west coast. Their territory included Deekyakus at the mouth of the Toquaht River and, moving southwest towards Ucluelet to Mahacoah, Chetquis, Chenathat, Dookqua, and Stuart Bay. The two main village sites were the Deekyakus and Mahacoah. In the winter months they dug for clams, fished for cod, herring and springs, and hunted for game in the McKenzie Range. March and April were the months for hunting fur seals. During the summer, they moved closer to Ucluelet to fish for coho, for halibut off Ten-Mile Bank, for seafood from Barkley Sound and to hunt for harbour seals from which they smoked the blubber.

Cecil's grandfather never moved from Mahacoah where he had a house and everything he needed. There were also two other families who lived there year-round. Years before, when the tribal wars broke out, the Ucluelets and Clayoquots turned against the Toquahts, and while they lost no land, they did lose band members. Only the McKay and Mack families were left. After the Second World War many in the tribe moved away, mostly to Ucluelet, because of the jobs and schools available there.

> I remember, when I was very young, that Captain out on his ship. His compass found the iron ore deposit up on the mountain. They didn't do anything about it for years, but now all the iron is gone. Now there are white men's traplines along the shore and across the reserve. Cecil used to be the best fisherman on the coast, but now there are no fishermen left in the band. They're all loggers, although at one time all used to own a boat and go fishing.[27]

The iron ore Jessie referred to came from Noranda's Brynnor Mine at Maggie Lake and was shipped through Toquart Bay. Cecil and Jessie Mack, like many other elders, tried to pass on to the next generation their culture, ceremony, songs, dance and legends. Their lifetime of hard work proved they could adapt to a white society but still maintain their heritage.

TOQUART BAY

The Toquart Bay area attracted attention for its mineral deposits before the turn of the century, but those early prospectors could not have foreseen the giant development that would be built at that location in the sixties. For seven years, giant ships docked at Toquart Bay to load iron ore for shipment to Japan. The Brynnor Mine was a profitable venture for the Noranda Mining Company.

In the sixties Japan was the spark plug for mineral development in the province. In 1965, it imported 205 million tons of raw materials from around the world. The Japanese signed long-term contracts for raw materials from mines in several countries, including Canada. They had to import iron ore to keep their steel mills operating. Japan spent millions helping to finance mines and docks as well as special ore carriers designed for transporting products across the Pacific Ocean.[28]

Surrey prospector Ed Chase staked his claim in January, 1960, where Draw Creek flows into Maggie Lake, a property he and his Vancouver financial backer sold to Noranda for approximately a million dollars. Chase only received a portion of the windfall as the case ended up in court. "His backer convinced the court that he had paid Chase something over and above the basic grubstake expenses which would have entitled him to fifty percent according to a well-established precedent. This decision put Chase in the status of an employee rather than a partner."[29]

On April 5, 1961, MacMillan Bloedel logging crews rushed to cut trees from the crown land to make way for the new mining industry. Diamond drills were already boring into the hillside below the loggers' spar trees. Kie Mines, a subsidiary of Peter Kiewit & Sons, sent in a crew to remove the over-burden in preparation for the start of mining operations. Plans were drawn up for the wharf and the magnetite ore concentrator plant. Draw Creek was slated for diversion from the site of the proposed diggings.

A rock crusher and concentrator were constructed on the foreshore of Toquart Bay, apparently to prevent pollution of Draw Creek and Maggie Lake. The machinery was designed to handle seven hundred thousand tons of iron concentrates annually. The docking and loading facilities were capable of handling vessels of forty-five thousand tons.[30]

In May, 1962, the MV *Tawatsam Maru* became the first freighter to load ore. Some freighters, like the *Belmona,* carried mixed cargo but most took only ore. The *Belmona* carried coal from Port Moody destined for Japan in her other bunkers.[31] The largest ore carrier to load at Toquart wharf was the *Santa Isabel*, 740 feet long with a 110-foot beam.

About five million tons of ore were shipped over the seven-year lifetime of the contract signed with Japanese buyers, and two hundred people were employed in the mining operation at its peak. Trailers, a bunkhouse, and cookhouse provided living quarters for some, but many others established their families in Ucluelet and made the village their home. Excavation was carried on until the pit was four hundred feet deep and down to sea level. In the meantime, exploration continued and holes were drilled twelve hundred feet, locating two or three deep seams which could have warranted the establishment of an underground show. However, when consideration was given to tunnel mining of the seams, Noranda decided the operation would not be economically feasible. But there were other problems at the mine that may have changed management plans.

Workers were disenchanted with a contract that gave only five cents an hour increase in wages. Another group made up of three separate unions stepped in and promised a dollar an hour if workers signed with them. They voted in the unions. When the company claimed it could not break the original contract previously agreed to, the workers went on strike—a strike that lasted one year. Many of the workers were transients and left the area. Others rode out the strike. When the mine did eventually get back in operation it was only to get rid of the ore already mined. This lasted only three months. During the strike, Japan had found other sources of ore and no longer needed the Toquart mine. The main customer had gone.[32]

When the Japanese chose not to renew their contract, the 148th and last shipment was loaded on July 4, 1969. The *Belmona* docked at the wharf and loaded the last cargo for Japan. The conveyor system with its sixteen-hundred-ton-per-hour capacity was dismantled. The crushing plant machinery and the milling plant were taken down. On the twenty-one-acre pit site, a new lake was formed. Seven miles of gravel road built by the company reverted back to the provincial government. Fifteen of the houses that had been transported to the mine site for workers were moved to Pine Street in Ucluelet. The mine had been good for Ucluelet.

Five years after the mine closed, only a watchman, Charlie Beamish and his Labrador dog, remained on the site. The silence of the west coast was broken only occasionally by the rumble of MacMillan Bloedel logging trucks off in the distance. The man-made lake offered recreational opportunities. Charlie often rowed across the lake in good weather and the sight beneath the water gave him an eerie feeling. "They never took any of the equipment or anything out of the pit you know. It's sort of a funny feeling, rowing around out there and suddenly seeing all sorts of machinery right under you."[33] The rock-crusher stood backed against the hill, it's final load unprocessed, and the massive service shop was now used by Coulson Forest Company for machinery repairs.[34] Down the road stood the largest teepee in the world, estimated to be about 150 feet high. The metallic cone was used during its heyday as a cover for the iron ore concentrates until the freighters manoeuvered their way into dock at Toquart Bay.

Local residents considered the road used by the massive belly-loaders transporting ore from the pit to the loading site to be one of the best in the country. A grader was employed full-time to keep the surface smooth and clear. The story is told about the driver who was known as Grader Joe. One night Joe drove his car to the end of the wharf, set fire to it and quite neatly committed what the RCMP considered suicide.[35] The burned and rusted remains of the car were still visible at the end of the wharf five years later, surrounded by a few tumble-down shacks used previously as service bays.

Much of the beach at the Toquart Bay recreation site is composed of mine tailings from this operation, and the pier pilings and concentrator hood can still be seen. The area is under lease to Coulson Forest Company as a log dump and booming ground.[36]

In July, 1998, a Vancouver Island road-building company was contracted to remove three hundred thousand tonnes of tailings from the mine. The tailings, mostly limestone, will be barged to the United States and the site eventually levelled and reforested. It is reclamation work that should have been done when the mine closed.

MEMORIES OF THE OLD CABLE STATION

When the new cable office was built in Port Alberni in 1959 and a new connecting cable laid from Bamfield, it was the end of an era for those who had spent a lifetime working in the grand old Bamfield Cable Station. The changeover took place June 20, 1959. Instruments that had over the years carried messages from one end of the globe to another now lay lifeless and obsolete. The beautiful McLure-designed building lay empty. Since 1950, the Bamfield Cable Station had been taken over by the federal government and operated under a crown corporation named the Canadian Overseas Telecommunication Corporation. When a system of tone control was devised, making it possible to control the cables from Vancouver, the decision was made to bypass the unproductive relay station in Bamfield.

Caretakers looked after the empty cable station for several years. The McLure-designed bachelor quarters and accommodation for married staff were bulldozed. Twelve houses used by married staff were burned. Junk dealers picked through the old equipment, its value recognised only by the Institute of Electrical and Electronic Engineers, which managed to retrieve some equipment and mount a permanent display in the British Columbia Maritime Museum in Victoria. In 1969, the 190-acre property was purchased by five universities for a Marine Biological Station.[37]

One man who knew as much as anyone about the Cable Station was Bruce Scott, a noted author and Bamfield historian who lived and worked at the cable station for years and published numerous articles about life there. In a 1979 interview he and his wife Pauline talked about their life in Bamfield.

Bruce Scott was born in Sidney, Australia, and had worked at the Fanning Island relay station and the Auckland, New Zealand station, before volunteering to come to Bamfield. He arrived in Bamfield in March, 1930.

> When I stepped off the boat at Bamfield, it was a case of love at first sight. I might add that when I did step off the boat, I was dressed just as I would have been as a man about town in Sidney. A bowler hat and tie and a silk scarf and walking stick and this sort of thing. And I can imagine what the other Cablemen on the dock must have thought but they didn't say anything. Within an hour of getting off the boat I was changed into old clothes and I was exploring the forest trails, which I did every day thereafter for all the time I was at the Cable Station.[38]

273

Bruce first lived in the bachelor quarters along with the other young men who worked at the station. He enjoyed the social life which virtually revolved around the arrival and departure of the coastal steamers filled with tourists calling in during the summer months. The station had a dance hall with music supplied by a five-piece orchestra composed of members of the staff. On Saturday nights, the staff also provided movie shows which were open to the public. There was also a billiard room and library.

Living in the station was like living at a country club. There was every facility for recreation: hiking over forest trails, swimming, boating, fishing, hunting, photography and two tennis courts. Highlights of the year were the annual tennis dance at the end of the summer, and the New Year's dance, to which people were invited from all around Barkley Sound—even as far away as Port Alberni. They travelled for hours by small boats, danced all night and went home the next day. The weather at this time of the year was usually wet and stormy, so ladies from across the Inlet had to protect their evening gowns by wearing slickers, sou'-easter hats and gum boots. After being ferried across the stormy waters of Bamfield Inlet, each emerged from her rain clothes like a butterfly from a chrysalis, resplendent in her finery.[39]

Social activities at the station were duly reported in the Port Alberni newspaper. One such account was of the annual tennis masquerade dance.

When R. G. Martlew's boat, the *M. J. Hodgson*, left Port Alberni wharf last Saturday *en route* to Bamfield, a capacity passenger list was aboard, all invited guests of the skipper and his wife, to attend the annual tennis masquerade dance at the Bamfield Cable Station hall. The Rhythm Aces orchestra occupied considerable space and provided vocal entertainment *en route* with headquarters in the pilot house. The passenger guests included Mrs. Kelvin Robinson, Mrs. J. L. Dunn, Mrs. Fike (pianist), Miss Bertha Phillips (soloist), Miss Nellie Bourne, Miss Gwen Toms, Messrs. H. O. Dunham, R. Gale and M. McVicar. Fancy costume was worn by the ladies of the party who were the house guests of Mr. and Mrs. H. M. Baxendale, Mr. and Mrs. Butcher, Mr. and Mrs. R. Rockley and Mr. and Mrs. Greenlees. The party was received at the Bamfield wharf by Messrs. Russell Rockley, W. Scott, W. Forsythe, H. E. Martin and M. H. Baxendale.

During the dance, which continued long past dawn, Mr. and Mrs. Behan and Mr. H. R. Martin were individual hosts at their residence to Mr. and Mrs. Martlew's Port Alberni guests. As the party moored at the Bamfield dock, the Rhythm Aces heralded their approach by beating of drums and sounding of trumpets, and as the party turned homewards, at the end of the perfect weekend enjoyment, opinion was unanimous that Bamfield hosts were masters of the art of hospitality and good fellowship.[40]

The day after the Second World War was declared, a detachment of the Canadian Scottish regiment guarded the Cable Station against sabotage.

They threw barbed wire all around the station and they took over our hall for accommodations for the soldiers, and we all had to have a password and couldn't venture on the station without the password. Bamfield was the first place in Canada to be blacked out. When the Japanese submarines shelled Estevan Point, it was thought, at least on the news and the BBC and also in Victoria, that the Cable Station was being shelled. But that was not so. Everyone was looking for submarine periscopes, but we never were really in danger.[41]

It was during the war Bruce met his wife Pauline during an impromptu dance in the cable station library. They corresponded and eventually married in 1942. She had lived in Seattle all her adult life and had attended the University of Washington and then taught public school music before working for a telephone company. Her first impressions of Bamfield had been in the summer, with the sun shining every day. Her first year living there in 1942 proved not so sunny.

We were married in September and, of course, the rains had begun on the west coast, where at Bamfield we could have a hundred or a hundred and ten inches of rain a year. And I swear, I thought it rained every day until mid May. It was rather depressing. We lived in a tiny little cottage, one of those that he had built for summer guests, and it was really tiny. And I used to sit there alone while he was gone on duty in the evening, and the walls would seem to press in on me. I had quite a claustrophobic feeling about the place.

Getting from one side of the inlet, or creek as the locals called it, was always an exciting experience as Pauline found out one evening when they decided to go to a Saturday night movie. They had only reached the middle of the inlet when a storm blew in, creating waves over four feet high. "I honestly didn't think we would ever get across that water." Bruce told her later he had wondered what the noise was coming from the bow; it proved to be Pauline panting in fear. On other occasions large fish boats were recruited to return everybody safely across the water.

Transportation was always a vital concern for residents of Bamfield, which is situated on Grappler Inlet and Bamfield Inlet, two waterways that divide the community into three different sections. A boat was essential to travel from one area to another. To get to work Bruce rowed back and forth to the cable station and in the winter time, with a wind blowing, it was no easy task. "I didn't like it at all, but I could do it. I would only do it to go on duty, but not for social reasons." Transporting household items was another matter.

The only major transportation was by wheelbarrow and I could wheel anything in a wheelbarrow provided I could see over the top of it. And when I couldn't see over the top of it, I'd have to put the wheelbarrow down every fifty feet or so and sight a line in front and see if there were any stones in the way and make a mental picture of them and try to avoid them when I came close to where they were.

Some of the material carried on the wheelbarrow included all the lumber and building material for their new home which Bruce built. Most of the time any transportation into and out of Bamfield was by water. In more recent years, planes have taken over from boats, although the *Lady Rose* still provides an essential transportation and freight service.

Their daughter was born in 1944 and Pauline found it was no easy task to raise a child in such an isolated place. "If I had questions about what to do for her health-wise, or personality-wise, I only had books to consult. We did have a Red Cross Outpost Hospital with a nurse in charge, but we had no doctor at any time." Bruce had served on the original board of directors when they purchased a small private house from a fisherman who had moved away, and he had transformed it into an emergency hospital with one or two beds and a trained nurse in attendance. The nurse performed emergency work and could phone a Port Alberni doctor for more advice. On some occasions patients were transported to West Coast General Hospital in Port Alberni by float plane.

The destruction of the McLure Bachelor Quarters building is still regretted today. Bruce blamed authorities in eastern Canada for having no understanding or appreciation of it.

> They don't know anything about it and they don't want to know anything about it. This building was vacant and I could have sold it several times over. In fact I sent one party who already owned a principal tourist resort up past Campbell River. They flew back to Ottawa to see the authorities and the authorities wouldn't say yeah and they wouldn't say nay. They just couldn't make up their mind what to do with it, so eventually they said, "Well, let's demolish it" and that would settle the question, and that's what they did. Pushed it over with a bulldozer. I couldn't bear to look at it while it was being done. Just in passing I would look at it out of the corner of my eye.[42]

Retirement in Victoria didn't sit kindly with Bruce, and he began digging into the history of the west coast at the archives in Victoria. "I spent three hours each afternoon in the winter delving into history and writing it up in longhand in notebooks. After about three winters I found I had enough information for about three books." He wrote about people, shipwrecks, and the history of Pacific Rim National Park area.

Pauline and Bruce returned to Bamfield and operated a tourist resort in their old home during the summer months. Some people thought they were crazy to invest in Bamfield but they believed "that one day it would become one of the principal seaside resorts in western Canada." Their property occupied Aguilar Point and had a panoramic view of Barkley Sound and the Pacific Ocean. "We felt we didn't own it but we just took care of it for a temporary period. We invited, or welcomed, people and visitors to come and enjoy the place and see the view."[43] After ten years they did sell and retired permanently to Victoria. The Scotts laid the foundation for the tourist business in Bamfield which continues to thrive.

Today the Marine Biological Station is used by the universities of Victoria, British Columbia, Simon Fraser, Calgary, and Alberta, and the station again has become a focal point in Bamfield. In 1977, a commemorative plaque was unveiled on the old grounds of the Bamfield Cable Station signifying the laying of the Pacific Cable in 1902.

Mary Rockingham Hughes returned to Bamfield in 1943 after an absence of ten years. As a wife of a Cable Company employee, she recorded her experiences living "off" the station:

Two other D/N wives and families have joined their husbands since our arrival, three of the permanent staff have married and all have to live "off." So we are quite a little community, sending our husbands off with their lunch pails—and the laundry in a suitcase on Saturdays—rowing over ourselves for a game of bridge or for the Friday night movie. In spite of the advantages of Company light and water and a Chinaman with a blow-torch to unfreeze our pipes during the January cold, I am glad to be where we are—within walking distance of school and the beaches and outside the narrow cantonment life.[44]

For the first nine months Mary lived with her husband Leslie and children in what she described as "a very ancient farmhouse in a state of extreme disrepair." A path had to be cleared to the front door before they could move in. But it had a bath, which had been retrieved from a shipwreck and still had the barnacles to prove it. Several times when Leslie worked the night shift, a storm sent the old house creaking and groaning "like a ship in full sail, and I prayed I would not be a widow before morning."

However, what the Hughes family lacked in physical comforts, nature repaid. "The beaches were glorious and within twelve minutes walk of the house." There were several other house moves before the family settled in a house with a three-piece bathroom and electric light, "which only worked half the time, being ancient and temperamental." Mary's only anxiety was crossing the water during a storm, in the dark, and being afraid of being run down by a boat.

During their tenure in Bamfield Canada was at war, and the Bamfield Cable Station was on high alert, completely blacked out and surrounded by barbed wire and garrisons. In contrast, the village, on the opposite side of Bamfield Creek, was brightly lit. The Hughes children attended the small school with an international assembly of Norwegians, Russians, children of fishermen, cable men, storekeepers, and before internment, Japanese children.

> Teachers were in short supply, the isolation and the very mixed student body in the one-room school did not attract the best. We had a collection of neurotics, cranks and even one sadist. It was worrying to have children in the school which only went to Grade VIII, but included as pupils some men in their teens, waiting around until they could start fishing.[45]

The Hughes children rowed to school in a dug-out canoe for half the year and in the worst months went by school boat, a launch that travelled from float to float picking up little groups of children on each.

> For several years it was run by a woman, who, like many west-coast residents, was a heavy drinker. Many mornings she came erratically alongside our float, once wearing only her slip under a slicker, and handed the wheel to our eldest daughter. It was only at the end of the year that we heard the truth when Valentine (daughter) showed us a very beautiful wide silver bracelet, and when we asked why she had been given the bracelet, she said casually, "Because I steer the boat when she is drunk."

During the war a Russian ship ran aground just beyond Pachena Lighthouse. Instead of sinking rapidly, as most have done in the Graveyard of the Pacific, this ship berthed itself on a shelf of a rock, firmly wedged and upright. "The weather was calm so a flotilla of small and large boats set out from Bamfield, ran around Beale Light and then along the shore to Pachena and the wreck. Every boat, no matter how small came back with loot; hundred-pound sacks of very fine flour, large rough bath towels, and the more portable things went first. Later fixtures were removed and we saw toilets sitting on floats around Bamfield, in front of houses that had no water laid on, or at best a pump."

This ship would have been the SS *Uzbekistan* that ran aground in April 1943 without loss of life.[46] The ship eventually broke up and sank.

There was always fear and tension the Japanese might surface off the west coast. On June 20, 1942, a Japanese submarine was sighted two miles off the coast of Estevan Point. It immediately began shelling the lighthouse, perhaps mistaking it for the Bamfield Cable Station. Instead of causing panic at the Cable Station, the event almost passed unnoticed. The staff's attention lay elsewhere—the wife of one of the Montreal staff had drowned that night in the canal, very close to Bamfield. The woman had been visiting her family in Port Alberni, and had encountered a group of friends, all men, who persuaded her to return with them to Bamfield on their hired launch.

From time to time we all hired the *Nalda*, on weekdays the school boat, to make the four-and-half-hour journey to Port Alberni for shopping, dentist and other chores. So the party embarked on the *Nalda*, and there was much good cheer and partying on the long trip. Twenty minutes out of Bamfield she went on deck for a breath of air, and one of the men stepped up after her, when to the horror of those in the cabin, they saw a leg with a high heeled shoe fly by the door and a shriek to say she had gone overboard.

The skipper of the *Nalda* was proud that he turned at once, practically on the boats length, which may have been fatal, as their guest never surfaced. All the men were waiting to dive, though only as a matter of form, as she was a champion swimmer. Every staff boat and launch spent the next two days searching Barkley Sound. The bereaved husband flew out from Montreal and relatives came from Alberni, but it was six weeks later the body was found on an island at the edge of the Pacific.

The expulsion of the Japanese from the west coast affected the Hughes family. They awoke one morning to find all the Japanese boats, "which were always the best kept and finest boats of the local fishing fleet," had been rounded up and were anchored across the top of the creek. The Japanese were now to be sent to internment camps in the interior of British Columbia. Some of the younger Japanese had been born in Bamfield and other settlements along the coast; they married and earned their living there. Japanese children had attended the same school. The older boys had been kind on the school boat, "not bullying as was the norm."

The Hughes family bought a house previously owned by the Japanese. It was built on piles over the water and on stormy nights they could hear waves breaking beneath them. "There was a Japanese bath in the back, made with no nails and a small brick fireplace underneath to heat it. We never used it, rather stupidly. There was also a small Buddhist shrine in the attic. Our children were small, but the expulsion of the Japanese upset them."

Mary wrote in April 1944:

We are in the middle of the wettest April for many years. It rains and blows every day. The Creek is full of large American fishing boats, riding at anchor. The big ones anchor alone, but the smaller ones line up side by side, sometimes as many as six joined together, and swinging to and fro with the tide. When we see the big fellows start to come in we put our slickers and gum-boots ready and say "Another South-Easter coming." The sound of the fishing boat engine is the heart beat of Bamfield.

Mary now resides in Port Alberni, but when she gets together with other Cable people she can look back and laugh at some of the adversities. From her point of view, life was particularly hard for women, because everything had to be done by boat and just maintaining them through several violent winter gales had been difficult. She often lay awake some nights wondering if the stringers had broken and the float drifted away. "The constant bailing, drying of spark plugs; having to shop, get to the post office or customs, hospital or school, by boat can be a misery. The wide roads of Port Alberni are a welcoming sight to me."

The Second World War drastically changed the vulnerable communities on the west coast after Japan attacked Pearl Harbour. Millions were spent fortifying beaches and shore installations. Long Beach had mines, pilings, and tank traps installed. An airport was built at Tofino, and Ucluelet became a major base for seaplanes. Radar and bunkers were installed at Radar Hill. An army camp was based in Port Alberni. The evacuation of Japanese to internment camps had an adverse affect on the fishing industry, reducing the number of boats available for fishing and almost idling shore workers and canneries. Boats were commandeered for patrol duties, and it became difficult to get machinery and building supplies. But it was a good time for the forest industry which supplied wartime lumber needs.

The two decades following the Second World War saw major changes in the landscape. Logging companies were granted Tree Farm Licences that divided up the region's forests. The fishing industry restructured from small canneries that once dotted the coast to fast refrigerated packing vessels. Some plants were dismantled, others sold. The largest cannery at Kildonan ceased operations in 1960, and two years later the buildings and wharves were demolished and burned. Those protective pilings installed during the war at Long Beach rotted for about ten years before they were finally removed. At Bamfield, the buildings used by the army were occupied for a time by members of the Ohiaht band, other buildings were destroyed or transported elsewhere to assume a variety of functions. The Ucluelet seaplane base eventually closed down. The hangers were used as a truck servicing area and warehouse. The Port Alberni army camp land was returned to the city along with all its buildings, providing much needed housing for veterans returning from war. The pulp-and-paper mill built in Port Alberni after the war brought renewed prosperity to the area. In the post-war period, the region settled back into its normal peaceful life.

CHAPTER ELEVEN

ECHO SOUNDINGS

LIVING WITH NATURE

The islands of Barkley Sound and the shoreline of the Alberni Canal have always attracted individuals retreating from the big cities and seeking a different way of life. They lived off the land, hunted, fished and spent their time enjoying nature. There are ninety-eight islands of varying shapes and sizes clustered in this giant bay surrounded by rugged mountains and impenetrable forests. Add coastal weather conditions, Pacific ocean swells and southeasterlies to the mix, and the picture leaves a perfect place to hide or to make your own world. Many of the islands bear scars of violent winter storms, windswept trees bent away from the ocean, barren cliffs difficult for even sea gulls to find a foothold, and deep mysterious caves carved by an ocean constantly lashing against the rocks. Amidst the islands are sheltered channels and protected beaches that today lure kayakers and canoeists.

Salal Joe found Turtle Island in the Broken Group Islands a place to call home. The hermit lived on a float cabin on a sheltered cove for about twenty years. He was known to thousands of fishermen and boaters as "the Mayor of the Broken Group"[1] because of his constant presence and respect in the area. He went missing in 1980 when a park warden discovered his cabin unlocked and his four-metre boat missing. His boat was later found with two holes in the hull and the engine throttle wide open at Dodd Island, not far from his cabin. Friends from around the sound, fishermen, the Coast Guard and the RCMP all joined in the fruitless search. Salal Joe had disappeared as mysteriously as he had lived.

His real name was Joe Wilkowski. There was confusion about where he was born. He told some people he was born in Iraq, others he told Iran; however, his employment record stated he was born in Poland, on March 19, 1919. He worked for a time at Sarita Logging Division. An aunt and uncle raised him when his parents were killed. He came to Canada after the Second World War, settling first on the prairies before moving to Turtle Island. He was naturalised in 1955.

Salal Joe first earned a living gathering salal and ferns, which he sold to florists in Vancouver and Nanaimo. He regularly boarded the *Lady Rose* when she passed his way and joined the crew for coffee or soup. He did odd jobs for Parks Canada and sold clams to Bamfield fish processors. When Turtle Island became part of the Pacific Rim National Park, park officials decided to put him to work as a caretaker of the islands. The rugged recluse appeared in the movie *I heard The Owl Call My Name* with Dr. George Clutesi.

The legend of Salal Joe is known throughout the Pacific Northwest. He was a very private man. His long hair and beard gave him a wild appearance. When strangers approached his cabin, he often hid in the bush until they left. But he did call a few people friends. Roy Forsyth and Malcolm and Betty Hedman were considered friends and saw another side of the "wild man." They saw a man in tune with nature, a man who loved birds and wildlife. Hummingbird feeders around his cabin were kept supplied with sugar water; seagulls followed him when he fished, knowing he would throw tidbits overboard for them.[2] In the summer months boaters made a point of stopping in to see him, bringing coffee or supplies. They were welcome if they brought sugar for the humming birds. The winter months were different; heavy snows and west-coast storms often threatened to sink his home as waves crashed on the shoreline. He spent months alone in the float house cabin, his cat Chico his only companion.

John Monrufet remembered the hermit rowing out to meet the *Lady Rose* to pick up his mail and deliver his bundles of salal.

He would bundle up salal in bundles you could hardly pick up. He was a big man, he had a stack on two cross sticks poles and squeezed it to stay together. The pieces of salal he used to cut off were a foot long and the leaves still on it. They were taken to Port and trucked over to Vancouver.[3]

Salal Joe became an attraction for tourists aboard the *Lady Rose* all eager to take photographs of the west-coast hermit as he pulled alongside the ship with his bundles. He never liked having his photograph taken and always had some comment to make to repel the intruder from his privacy. "He always maintained that more than two vessels in Barkley Sound at one time meant, 'The damn place is getting too damned crowded.'"[4]

For over two decades he watched diligently over Barkley Sound taking his position as caretaker seriously.

Salal Joe saw the potential in collecting and selling salal, but this was not so with others who saw the plant as an encroachment on their land. Such was the case with the owner of Clarke Island, who built a lodge and got tired of cutting salal. He decided the only solution was to import a few goats that would hopefully graze on the plant. Unfortunately the goats ate everything except the salal. The goats were probably the *Lady Roses's* most unusual cargo. John Monrufet and Dick McMinn agree it was the "orneriest cargo" they had ever carried.[5]

The goats obviously did not like Clarke Island as they swam off to a nearby island and were never seen again. The owner of Clarke Island was not too unhappy to see them go. They had not been the ideal solution to the salal problem.

The fox farm at Link and Weld Islands did not have too much luck either. In 1925, a Mr. R. Springer of Victoria purchased the two islands opposite Ecoole, with the intention of breeding and raising valuable blue foxes. The location had more to do with the proximity to the fish packing plants than the habitat for raising foxes. Fish and fish offal are the main foods for foxes, and there was no shortage for the farm. Eight pairs of foxes were brought in for starters. Springer planned to divide off the islands into sections with wire netting.[6] No one really knows what happened to the fox farm except to say it was another scheme gone awry.[7]

Float homes are not an unusual sight in the sound or in bays and inlets along the canal. A study done in 1983 reported about sixty-five floating cabins, the majority being at Sunshine Bay and Uchucklesit Inlet.[8] The homes were controversial, as they were not sanctioned by any government official. Many were owned exclusively by residents of Port Alberni and were used primarily as summer base camps for fishing or boating. The floating cabins competed for the foreshore with boat anchorage and marinas, log storage and dumping, fish and shellfish habitat, and other shore-based activities. In 1994, there were ninety-three floating cabins, an increase of forty percent, only fifty-eight authorised.[9]

Not everyone who claimed an island home was a hermit, some were described as individualists. This was the case of Nelson and Myra Dunkin who lived on Tzartus (Copper) Island. They were a sociable but independent couple who enjoyed the isolation of the sound. In the fifties, Nelson acquired Captain William Spring's old trading post on the island, near Clifton Point. The over one-hundred-acre property was mostly water frontage, and included a sandy beach, a waterfall and the slope of Copper Mountain, the site of many old mining claims.[10] One of the claims happened to be the original claim worked by Captain Stamp.

Myra was born on the Isle of Lewis, in Scotland, and came to Canada as a war bride. Her first home was at Port Albion, where Nelson worked for the Nootka Bamfield Packing Company. They lived on a float house at Kildonan for a time before buying the property on Tzartus Island.[11]

Nelson Dunkin built his house with found materials on the shoreline, just as Anderson had done those many years before. Their three-storey house was built on pilings over the water so that at high tide the water lapped beneath the floorboards. A small bridge connected to the shore. The house was built over the water to avoid having to clear the land. By the time the home was ready for occupancy, the Bamfield Cable Station was being disposed of and the furniture and equipment sold. Bruce Scott met the couple during one of their expeditions to pick through the furnishings. "He and his wife haunted the Station for several weeks, picking up many antique pieces as well as modern furnishings for a song. I was the one who was disposing of these assets for the Cable Station."[12]

The Dunkins' nearest neighbours lived at the Native reserve at

Sarita; Bamfield, the nearest village, was about ten miles down Trevor Channel, and Kildonan was five miles away in Uchucklesit Inlet. Without roads, telephone or television, their only connection with the outside world was a transistor radio. Although isolated, they were never bored. Nelson had a reputation for carving folk art. "On the birth of his grandson, he made and carved a cradle, inscribing the sides with biblical quotations and painting a bagpipe-playing angel at the head—thereby inferring that all, or most, angels are Scottish."[13]

Twice a week, on Tuesdays and Thursdays, Nelson made the trip to Bamfield in his commercial fishing-type boat *Raven* to collect mail and buy groceries. If there was any freight destined for him, the *Lady Rose* delivered it to his own float at Clifton Point. When the Dunkins wanted the *Lady Rose* to call in, all they had to do was flag her down. Visitors who called in while on boating trips always found the Dunkins' welcome mat waiting.

Nahmint Lodge was another point of interest along the canal. The wooden structure built over water on the south shore of Nahmint Bay became a haven for fishermen. Retired fisherman, Gus Beurling, known to local fishermen for the development of the Beurling plug made of yellow cedar, built the fishing lodge and operated it for over twenty years in what he considered "the hottest salmon spot I've ever come across."[14] When he discovered how plentiful the big fish were at that location, he decided to open a lodge. Beurling started with just one building on floats and kept expanding until he could accommodate up to thirty-five people a night. One of the buildings had bunkhouse-style accommodation, which the fishermen seemed to enjoy. Perhaps it brought back memories of their childhood summer camps.

Viewed from the water, the motley cluster of floating buildings gave no hint of being one of the most popular fishing lodges in the province during the fifties and sixties. The original building, surrounded by bedrooms, was painted green. A recreation-dining room had another cluster of airy bedrooms. The bright, roomy recreation room was decorated with interesting objects such as shell work, burl carvings, Native artefacts, and antique furniture. People from around the world flew in for some fishing. "This place seemed like a small United Nations. People come from France, Australia, Honolulu, the Scandinavian countries, even had one guy here from New Zealand, who flew over for just one day's fishing, then flew back home again."[15] The majority of visitors, however, were from the United States. Men who wanted nothing more than to get away for a few days fishing. Guests paid $35 per day, which included everything except alcoholic beverages. Most guests brought their own bottles.

The attraction may also have been the ready supply of fish nearby. Within five minutes of the lodge, a fisherman was almost guaranteed to catch a salmon weighing around thirty-seven pounds. Gus liked to brag about the biggest. "Biggest I ever saw was a ninety-two pounder, caught twenty-one years ago. I've had others that I've had right alongside the boat before they got away."

One of the oldest visitors to the lodge was a ninety-year-old man from the southern United States whose health was not the best. The gentleman required an oxygen tank every time he went fishing. One day he and Gus were out fishing. "We hooked on to a fair-sized fish this one time we were out, and he tried to land it. The way it worked out though, I ended up with one hand on the fishing pole, and the other on the oxygen tank, trying to land the fish and give him air all at the same time. Guess it must have looked a little comical."

Gus enjoyed telling fishing and people stories, some happy, sad, or funny, many collected over his twenty years dealing with everything from bank presidents to postal carriers. He could reel them off as easily as he reeled off the best spots for fishing. Nahmint Lodge was one of the first successful fishing lodges in the area. After closing in 1974, the lodge was towed to Congreve Bay where it still operates today as Barkley Sound Resort under another owner. Gus died in December 1987. Today there are many wilderness and fishing lodges, campgrounds, marinas, all catering to a growing tourism market.

COUGAR BROWN

Cougar Brown lived in an old shack down a gravel road in the Franklin River area. There was no electricity, no telephone, and his running water came from a mountain stream up the hillside. His sole source of light was a trio of Coleman lanterns, and heat

Fish processing. PN 9286

Fish boats docked in Port Alberni.

Captain Richard McMinn.

Lady Rose. <small>PN 13607</small>

Captain John Monrufet.
PHOTO COURTESY OF DICK MCMINN.

*Harry "Cougar" Brown with his
hound and a cougar skin.*

Bamfield Cable Station with cable repair ship Restorer *docked.* PN 4471

Preparing for boat race on the Somass River. PN 616

The Maquinna *docking at Port Alberni.* PN 595

John Evans recalled a memorable landing from Princess Maquinna.
PHOTO COURTESY
LAURA EVANS

Amphitrite Point lighthouse, July 1954. DORRIT MCLEOD PHOTO.

*George Fraser
with brothers
James and William.*

*Visitors enjoy George Fraser's garden in Ucluelet. Fraser in shown in upper right
hand corner.* PN 12424

Gus Beurling, left, with a catch at the Nahmint Fishing Lodge on the Alberni Canal.
PHOTO COURTESY OF
SON, HAROLD BEURLING.

Stone & Blandy Shipyard. PN 3903

The SS Tees, *docked in New Alberni at the Waterhouse Wharf.* PN 392

The Four Winds *docked at Port Alberni.* PN 597

A view of the busy waterfront in Port Alberni. Somass Sawmill built in 1934 in background; E & N Railway in foreground. Photo Clegg's Studio. PN 2255

Miners taking a break at the Big Interior Mountain mine in 1913. Those identified in photo include George Drinkwater, Cliff Pineo, C. Hicks, Ernie Woodward and A. L. Withers. PN 803

Kildonan Cannery. BCRSA D-00594

Whale being processed at Sechart Whaling Station. BCRSA A-09217

Mountain of whale bones at Sechart Whaling Station. BCRSA D-03825

Aerial photo of Port Alberni, Stamp Harbour.

Giant oil rig, the Ocean Ranger, *in Stamp Harbour, Port Alberni.* PHOTO COURTESY OF PORT ALBERNI HARBOUR COMMISSION.

A view of the giant propellers of the Ocean Ranger. PHOTO COURTESY OF PORT ALBERNI HARBOUR COMMISSION.

Destruction in the aftermath of 1964 tsunami in Port Alberni.
PN 9512

The Tidal Wave resulted in some unusual sights on the streets of Alberni. This boat was swept hundreds of yards from its mooring and was found in the centre of River Road. Work crews moved it to the roadside. PN 9525

The Haida Carrier, *a self-dumping log barge, with* Victory V.

Saunders' Alberni Trading Store. PN 1491

Bamfield Marine Biological Station.

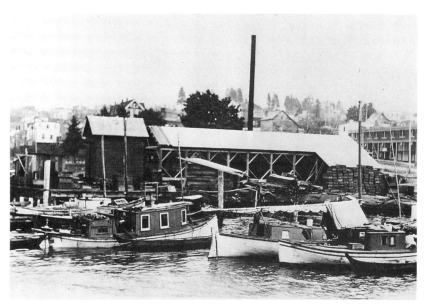

George Bird's sawmill on the waterfront at Port Alberni.

Fishing fleet at Fisherman's Wharf, Port Alberni.

for the uncarpeted, uncurtained shanty came from a massive woodstove. A portable radio was his only connection with the outside world. He would have been considered a hermit by today's standards, but this was a lifestyle he chose—out in the wilderness with his faithful cougar hounds as companions. Occasionally a passing logger would drop by to make sure he was all right. Cougar Brown lived the good life into his nineties until failing health forced him to move to Port Alberni.

Harold Brown was born in Washington and grew up in a small Texas town at the turn of the century, and by 1909 earned a living hunting cougars. In Texas he was paid $15 a cat; in later years in British Columbia, he was paid $40. He came to British Columbia when he was thirteen years old. Here he met up with an old trapper named "Snow" and they headed up to Alaska. He tried marriage in 1927 but said it was the biggest mistake he ever made. There were no children from the marriage. He worked for a time on the east coast of Vancouver Island in the forest industry, then came to Port Alberni in 1935 because, as he said, "There were more game here."

Cougar Brown arrived at a time when it seemed the west coast was over-run with cougars. The big cats had grown so bold that parents were afraid to let their children out of sight and in some cases kept them home from school rather than risk even a short walk.[16] There were so many cougars roaming around killing off the deer population, that the local Game Association passed a resolution asking the Game Board to send in one of their professional hunters.

A 1934 government annual report recorded 423 cougars killed on Vancouver Island and another sixty destroyed by game wardens. This compared to a yearly average of around eighty.[17] These were recorded kills with bounty paid. No doubt there were many more killed by hunters who were not designated "cougar hunters." A non-designated cougar hunter received only $20 whereas a professional hunter received $40.

Cougars are the largest wild cats native to British Columbia and imposing but elusive members of the province's wildlife. They are capable of killing a six-hundred-pound elk, so attacks in populated areas had people fearing for their lives. A cougar weighs between 190 and 210 pounds, and adult males can measure nine feet in length, including a thirty-inch tail. Normally cougars avoid human contact although sometimes show harmless curiosity towards man. Attacks on humans are usually attributed to old, starving cougars, or cougars defending their young. The mid-thirties were not normal times, but by 1936, the problem seemed to have abated somewhat. During the first two months of that year, Alberni government agent W. H. Boothroyd paid bounty on only sixty-nine cougars.[18]

Cougar Brown later boasted to newspaper reporter Shirley Culpin, "Got the highest monthly total of my life here—thirty-one cats in one month, which wasn't bad. I guess through the years I've killed as many or more'n any other man that ever hunted cougars in B.C. Yup, I was a cougar hunter. I wasn't no amateur. An' where my dogs went, I went."[19] For sixty-five years he raised cougar hounds and his affection for the animals never diminished. "Y've just gotta have patience with 'em, an' be gentle, an they'll be as good a friend as ya could ask." A series of strings, pulleys and weights between the bed and door allowed Brown to let his dogs out of the cabin without having to get up.

When he was not out hunting cougars, Brown worked on logging operations during the summer, then returned to hunt cougars in the winter. He also maintained a small trap line, which he gave up in 1971. In his advanced years, he played the violin for his own amusement, but when younger, he played for dances in the Gulf Islands and around Campbell River. He had a reputation as a fine violinist. He sold his original violin for $500 in 1924, but missed it, then bought another for $40. The violin had pride of place in his cabin, along with his two guns, a .30-30 and a .303.

About twice a week he drove into Port Alberni using one of the two cars he kept handy for transportation, a 1926 Chev. four-door sedan and a 1927 Chev. sedan. "I keep two just in case one doesn't run."[20] He wished he had kept his 1928 Model A Ford as he used it to pull out his other cars when stuck in the snow.

When this author interviewed him in 1984 he was celebrating his 99th birthday, although some doubted the accuracy of the years. Who could argue with this crusty old character that loved to tell stories of his exploits hunting cougars?

It was about 1950 and I was up in the Museum Creek area. My

dogs were with me. There were lots of deer around then but the dogs never harmed the deer. I put them out on the road and the dogs would just keep going while I drove behind. Then all of a sudden, they took off. It had snowed up the mountain and it was raining lower down. I parked the car and went up the mountain but the dogs kept on going. I went back to the car and drove down to China Creek booms and got four more dogs and then went back and turned "Old Hunter" loose. That was my favourite dog. He could smell the county. Just about dark, the eight dogs had the cougar trapped. I just shot it down. Then when I opened it up, there were seven cougar kittens in there. So I took them out of the stomach and put them in my packsack.[21]

He placed the kittens beside one of his old dogs that took to them immediately and began licking them all over. Not wanting to miss out and lose the bounty, Cougar Brown returned to the kill.

I was walking along the old railway grade when this big black thing appeared. It was nothing else but a bear. I took the rifle out and took aim and killed it. Then the dogs came alive and began barking. They had never barked at a bear before I shot it. Well, Barney Bordeleau, who ran Franklin River, wanted the bear skin, so it was skinned and he got it.

The year was 1951 and Cougar Brown had just bagged his two-hundredth cat.[22] He raised five of the kittens; one he sold to a zoo in Washington State. Then he told the story of the biggest cougar he ever shot.

Al Bronson was the manager at Franklin then when he and I went hunting. I had fifteen hounds with me at the time. We hunted for four days and nights then at Camp A, just before Franklin, this big cougar jumped off a cliff onto the railway bridge. One of my dogs disappeared. The next morning, the old dog was back and we found where the cougar had killed a beaver who had been cutting down a tree. Al and I got up there with those dogs and the dogs were barking all around Al and the cougar. I took the ice out of the gun and whoa! this big cougar jumps on the limb of a tree right in front of me. I just put up my gun and boom, it was dead. I said to Al I would bet him $100 that the cougar weighed more than 120 pounds. I was the biggest I ever did see. He had to return by boat to pick it up. The cougar weighed two hundred pounds.[23]

The decision by the provincial game department to take the bounty off cougars in the mid-fifties put Cougar Brown and his dogs out of business. "I've refused to kill cougars since they took the bounty off. I've only done it as a special favour to get a skin for a friend now and then." In retirement, he enjoyed watching hockey on television, especially games between the New York Islanders and the Edmonton Oilers. Cougar Brown was photographed in 1984 by French photographer Arnaud de Wildenberg for the book *A Day in the Life of Canada*.

THE WHEELHOUSE POET

Let no man boast
In his tiny voice that his ship is best
When the Southeast god walks in the West.

From "Storm" by Dick McMinn.

Dick McMinn never intended to be a poet. He had spent a lifetime on the sea criss-crossing island waterways up and down the coast of British Columbia, until he settled in Port Alberni. And then it came to him by accident; a need to express the beauty he saw around him. One day he was returning from Ucluelet; the sea was at his back as he skippered the *Lady Rose* down the Alberni Canal to Port Alberni. In the wheelhouse he reached for a pen and paper and wrote his first poem which he titled "Storm." He remembers looking at it and thinking, "That's not only easy but it's not bad," and he has been writing ever since.[24]

McMinn was born in Ladysmith in 1914. His mother was born in South Africa, of English parents who had a large farm there. She met McMinn's father, who was born in Ireland, during the

Boer War when he served with the Cape Mounted Rifles. He had also fought in the Zulu Rebellion. They then came to Canada. When the First World War erupted in Europe, his father, Robert E. McMinn, joined the Canadian Army. His mother refused to remain in Canada when her husband was in France, so the family returned to Ireland. His father came back from the war gassed, wounded, and shell-shocked. The family returned to Canada and settled in Port Alberni where Robert secured the position as Chief of Police.

Robert's physical condition did not improve and seemed to worsen with the west-coast weather. Doctors recommended a warmer climate. Dick's mother had relatives in South Africa, so he went back there, leaving his wife and children behind in Port Alberni. "I never saw him again for ten years. Those were ten tough years, not so much on our younger ones, but on my mother, with five young mouths to feed." His mother gave music lessons to provide for her family and during the period of silent movies, played the piano accompanied by Mr. E. Brown on the violin, for the theatre in Port Alberni.

The Port Alberni waterfront always attracted Dick. He delivered papers to the trollers on the waterfront; this was his first contact with small ships. The fishermen got to know their newspaper boy and sometimes hired him to pump out their boats during the winter when they were away. When they returned in the spring he was awarded a dollar or two. It was a case of earning a few pennies in whatever way he could.

It was part and parcel of those days, as a youngster, better than crawling under the board sidewalk at the Somass Hotel, where anybody that staggered out dropped their nickels through the cracks in the boards. You could pick up quite a bit of change there. And diving for dimes was quite a business down at the floats. The fishermen would toss them in. You got so you could dive below, and see them coming down like leaves and pick them up, no problem at all. You even went down to the old CPR Dock and the old Waterhouse dock, catching a sackful of perch and selling it. There were two laundries at the foot of Third Avenue hill. One was the Yee Lee Laundry and for a sack of perch you could get two bits. All this was part of my first contact with the sea.

One summer, when he was ten, "heaven smiled," and fisherman Collie Hill invited Dick to join him during his school summer holidays. He spent a boy's adventuresome summer at Effingham Inlet and had the use of the fisherman's dug-out canoe. The next year he was invited along again, this time they fished out of Dodger Cove, situated between Diana Island and Edward Island.

> It was a big place then. There were hundreds of Indians living there. There were fish camps that bought fish, B.C. Packers. We used to lie in there at anchor, then at two o'clock in the morning we would get up and go fishing. We went out the other side of Dodger Cove and out beyond Cape Beale to the S.E. bank and various places. Then we'd come in at three o'clock in the afternoon and go straight into Bamfield where Collie would sell his fish. As soon as he sold his fish we'd take off for Dodger Cove and drop the anchor and go to sleep. I thought it was wonderful.

They never stayed in Bamfield harbour because it was too congested with lots of fish packers. A top spring salmon could get seven cents a pound. There were times during those summers when his fisherman friend, Collie Hill, would suddenly stop the boat, rush down below to get his high power gun and shoot a deer. This was during the Depression and the crew needed meat. The deer was hauled onto the ship, then divided up among the fishermen and their families.

Dick finished high school just at the beginning of the Depression and got his first job as tail sawyer at the R. B. McLean Sawmill, a job that lasted only two weeks. At an hourly pay of only twenty-five cents, it was a less than happy experience. "Nobody ever got me back in a sawmill again." He packed his bags and left Port Alberni, walked over the Horne Lake Trail, down to Lost Lake and the Big Horn River, where he came across Thompsen & Clark logging camp and was hired as a chokerman. The next morning he boarded a speeder for the early shift and was on his way up the mountain for $3.50 a day. He stayed in logging camps for the next few years until he had enough money to buy his first boat, a Columbia River boat.

I took this boat out and I think I lived on it for about two years. I used to travel from logging camp to logging camp, extremely independent, because if I got dissatisfied slightly I would move out, get on my boat, and disappear to the next logging camp. This was not considered bad in those days. Logging camp employees turned over with monotonous regularity. If you stayed longer than six months, somebody was going to call you a homesteader. These two or three years living on that little sail boat, I consider were the happiest years of my life, the freest, maybe.

The McMinn family were reunited when Robert returned from South Africa and got a job with customs at William Head in Victoria. Dick had become independent, and as a logger he had no problem getting a job. He returned each spring to Vancouver to be hired out to another logging camp, and he witnessed first hand the difficult times in British Columbia. "I used to see these fellows sitting around in Vancouver. I remember walking past the post office and they were lying in there—there must have been a hundred of them. They'd ask you for two bits and you'd give them a dollar."

Dick had become a skilled chokerman, but he disliked the bugs; the no-see-ums, and mosquitoes. "You're sweating, and they're chewing the hell out of you." Then one day he looked out across the strait and saw in the distance a ship "going by like a bucket of ice cream." He decided there and then he wanted to be on the water. The next time he was in Victoria he investigated the possibility of being hired on a crew with one of the Canadian Pacific Railway steamships. He met a Mr. Appleyard who did the hiring and who gave him his first job in the shipping industry.

He was assigned to the "bull gang" which meant he was not assigned to any particular ship, until a superior discovered he could tie a knot and immediately recognised he had someone with experience. Dick joined the *Princess Charlotte* and would serve on the *Princess Maquinna, Princess Elaine, Princess Joan, Princess Elizabeth, Princess Marguerite,* and *Princess Kathleen.* This experience earned him a mate's ticket and ultimately a master's ticket.

When the Second World War erupted in Europe he enlisted in the navy but ended up stuck in Esquimalt with no prospects of going overseas, so he deserted. "I picked up my gear and went to Vancouver and went before the shipping master and demanded to be placed on a deep sea ship." The shore patrol caught up with him and he was escorted back to Esquimalt to face discipline. "I got out of jail and they made me an officer. It was strange. They put me on a bangor and sent me back to where I had come from, Alaska. I never saw any war at all." He was navigating officer on the Bangor minesweeper.

After the war ended he returned to school, to Victoria College, for a year. After some soul searching he decided he was not suited for work within a large corporation and liked the independence of being on ships. In 1946, George McCandless and Essen Young called; they had just founded the Barkley Sound Transportation Company. They invited him to work for them aboard the *Uchuck*. The telephone call sealed his fate and brought him back to Port Alberni. "I thought this would be a wonderful thing, because I like this country. They said, 'Bring your master's ticket. You'll be home every night.'"

After several years as skipper of the *Uchuck I*, *II*, and *III*, he and John Monrufet, who had been engineer aboard the *Uchuck II*, decided to go into business for themselves. They formed the Alberni Marine Transportation Company and purchased the *Lady Rose*. Over the years the *Lady Rose* only missed one trip; the winds had blown all the logs loose on the canal and the ship could not leave the deck with booms wrapped all around.

I'm well aware of the fact that weather can stop any ship. Show me the man that beats his little chest and says "my ship can take anything" and I'll show you a man who's going to get into trouble at sea. The sea is a big place. The worst we took it (*Lady Rose*) through was eighty miles an hour—a wild ride that was. These things happen to all ships.

The inlet is not particularly good sailing. Most inlets are not on this coast. There's either so darn much wind or there's no wind at all. It nearly always blows in one direction. You can get very strong winds here in Port Alberni harbour when there's no wind out there at all. This quite often happens in the summertime because you have a monsoon effect. As your valley heats up, the air rises—when it rises it sucks the air in up the inlet and causes wind. In the wintertime its slightly different. There's roaring gales out there and not that much in here although an occasional one will sneak in here and give you a blast.

It was the effect of the wind on the water as he headed back from Ucluelet one day that inspired his first poem. Now there are fifteen notebooks full of poems of his life experiences. Dick has a dream:

I'll get my sail boat built. I'm going to anchor it in a lot of lonely little bays but one day I'm going to come up on deck and write the best darn poem that's ever been written on the west coast and when I recognise that it is, I'm going to frame it and stick it in my boat. Nobody will ever read it. It will be the best I could do. That's as far as you can go.

Today Dick McMinn lives out his retirement years in Port Alberni with wife Pat Grace and pet crow named Joe. He arrived home one day to find the injured crow under a maple tree. His pet dog was wagging its tail while the crow flapped around in terror. He rescued the crow (it had a broken wing) and took it to the vet who declared that the muscles of the bird's wing could not be repaired and that he would never fly again. Dick took the bird home, constructed a wire net around the maple tree and there Joe lives out his life unafraid of the hawks that occasionally swoop down and attempt to scoop him up. Joe the Crow has been a companion for fifteen years.

ISLANDS

by Dick McMinn

And islands grow
Their ragged trees,
Beyond the hills
Toward the seas,

And each exquisite,
Secret pass

Mirrors its cedars
In gold-green glass,

And eel-brown kelp
Hides hidden reefs,
Like shimmered shades
Of vague beliefs.

Islands are poems
Of bone-white drift
From shattered songs
Of the big sea-lift.

Islands are small
And perfect places
Like little worlds
With quiet faces.

WHEN THE EARTH SHOOK

The west coast of Vancouver Island lies within an earthquake-prone zone that girdles the entire Pacific Ocean. About eighty percent of the earth's seismic energy is released in this region, and it is here that some of the world's most disastrous earthquakes occur. Enormous land-masses, known as tectonic plates, cover the earth's crust. These masses are in constant motion, grinding against or slipping under and over each other, or spreading apart.

About five hundred measurable earthquakes occur each year along the fault lines, or boundaries, between the plates. Off the coast these massive plates move four or five centimetres a year, causing great stresses as they rub against one another. Each time some of that stress is relieved, an earthquake occurs. If a large mass of rock along one of these underwater faults suddenly drops or rises, the water above moves with the seabed.[25]

There have been earthquakes, landslides, and tsunamis for hundreds of years along the coast. Researchers at the Pacific Geoscience Centre in Sidney, British Columbia, have determined that the oceanic crust is no longer sliding smoothly beneath us and that the crust of Vancouver Island is being strained. Geologists noticed the earth's crust in central Vancouver Island is being squeezed at different rates. Perhaps this is an early warning signal of the Big One.[26]

Tidal marshes, outcroppings, and excavations in estuaries show clear evidence of past earthquakes and tsunamis. Layers of buried peat exposed at Tofino revealed a record of past ground-shaking and abrupt land changes. Sheets of sand were deposited by tsunamis that rushed into the coast and buried the peat layers. An analysis of plant and animal fossils show what was buried many years before. Radiocarbon dating and tree growth rings suggest the last earthquake occurred about three hundred years ago and that hundreds of kilometres of coast line subsided during this event. There are records of a tsunami at a number of sites along the Japanese coast on January 27, 1700.[27] There is no indication of a British Columbia earthquake at this time, but researchers, having eliminated other sources, concluded that an earthquake along the Cascadia subduction zone generated the tsunami during the evening of January 26, 1700.

Most of the tsunamis reported within recorded history were relatively small and caused no destruction, with the exceptions of the 1707 Hoei Tokaido-Nanaido Japanese tsunami which killed thirty thousand people; the 1868 Peru tsunami which caused twenty-five thousand deaths, and the 1896 Meiji Sanriku tsunami in Japan which killed 27,122 people.[28] This 1896 tsunami was felt along the length of Vancouver Island but did little damage. The *Colonist* reported:

It is very seldom that a tidal wave is so far reaching, and at the time, the first reports of the one on the Vancouver Island shore were telegraphed from Carmanah signal station; it was supposed that the disturbance was caused by subaqueous eruptions not many miles off the land. For upwards of three hours the water rushed inland for miles, moving strangely to and fro at a velocity of nearly eight miles an hour. The steamer *Maude* which returned yesterday from west-coast ports was at Kyuquot at the time, and her officers, crew and passengers watched with curious attention the novel movement of the waters, estimating that at Kyuquot during the few hours of the inundation all the sea-skirting land was submerged to a depth of four or five feet.[29]

In more recent history, three tsunamis along the Pacific Coast caused major destruction. The Great Aleutian tsunami of 1946 killed 173 in Hawaii when waves of over fifty-five feet (17 m) above the normal sea level swept through coastal villages. Other deaths have occurred as a result of tsunamis in the Pacific.

The Japanese word "tsunami" has replaced the term "tidal wave" in order to differentiate between waves produced by earthquakes and waves associated with tides. Generally a tsunami is a wave produced by an earthquake, landslide, volcano, or large explosion. It is usually applied to ocean waves as opposed to lakes.

Most west-coast tsunamis have occurred as a result of earthquakes in other areas such as Alaska, Japan, and by local submarines slides. Sydney O. Wigan of Fulford Harbour studied the tidal data at Tofino and identified forty tsunamis in eighty years.[30] On February 9, 1928, an earthquake rattled Bamfield around 3:00 a.m. The instruments at Pacific Cable Station noted the surge from the shock and fishermen reported two large tsunamis. The quake was also felt in Alberni.[31] A minor earthquake was also felt in the Albernis on March 5, 1936.[32] There was little damage in either event.

The 1946 earthquake at Courtenay, on the east coast of Vancouver Island, was one of the few documented cases where a tsunami was generated following a British Columbia earthquake.[33] This tsunami, which led to one death, produced waves of about eight feet near Texada Island. This same earthquake resulted in a large submarine slide and the loss of a lighthouse on Comox spit. The 1946 earthquake struck Sunday morning, June 23rd, with a magnitude of about 7.3 on the Richter scale. The epicentre was on land but close to the shoreline of the Strait of Georgia.[34] It was felt in many Island communities, on the Lower Mainland, and as far south as Portland, Oregon, north to Ocean Falls and east to Kelowna in the Okanagan. At Kildonan, the pier and the ice crusher collapsed into the water. At the time, ice was being crushed for shipping fresh salmon. The crusher was operating on the wharf. When the slump occurred, the machine fell into the water, carrying the operator along with it. He was unable to swim, and with a broken shoulder, was in some danger. He was rescued and sent to West Coast General Hospital.

In the Alberni District chimneys toppled, windows broke, dishes came crashing down, and furniture went flying. In its wake, the earthquake left two people injured, four families homeless, and did thousands of dollars damage to property. Eyewitnesses saw the Motion Block facade break away, damaging the building. Other masonry buildings suffered a similar fate in Port Alberni. There were a number of chimneys damaged, including one at the hospital, which resulted in some anxious efforts to rebuild it and restore full hospital service. Most of the damage occurred in sections of town built on low-lying land; those houses built on rock suffered little damage. The liquor store reported "no damage to the Scotch and only a few bottles of gin, rye, and beer." This store was built on a rocky base. The tower of the post office in Port Alberni was damaged by the heavy clockwork shifting in its base. The front of the building was barricaded and business continued as usual, with customers having to use a rear entrance.

Captain Essen Young, aboard the *Uchuck* on his way to Bamfield with a party of picnickers, felt the earthquake just off Franklin River. He noticed the rumbling and grating as if the boat was running over rocks. He stopped the engines and his mate George McCandless checked the ship over for serious damage. About fifteen minutes later, five-foot swells began rolling up the canal. Only then did the ship's crew suspect an earthquake. Five dead whales were seen floating on the ocean surface off Cape Beale immediately after the quake.[35]

Serious damage was caused to the CPR Telegraph cable in the Alberni Canal near Franklin River. The earthquake was witnessed at Franklin River when a ridge of water, estimated to be twenty or thirty feet high, rose in the middle of the canal, extending in a north and south direction. This rise in the water level caused a small tidal wave on each side of the waterway.[36]

The strongest earthquake of this century, which struck on Good Friday, 1964, off Anchorage, Alaska, measured 8.5 on the Richter scale. The energy released was estimated to equal the detonation of thirty-two million tonnes of TNT, or two thousand of the atomic bombs dropped on Hiroshima and Nagasaki at the end of World War II. A section of the ocean floor rose forty-nine feet and the resulting tsunami raced down the coast at speeds of up to 450 miles an hour. Alaska was declared a disaster area with hundreds of people missing.

The southwest coast of the Island bore the brunt of the tsunami. Eighteen houses in Hot Springs Cove were torn from their foundations. Basements flooded and gardens washed away at Bamfield before the waves travelled up the canal to swamp the streets and the lower areas of Alberni and Port Alberni. Miraculously, no one was killed, but the tsunami continued down the coast to California where eleven people drowned at Crescent City, 1562 miles from the earthquake's epicentre.[37]

Alberni resident May Luecke has written about her personal experience during the 1964 tsunami. She remembered it had been an ordinary night with no hint of impending disaster. Her home hummed happily with activity as the family looked forward to a visit from May's sister and her husband from Vancouver who were coming to spend Easter with them. The house was filled with the aroma of hot cross buns, pies, and cakes. After supper, the men, listening to the news in the living room, called out that there had been an earthquake in Alaska. A brief announcement later that evening informed them that a tidal wave was rolling southward. They felt sorry for those suffering in Alaska, but were not alarmed about the news of the tidal wave. Alaska lay thousands of kilometres north and the vast Pacific would break up the wave. Besides, the Albernis were not directly on the coast; the long natural canal would provide protection. The tidal wave forgotten, the family enjoyed a bedtime cup of tea.

Shortly before midnight, the sound of water lapping against the side of the house brought the household to attention. They were completely surrounded by a few inches of water. Impossible, they thought, they were more than a block from the river. Unbelieving, they turned on their radio and sat bewildered as they listened to an excited announcer: "This is the first wave, it will be followed by a larger wave. All those living in low-lying areas are advised to seek higher ground at once. Stay tuned."

They were reluctant to leave the family home as they had only lived in it for five years and had just begun to make it comfortable, with new furniture, fresh paint, and colourful rugs. The water around the house had receded as quickly as it had come. They procrastinated, thinking they could save personal possessions and furniture. As they put on their coats, and called the family dog and headed down the front stairs to the car, they heard the angry river and their hearts jumped. "Only then did we realise that we were in real danger. Our lives were threatened by our lovely river. As we reached the car, water swirled around our ankles, rising quickly. We had delayed too long."[38] May's father shouted for them to make a run for the hotel. The two hotels in Alberni, the Greenwood and the Arlington, became safe havens for many refugees from the tsunami that night.

On Easter weekend, in 1964, an earthquake in Alaska generated a tsunami which swept down the west coast and silently crept up the canal, covering everything in the low lying areas. Residents of Alberni have never forgotten that night of terror.

The *Lady Rose* was tied up in dock. McMinn got a call from Jock McKay, a watchman at the harbourfront, telling him there was a tidal wave. McKay was getting on in age and perhaps drank a little more than he should have, so McMinn didn't believe him and told him he was drunk. McMinn decided to investigate anyway:

> I was driving a little Volkswagen in those days. I could see a gleam in the headlights right across the road and the water was running from the pulp mill out across the road towards the railroad tracks. I thought, my God, what is that, there must have been a tidal wave. It spilled up the river, it has come through the pulp mill and over the top and that is it in front of me. Well, I thought, these damn Volkswagens float anyway! So I drove the Volkswagen into it and the water came up, not quite half-way up its wheels.[39]

The headlights picked up nothing but water as McMinn drove down Third Avenue. There was water everywhere. He turned up the hill, went along Eighth Avenue and down Argyle Street, but could only get as far as the Somass Hotel. He stood there awhile pondering what to do, then waded into it. "What the hell, I could see these waves going out as fast as they were coming in, I guess, because the dock was almost dry when I got down to the docks. And the *Lady Rose* had been sitting on the bottom. She had broken a couple of her lines, but two were still holding. I got on her and put another one on, then Johnny turned up."

303

McMinn urged Monrufet to get aboard and start the engine. Logs covered the harbour. Slowly they nudged the ship out of dock, pushing away the logs and began working their way out to Polly Point, to the south of the harbour. They soon realised there would be no point in going further out as there would be logs everywhere along the canal. So they waited and waited and listened to the radio. When it was announced another wave was coming up the canal, they decided it would be better to meet it head on, than to be tied up to a dock.

So we carried on towards Dunsmuir Point, dead slow, pushing at a log here and there, but there was no tidal wave. So we turned around and churned our way back to the dock, pushing our way in among the logs and shouldering this and that, and got alongside and put some good strong lines on her. Now all we could do was wait. So we hung around the radio waiting for more reports, but there were no more. We figured this was it. The tugs were already out. Whatever tugs MacMillan Bloedel could get, were out collecting logs. So it was just as wise to stay at the dock.

The *Lady Rose* had survived the tidal wave, but it was a night few residents of Port Alberni and Alberni will ever forget. It was business as usual the next day for the little ship.

Meanwhile the Alberni Valley Search and Rescue Squad had been mobilized, as had the Salvation Army and Civil Defence. These volunteers began waking up residents in the flood prone area and assisting others fleeing for safety. In a Rescue Squad account of that fateful night, a volunteer recounts his experience as they prepared to evacuate some residents:

My eye was caught by a low white line that looked like a six-inch high veil of mist approaching from the direction of the river. I shouted to the man nearest it, that it might be water, but it was slightly foggy and hard to see, and he thought it was mist. In about thirty seconds it was at our feet and welling up, and we yelled to the nearest people who were on a low verandah with three youngsters to get in the car. As soon as everyone was crammed in I tried to drive off, but could only go about ten feet when the water flooded the engine and the car stalled. At first we jumped out and lifted the children on the car roof but realized that if the water continued to rise, that would be useless, so instead, decided to get to the nearest high porch.

We waded up to our thighs through the water and managed to get above it. By this time the water was about three feet deep in this area, which is a large flat piece of ground, causing a quicker levelling out of the wave. We missed the full brunt of the wave in this area. There were three people in their seventies, a young man and his wife and their baby and two little boys on the porch together.[40]

They waited until the water receded and it was safe to move to higher ground. The Albernis were in a state of shock. In the next few days and weeks tales emerged of heroism, neighbour helping neighbour, and general relief there had been no deaths. Outside help arrived to bolster local authorities trying to cope with the relief effort. Of the 694 registered evacuees, 130 were placed by the Welfare Department and Red Cross, the rest made their own arrangements with friends and relatives.[41]

The following day, March 28th, there was considerable concern expressed by provincial officials for other west-coast communities. The Search Sea Rescue Co-ordination Centre in Vancouver began to collect data from the Canadian Coast Guard, RCMP, airlines, logging camps, and canneries.

At Hot Springs Cove, the Search Sea Rescue Centre informed provincial authorities of the damage in that community, where sixteen of the eighteen houses were destroyed. The Indian Affairs Department Agent in Alberni coordinated efforts to house and clothe the evacuees. A group of forty people were taken by boat to Ahousat.

At Zeballos, thirty homes were knocked off their foundations and considerable damage done to personal property. The small logging community of Amai was hard hit by the tsunami which struck ten buildings and caused considerable damage to personal property. Five families involving about twenty-five members and twelve single people were temporarily homeless and spent two nights in the open. Their telephone system was knocked out by the wave but they took care of themselves and made their own survival arrangements.

Many of the cabins in the Broken Group Islands were damaged. Salal Joe on Turtle Island commented it was no big deal. "The float went up and then came down."[42]

Tofino and Ucluelet were also hit. Fishermen alerted by radio stood by their boats when the wave struck, thus saving many from damage by the swirling waters. In Ucluelet harbour, log booms scattered. One boom containing five million feet of timber broke up but was later recovered. The water main bringing water to Ucluelet from Port Albion was carried away in the surging tide. Divers Lou Klock and Jimmy Hill worked for two days to repair the break. Telephone and television cables were also broken and power cables shifted from position. In Tofino, the water main from Meares Island lay twisted like a huge snake on the mud flats where the tidal surge had thrown it. The airplane float at the government dock had broken from its moorings. The village tide gauge recorded an eight-foot above-normal crest shortly before midnight. Tide plus the tidal wave brought the height of water to sixteen feet.[43] The Mayor of Port Alberni, Les Hammer, and his wife were enjoying an Easter weekend at the Clayoquot Hotel when news of the disaster reached them. He immediately returned home to join Alberni Mayor Fred Bishop in facing the disaster.

Cleaning up after the tsunami was a major undertaking, considering the muddy deposits which accompanied the flooding. At the MacMillan Bloedel pulp-and-paper mill, the fifty-four-inch water pipeline supplying the plant was taken out by logs which collided with it as they were carried along by the wave. The line had been mounted on trestles and crossed the Somass River estuary near the head of the canal. The sewage disposal basin was filled with logs, but there was no permanent damage to the system.[44] Engineering and warehouse buildings near the Canadian Pacific and Dominion Government Wharf were affected. The wharf structure damage was due to the decks rising with the wave and then hanging up in some parts during the recession.

The 1964 tsunami created a situation different to that normally presented in flood disasters. The second wave, travelling 240 miles per hour on top of a tide created by the first wave and already eight feet higher than normal, smashed everything in its path and tossed enormous logs and other debris, including buildings, boats and automobiles, up to a thousand feet. It then receded to be followed by a succession of lesser waves. The wave surge continued in the canal for approximately eighteen hours.[45]

The destruction occurred practically without warning. No warning system then existed for Civil Disaster. The disaster was estimated at five million dollars. In a way it was a cheap lesson for other communities to learn to prepare for such emergencies. The earthquake which struck Alaska could equally have struck the Albernis or Vancouver.

The strength of the tsunami was such that a considerable portion of Stamp Harbour's bottom was moved about by the force of the surging waters and this created new and unknown problems for shipping. A complete new survey of the harbour was undertaken in May, 1964. Some sections that had been raised by the movement of the earth were charted and dredged for the safety of ships.[46]

There have been other earthquakes recorded in recent years. Now Port Alberni has a tsunami warning system in place to alert residents to the potential tsunami and earthquake danger. There is also a Provincial Emergency Program in place to deal with such emergencies. Who can forget the Mexican earthquake of 1985, or the California quakes of 1989 and 1994, or the Kobe, Japan, quake of 1995? Earthquake initiatives have intensified, and education in schools about the potential danger is more common. Buildings such as schools and hospitals have been tested, upgraded, and in some cases replaced. British Columbians have been warned the next earthquake could be "The Big One."

CHAPTER TWELVE

NEW DIRECTIONS

PACIFIC RIM NATIONAL PARK

Pacific Rim National Park has greatly affected Barkley Sound and the surrounding area. Established in 1971, Canada's first marine park includes Long Beach, the Broken Group Islands, and the West Coast Trail. The history of the park goes back to the twenties when the federal government reserved 232 square miles between Port Renfrew and Sarita River for a national park.[1] In 1930, representatives from the Department of the Interior visited the west coast to select a site for a "seaside national Park" and the choice appeared to lie between Carmanah Beach and Long Beach.[2]

While everyone favoured the site, the biggest stumbling block remained: the provincial government refused to waive mineral rights to the federal government who insisted this be part of the agreement, to ensure there would be no commercial activity within the park. The whole project failed when the federal government withdrew its proposal. This prompted an editorial in the *Port Alberni News*:

> The same old thing is happening again. Down in self-centered Victoria, where conspiracies of greed are ever at work, with

political wires, to block all public development on Vancouver Island unless such development is directly tributary and immediately profitable to that city, certain elements have combined to knock the Long Beach National Park proposition. These elements profess to be in favor of the Sproat Lake Long Beach road, which is a shallow profession, inasmuch as the building of this road is dependent upon the selection of Long Beach as the West Coast park site. Influences in Victoria are promoting Carmanah in preference to Long Beach, and recent manoeuvers give rise to the suspicion that their campaign is not being conducted entirely in the open.[3]

Public interest in the park had been aroused and a movement began to reserve just a small portion at Cape Beale as a provincial park. Bamfield author Bruce Scott took a keen interest in promoting this idea and began pressuring government to make a decision. From the moment Scott stepped off the boat at Bamfield he fell in love with the area and over the years explored it on land and sea. He firmly believed it should be preserved for a park and advocated this to anyone who would listen. For over forty years he wrote articles to the newspapers including photographs of the west coast, but it was not until he presented slide shows that he got any reaction from the public. "One good picture is worth a thousand words," he noted in an interview.[4]

In July, 1964, the same month as the Bamfield road link opened to Port Alberni, a new luxury hotel opened on Long Beach. The Wickaninnish Inn was designed to become a destination point for those travelling to the west coast. The principals involved in the venture were Bob Fells, the general manager, formerly of West Vancouver; Jeff Crawford, owner operator of the Geisha Gardens restaurant in Vancouver, and Ucluelet magistrate Joe Webb, the former owner of the Wickaninnish Lodge.[5] The lodge had been a small resort created by Webb from an old hospital building used during wartime at the airfield in Tofino.[6]

In 1968, the idea of a National Park on the west coast continued to have momentum, prompting a visit from MP Jean Chretien, Minister of Indian Affairs and Northern Development,[7] now the Prime Minister of Canada. Before heading out to Long Beach, at a stop-off in Port Alberni, Chretien posed for photographs and boasted to reporters he was just "an average small-town boy, even if he was a cabinet minister at the age of thirty-four." The press noted: "The craggy-faced, fair-haired minister was probably the most approachable cabinet minister on the Ottawa scene." Appealing to his home-town boy image, Chretien said: "Why not? I am the eighth of nine living children. My father worked in the paper mill at Shawinigan Falls. I worked in the paper mill summers during high school and university. I'm just a typical Port Alberni boy."[8] Before entering politics, Chretien had been a lawyer, a 1959 graduate of Lasalle University, and was known to despise red tape. He appeared to be the man who could make things happen for the park.

The provincial government had already established campsites and beach frontage acquired when the area was released from National Defence after the Second World War.[9] As well, a number of people had privately owned properties along the beach. This concerned the federal government because it did not want to be plagued with the problems of townsites as it had in Banff and Jasper. Traditionally Ottawa only established parks on land free of all encumbrances.

In 1966, provincial Recreation and Conservation Minister Ken Kiernan announced the province was willing to co-operate with Ottawa in establishing a west-coast national park centring on Long Beach. It would hand over existing Crown park reserves—providing Ottawa would acquire the remaining land needed. Federal Resources Minister Arthur Laing said he "would act with the speed of light" to follow up Kiernan's offer.[10]

The subject was raised again in the 1967 session of the British Columbia Legislature by MLA Howard McDiarmid, in whose riding Long Beach was situated. This same year federal parks officials carefully studied the west coast with a view to drawing up a major proposal. Harold McWilliams, director of British Columbia's Provincial Parks Branch, noted officials were "quite favorably impressed with Long Beach and Tofino areas which themselves covered ten miles of coastline, and three thousand acres of provincial park reserve, and were drawing up a feasibility study on such a park."

The federal government dragged its feet in making the final decision to establish the park. Laing's promise of acting with speed had reached a red light when the subject of purchasing private property was concerned. Every year the government procrastinated, the value of the alienated land increased in value, from an estimated two million dollars to three million dollars.

Finally in 1969, the provincial and federal governments reached an agreement to share equally the cost of acquiring land for the national park. Bill 73 was introduced in the legislature on March 20, 1969, to provide the basis for further negotiations between federal and provincial authorities in acquiring new parkland. Besides the 4,700 acres of parkland held at Long Beach there would be sixty-five miles of parkway between Tofino and Port Renfrew, including Effingham Island.[11]

There were almost fifteen thousand acres of provincial crown lands within the proposed park boundaries under forest management licences. The harvesting rights would be bought back from the companies involved, or exchanged for other forest area. The Wickaninnish-Long Beach national park would be ready for the centenary of British Columbia joining Confederation. Stage two would include Effingham Island. Stage three would be the narrow strip of land, one-quarter mile wide, along the coastline from Pachena Bay to Owen Point at the entrance to Port San Juan Harbour. The total park area would cover thirty-four thousand acres.

A formal agreement was signed in April of 1970, reserving the coastal strip between Chesterman's Beach, near Tofino, and Port Renfrew. The old West Coast Lifesaving Trail had been included. The idea of Effingham Island being included was shelved in favour of including all the Broken Group Islands. Chretien was present when Princess Anne officially opened the park on May 4, 1971.

The park meant the end of the old Wickaninnish Inn on Long Beach. Instead of anticipating increased tourist trade Fells prepared the hotel for closure. The old weather-beaten hotel that had faced many storms from the Pacific Ocean could not fight park regulations dictating there would be no commercial resort development within park boundaries. Fells, who had planned to stay there for the rest of his life finally acknowledged he would have to go.[12] The twenty-two-room resort became the interpretive centre for the park.

Today Pacific Rim National Park Reserve is visited by thousands of visitors from around the world who enjoy the beaches, trails, tidal pools, and ocean-swept rocks. The interpretive centre has become an integral part of the park and now looks as wind-swept as the original Wickaninnish Inn. So many people want to hike the West Coast Trail that reservations are now required. The *Lady Rose* continues to drop off canoes and kayaks for travelling in the sheltered waters of the Broken Group Islands. Ucluelet and Tofino have developed a thriving whale-watching industry, and Bamfield has become a stopping off point for those venturing on the West Coast Trail. All west-coast communities have benefited from the park's presence. A new Wickaninnish Inn has since opened outside the park boundary, at Chesterman's Beach, near Tofino, attracting tourists from around the world.

WRECK OF THE VANLENE

History has shown there have been many shipwrecks off the rugged west coast. New navigational aids and modern technology minimized the risk, so the wreck of the *Vanlene* on March 14, 1972, on Austin Island in Barkley Sound, took everyone by surprise. The Panamanian-registered 10,500-ton freighter carrying a thirty-eight-man Chinese crew and a cargo of three hundred Dodge Colt automobiles, left Nagoya, Japan, on February 24, 1972. The freighter had been *en route* to Vancouver when it sent out a distress signal about 9:00 p.m. The ship was originally reported in distress off the Washington coast.

The *Vanlene* ran aground on a rock, piercing a huge hole through her belly. Water entered the engine room from the port side below the floor plates. The captain ordered the pumps started, but they could not cope with the volume of water and the ship listed to port. Soon the port generator was under water, and the chief engineer ordered his staff to abandon the engine room and seek safety on deck. Before long, the starboard generator was flooded, cutting off all electricity except for emergency battery power for the radio. Half an hour after the grounding, the captain broadcast the SOS distress call.[13]

The distress signal was received by Tofino Radio and relayed to the Search and Rescue centre. The Bamfield lifeboat was alerted and the search began of the shoreline between Bamfield and Clooose Bay. This proved fruitless. It was not until a radio direction finding was taken from two other vessels and a U.S. Coast Guard aircraft that the stricken vessel was located closer to Cape Beale.

Six other vessels joined in the search, and the freighter was finally sighted on Austin Island, about fifty-eight miles from where it was originally reported. The ships involved in the search were the British ship *Victoria City*, the Liberian ship *Coral Stone*, the Russian ship *Tiksi*, and the Bamfield lifeboat. Two tugboats helped in the rescue; they were the *Neva Straits*, owned by Rivtow Straits Ltd., of Vancouver, and the Canadian naval auxiliary ship, *Laymore*.[14]

The crew of the *Vanlene* was taken to Port Alberni and housed at the Somass Hotel before being transported to Vancouver. Captain Lo Chung Hung, obviously distressed at the outcome, claimed he had navigated across the Pacific Ocean using only a compass but had then experienced dense fog as he approached the west coast. The ship was over twenty years old.

> We had reduced our speed to a crawl but got picked up by the strong current at the mouth. I wasn't really sure where we were, that's why the confusion about our position. All our navigation aid was broken down. I requested of the ship's owner that it be fixed before we left Japan, February 24, but this is the option of the owner. I am very unhappy about it all.[15]

The captain, only twenty-nine years of age, had been at sea for thirteen years and had been a master for four. All of the crew was from Hong Kong and some had just joined the ship. This happened to be the first voyage for the twenty-year-old radio officer, Yeung Shun Wai, who remained at the controls of his radio, using battery equipment after the engine room had flooded. Water in the engine room had risen about fifteen feet when he was called from the depths of the listing ship as the rescue vessel *Laymore* stood by. The young man was so terrified he had difficulty climbing the ladder to safety. The ship listed about twenty-five degrees as he climbed from below deck to join other crew members on the coast-guard vessel.[16]

Almost immediately the wreck of the *Vanlene* became a bit of a curiosity on the coast; this giant freighter suffered the indignity of being hung up on a rock unable to move. *Alberni Valley Times* reporter Rollie Rose took a trip out to see the ship and got within one hundred feet of her, through the good seamanship of deep-sea skipper Zig Treit and his sixty-five-foot vessel *Leik*. Aboard were others interested in seeing what had happened to the ship: Zig's wife Val, and fishermen Paul Tennant and Paul Lavallee. None could understand how the *Vanlene* managed to hit Austin Island, which was no bigger than a rock when compared to Effingham Island. To get to it, the *Vanlene* had managed to navigate through a checkerboard of large rocks. Rose described the scene:

> She looked lonely there this morning. It was as if she was appealing to the tugs at her side all night, to try and do something, anything. She's a clean ship compared to some which pass her way and looks to be well-maintained. In her stern are three hundred Datsun [*sic*] cars. Everyone here today is talking about these cars. Someone on board the *Leik* suggested we should drag for a car since we were a deep-sea troller but someone else said perhaps we had better not, because we might bring up the navy submersible which is operating in the area. The feeling is it all depends on which hold the cargo is in, whether or not these vehicles will ever drive a Canadian road. If they are in the stern, they are lost, because the stern is awash; but if they are forward, there might be some salvage.[17]

Salvage attempts were made by the tugs *Neva Straits* and *Sudbury II*, when at high tide they attempted to pull the ship free. Fisheries officers were concerned about the diesel and bunker oil aboard the ship, which began to spill into Barkley Sound. The ship had more than a hundred thousand gallons of bunker oil in her tanks when she grounded and, by the next day, 17,500 gallons had leaked out on the surface.

Already reports indicated there was oil one inch thick in the area of the wreck and throughout the Broken Islands. Oil slicks had been spotted on Coaster Channel; there was an oil slick in Newcombe Channel, and as far away as Loudoun Channel. Twelve miles of beach were covered with a one-foot wide band of oil. Authorities were completely unprepared for the oil spill and attempted to do what they could with what was at hand. A boom of logs was tried but proved ineffective as the oil simply swept over the boom with the action of the waves. The naval tug *St. Anthony* towed a thousand-foot boom, and the naval auxiliary vessel *Laymore* towed another six-hundred-foot boom and a slick-licker to the scene from Vancouver. Canadian navy ships *Ready* and *Camsell* transported three hundred bales of peat moss for mopping up, and an oil barge was towed to the scene to contain the remaining oil pumped from the *Vanlene* bunkers.

Conservation groups raised the alarm about the wildlife that could suffer as a result of the oil. Offers were made to transport oil-soaked birds to Victoria for treatment. In the end it was nature herself who helped the situation. Gale-force winds, torrential rain and the highest tides of the year helped dissipate the oil and carry it out to sea. The oil remained floating, but out in the Pacific Ocean, where not much thought was given to pollution.

Dr. William Austin, a marine biologist at Simon Fraser University, conducted a study into the oil spill. Although the spill had been minor, it pointed out some major flaws in preparedness for an oil spill on the west coast. An inquiry drew attention to the lack of training and experience of the ship's officers, whose certificates of proficiency had been issued by the Republics of Panama and Liberia—in the case of the radio operator, without examination.[18] In the opinion of the inquiry, the grounding of the *Vanlene* had been due to errors in navigation, which could and should have been detected and remedied.

Six days after the grounding there appeared little hope of recovering the *Vanlene* because of the massive damage to her hull. The *Lady Rose* carried Comox-Alberni MP Tom Barnett to the scene of the wreck where evidence of the oil slick had all but disappeared. Crews pumped a second tank-hold of oil from the freighter. Barnett, accompanied by Navy Lieutenant Commander Sid Fairbairn and Rollie Rose, toured the wreck. They found it was not only the sea that was raping the ship; during the night she had been ravaged by scavengers.

They've already taken her wheel, who knows what else, and Lt. Cmdr. Fairbairn is upset because these scavengers also took one of his portable pumps. At first you get the feeling you hadn't better stay aboard too long because she might roll over and go down. But after awhile you lose this feeling. You begin to sense what was but is no longer. The cars (Dodge Colts) in her forward hold are still tied down. They appear to be okay. But in her stern there are more cars, awash for seven days now. On the bridge it's easy to see where the scavengers have been. Everything has been tossed around and, like the navy said, her wheel is missing. So is one of the telephones to her engine room.

This is the first good day since the wreck. Outside there is sunshine, a ripple and light swell on the water, but inside here it is cold, and quiet. Sad. At the stern of the ship, the sea slops over her decks. Every now and then there is a banging noise, a loose chain. A sailor, using a walkie-talkie, keeps in touch with his buddies on the water. Some are pulling booms, others ferrying personnel. On the deck below, salvage men go about their business. In the meantime, the *Vanlene* is being readied for committal to the sea. She lived twenty years and there is a story here that this was her second-to-last voyage. May she rest in peace and be soon free of the scavengers who tear at her.[19]

Before salvage operations could begin to lift some of the cars in the hold, scavengers had carted away engines, seats, and wheels, leaving behind only dented bodies and smashed windows. However some cars were safely removed. Dick McMinn witnessed the operation. "They picked the cars up—moored a scow on this side of Effingham, the lee of Effingham Inlet was quiet. Picked the cars up out of the front hold. It was the only hold they could get the cars out, because it was above water. They took all the cars out by helicopter. I don't know how they did it."[20]

About a year later, west-coast storms and seas accomplished the final affront on the *Vanlene*. The main body of the ship broke apart from the bow section, which remained firmly embedded into the shoreline of Austin Island.

The wreck of the *Vanlene* still stirs the memories of many mariners. It was a tourist attraction for many years. "The *Lady Rose*, on its Sunday cruise, used to go between the islands. And when the wreck was there, it was a big tourist attraction. Slowly the ship drifted apart into two pieces, then the skipper used to go through the middle and people would be hanging over the sides."[21]

There were some lighter moments as experienced by John and Kay Monrufet as John skippered the *Lady Rose* between the two pieces of the ship for the amusement of the passengers. John would call out to the wrecked ship and inquire if they needed assistance. One day the joke was on him. Kay tells the story:

> I was on board that day and John was at the wheel, and the deck hand, who was a pal of the young fellow the engineer, who just happened to be John's son, was down below. They had an arrangement for some sort of signal and just as the *Lady Rose* got right in the middle, there was a horrible grating noise. John's face looked startled. And Bill Garden was on board that day too and wondered what's that. We noticed one conspicuous thing, the deck hand had disappeared out of the wheelhouse. He was gone. Then John knew someone was playing a joke on him. He had caught on to it right away.[22]

The grating noise heard up in the wheelhouse had been a sound of a length of heavy chain being pulled over the side of the ship.

There were many things learned from the wreck of the *Vanlene* about oil spills, transportation of oil, and traffic control in coastal waters. To minimise the number of marine mishaps, the Canadian government installed a system known as Vessel Traffic Control, similar to air traffic control systems, to regulate all inbound and outbound marine traffic. Safety measures were also instituted to prevent sea pollution from oil tankers. All ships over ten thousand gross tons were required to have two radar systems capable of operating independently, and all new crude oil tankers over twenty thousand deadweight tons were required to be fitted with separate ballast tanks and a high-pressure spray system for cleaning the tanks.[23]

THE SEDCO *AND THE* OCEAN RANGER

Concerns about oil polluting the west coast of Vancouver Island did not translate into public condemnation of oil drilling until the early eighties when hearings were held and all drilling eventually abandoned. By then exploratory drilling had continued off the coast since the late sixties. The first evidence of this and the business impact of the industry was experienced in Port Alberni in October 1967 when the *Sedco 135-F* drilling rig was towed into the harbour for modifications to its anchor system. "The sight of this sea-going drill rig caused travellers in Barkley Sound and the Alberni Inlet to stare in disbelief at its immense size."[24] The rig had been exploring the continental shelf off Vancouver Island, the Queen Charlotte Islands, and in Hecate Straits.

As the rig entered Barkley Sound, airplanes flew overhead taking in the scene. Guiding the eighty-foot drilling rig through the narrow passages of the Alberni Canal was the task of the vessels *Gulf Joan, Min Tide*, with the *Island Warrior* in the lead, while the *Island Commander* and the *Canadian Tide* towed in reverse keeping the vessel straight on course. The armada slowed to a crawl coming through Sproat Narrows. The RCMP vessel preceded the tow and the *P. F. Stone* acted as guide. This was probably the biggest towing job ever undertaken in the history of the canal to this time.

The *Sedco 135-F*, which cost ten million to construct, was then the largest vessel of its kind in the world. It was owned by Southeastern Commonwealth Drilling Ltd. of Calgary and Dallas, and leased to Shell Canada Ltd. for its drilling operations on the coast.

By May, 1969, the *Sedco* had been stripped down to its bare essentials, ready to embark on a six hundred thousand dollar cruise to New Zealand. A thousand tons of equipment had been removed and a steady flow of repair parts, water, and groceries had been loaded. The next project was offshore drilling around New Zealand for Todd Oil Services and Shell B. P.[25] Another *Sedco*, the *708*, made a winter lay up in Port Alberni in 1977-1978. This rig had been drilling in Kodiak, Alaska.[26]

One year later, in December 1978, another rig entered the sound. It was the ill-fated *Ocean Ranger*, then the largest oil-drilling rig in the world, having eclipsed the size of the *Sedco 135-F*. The rig was 340 feet high with a length of nearly four hundred feet and a width of 298 feet. At maximum draft its displacement was 38,940 tons. The rig is remembered for its unfortunate capsizing February 15, 1982, off the southeast coast of St. John's, Newfoundland, with a loss of all eighty-four crew members.

Back in 1978 when the *Ocean Ranger* entered the harbour in

Port Alberni, it was a sight to behold, almost dwarfing the mountains on either side of the canal. During the Christmas season, the huge rig lit up the harbour like a giant Christmas tree. Power for the rig, for drilling and ocean voyages, came from four diesel engines, each generating 3,400 horsepower. The future looked bright for the engineering firms in Port Alberni who hoped to see increased business in servicing the oil rigs operating on the west coast.

Living quarters had space for one hundred men, but while in Port Alberni, only nine men manned the rig, including Captain Peter Bamber who controlled the massive vessel from a small bridge. The rig had made the trip by itself from the Gulf of Alaska, making eight knots on a good day. Stiff head-winds could bring it to a standstill even though it was considered immune to wind and wave. Its platform was roughly the size of three football fields, above two pontoons joined to it by eight legs.

> The supporting columns rest on two huge pontoons underwater, two columns to a pontoon. These contain ballast tanks, which, when flooded or emptied, lower or raise the entire rig. The rig can sink until its draft is 80 feet. Even high seas pass harmlessly underneath the main platform, with nothing more to push against than the supporting columns. The *Ocean Ranger* can withstand 100-foot waves and 100-knot winds, a full-blown hurricane.[27]

The *Ocean Ranger* was considered one of the safest rigs built, but it became the second rig to sink, the first being one lost in the South China Sea in 1979. There were many theories why it sank with such a tragic loss of life. One said human error; another said it was struck and holed by a Soviet cargo ship which sank a day later; another believed it was battered by "100-year storms," the worst of the century.[28] Whatever the theory, no one could dispute this was no dinky vessel; it was a super rig, reinforced to withstand heavy winds and waves. Owners Ocean Drilling and Exploration Co. of New Orleans,[29] had the rig built at Hiroshima, because Mitsubishi happened to be the leader in development of cold-stressed steel.

The *Ocean Ranger* was launched in traditional Japanese fashion and ceremony. In May, 1976, bands played and flags fluttered at dockside at Hiroshima, as crowds gathered to launch the oil rig. The company that built it, Mitsubishi Heavy Industries, was proud of the work done. The future looked bright for oil-rig construction. As a tape was cut, balloons and white doves soared over the rig, and slowly the *Ocean Ranger* was pulled away from dockside by two tugs. A man jumped on stage shouting *Banzai!* meaning "long life" and the crowd joined in the chorus.

The party moved to a hotel where a cask of rice wine sat in the foyer. A man in traditional Japanese dress jumped on the cask and smashed the lid with a blow from a wooden hammer. Sake splashed on the floor and the audience burst into applause. The ceremony, called *kagami wari*, is staged to celebrate a ship launching and other festivals. The guests rushed to get square wooden cups, made for the occasion and salted to ward off bad luck. Only after the cups had been filled with wine and slowly emptied was the *Ocean Ranger* truly launched.[30]

The *Ocean Ranger's* maiden voyage crossed the Pacific Ocean to the Gulf of Alaska. It "sea-crawled" across the ocean under its own power, driven along at maximum six knots by gigantic propellers in its pontoons. It made the three-thousand-mile journey in thirty days. The Gulf of Alaska became its base for two years. Then in 1978 it lifted anchors and moved south past the Queen Charlotte Islands, south to Barkley Sound and up the Alberni Canal to Port Alberni.

Alberni Valley Times reporter Carl Vesterback visited the rig and was impressed with its size. He described his visit:

> The tug which had brought us out to the rig had seemed big to a landlubber. It was a flyspeck beside the Ranger. Four enormous columns supported the main platform 150 feet above us. The derrick itself towered another 190 feet above that. We were expected, and as the tug backed in to the rig's northeast corner, a crane on the platform lowered a flimsy-looking basket to carry our party of seven aboard. No elevator, no stairs, Just this basket.
>
> Not wanting to think too much, I jumped onto the basket in the first group of four people. Feet on a ring on the bottom, hands locked in a terror-inspired grip around rope netting, we

were whisked over 150 feet into the air, swung over the platform and lowered to the deck. Once aboard, Captain Peter Bamber welcomed us with coffee and sympathy as eyes slowly unglazed and fingers loosened. Finally, when we could all function again, we started off on the tour.[31]

After the tour and some more coffee, it was time to return to the basket for the final invigorating swing over the side down to the waiting tug. "Willie, the gentle giant from Louisiana, who works the crane, put us down gently on the tug's stern and waved goodbye. 'Y'all come back now, heah?'"

After the modifications were made in Port Alberni, the rig began an epic journey, 14,500 miles in 120 days, around both American continents to Baltimore Canyon, a trench off the New Jersey coast. There drilling continued for five months before the rig was towed to Porcupine Basin off the Irish coast, where seas were as rough as any experienced. The *Ocean Ranger* had travelled all this distance without incident, and industry still regarded it as the ultimate in oil rig design.

In October 1980 the *Ocean Ranger* finally reached the Hibernia oil fields off Newfoundland, where a consortium of oil companies had waited a year for the rig. Over the next two years it moved several times to different locations in Hibernia. Work about the rig was dirty and boring, isolation being the biggest problem for crews away from home for weeks at a time. Towards the fateful day there was growing criticism about safety, lack of adequate maintenance and insufficient training procedures. There were warning signs of things to come when only one week before the disaster, the oil rig developed a sudden list of five degrees and the crew was ordered to the lifeboat. Not only could the lifeboat not accommodate all the crew but most of the crew were not wearing life preservers, and the lifeboat motor would not start. Alarms bells should have rung but did not. The list was corrected and the problem attributed to human error; someone had opened the wrong valve and let too much water into a pontoon. A week later the *Ocean Ranger* vanished taking eighty-four men with it.

There was a sense of sadness when news of the *Ocean Ranger* disaster reached Port Alberni. Many remembered its bright lights in the harbour, others recalled their association with the workings of the giant rig. The terrible lost of life was regretted by everyone. The *Ocean Ranger* had travelled thousands of miles, through strong winds and treacherous seas, after leaving Port Alberni's quiet, safe harbour.

A subsequent royal commission found that the rig toppled because of design flaws and inadequate training of the crew. It said workers might have been saved with better safety education, survival suits, and adequate lifeboats.

The demise of the *Ocean Ranger* has not stopped Newfoundland's offshore oil boom, but it has forced stricter regulations and safety procedures. The biggest test has come with the huge *Hibernia* platform in place. The *Ocean Ranger* had been nicknamed the Cadillac of rigs; the *Hibernia* is now dubbed one of the wonders of the world.[32]

FORESTRY CAPITAL OF CANADA

In 1986, Port Alberni was declared the Forestry Capital of Canada. Mayor Gillian Trumper planted MacMillan Bloedel Ltd.'s sixty-millionth seedling in the region; truck loggers paraded the latest in forestry equipment through the streets of the city; it was a giant celebration during the heady days of Expo year in Vancouver and British Columbia. There was no one in Port Alberni who did not believe their future in forestry seemed secure. MB's chief forester assured there were still fifty-five years of old growth timber left at current harvest levels. When that was gone, the future of the industry would depend on how well the second growth compared to the standards of the old growth forests.

Port Alberni has a long history of forestry beginning with the Anderson Sawmill in 1860. In many ways, the history of the region has been tied to the forest industry, beginning with the first rough lumber cut for ship spars, and shipped in sailing ships to ports around the world. The second venture, the first paper mill in the province, the British Columbia Paper Manufacturing Co. lasted only four years before it was disbanded. But early pioneers recognised the forests could be made to produce an economic product. Many made their living from small sawmills and logging.

The emergence in 1904 of the Barclay Sound Cedar Company

sawmill gave the first continuity in the industry, providing valuable jobs in the community. The mill had changed hands a few times before Harvey Reginald MacMillan purchased it in 1936. Another company, Bloedel, Stewart & Welch was firmly entrenched in the Albernis, having a sawmill at Great Central Lake and extensive timber rights at Franklin River. To harvest this forest, the company built the Somass sawmill, a shingle mill, and developed the Franklin River Logging Camp, all during the Depression.

The Second World War brought more growth to the city with MacMillan's plywood plant in 1941, built to satisfy a wartime demand for waterproof bonded Douglas-fir plywood. After the war, Bloedel, Stewart & Welch added a pulp mill and opened up Sarita River logging. The city and the region were booming. In 1951, the merger of these two competitive forest industry giants became one of the world's largest forest companies, MacMillan Bloedel Ltd.

In 1978, the old Alberni Pacific sawmill was replaced with a fifty-million-dollar mill; the plywood mill was modernised, and newsprint machines were added to the pulp mill. By 1981, MB's Alberni Valley operations had a total of 5,600 hourly and staff people of the community's total population of twenty-five thousand with a gross payroll of $157 million. The company slogan "Here today and here tomorrow" provided assurance good fortunes would continue.

In the business world nothing is forever, and it was this way with MacMillan Bloedel Ltd. Noranda, the company that had mined the ore at Toquart, succeeded in amassing just under fifty per cent of MB shares. It in turn lost controlling interest in its own company to the giant Brascan. MB regionalized, giving decision-making power to regional managers and taking it out of the hands of plant managers. As the operations were restructured, MB became a much leaner and a more cost-effective organization, which needed fewer employees. The early eighties recession sharply reduced demand for forestry products, and compounding the problem, higher interest rates curtailed any recovery. The company needed millions to modernise its plants if it was to survive.

There were warning signs in the early eighties that land use issues would arise. The Nuu-chah-nulth Tribal Council had found a voice and used it to condemn the company's forest practices and the lack of funds for reforestation from the province and federal government. Slash burning, clear-cut logging, and management of the land, the "multiple-use dilemma," were all cause for concern. Some forest analysts predicted that by the year 2000, as many as a hundred forest-based communities would be threatened with survival. Old loggers could easily tell what was happening to the forest; the trees were not as big as when they first started logging; they were going higher up the mountains, and all that was left was decadent wood.

When MB decided to log Meares Island, the little island within view of Tofino, it opened up an environmental Pandora's Box. The company had a cutting permit awarded by the provincial cabinet after three years of work by a planning team trying to harmonize conflicting viewpoints. The Ahousat and Clayoquot bands claimed the island as part of their aboriginal land claims. Environmentalists joined in the Native protest, and the whole issue ended up in the Supreme Court of Canada. From a public relations point of view, it was a disaster for MB. Television crews only heightened the confrontation.

Images of people blocking logging roads and being arrested by police were shown in daily news reports around the world, but there was little in-depth investigative reporting on the issues surrounding forestry in British Columbia. The world witnessed the largest mass arrest in Canadian history when more than eight hundred people were charged for defying a court order against disrupting MB operations. MB attempted unsuccessfully to counter the bad image being portrayed for its logging practices. There would be no logging on Meares Island, or in the Walbran or Carmanah forest, and only limited logging in Clayoquot Sound.

This historical essay has focused on Barkley Sound and the Alberni Canal, but issues in Clayoquot Sound to the north had major ramifications throughout the entire Alberni-Clayoquot Regional District, particularly in Port Alberni and Ucluelet, where loggers and sawmill workers and their families lived.

Today, MB logging operations at Kennedy Lake, Franklin River, and Sarita are either merged, gone, or drastically reduced. Logging contractors have laid off crews. Loggers are taking computer courses instead of cutting down trees; others are being counselled on how to start a new career at age forty-five or fifty-five. The future does indeed look bleak for forestry within the region. There have, however, been cyclical downturns in the past; Ucluelet and Port Alberni have survived, and will do so again. There is a scientific panel at work giving advice to government on how best to use the forest. While Natives are busy negotiating land claims settlements, they are also seeking a deal between green groups and forestry companies. How all the issues within the region will be resolved remains to be seen. H. R. MacMillan once said, "The forest is by far the most important crop to the public, now and for the long pull." As the fortunes of forestry go, so goes the province.

EPILOGUE

The people who journeyed to the west coast of Canada came from many lands; they travelled great distances seeking a future in the new world. Banfield, who had been at sea all his life, saw the opportunity of acquiring a small piece of land on which to spend the rest of his life. His greatest concern was that the government would not recognise his land transaction with the Natives.

The Roman Catholic missionaries, the Methodists, the Presbyterians and the Shantymen came hoping to make a difference in the lives of the First Nations people and to convert them to Christianity while serving the needs of the first settlers.

The miners came looking for gold, copper, and other minerals, having given up hope in the Cariboo, Klondike, and California gold rushes. Few made any money. Mine after mine reached the production point only to be stymied by insufficient product. The miners abandoned their dreams and settled in small communities like Alberni, Ucluelet and Bamfield, and points along the canal.

Fishermen had an easier time, for there was an abundance of marine life and few fishing restrictions. The whalers arrived from Norway and Newfoundland and they shared the skill of hunting whales.

Farmers were seen as desirable settlers, but on the west coast there was not much arable land free of trees. Some settled in Ucluelet, most others in the Alberni Valley.

The Bamfield Cable Station brought immigrants from Australia and New Zealand, and other relay stations around the globe, in an effort to establish the greatest communication network, the "all red route." These gentlemen of the British Empire were some of the first settlers in the small coastal village.

Others saw opportunities in the great forests that marched down the mountainsides to sea level; sawmills, shingle mills, and logging camps were built to capitalize on the resource. A man could make a living cutting a few trees up a hillside then float them down the canal to the sawmill. British Columbia's largest forest integrated community developed at Port Alberni.

Throughout the past century coastal steamers and mail boats kept settlers linked geographically and socially. These gallant little ships were bright lights in an otherwise remote existence until roads were built.

All arrived on the west coast with great expectations that they could put down roots, farm the land, harvest the sea, or develop a business in a new land full of opportunity. Most spoke English, others came from countries around the world.

Today, the area faces many challenges. There is increased pressure for commercial development and recreational opportunities. Statistics from 1993 show there are currently about twenty-two thousand people living in the Barkley Sound-Alberni Canal area. The shoreline of the region is not as isolated as it once was. There are almost one hundred float cabins tied up a various spots, the largest concentration being at Julia Passage and Kildonan. Today float planes make regular flights into Bamfield. Recreational fishing camps dot the inlet and sound, and fish charter vessels ply the waters. The *Lady Rose* and the *Francis Barkley* continue to make regular scheduled visits to Bamfield and Ucluelet and all points in between. Pacific Rim Highway to the west coast carries hundreds of thousands of tourists yearly, and the partially paved road to Bamfield gets its own share of traffic.

Port Alberni is the mainstay, or service centre of the region, and the dropping-off place for those embarking on hiking, canoeing, or kayaking adventures on the coast. Recreation development sites are located at Newcombe Channel, Haggard Cove, Mayne Bay and Headquarters Bay. There is increased pressure to release crown land for recreational cottages. Those applications have so far been rejected.

Trevor Channel and the Alberni Canal continue to be the main navigational channels for ships coming to and from Stamp Harbour in Port Alberni. With freighters becoming larger and larger, there has been a decline in the number of ships now navigating the channel; however, the increase in recreational boaters more than makes up for the loss.

The forest industry continues to be an important fact of life in the region and is the driving engine of the economy. New forestry practices, environment issues, and decreases in log allocation within the Alberni-Clayoquot Region, have reduced the work force considerably.

Commercial fishermen now find it increasingly difficult to make a living from the sea. They must cope with changing regulations, declining stocks, and unpredictable markets. It is unlikely that employment levels in fishing will return to those experienced in earlier times.

There are now eight recreational lodges within Barkley Sound: Barkley Sound Resort at Congreve Island; Seacrest and Kildonan Cannery Lodges at Kildonan; Ocean Sport Enterprises at Cigarette Cove; Effingham Lodge at Jane Bay; Canadian King Lodge at Robbers Passage, Tzartus Island; Murphy's Lodge at Sunshine Bay; Rendezvous Dive Charters at Rainy Bay; and Pinkerton Island Resorts at Pinkerton Islands. As well as hotels in each community there are also moorage and campground facilities at Poett Nook and Murphy Bay, plus marinas at Ucluelet, Bamfield, China Creek and Port Alberni.

The biggest change has been within the Native population as it struggles to settle land claims with federal and provincial governments and to cope with high unemployment.

Port Alberni has also changed. Amalgamation in 1967 joined two cities into one. Some old-timers still refer to "old town" Alberni, today the North Port district of Port Alberni. The pulp mill has closed and with it has gone the smell, or as some once put it, "The smell of money." Today the modernised plant produces fine paper for world markets. The plywood plant has been demolished after sitting empty for a number of years, but two sawmills still produce lumber for markets around the world.

In conclusion, each of the first economic attractions to the west coast, fur trading, seal hunting, whaling, fishing, mining, and logging, had its heyday as man exploited the area's natural resources and adapted to the west-coast environment. Canneries and salteries disappeared as fish processing technology improved. Communities that once thrived from resource development now rely on tourism to generate jobs. To develop the area economically while maintaining the balance of nature and man's desire will require vision and imagination. The life journeys of the men and women who pioneered the last frontier of Canada are not forgotten.

APPENDIX ONE

PLACE NAME GUIDE

This list has been assembled as an easy reference place name guide. It is by no means a complete list of all of the places within the Alberni Inlet and Barkley Sound, but it does contain places relevant to this manuscript. The author acknowledges the research of R. Bruce Scott, the Alberni District Historical Society, Dale Schroeder, and the Barkley Sound Planning Committee.

AGUILAR POINT: Location: Tip of Mills Peninsula on the east side of Trevor Channel at Bamfield. Named for Captain Henry Aguilar, RN Second Master, Navigating Officer of HM gunboat *Grappler* that transported Captain Richards on his survey of Barkley Sound in 1861.

ALBERNI INLET/CANAL: Location: Northeast of Barkley Sound. Named in 1791 by Lieutenant Francisco Eliza to honour Don Pedro de Alberni. Name was changed in 1933 to waylay fears of shipping captains it was a man-made canal and fees would be levied.

ANDERSON LAKE/RIVER: Location: Head of Uchucklesit Inlet. Name changed to Henderson Lake/River. The origin of the first name is unknown, although it was presumably named for the Anderson Company, owners of the Alberni townsite in 1860.

ALBERNI: Location: Head of Alberni Inlet. The original townsite of Alberni was named in 1861. The *British Colonist* reported on May 31: "Captain Stamp's place has been named Alberni by the Survey." This was the site of the Anderson Mill. In 1886 when settlers arrived, a community developed two miles north. This became the old town of Alberni, incorporated in 1913.

AMPHITRITE POINT: Location: South point of Ucluth Peninsula at Ucluelet. Named for the frigate HM *Amphitrite.*

AUSTIN ISLAND: Location: West side of Imperial Eagle Channel, south of Effingham Island.

BAMFIELD: Location: West and east sides of Bamfield Inlet. Named for William Eddy Banfield who settled here in 1859 and became Government Agent. He explored Barkley Sound and the Alberni Inlet providing valuable ethnological information on the Native population and geographical data of the surrounding area. He died in 1862. Some say he drowned; others claim he was murdered. The "n" became "m" through common usage. Population—516 (1996).

BAMFIELD INLET/CREEK: Location: Inlet location east of Trevor Channel and Mills Peninsula. Creek on the east shore of Bamfield Inlet. Both named for William Eddy Banfield.

BARKLEY SOUND: Largest sound on the west coast of Vancouver Island. Divided into three channels, Loudoun, Imperial Eagle and Trevor Channel. Contains Broken Group Islands. Named in 1787 by and for Captain Charles William Barkley of the British trading ship *Imperial Eagle.*

BENSON ISLAND: Location: In the Broken Group Islands, north of Coaster Channel. Named for John W. Benson who settled there in 1893. Named changed from Hawkins Island in 1933 to reflect original owner.

BRABANT ISLANDS: Location: In the Broken Group Islands, north of Peacock Channel. Named for Reverend A. J. Brabant, a Flemish Oblate father who established a mission at Hesquiat in 1875.

CAPE BEALE: Location: A rocky headland at the entrance to Barkley Sound. The first lighthouse on the west coast was constructed here in 1787 and named for John Beale, the purser on the trading ship *Imperial Eagle*. Beale and his crew were killed by Natives in a small river near Destruction Island the same year.

CHINA CREEK: Location: Creek drains into east side of Alberni Inlet near Underwood Cove south of Port Alberni. Originally known as Gold Creek for the Chinese who panned for gold in the 1860s. The creek later became the site of extensive prospecting around 1890 and several mines were located nearby.

CLARKE ISLAND: Location: Broken Group Island, north of Coaster Channel. Named for William R. Clarke. It was here the owner of the island, built a lodge and got tired of cutting salal. He imported a few goats with the hope they would graze on the salal. The goats swam off never to be seen again.

CLO-OOSE: Location: Midway between Port Renfrew and Bamfield on the west coast. Originally home to 400 warriors of the Nitinaht tribe. The isolated village became a real estate developer's dream that failed to materialize. Prospective buyers came from around the world to settle in this promoted utopia, only to find they had to battle rough sea, heavy rainfall and endless fog. Few stayed; most moved on to Victoria or Bamfield. The beach became known for treacherous landings from the steamer *Princess Maquinna*.

COLEMAN CREEK: Location: Flows into the east side of Alberni Inlet. Location of early Alberni Pacific Lumber Company logging camp.

CONGREVE ISLAND: Location: East of Tzartus Island, on the east side of Trevor Channel.

COPPER ISLAND: Location: East side of Imperial Eagle Channel. Renamed Tzartus Island in 1933. It was the site of the first attempt at mining in Barkley Sound. Captain Edward Stamp prospected and performed some shafting work on the island. Spring's trading post was located at Clifton Point. It was here the Cox family waited out the weather until they could be transported to Cape Beale lighthouse.

CRAWFORD LAKE: Location: North of Sechart Channel. Named for Eliza Crawford, wife of Mason Anderson and the mother of prospector Captain James Crawford Anderson. Anderson's unique residence at Sechart was admired throughout the Sound. The picturesque house was constructed of lumber, doors and windows salvaged from shipwrecks.

DIANA ISLAND: Location: West side of Trevor Channel, west of Bamfield. The *Diana* was a steam towboat purchased in San Francisco by Captain Stamp for towing ships in and out of Stamp Harbour for the Anderson Mill.

DODGER COVE/CHANNEL: Location: West side of Diana Island, north of Trevor Channel. For weeks, the schooner *Saucy Lass* waited out a storm in Barkley Sound, "dodging the weather." When charting the waters, Captain Richards learned from Captain Pamphlet that "it was a fine place to dodge the weather in," he declared that should be its name. Father Brabant conducted the first Roman Catholic mass in the home of storekeeper Andrew Lang who managed Spring's trading post.

ECOOLE: Location: South side of Seddall Island on Rainy Bay. Trading post and fish curing plant located here. In 1889 dogfish oil was being processed. Butterfield Mackie and Co. built a saltery and smokehouse in 1916. For several decades various companies processed fish. There was a store, post office and school.

EDWARD KING ISLAND: Location: West side of Trevor Channel, south of Diana Island. Named for Captain Edward Hammond King who was accidentally shot on the island while on a hunting expedition. He was the founder of the *New Westminster Times* and the *Victoria Gazette*. He died three days later *en route* to Alberni where he was buried.

EFFINGHAM ISLAND: Location: Broken Group Islands south of Coaster Channel. Originally named Village Island. The Geographic Board of Canada changed the island name in 1905. Captain Meares named the Island in 1788 in honour of the Third Earl of Effingham, the Rt. Hon. Thomas Howard. Reverend Melvin Swartout and company made a historic journey to the island in 1896 to preach to the Tseshaht who had a village on the northeast side.

EXECUTION ROCK: Location: Eastern shore of Trevor Channel, south of Bamfield. Site of the original Ohiaht summer village of Keeshan. A feud between the Ohiaht and the Clallam almost eliminated the Ohiaht tribe. The rock takes its name from the resulting slaughter.

FLEMING ISLAND: Location: West side of Trevor Channel, and south west of Tzartus Island. Named to honour Sir Sandford Fleming who persisted and against all odds, brought the All Red Route, a British Empire round-the-world communication system, to a successful conclusion. Bamfield Cable Station was part of that system. The cable arrived in Bamfield in 1902.

FLORENCIA BAY: Location: Northwest of Ucluelet between Qusitis Point and Wya Point. Name changed from Wreck Beach where black sands held placer gold deposits and yielded promises of gold.

FRANKLIN RIVER: Location: Flows into the Alberni Inlet on the east side at Stamp Narrows. Two large logging camps were located here to serve the Bloedel, Stewart & Welch sawmill in Port Alberni.

GEORGE FRASER ISLANDS: Location: South of Ucluelet Inlet. Named for renowned horticulturist George Fraser who settled in Ucluelet and developed a large garden and nursery of trees and shrubs.

GRAPPLER INLET: Location: East of Bamfield Inlet and Trevor Channel. Named after HM gunboat *Grappler* that transported Captain Richards in the 1861 survey of Barkley Sound.

GREEN COVE: Location: East side of Uchucklesit Inlet, near Kildonan.

HAMMOND PASSAGE: Location: East of Imperial Eagle Channel and northwest of Cape Beale. Another area named for Captain Edward Hammond King who died tragically from gunshot wounds in 1861.

HAWKINS ISLAND: Location: Broken Group Islands, north of Coaster Channel. Original name of Benson Island.

HAYES LANDING: Location: West side of Alberni Inlet, half a mile south of Nahmint Bay and 14 miles from Port Alberni. Named for Colonel G. H. Hayes of the Nahmint Mining Company, Portland, Oregon, who developed a mine at this site. In 1898 120 tons of ore were shipped containing copper, gold and silver.

HEADQUARTERS: Location: South of Underwood Cove on the east side of the Alberni Inlet. The site of a large construction camp for the Canadian Northern Railway which attempted to build a railway from Victoria to Port Alberni prior to the First World War.

HELLS GATE: Location: Pocahontas Point on the west side of the Alberni Inlet. The channel narrows and deepens to about 163 fathoms. Here the *Pocahontas* anchored during a violent winter storm in 1862 and the crew painted the words Pocahontas '62 on the rock face. Natives believed a monster described as a whale lived here. They named it Klu-quilth-soh.

HENDERSON LAKE/RIVER: Location: Northeast of Barkley Sound, and west of the Alberni Inlet. Named for Captain John Henderson, skipper of the *Woodpecker*, who transported the machinery to the Anderson Mill in 1860. Original named Anderson Lake/River. Henderson Lake has the highest rainfall in Canada. The greatest 24 hour rainfall recorded was over 16 inches.

HILLIER ISLAND: Location: West end of Pipestem Inlet, east of Toquart Bay. Named for Ucluelet pioneer, Herbert J. Hillier, who arrived in 1898 and served as government lineman and agent for fifty years. The Island is an important waterfowl migration and wintering area.

IMPERIAL EAGLE CHANNEL: Location: Middle channel of Barkley Sound. Named for the *Imperial Eagle*, the ship commanded by Captain William Barkley.

KVARNO ISLAND: Location: North end of Ucluelet Inlet. Named for Norwegian John Hartwick Kvarno, a pioneer who settled and farmed in Ucluelet.

KILDONAN: Location: North side of Uchucklesit Inlet. Site of the largest fish processing plant on the west coast. The Wallace Brothers changed the original name to Kildonan after their hometown in Scotland. Their company, Wallace Fisheries, built a small community complete with electric light, water and sewage system. It had its own store and school plus accommodation for Native and oriental workers. The cannery buildings and wharves were demolished and burned in 1962.

LINK ISLAND: Location: Junction of Imperial Eagle Channel and Junction Passage. An unsuccessful attempt was made to establish a fox farm on the Island in 1925.

LONE TREE POINT: Location: Stamp Narrows on Alberni Inlet.

LOUDOUN CHANNEL: Location: West side of Barkley Sound. Named for the original name of Captain Barkley's ship, the *Loudoun*, later renamed *Imperial Eagle*.

MAGGIE LAKE: Location: Southeast of Kennedy Lake, west of Toquart Bay. Rich ore deposits found in the area led to the establishment of Noranda's Brynor Mine in 1962. Ore processed here was shipped through Toquart Bay to Japan.

MONITOR LANDING: Location about 18 miles south of Port Alberni. The Monitor mine, located here at the turn of the century, shipped 992 tons of copper ore to the Tacoma smelter and employed about 20 men.

NAHMINT BAY/RIVER: Location: Western shore of the Alberni Inlet. Named by the Vancouver Island Exploring Expedition (1863-4) for the Native tribe living in the area. Site of early mining prospecting. In 1894, Frank Garrard and family settled here. Later Nahmint Lodge provided accommodation and hospitality for fishing visitors from around the world.

NEWCOMBE CHANNEL: Location: West side of Barkley Sound. Named for anthropologist Dr. Charles F. Newcombe who studied Natives of the west coast.

NUMUKAMIS BAY: Location: East side of Trevor Channel, opposite Tzartus Island. Father Brabant established a mission at Numukamis, near the mouth of Sarita River. Large population of Ohiahts once lived in the area. The Bay is under environmental protection because of the seabird nesting colony.

PACHENA/BAY/RIVER: Location: Southeast of Barkley Sound. Named for the Natives of the area.

PIPESTEM INLET: Location: East of Toquart Bay, west of Effingham Inlet. It was here the patrol vessel, HMCS *Armentieres* struck an uncharted rock and sank in 1925. She was refloated. Fish and wildlife reserve.

POCAHONTAS ROCK: Location: At Hells Gate. Named for the sailing ship *Pocahontas*, skippered by Captain Cyrus Sears, which anchored here in the winter of 1862 during a storm. A crew member painted the ship's name on the rock.

POETT NOOK: Location: East of Imperial Eagle Channel, south of Christie Bay. Named for Dr. Jos. Henry Poett who arrived in the United States in 1848 aboard the *Virginia*. He had a medical practice in San Francisco and held mining interests on Copper Island (Tzartus). Present site of commercial campground and moorage operation.

POLLY POINT: Location: South end of Port Alberni, east side of Alberni Inlet. Reserve of the Tseshaht; named for Polly, matriarch of the Tseshaht tribe. The first Native woman in the Alberni Valley known to take a white husband. She was a midwife and healer of her people.

PORT ALBERNI: Location: At the head of Alberni Inlet. Incorporated in 1912, it amalgamated with Alberni in 1967. The first two towns in Canada to voluntarily amalgamate. Site of the Anderson sawmill established in 1860. Population 1996—18,669.

PORT ALBION: Location: Northeast side of Ucluelet Inlet. Earliest settlement of Ucluelet. Mission, school and church were located here, as were the Sutton sawmill and later the reduction plant of the Bamfield Packing Company. Emily Carr visited here in 1898 and wrote of her experience. Later incorporated into the Municipality of Ucluelet.

RAINY BAY: Location: Northeast of Tzartus Island. Present site of private recreational subdivision and dive charter operation.

RITHERDON BAY: Location: East side of Trevor Channel. Site of early Japanese salmon saltery.

SANFORD ISLAND: Location: East side of Imperial Eagle Channel, southwest of Fleming Island. Named for Sir Sanford Fleming, Chief Engineer of the Canadian Pacific Railway. See also Fleming Island.

SAN MATEO: Location: East side of Trevor Channel. Site of early fish processing operations. Japanese had boat building operation here until Second World War evacuation.

SANTA MARIA ISLAND: Location: Southwest of Sarita River and east of Tzartus Island. Large shellfish resource.

SARITA BAY/RIVER: Location: East side of Trevor Channel, between Christie Bay and Poett Nook. River flows into Numukamis

Bay. Site of winter encampment for the Ohiahts, also Roman Catholic mission. Sarita Logging Camp established here to salvage trees infested by hemlock looper. The Sarita River estuary is rich in fish and waterfowl. Trumpeter swans over-winter in the marshes.

SECHART: Location: Equis Beach north of the Broken Group Islands, near the entrance to Pipestem Inlet. The site of the first whaling station on the west coast established in 1905.

SNUG BASIN: Location: Head of Uchucklesit Inlet and site of early mining ventures. Location of boom and dumping forestry operations.

SPRING COVE: Location: West side of Ucluelet Inlet. Named for Captain William Spring who established a trading station in the area in 1869.

STAPLEBY: Location: Pioneer settlement at the head of Ucluelet arm with its own post office, store and school.

STUART BAY: Location: East side of Ucluelet Inlet. Named for Captain Charles Edward Stuart, of Nanaimo, who established a trading post at this location in 1860.

SWISS BOY ISLAND: Location: East side of Imperial Eagle Channel, west of Tzartus Island. Named for the US brig *Swiss Boy* incident (1859), in which the ship was seized and pillaged by Natives when it sought anchor for repairs. Captain and crew were held prisoner for several days before being allowed to leave.

THIEPVAL CHANNEL: Location: Broken Group Islands, north and east of Turret Island. Named for patrol vessel, HMCS *Thiepval* which in 1930 struck an uncharted rock in the middle of the channel and sank.

TOQUART BAY: Location: West side of Barkley Sound, at north end. Site of Brynnor Mine ore shipping operation in the sixties. Ministry of Forests recreation reserve.

TREVOR CHANNEL: Location: East side of Barkley Sound. Named for Frances Hornby Trevor, wife of Captain Barkley who discovered the Sound in 1787. Main shipping channel for the Alberni Inlet. San Jose Islets in Numukamis Bay have a seabird nesting colony.

TURTLE ISLAND: Location: Broken Group Islands, north east of Turret Island. Salal Joe settled here making a living by collecting salal in bundles and shipping to Vancouver markets. He became known to fishermen and boaters as "the Mayor of the Broken Group."

TZARTUS ISLAND: Location: East side of Imperial Eagle Channel near north end. Previously known as Copper Island. Site of early mining activity and Captain Spring's trading post at Clifton Point. Anderson Company attempted to start a mine here in the early 1860s.

UCHUCKLESIT INLET: Location: North of entrance to the Alberni Inlet. Named for the Uchucklesaht tribe that frequented the area. A prime fish and wildlife habitat. Post office and wharf at Kildonan visited by *Lady Rose*. Inlet used for forestry booming grounds. Old townsite of Barclay on west side. There are 27 float cabins located in the inlet.

UCLUELET: Location: West shore of Ucluelet Inlet. Named for the Yuclutl-ahts tribe. Words mean "People with a safe landing place." First settled by former Hudson's Bay Company employee from Nanaimo, Captain Charles Edward Stuart, who had a trading post. Village grew in importance as major fishing and logging centre. Population 1996—1,658.

UNDERWOOD COVE: Location: South of China Creek and north of Franklin River on east side of Alberni Inlet. Named for Walter Underwood who came to work at the Anderson sawmill. He married Polly of the Tseshaht tribe. Site of early logging camp.

VERNON BAY: Location: East of mouth of Effingham Inlet. Fishermen found skeleton of sea creature thought to be a sea serpent. Verified later as a large basking shark.

VILLAGE ISLAND: Location: Broken Group Islands, south of Coaster Channel. Named changed to Effingham Island. Large summer reserve of the Tseshaht tribe located here. Named by Captain Barkley during his exploration of Barkley Sound because of the large Native village. The Reverend Melvin Swartout and Alfred Carmichael made their memorable canoe journey here from Ucluelet in 1896.

WELD ISLAND: Location: East side of Imperial Eagle Channel, west of Tzartus Island. Fox farm located here during the twenties. See Link Island.

WRECK BAY: Location: Northwest of Ucluelet, south of Long Beach. Name changed to Florencia Bay. Site of early gold mining activity believed discovered by Captain Binns in the late 1890s.

OTHER INFORMATION ABOUT THE AREA

- Fifty-five salmon-bearing streams
- 100 bald eagle nests
- 18 seabird colonies
- Herring spawning northern shore of Loudon Channel
- Important eel grass and kelp beds
- 30 sites for harbour seals, California & Stellar sea lions
- Two wildlife species endangered
  —Trumpeter swans and Marbled Murrelet
- One ecological reserve at Baeria Rocks, Imperial Eagle Channel.
  —53 hectare seabird colony & subtidal marine life
  —237 breeding pairs of three species
- 29 shellfish leases and four fish farm leases
- several seaweed culture operations
- 376 recorded archaeological sites
- 38 recorded "culturally modified trees"

APPENDIX TWO

CHRONOLOGY

1787—Captain Charles William Barkley with trading ship *Imperial Eagle* sailed into Barkley Sound.

1791—Alberni Canal/Inlet named to honour Don Pedro de Alberni, a lieutenant-colonel with the Spanish navy who led the Spanish Catalonian troops to Nootka Sound.

1859—William Eddy Banfield settled in Bamfield, became agent for the Colonial Secretary in the region. Provided valuable ethnological and geographical information.

1860—The *Meg Merrilies* transported workmen to the head of the Alberni Canal to construct the Anderson Sawmill.

1861—Captain Edward Hammond King fatally injured in a shooting accident while hunting in Barkley Sound.

—Victoria newspaper reported sawmill settlement had been named Alberni.

—Captain G. H. Richards surveyed Barkley Sound.

1862—Word reached Victoria of Banfield's death by drowning. There were conflicting versions of what happened. Native was brought to trial and acquitted.

1864—Anderson Sawmill closed due to shortage of available timber. Charles Taylor stayed on in Alberni to manage the Anderson Farm.

1867—Anderson Company agent, Gilbert Malcolm Sproat, complained to Colonial Secretary about the hostile and unfriendly attitude of Natives towards west coast traders.

1871—Anderson Company land finally surveyed in Alberni. Other surveys conducted in 1881 and 1886.

1874—Cape Beale lighthouse completed and a trail made to the head of Bamfield Inlet.

1875—Father A. J. Brabant established Hesquiat mission and another at Numukamis.

1878—Cox family arrived at Cape Beale to take on lightkeeping duties.

1881—Harry Guillod appointed the first Indian Agent for the West Coast Agency. Opened office in Ucluelet.

1883—Settlers began arriving in the Alberni Valley.

1888—Wreck of the *Woodside* created mystery as conflicting reports emerged about the disappearance of baby Albert Waring.

1890—Presbyterian mission opened at Ucluelet with the Reverend J. A. MacDonald.

1892—Gus Cox made special constable with the British Columbia Provincial Police. In 1904 he is appointed chief constable for the West Coast District.

—George Bird sailed the *Lily* single-handed to Alberni.

—Barclay Townsite planned.

1894—Mining boom in region.

—John Webb Benson built hotel on Hawkins Island.

1894—George Fraser started nursery business in Ucluelet and became celebrated horticulturist.

1896—Alfred Carmichael and Reverend Melvin Swartout made missionary journey from Ucluelet to Village Island.

1902—Bamfield Cable Station constructed. Trans-Pacific Cable laid creating a round-the-world communication system. People began settling in Bamfield. Lifeboat stationed here.

1905—Sechart Whaling Station established.

1910—Kildonan is site of largest fish processing plant in the region, operated by Wallace Fisheries. Start of fishing bonanza; other canneries and fish processing plants followed.

1911—Stone shipyards established. Brothers Doug and Percy Stone took over mail run to Bamfield and Ucluelet. Began famous *Victory* fleet.

1912—Port Alberni incorporated.

1913—Alberni incorporated.

—*Princess Maquinna* maiden voyage to Port Alberni.

1919—Eberts Fishing Inquiry into the declining fish stock in Barkley Sound held in Port Alberni.

1934—Franklin River logging camp opened to serve Bloedel, Stewart & Welch sawmill in Port Alberni.

1937—Dorothy Blackmore became first Canadian women to hold a master mariner certificate. With father, operated pilot boat service on Canal.

1939—World War II. Region prepared for war. Seaplane base established at Ucluelet; Army camp in Port Alberni.

1941—Captain Richard Porritt's *Uchuck I* began serving logging and fishing camps and coastal communities.

1942—Estevan lighthouse shelled. Japanese evacuated from region.

1945—War ended. Communities returned to normal. Military camps closed.

1946—Essen Young and George McCandless purchased *Uchuck* business and formed the Barkley Sound Transportation Company. They added *Uchuck II* and *Uchuck III* to service.

1948—Sarita River logging camp founded to harvest bug-infested timber.

1950—Alice Riley continued pilot boat service when husband drowned at sea.

1952—Ucluelet became Village municipality.

1959—Road opened from Alberni to west coast.

1960—Partners Dick McMinn and John Monrufet purchased the *Lady Rose*. Ship began long career servicing Ucluelet and Bamfield.

1962—Noranda opened mine at Toquart Bay.

1964—Earthquake in Alaska caused tidal wave in Alberni Canal. Devastated low-lying areas of Alberni and Port Alberni, and damaged west coast communities.

—Road opened to Bamfield.

1967—Amalgamation of Alberni and Port Alberni.

1971—Pacific Rim National Park opened.

1972—Wreck of the *Vanlene*.

1978—*Ocean Ranger* arrived in Port Alberni for repairs.

1986—Port Alberni declared Forestry Capital of Canada.

APPENDIX THREE

SHIPS AND SHIPPING COMPANIES

Alberni: The 87-foot schooner was the first wooden ship constructed in Alberni in 1861 for the Anderson Company. She was first used in coastal trade but later made a number of voyages to Honolulu.

Archangel: On March 31, 1966, as the lumber carrier loaded packaged lumber, its cargo shifted causing lumber to hail down on longshoremen. One man died, others were injured.

Armentieres: The trawler served the West Coast as a patrol vessel. The ship was stationed at Bamfield.

Boston: On March 23, 1803, while anchored in Nootka Sound, Natives attacked the ship. Twenty-five of her 27 crew were massacred, their heads "arranged in a line" for survivor John R. Jewitt to identify. He and another survivor, John Thompson, became two of some 50 slaves owned by Chief Maquinna.

City of Alberni: This was the last of the beautiful five-masted wooden sailing ships to sail West Coast waters with a cargo of lumber. She was built in 1920 at Hoquiam, Washington. First named the *Vigilant,* the ship was described as a "winged queen of the seas" when she sailed to Honolulu from Puget Sound for the E. K. Wood Lumber Company. She was purchased from her American owners by H. A. "Archie" Stevenson, manager of H. R. MacMillan's shipping subsidiary, the Canadian Transport Company, and came under the Canadian flag as the City of Alberni.

Colonia: The ship laid the underwater cable to Bamfield.

Cutch: Designed in India for the Maharaja of Cutch. Brought to British Columbia in 1890. A schooner-rigged vessel, she was built in 1884 in Bremner and Company of Hull, England. Her registered tonnage was 324 and she was licensed to carry 150 passengers. She first transported mail and passengers between Vancouver and Nanaimo. After being shipwrecked in 1900, she was rebuilt at Seattle in 1901 as the *Jessie Banning* and was placed in service briefly there. Her final service was in Colombia, South America, as the gunboat *Bogota*.

Devastation: The Colonial government sent police with the warship to Bamfield to investigate the death of William Eddy Banfield.

Favourite: A sealing schooner owned by trader Captain Spring.

Fernglen: The Norwegian lumber freighter was the first "motor ship" to load lumber from Port Alberni. She travelled from New York via the Panama Canal in less than twenty days arriving in February, 1931.

Givenchy: The trawler served as a minesweeper during the First World War, then on the Atlantic coast as a Fisheries patrol vessel before being brought to the West Coast to serve Fisheries here.

Haida Brave: The barge was built in 1978 for Kingcome Navigation Co., a subsidiary of MacMillan Bloedel Company. It was self-propelled, self-loading and self-dumping. During the actual dump when the vessel was listed over as far as 30 degrees she was held in place by tugs fore and aft to ensure that the logs were deposited in locations prepared for the purpose.

Hecate, HMS: The Royal Navy survey vessel used by Captain G. H. Richards in charting the West Coast.

Imperial Eagle: Previously named the *Loudoun*, the British trading ship was a fine vessel of 400 tons, ship rigged with 20 guns. The ship sailed from the River Thames, London, England, in August 1786, under Captain Charles William Barkley, and arrived at Nootka in June 1787. Barkley named many of the places in Barkley Sound.

Iris: A twin-screw steamer, 295 feet in length, built in Scotland specifically for servicing submarine cables. She went into service in 1902.

Lady Rose: The ship was built on the River Clyde shipyards in Scotland in 1937 and designed for British Columbia waters. Launched as the *Lady Sylvia,* she was built with a four-stroke, six-cylinder 220-horsepower diesel engine with an oil-operated, re-verse-reduction gearbox. Her dimensions were 105 feet overall by 21-foot beam and 14-foot depth with a 25-ton cargo capacity, with speed of 11 and one-half knots. She steamed into Vancouver Harbour in July 1937 to join the Union Steamship fleet. Her name was changed to the *Lady Rose* as another Canadian vessel already bore the name *Lady Sylvia.* She served the Howe Sound run until 1941 when she was taken over by the military and assigned to run in Barkley Sound between Port Alberni and Ucluelet. After wartime service she served various lower mainland ports. In 1960 she began her present work moving passengers, freight and mail between Port Alberni, Bamfield, Ucluelet and other points in Barkley Sound.

Leonede: A small sloop owned by Captain Peter Francis used by William Eddy Banfield to explore the West Coast.

Lily: The ship was forty feet long and very wide of beam. Her boiler was set in brick. She was previously owned by Robert Dunsmuir and used in the construction of the Esquimalt Drydock. She was turned over to Mr. Foster of Departure Bay, Nanaimo, who used her to carry fresh water to sailing ships loading coal. She was brought to Alberni in 1892 by George Bird to serve the paper mill there.

Machigonne: A 110-foot submarine chaser bought by the Gibson Brothers in 1946 from War Asset Disposal. Carried passenger and freight from Port Alberni to West Coast points. Later went on the Horseshoe Bay to Gibsons Landing run.

Malahat: The Cameron Genoa Mills Shipbuilders Ltd. in Victoria built the schooner in 1917 for the Canadian Steamships Company. Her length was 245 feet, her breadth 43 feet and her depth 23 feet. The 1,543-ton ship was launched August 11th, 1917. The ship is most famous for her rum-running career. She was acclaimed "Queen" of the liquor fleet and often carried 60,000 cases of liquor. The Gibson Brothers purchased her in 1935 and she became a log barge.

Maude: Captain Joseph Spratt built the side-wheeler steamer in the San Juan Island territory in 1872. The ship was listed as 116 x 21 x 9 but her dimension changed with various conversions. She was converted to a steamer in 1885 and used two-cylinder engines. She was sold to the Canadian Pacific Navigation Company and claimed to be the first "ferry" on the Strait of Georgia and for many years made regular trips to the West Coast and into Alberni. For a time she was a freight barge and during her latter years was a salvage ship.

Meg Merrilies: The schooner, skippered by Captain Tom Pamphlet, brought the first white settlers to Alberni on June 29, 1860 to build the Anderson sawmill. The first shipment of lumber from the mill was carried to Victoria by the ship in July 1861.

Pocahontas: The ship, skippered by Captain Cyrus Sears from Baltimore, Md. lay stranded in Alberni for several weeks when the Alberni Canal froze during the winter of 1861-62. It took on a shipment of lumber for the US. Sears later wrote of his experience.

Princess of Alberni: The steamer became the Nootka Prince.

Princess Maquinna: The ship was a single-screw vessel of 1,777 tons and had accommodation for 400 day passengers and sleeping facilities for 100. She was 232.5 feet by 38 feet by 14.5 feet. She was the first British Columbia vessel launched under Yarrow designation. Retired in 1952, she was stripped down and engines removed and became the ore carrier *Taku*. She was called "Old Faithful" and loved by all who travelled the rugged West Coast.

Princess Norah: She was built at the Fairfield yard at Goven, Glasgow in 1928 and designed for West Coast waters. The ship alternated service with the *Princess Maquinna*. She was a single-screw, single-stack vessel of 2,731 tons, length 250.1 feet, width 48.1 feet and depth of 23 feet. She had 2,750 horsepower reciprocating engines that gave a speed of 16 knots. She could carry 700 passengers and 179 people in 61 staterooms. In 1955 she became the *Queen of the North*. She was sold in 1958 and renamed the *Canadian Prince*. Sold again in 1964, she became the hotel-cabaret Beachcomber in Alaska.

Plumper, HMS: Captain G. H. Richards used this Royal Navy vessel in surveying the Pacific Coast.

Quadra: The Canadian government patrol vessel replaced the old lighthouse tender *Sir James Douglas*. In 1891, she was built of steel, 265 tons register, length 174.5 feet, beam 31.1 feet, quadruple engines, 120 horsepower with speed of 11 knots. Her equipment included heavy lifting gear. In 1906 the ship rescued all hands from the wrecked *Coloma*. In 1917 she collided with the *Charmer* in Nanaimo harbour. Salvaged, she became a zinc ore carrier for Britannia Mines in Howe Sound. In 1924 she was chartered by a rum-running company and was seized in San Francisco along with the schooner *Coal Harbour*. She sank in the Bay, was salvaged and sold for junk.

Rainbow: The ship was built for the Gulf of Georgia and Fraser River service, and was too top heavy for safety and comfort to travel on the open ocean. For a time she served the West Coast when the *Maude* was out of service.

Saucy Lass: A schooner used in the hunting-fishing trip of Captain Edward Hammond King in 1861 in Barkley Sound. King accidentally lost his life and was the first white person buried in Alberni.

Sir James Douglas: In 1866, with skipper Captain Clarke, the ship carried mail and passengers between Victoria and Nanaimo twice a month. It was also a lighthouse tender that serviced Cape Beale.

Surprise: A sailing ship owned by trader Captain William Spring. The ship transported Father Brabant on his visit to the West Coast.

Tees: The ship was built in 1893 at Stockton-on-Tees by Richardson and Duck and for a short time served the Hudson's Bay Company. She arrived in Victoria in 1896 and made her maiden voyage into Alberni in August the same year. The *Tees* saw plenty of action between 1900 and 1925 before her purchasers turned her into the *Salvage Queen.* In 1937 the old ship was scraped and torched. The *Tees*, skippered by Captain John Irving, earned a place in the hearts of all that travelled aboard her.

Thiepval: Built in 1917 by Canadian Vickers Ltd. and commissioned into the Royal Canadian Navy in 1918, she was transferred to the Marine and Fisheries department in March 1920 to be used as a patrol vessel. In 1930, the ship was grounded in an uncharted channel north of Turret Island and sank. Thiepval Channel is named in her honour.

Tonquin: Natives attacked the Boston sailing ship June 1811 at Village Island. Only a Native interpreter survived.

Warspite: The Royal Canadian Navy vessel from Esquimalt was dispatched to Barkley Sound to locate a missing child from the wreck of the Woodside.

Veta C: Renamed the *Chelan,* was a 145-foot cargo vessel of 541 gross tons. She was originally built as a United States army transport for the Aleutian Islands and later converted for cargo.

William J. Stewart: The hydrographic survey ship now welcomes tourists to Ucluelet as the *Canadian Princess,* a hotel-restaurant.

Willie: Captain George Albert Huff's stern-wheel steamer, or the "*Weary Willie*" as it was sometimes known, was familiar during the early days of settlement on the canal. She was available for charter and made regular trips to the mines and points along the waterway.

Woodpecker: The schooner was used to transport machinery to Alberni for the Anderson Sawmill in August 1860.

SHIPPING COMPANIES AND THEIR VESSELS

Barkley Sound Transportation Company

Fleet: *Uchuck I, II, III,*

Blackmore Marine Service

Vessels: *Blue Swallow, Moon Dawn, Skidoo*

Brynnor Mine

Ore carriers: *Belmona, Santa Isabel, Tawatsam Maru,*

Canadian Fishing Company

Fish boats: *Canfisco, Cape Batherst,*

Cape Mark, Cape Perry

Gibson Brothers:

Company vessels: *Otter, Maid of Orleans*

Nootka Packing Company

Fishing boats: *Midnight Sun, Pacific Queen, Pacific Sunrise, Pacific Sunset*

Riley's Boat Service

Vessels: *Black Hawk, Maureen R., RE Riley, RE Riley II, RD Riley*

Stone Bros. ships*:*

Mayflower, May Fly, May Queen, Oh Mi Mi, Somass Queen,
Victory Fleet:
Victory I, Victory II, Victory III, Victory IV,
Victory V, Victory VI, Victory VII, Victory VIII
Victory IX, Victory XI,
Anglo Canadian VIII

Ucluelet Transportation Company

Vessels: *Merry Widow, Tofino, Roche Point*

Union Steamship Company

Coastal fleet: *Princess Charlotte, Princess Elaine,*
Princess Elizabeth, Princess Joan, Princess Kathleen,
Princess Maquinna

West Coast Marine Mission: (United Church Marine Service)

Ships: *Broadcaster, Melvin Swartout, Messenger II*

Whaling fleet:

Germania, Orion, Sebastian, St. Lawrence
Rainbow fleet: *Black, Blue, Brown, Green, White*

OIL RIGS

Sedco 135-F drilling rig was towed into Port Alberni in October 1967 for modifications to its anchor system.

Towing vessels: *Canadian Tide, Gulf Joan, Island Commander, Island Warrior, Min Tide, P. F. Stone*

Sedco 708 drilling rig wintered in Port Alberni in 1977-78.

Ocean Ranger drilling rig arrived in Port Alberni in December 1978. It was 340 feet high; length 400 feet and width 298 feet. At maximum draft her displacement was 38,940 tons. The rig capsized February 15, 1982 with a loss of all 84 crew.

SHIPWRECKS

Amethyst: The schooner was abandoned by her crew in April, 1902, and later found adrift in Barkley Sound.

Coloma: The ship was wrecked December 6, 1906.

Florencia: The sailing ship was wrecked November 14, 1860, about five miles west of Amphitrite Point, near Ucluelet. It had been *en route* to Hawaii with a cargo of lumber.

Glen Fruin: Ship was wrecked on Danger Rock at the entrance to Barkley Sound in December, 1880.

Orpheus: The schooner collided with the SS *Pacific* and sank off Cape Flattery in the winter of 1876. Two people survived.

Uzbekistan: The Russian ship ran aground near Pachena Lighthouse in April, 1943, without loss of life. The ship eventually broke up and sank.

Valencia: The American steamer left San Francisco on January 20, 1906, *en route* to Victoria with 164 passengers and crew. The following day, due to poor visibility, the ship missed the entrance to Juan de Fuca Strait and edged its way up the West Coast. Just after midnight on January 22, the ship grounded at Pachena Point. Only 38 survived; 59 bodes were recovered. The others were declared missing and presumed drowned.

Vanlene: The Panamanian registered 10,500 ton freighter with a 38-man Chinese crew, left Japan February 24, 1972. The ship grounded on a rock piercing a hole through her belly at Austin Island on March 14, 1972.

Search vessels: *Bamfield Lifeboat, Coral Stone, Victoria City, Tiksi, Neva Straits, Sudbury II, Laymore, St. Anthony, Ready Camsell.*

Woodside: The steamboat was built by Muir Bros. and launched at Sooke in June 1878. The steamer carried passengers and freight between Victoria and Alberni. In 1888, the ship was returning to Alberni when it was caught in a storm and lost its rudder. All passengers landed safely about three miles from Pachena.

NOTES

Chapter One

1 Morris Swadesh, 76-93.
2 Alfred Carmichael's "Revenge of the Clallams." See also R. Bruce Scott, 253-56.
3 Jim Pojar and Andy MacKinnon, 52.
4 Della Kew and P. E. Goddard, 31.
5 See Swadesh, Text 1. Legend as told by Tom to Sapir.
6 John R. Jewitt, 16.
7 Pacific Rim National Park Human History Study: Box E, vol 2, 18, AVM.
8 Banfield letters 1858: Ethnology Regional Research File Box, vol 1, AVM.
9 *Ibid.*, 28 Aug. 1858.
10 Captain John T. Walbran, 31.
11 Banfield report, 24 Oct. 1859.
12 Banfield file 38.17.
13 Banfield Reports to the Colonial Secretary W. A. G. Young, 24 Oct. 1859, Ethnology, vol 1, AVM.
14 *Ibid.*
15 *Ibid.*, Report, 3 July 1860.
16 *Ibid.*, statement of land transaction, 11 Feb. 1860.
17 See Banfield reports, 3 July 1860.

18 *Ibid.*, 4 Mar. 1860.

19 *Ibid.*, 30 Jan. 1862.

20 Stuart family history file, Hudson's Bay Company archives, Winnipeg, Manitoba. Nanaimo Community Archives.

21 Alan D. McMillan & Denis E. St. Claire, 10.

22 Banfield report, 4 Mar. 1860.

23 *British Colonist* 27 Mar. 1861.

24 *Ibid.*, 11, 12 Jan. 1861.

25 See Walbran.

26 *Ibid.*

27 See Stuart file.

28 See Banfield, 20 July 1860.

29 *Ibid.*, 30 May 1861.

30 *West Coast Advocate* 30 May 1935. Alex Sproat recalls his father's story of the winter of '62 and the *Pocahontas*.

31 Cyrus Sears letter, published in *Alberni Pioneer News* 24 Feb. 1912.

32 British Columbia pamphlets 1858-1872, Appendix B: Anderson Sawmill file No. 45.9, Parliamentary Library, Ottawa.

33 W. Kaye Lamb, 104.

34 R. Bruce Scott, part 5.

35 L. V. Kelly re: Captain Tom Pamphlet association with W. E. Bamfield. Undated article from George Bird papers, W. E. Banfield newspaper biographical file.

36 G. M. Sproat file 35.18, Alberni Mill Lands correspondence, 175.

37 *Ibid.*, 174.

38 George Bird, 98.

39 T. A. Rickard, "Gilbert Malcolm Sproat," 21-32.

40 Gilbert Malcolm Sproat correspondence to the Colonial Secretary 1 Nov. 1864, Alberni Lands correspondence: File 35.18.

41 Craig Brown, 47.

42 Gilbert Malcolm Sproat, 99-102.

43 *Ibid.*, 101.

44 *Ibid.*, 103.

45 Alberni Mill Lands correspondence: File 35.18, 176.

46 *Ibid.*, 185.

47 *Ibid.*, 187.

48 *Ibid.*, 188.

49 See Bird, 99.

50 Alberni 1871 survey, File 21 19, Accession 977.4-ADHSA.

51 See Bird, 52; see also Charles Taylor: File 51.30.

52 Charles Taylor: File 51.30, ADHSA.

53 Alex Sproat, "West Coast Lore," *West Coast Advocate* 29 Aug. 1935. Alex Sproat is the son of G. M. Sproat.

54 Guillod reports, 11 Oct. 1882.

55 Ruth Kirk, 239.

56 Charles Taylor: File 51.30.

Chapter Two

1 See Pacific Rim study.

2 *West Coast Advocate* 2 Oct. 1947.

3 Moser.

4 See Walbran.

5 See Banfield reports, 39.

6 John Ross, "A Pioneer Family of the West Coast," *West Coast Advocate* 2 Oct. 1947.

7 Alex Sproat, "West Coast Lore," *West Coast Advocate* 3 Jan. 1935.

8 See Scott, 78.

9 Doris Farmer Tonkin, interview with Pattie Haslam, "My Two Fair Ladies," *Daily Colonist* 23 June 1968.

10 Gus Cox memoirs, ADHSA.

11 See Bird, 208.

12 Gus Cox memoirs.

13 John Ross, *West Coast Advocate* 2 Oct. 1947.

14 Pioneer Parade 76.2; see also Nicholson, 144.

15 Tonkin, interview with Pattie Haslam, *Daily Colonist* 23 June 1968.

16 See Nicholson, 140.

17 Tonkin, *Daily Colonist* 23 June 1968.

18 See Bird, 208.

19 Gus Cox memoirs.

20 Goodall, 92.

21 "Indian Commission," *Port Alberni News* 9 May 1914.

22 McKenna-McBride Commission. Minutes of the West Coast Agency hearings, 904.

23 Bob Soderlund, "From Nations to Reservations," *Ha-Shilth-Sa*, 6 May 1976: 4.

24 McKenna-McBride Commission. Summary of West Coast Agency hearings, 851.

25 *Twin Cities Times*, 11 Dec. 1953.

26 Cox family history file, ADHSA.; see also Muriel Cox obituary, *Alberni Valley Times* 15 Mar. 1978.

27 Peterson, *Twin Cities*, 169.

28 Department of Indian Affairs, Annual Report, 1882, 161.

29 Guillod family history file; see also Guillod: File L.9.18.

30 *British Columbia Historical Quarterly*, 19.3-4: 187.

31 *Ibid.*, 191.

32 Indian Agent Reports (Alberni) 1881-1885, Alberni Valley Museum. Harry Guillod report, 22 Sept. 1881.

33 Guillod reports 1881-1903, 980.22a, ADHSA.

34 *Ibid.*, report of 1885.

35 Frederick Christian Thornberg: File L.15.18, ADHSA.

36 Paul Tennant, 51.

37 Guillod reports, 9 Oct. 1882.

38 K. E. Guillod, "Women who Pioneered," unknown newspaper clipping, 19 Nov. 1933.

39 See Bird, 49.

40 Alex Dunn, 30.

41 *Ibid.*, 31.

42 James K. Nesbitt, "Shipwreck survivor gives plaque to Victoria," *Daily Colonist* 25 Nov. 1962.

43 "Granny" McFarlane Dies: Was Pioneer of Old Town," *West Coast Advocate* 20 Feb. 1936.

Chapter Three

1 Exploring Expedition, Box 12, File 19, ADHSA.

2 Frank C. Garrard memoirs, Legal Box #13, ADHSA.

3 National Archives of Canada File 8052-86-A/1416.

4 National Archives of Canada, Annual report 1900 for Public Works, Sessional Paper No. 9.

5 G. M. Sproat: File 35.18, ADHSA.

6 *Daily Colonist* 18 July 1864: 3.

7 Father Brabant journal, Alberni Valley Museum.

8 See Bird, 55.

9 Obituary of Mah Bing, *West Coast Advocate* 8 Sept. 1938.

10 See Bird, 55.

11 See Scott, 183.

12 See Bird, 19.

13 *Ibid.*, 19, 20.

14 T. W. Paterson, 62.

15 Annual Mining Report, 1893, 1080.

16 See Bird, 27.

17 *West Coast Advocate* 11 April 1935.

18 See Mining Report 1893, 22.

19 *Nanaimo Daily Free Press* 19 March 1897.

20 See Bird, 62-63.

21 *West Coast Advocate* 11 April 1935.

22 Ben Hines, 13.

23 *West Coast Advocate* 11 April 1935.

24 *Nanaimo Daily Free Press* 25 Oct. 1897.

25 See Hines, 19.

26 *Ibid.*

27 Ruth Green, 155-6.

28 *Nanaimo Daily Free Press* 15 April 1897.

29 *Ibid.*

30 Anthony Watson: File L.36.11. Mary Oliver interview with Ty Watson.

31 E. A. Hillier, unpublished manuscript, "History of Ucluelet, 1899 to 1954," 2.

32 See Watson file.

33 See Bird, 200.

34 See Paterson, 60.

35 See Watson file.

36 *West Coast Advocate* 18 April 1935.

37 *Ibid.* 26 July 1934.

38 *Ibid.* 10 Nov. 1938.

39 Annual Mining Report, 1944, G147. See Hines, 58.

40 See Paterson, 58.

41 See Nicholson, 132.

42 British Columbia Provincial Archives: File L.616.9(15) C891b - 1890.

43 See Bird, 201-202.

44 See Garrard file, Legal Box #13, 129.

45 Barkley Sound Plan, Regional District of Alberni-Clayoquot, March 1983, 49.

46 See Hines, 46. Annual Mining Report, 1909.

47 *Alberni Pioneer News* 4 June 1910.

48 Report of the Alberni coal-field. Department of Mines, May 14, 1922. ADHSA File No. L.6.10.

49 "Railway graders cut into coal seams in Port Alberni," *Alberni Pioneer News* 7 Jan. 1911.

50 "Authority pronounces on Port Alberni coal," *Ibid.* 15 July 1911.

51 "Diamond drill ordered," *Ibid.* 22 July 1911.

52 *Port Alberni News* 13 Aug. 1919.

53 *Ibid.* 27 Aug. 1919.

54 "E & N refuse permission to reopen old tunnel," *West Coast Advocate* 27 Oct. 1932.

Chapter Four

1 Accumulation of fishing history of the Alberni Inlet/Barkley Sound 1800-1980, file, Alberni Valley Museum.

2 See Jewitt, 12.

3 Royal Commission on Indian Affairs for the Province of B.C. Meeting with the Tseshaht Band or Tribe of Indians, held on their No. 1 reserve, 11 May 1914.

4 See Bird, 46.

5 "Alberni Valley Museum fishing history, Alberni District 1856-1900"; "Letter from Barclay Sound, 23 Aug. 1861," *Daily Colonist* 23 Aug. 1861.

6 *Ibid.*, 16 Aug. 1861.

7 See Fishing Industry file, Alberni Valley Museum, Department of Fisheries Annual Report 1886.

8 *Ibid.*, sealing.

9 See Hillier, 1.

10 George Nicholson, 211.

11 Irma Cashin interview by Edwin Hubert, 23 Nov. 1994, BOHP.

12 *Ibid.*

13 *Alberni Advocate* 26 April 1912.

14 See Fishing Industry file, sealing, AVM.

15 W. E. Barraclough, "The Development of the Dogfish Fishery in British Columbia," Seventh Pacific Science Congress 1949, 513, PBS.

16 *Port Alberni News* 16 Aug. 1916.

17 Alex C. Anderson, Inspector of Fisheries, 1877.

18 *Ibid.*, 1878.

19 Thomas Mowat, Inspector of Fisheries, 1887.

20 See Bird, 182-83.

21 E. G. Taylor, Inspector of Fisheries, 1915-16.

22 Fishing industry file, herring, Alberni Valley Museum.

23 "Fish illuminate water of canal," *Alberni Pioneer News* 16 Oct. 1909.

24 *Port Alberni News* 17 Feb. 1915.

25 Pioneer Parade, ADHSA, File 76.14.

26 Jon Van Arsdell, 28.

27 See Jewitt, 85.

28 See Bird, 49.

29 Joseph E. Forester and Anne D. Forester, 186.

30 Robert Lloyd Webb, 151.

31 C. W. Sanger and A. B. Dickson, 14.

32 See Webb, 156. James Clark to the Department of Labour, New Alberni, B.C., 27 April 1905. National Archives of Canada (NAC), RG 23, Vol 242, File 1536 (1), 219.

33 *Ibid.*, 157.

34 *Ibid.*, 173. George A. Huff to L. P. Brodeur, application for whaling licence, Victoria, 10 September, 1907. NAC, RG 23, Vol 242, File 1536 (1), 535.

35 *Alberni Pioneer News* 5 Sept. 1908.

36 See Webb, 169.

37 Vi Henderson, 3.

38 See Forester, 190.

39 William Roff lectures, File 51.6, ADHSA.

40 *Alberni Pioneer News* 26 June 1909.

41 See Fishing Industry file, Whaling, AVM, 1913.

42 Pioneer Parade, ADHSA, File 76.14.

43 *Alberni Pioneer News* 11 April 1914.

44 See Forester, 190; also Webb, 186.

45 Pioneer Parade, ADHSA, File 76.14.

46 *Ibid.*

47 See Scott, 184.

48 See Paterson, 62.

49 Mary Wood, ADHSA, File 4.13.

50 See Webb, 182.

51 See Sanger and Dickinson, 19.

52 Bill McDermid interview by Edwin Hubert, 10 Jan. 1995, BOHP.

53 *Port Alberni News* 24 Feb. 1926.

54 Gordon Gibson with Carol Renison, 209.

55 *Ibid.*, 221.

56 Progress reports of Pacific Coast Stations, No. 70, March, 1947, p. 30-31, PBS.

57 *Ibid.*, 31.

58 See Forester, 199.

59 Elsie Hillier, "Reflections and reminiscences," *The West Coaster* 20 Oct. 1960. Information about Jansen comes from this source.

Chapter 5

1 See Tennant, 76.

2 Undated newspaper article, Church History of Alberni, ADHSA.

3 Howard, 155.

4 "Swartout," *West Coast Advocate* 5 Dec. 1935: 7.

5 Shadbolt, 24.

6 Emily Carr, 3.

7 See Carr, 5.

8 *Ibid.*, 4.

9 Ira Dilworth, foreword, *Ibid.*

10 *Ibid.*, 7.

11 *Ibid.*, 10.

12 Alfred W. Carmichael, "To Village Island and Back, Narrative of a Journey from Ucluelet to Village Island, Barkley Sound, 1896." Part 11, Provincial Archives of British Columbia, Carmichael file, AVM, Information about this story comes from this source, unless otherwise stated.

13 Carmichael file 48.5, ADHSA, 95.

14 See Bird, 36.

15 Carmichael file 48.5, ADHSA, 97.

16 *Ibid.*, 100.

17 *Ibid.*, 101-102.

18 See Graham, 195.

19 See Scott, 136.

20 See Nicholson, 135.

21 See Howard, 220.

22 Interview with Chief Cecil and Mrs. Jessie Mack of the Toquaht Band by Jill Lewis, *Ha-Shilth-Sa* 6 May 1976.

23 *Ibid.* Interview with Mowachaht band member Maurus MacLean.

24 See Bird, 3.

25 *Ibid.*, 2.

26 *Ibid.*, 45.

27 *Ibid.*, 4.

28 *Ibid.*, 16.

29 Jan Peterson, *The Albernis*, 79.

30 See Bird, vii.

31 See Hillier, 1.

32 *Ibid.*

33 Bill Dale, American Rhododendron Society, Summer 1990: 125. See also undated article in *The Northern Scot*, Elgin, Scotland. "Rare gardening honour for a pioneering son of Moray."

34 George Fraser, AVMSA, file 1.20.

35 *Ibid.*, Marion Crossley article, "George Fraser's Garden," 5.

36 See American Rhododendron Society, 127.

37 "Activity and beauty along Tofino's route," *Alberni Pioneer News* 4 March 1914.

38 "Flower show and dance of Alberni Horticultural Society," *Port Alberni News* 19 April 1922.

39 See American Rhododendron Society, 127.

40 *The Northern Scot*, undated.

41 "Ucluelet—Oldest settler honoured," *West Coast Advocate* 31 Oct. 1935.

42 "Ucluelet—Fraser honoured," *Ibid.* 6 Aug. 1936.

43 George Fraser, letter to the editor, *Ibid.* 1 April 1937.

44 "Mr. Fraser is 82 years old," editorial, *Ibid.* 15 Oct. 1936.

45 *The Northern Scot*, undated.

46 See Bird, 198.

47 Geoffrey Castle, "Corrupted Town Name Honours Carpenter," *Times Colonist* 25 Nov. 1995.

48 *Port Alberni News* 29 July 1914.

49 Interview with Bruce and Pauline Scott in 1979, BOHP.

50 *Port Alberni News* 29 July 1914.

51 *Ibid.* 21 Dec. 1907.

52 *Ibid.* 28 Dec. 1907.

53 *Ibid.*

54 *Ibid.* 11 Jan. 1908.

55 *Ibid.* 25 Jan. 1908.

56 *Alberni Pioneer News* 17 Aug. 1907.

57 Scott interview, BOHP.

58 *Ha-Shilth-Sa* 17 March 1975.

59 See Bird, 42.

60 *Ibid.*, 209.

61 "Another motor lifeboat to be established at Bamfield Creek," *Alberni Pioneer News* 4 Sept. 1909.

62 *Ibid.*, 25 Sept. 1909.

63 "Bamfield holds first school meeting," *Ibid.*, 26 Dec. 1908.

64 "Bamfield Report," *Alberni Advocate* 17 May 1912.

65 Jean Buck Wallbank, Benson Island, 3. Information about the island comes from this source, unless otherwise stated.

66 See Pacific Rim National Park study, 77.

67 See Wallbank. 2.

68 "Benson looks for market for his logs," *Port Alberni News* 12 Oct. 1907.

69 See Bird, 213-14.

70 See Nicholson, 146.

71 "Enjoyable excursions to Hawkins Island," *Port Alberni News* 11 Sept. 1918.

72 "Hawkins Island launch goes for trial trip," *Ibid.* 12 Nov. 1919.

73 "Big fish caught," *Ibid.* 21 April 1920: 4.

Chapter Six

1 Mr. and Mrs. Arthur Baird interview by Larry and Grace Krueger, Pacific Rim National Park Study, vol 2, 149.

2 Bill McDermid interview by Edwin Hubert, 10 Jan. 1995, BOHP.

3 *Ibid.*

4 *Ibid.*

5 "Shark fishing industry to be located on Alberni Canal," *Port Alberni News* 31 Aug. 1921.

6 Joe Garcia interview by Tanya Porter, BOHP.

7 "Huge knife sliced Basking Shark," *Times Colonist* 27 Sept. 1992: M2.

8 Johnny Williams Sr., "This land, These rivers," *Ha-Shilth-Sa*, 6 May 1976: 5.

9 R. E. Foerster, paper, Seventh Pacific Science Congress 1949, Pacific Biological Station, Nanaimo, 417.

10 See McDermid interview, BOHP.

11 Roald Ostrom interview by Tanya Porter, BOHP.

12 Grace Tuttle journal, ADHSA.

13 See McDermid interview, BOHP.

14 Ardie Logan interview by Tanya Porter, Nov. 1994, BOHP.

15 "Sea Serpent at Ucluelet," *West Coast Advocate* 9 May 1935.

16 "Sea Serpent in Barkley Sound," *Ibid.* 4 April 1935.

17 *Ibid.*, May 9, 1935.

18 *Ibid.* 18 Aug. 1935.

19 "Caddy rears head before fisherman," *Ibid.* 15 Oct. 1936.

20 "Port Alberni residents discover skeleton of 40-foot monster," *Twin Cities Times* 8 Dec. 1947.

21 *Ibid.* 15 Dec. 1947.

22 File 36-16 Sharks - General 1944-56, Vol II. PBS. Correspondence comes from this source.

23 See Scott, 258.

24 Dr. Craig P. Staude, "Amphipacifica," *Journal of Systematic Biology*, vol. I Supplement I, April 20, 1995.

25 "Fifty Scotch families on way to West Coast," *Port Alberni News* 10 Sept. 1924.

26 Announcement by Hon. T. D. Pattullo re: Hebrideans," *Ibid.* 24 Sept. 1924.

27 *Ibid.*

28 "The Hebrideans—How to get them and How to hold them," *Ibid.* 1 Oct. 1924.

29 "Preference for Alberni District," *Ibid.* 22 Oct. 1924. (Reprint from *Vancouver Daily Province*.)

30 Pattullo Papers, Add. Ms. 3, Box 21, File 8, BCARS Archives.

31 *Ibid.*

32 *Ibid.*

33 "Hebridean Settlers Here in the Spring," *Port Alberni News* 12 Aug. 1925.

34 Interview with Pete Gregory and Stan Littleton, Fishing file, Alberni Valley Museum.

35 *Port Alberni News* 21 March 1917.

36 Lyons, 284-85.

37 Department of Fisheries Annual Report 1911-12, Alberni Valley Museum fishing file.

38 Chalmer Ternan obit. *Port Alberni News* 29 August 1917.

39 *Ibid.* 10 March 1916.

40 *The Alberni Advocate* 8 Aug. 1913.

41 *Alberni Pioneer News* 3 Feb. 1912.

42 *Ibid.* 23 Dec. 1912.

43 *West Coast Advocate* 15 July 1937.

44 *Alberni Pioneer News* 1 April 1911.

45 "Golden Jubilee, 1874-1924," *Nanaimo Daily Free Press* undated, Nanaimo Community Archives.

46 *Daily Times* 21 March 1931.

47 "Fish Plant nears Completion," *Port Alberni News* 30 Jan. 1918.

48 See Goodall, 83.

49 *Port Alberni News* 22 July 1937.

50 See Hillier, 3.

51 See Fishing History file, Alberni Valley Museum.

52 Peterson, *Twin Cities*, 48-49.

53 A. H. R., "Over a Million Fish a Year," *West Coast Advocate* 1937. Interview with Ucluelet pioneer. Information about Mr. Lyche comes from this source unless otherwise stated.

54 "Ottawa is opposed to Cannery Licence," *Port Alberni News* 27 March 1918.

55 *Ibid.* 22 May 1918.

56 *Ibid.*

57 *Ibid.* 19 Feb. 1919.

58 *Ibid.*

59 *Ibid.* 26 March 1919.

60 *Ibid.* 29 Oct. 1919.

61 *Ibid.* 9 Nov. 1921.

62 Annual Report of the Fisheries Branch, Department of the Naval Service, 1919.

63 Young and Reid, 43.

64 See Forester, 155.

65 See Foerster paper, 414.

Chapter Seven

1 *Alberni Valley Times* 13 March 1985.

2 *The West Coaster* 10 May 1962.

3 See Annual Fisheries Report, 1919.

4 See Nicholson, 200-203.

5 See Starkins, "Rum Running," 19.

6 *Port Alberni News* 12 Aug. 1925.

7 See Nicholson, 200-203.

8 See Greene, 220.

9 Eric Newsome, 108-110.

10 Dorothy Wrotnowski, "Island's Ernie May sailed on Great Ship," *Daily Colonist* 7 March 1971.

11 See Gibson and Renison 86.

12 See Greene, 225.

13 *Ibid.*, 87.

14 *Vancouver Sun* 23 March 1944.

15 *West Coast Advocate* 30 March 1944.

16 See Gibson, 120.

17 See Nicholson, 172-175.

18 See Starkins, 19.

19 "Board endorses request from Ucluelet," *Port Alberni News* 20 June 1908.

20 *Port Alberni News* 25 March 1911.

21 Ucluelet report, "Meeting of Vancouver Island Development League held," *Alberni Pioneer News* 27 Feb. 1909.

22 Grant Obituary, *Port Alberni News* 5 Nov. 1921.

23 *Alberni Pioneer News* 26 June 1909.

24 See Nicholson, 281.

25 *West Coast Advocate* 4 Dec. 1952.

26 "Burde Announces Road Grant," *Port Alberni News* 12 July 1922.

27   "Big Plans include road from Alberni," *Port Alberni News* 22 Aug. 1923.

28 Mr. and Mrs. Arthur Baird Interview by Grace and Larry Kreuger, 7 July 1973, Pacific Rim National Park Study, Vol. 2, 161.

29 *West Coast Advocate* 4 Dec. 1952.

30 Interview of Mrs. Sheila Mead-Miller by Grace and Larry Keuger, 18 July 1973, Pacific Rim National Park Study, Vol. 2, 143.

31 School register, ADHSA.

32 See Hillier, 4.

33 *Port Alberni News* 19 May 1920.

34 *Ibid.* 16 June 1920.

35 See Mrs. Sheila Mead-Miller interview, 136-8.

36 Johnson, 89.

37 See Hillier, 6.

38 *West Coast Advocate* 2 April 1958.

39 *Ibid.* 4 Dec. 1952.

40 Walter Guppy, Clayoquot Soundings, 41-42.

41 *West Coast Advocate* 20 March 1952.

42 See Peterson, 284-85.

43 *West Coast Advocate* 22 July 1937.

44 See Fishing Industry file, AVM.

45 School register, ADHSA.

Chapter Eight

1 "This is Franklin River," Harmac News, undated, from Logging and Sawmill file, AVM.
2 "Franklin Creek Camp Open Soon," *West Coast Advocate* 27 Sept. 1934.
3 *West Coast Advocate* 4 Oct. 1934.
4 *Ibid.* 19 Jan. 1935.
5 *Ibid.* 8 June 1939.
6 *Ibid.* 11 July 1946.
7 *Ibid.* 12 Aug. 1948.
8 "This is Sarita River," Harmac News, undated.
9 Information from Joe and Jane Stanhope, daughter and son-in-law of Bob Banks. The author appreciated the assistance received from this source about Sarita and Franklin River Logging Camps.
10 *Twin Cities Times*, undated, newspaper clipping file, ADHSA.
11 *West Coast Advocate* 27 Jan. 1949.
12 *Ibid.* 30 March 1950.
13 Heart of the People, film, Knowledge Network.
14 *Port Alberni News* 15 May 1918.
15 *Ibid.* 14 April 1920.
16 Logging and sawmill file, AVM.
17 MacKay, 188.
18 *Ibid.*, 199.
19 McDermid interview.
20 See Gibson and Renison, 45.
21 See Hillier manuscript, 7.
22 Memorandum by C.H.S. Vancouver, B.C., May 24, 1945. Information about excursion to Franklin River is from this source.

Chapter Nine

1 Mary Rockingham Hughes, "Bamfield Again," *Zodiac*, a journal of the Bamfield Cable Station, Sept. 1944, 204.
2 See Bird, 49.
3 "Trail Blazers," *West Coast Advocate*, 10 April 1941.
4 Pioneer Parade 76.2.
5 Interview with Jack Thomson, *West Coast Advocate* 21 March 1946.
6 See Green, 54.

7   *Ibid.*

8   See Bird, 143.

9   "New West Coast Enterprise," *Port Alberni News* 23 July 1910.

10 *Port Alberni News* 29 July 1911.

11 *Ibid.* 17 Sept. 1913.

12 *Ibid.* 4 Aug. 1915.

13 *Ibid.* 29 July 1911.

14 "Port Alberni has its Mayflower," *Alberni Valley Times* 9 Feb. 1970.

15 "Stone wins Nanaimo Regatta Cup," *West Coast Advocate* 17 Sept. 1931.

16 Ruth Roberts, "Waterway family serves valley," *Alberni Valley Times* 15 June 1977.

17 *Port Alberni News* 5 Oct. 1912.

18 Douglas Stone Jr. interview by Jan Peterson, 20 Aug. 1996.

19 Stone Brothers file, ADHSA. See also *Port Alberni News* 20 July 1921.

20 "New Mail Boat for Barclay Sound Run," *Port Alberni News* 18 March 1925.

21 Stone interview.

22 *Port Alberni News* 6 Jan. 1926.

23 Stone interview.

24 *Ibid.*

25 *Port Alberni News* 6 Jan. 1929.

26 *West Coast Advocate* 26 July 1934.

27 See Stone file, ADHSA.

28 "New Tug Boat for Stone Bros.," *West Coast Advocate* 7 Nov. 1940.

29 Stone interview.

30 *West Coast Advocate* 9 April 1959.

31 *Twin Cities Times* 4 Oct. 1967.

32 "Life on West Coast Waters," *Alberni Valley Times* 1 June 1977.

33 Dick McMinn interview, 9 Aug. 1983.

34 Morris, 4.

35 McMinn interview.

36 *Ibid.*

37 *West Coast Advocate* 14 April 1955.

38 Dick McMinn file.

39 McMinn speech to Alberni District Historical Society.

40 John and Kay Monrufet interview by Edwin Hubert, 3 Feb. 1995, BOHP.

41 "Barclay Sound Uchuck 111 being withdrawn," *West Coast Advocate* 2 June 1960.

42 *West Coast Advocate* 21 July 1966.

43 *Times Colonist* 10 May 1997.

44 McMinn speech.

45 *Ibid.*

46 Saul, A Course Was Laid.

47 *Ibid.*

48 Dick McMinn file.

49 Rushton, 141.

50 See Morris, 24.

51 See Rushton, 146.

52 The Ship's Log, [Alberni Marine Transportation Co.] 1.2 (1993): 5.

53 See Morris, 35.

54 Bill Moore, "The Good Ship Maquinna," *The Westcoaster* 12 Oct. 1977: 11.

55 *Port Alberni News* 19 July 1913.

56 Cpt. H. D. Halkett, "The Good Ship Maquinna," *The Islander* 18 May 1980.

57 See Green.

58 Irma Cashin interview by Edwin Hubert, 23 Nov. 1994, BOHP.

59 Bruce and Pauline Scott interview by June and Kirk Kerstetter, 1979, BOHP.

60 *The Islander* 18 May 1980.

61 *The Westcoaster* 12 Oct. 1977.

62 Scott interview.

63 See Nicholson, 94; see also *The Islander* 18 May 1980.

64 *Port Alberni News* 29 May 1930.

65 Shipping file, ADHSA.

66 "SS Chilliwack to replace Maquinna," *West Coast Advocate* 4 Sept. 1952.

67 See Scott, 176.

68 Laura Evans, "To Carmanah Point on the Princess Maquinna." First published in Discovery, a booklet by the Alberni Valley Creative Writers' Group for the Captain Cook 200th anniversary in 1978, 17-24. With permission of the author.

69 "Machigonne beings service," *West Coast Advocate* 9 Jan. 1947.

70 *West Coast Advocate* 9 Dec. 1937.

71 "Pilot Boats' Story told," *Twin Cities Times* 18 Jan. 1967.

72 Joseph Clegg file, L.8.28.

73 *Alberni District News* 3 Oct. 1940.

74 *Alberni Valley Times* 1 June 1977.

75 Longshoremen file No. 17.16. ADHSA.

76 *Ibid.*, Bud Handley research. The following information comes from this source.

77 See Goodall, 115.

78 *Ibid.*

79 "Lumber Shipments," *Port Alberni News* 28 July 1926.

80 "Hugh Watts Retires," *Alberni Valley Times* 9 Oct. 1968.

81 *Alberni Valley Times* 12 Feb. 1931.

82 See Peterson, *Twin Cities*, 132.

83 *West Coast Advocate* 19 April 1934.

84 Bud Handley, "Wars, the Union, into the present," untitled newspaper, 30 Dec. 1976, ADHSA.

85 "Shortage of Ships worries Sawmills," *West Coast Advocate* 26 Oct. 1939.

86 See MacKay, 142.

87 Remember When," *Alberni Valley Times* 16 Oct. 1968.

88 Waterfront News, 13.1 (April 1993). Information on this incident is from this source.

89 *Ibid.* Larry Mannix, President, Local 503, Port Alberni.

90 "Harbour Jobs aren't there," *Alberni Valley Times* 16 May 1983.

Chapter Ten

1 Howard, Godships. Passages of this book are quoted frequently with permission of the author.

2 Laite file, United Church Archives.

3 "History of Strangers' Rest," *West Coast Advocate* 11 Sept. 1947.

4 *Port Alberni News* 10 Sept. 1924.

5 *West Coast Advocate* 16 April 1936.

6 Gwen Howe, "Looking Back," unpublished manuscript, 7 April 1981, File No. 6.16.

7 Johnson, Not Without Hope. With permission of the author.

8 *Ibid.*, 40.

9 "First Explorers," *Ha-Shilth-Sa* 6 May 1976: 6.

10 Mabel Taylor interview, 27 July 1981, Alberni Valley Museum Fishing History file.

11 Barman, 167.

12 See Brown, 57.

13 Mabel Taylor file, AVM.

14 See McMillan and St. Claire, 29.

15 *Ibid.* From article by Denis E. St. Claire.

16 *Ibid.* Information following from this file source.

17 Annie Clappis interview by Jean McIntosh, 1986, Alberni Valley Museum basket weaver file. Information in this section comes from this source.

18 Basket weaver file, AVM

19 Angie Joe interview, BOHP.

20 See Tennant, 81.

21 *Alberni Valley Times* 2 April 1975.

22 *Ibid.* 4 April 1973.

23 *Ibid.* 14 Oct. 1976.

24 Agnes Dick, interview with author, July 1981.

25 *Alberni Valley Times* 14 Oct. 1976.

26 Loraine Littlefield, "Gender, Class and Community," thesis, UBC, October 1995, Nanaimo Community Archives.

27 Interview with Chief Cecil and Mrs. Jessie Mack by Jill Lewis, *Ha-Shilth-Sa* 6 May 1976. All information about the Toquaht tribe comes from this source.

28 McDonald, 45.

29 Guppy, Wet Coast Ventures, 117.

30 Barkley Sound Plan, Regional District of Alberni-Clayoquot, 1983, 63.

31 Newspaper clipping file, undated, ADHSA.

32 George Karpoff interview, 16 Oct. 1997.

33 *Alberni Valley Times* 26 Sept. 1973.

34 *Ibid.*

35 *Ibid.*

36 See Barkley Sound Plan.

37 See Scott, 164.

38 Bruce and Pauline Scott interview, by June and Kirk Kerstetter, 1979, BOHP.

39 R. Bruce Scott, "Bamfield holds fond memories," *Times-Colonist* 11 April 1993.

40 *West Coast Advocate* 23 Sept. 1937.

41 Bruce Scott interview by Brian P. White, 21 Dec. 1973, Pacific Rim National Park study, vol. 2.

42 Bruce and Pauline Scott interview, BOHP.

43 See White interview, 11.

44 *Zodiac*, June-July, 1943: 127.

45 Mary Hughes file No. 12.3, ADHSA. Information in this section comes from this source.

46 Donald Graham, 188.

Chapter Eleven

1   *Alberni Valley Times* 8 Aug. 1980.

2   Ramon Kwok, "Salal Joe is Missing," unpublished manuscript. With permission.

3   John Monrufet interview, BOHP.

4   See Morris, 33.

5   See Monrufet interview. Also see Morris, 34.

6   *West Coast Advocate* 16 Dec. 1925.

7   Brian P. White, Pacific Rim National Park Study, Vol. 2, 164. Reference to Link Island fox farm.

8   Barkley Sound Plan, Regional District of Alberni-Clayoquot, 1983.

9   Barkley Sound Planning Strategy, January 1994, prepared by Barkley Sound Planning Committee.

10 R. Bruce Scott, "Independent People," *Daily Colonist* 9 Feb. 1969.

11 'Copper Island Resident Buried Locally," *Alberni Valley Times* 15 Nov. 1977.

12 *Daily Colonist* 9 Feb. 1969.

13 *Ibid.*

14 Shirley Culpin, "Gus tells his Tall Tales well," *Alberni Valley Times* 21 July 1972.

15 *Ibid.*

16 *West Coast Advocate* 13 Dec. 1934.

17 Ministry of Environment Library, Victoria, Annual Reports.

18 *West Coast Advocate* 5 March 1936.

19 Cougar Brown interview by Shirley Culpin, *Alberni Valley Times* 24 Jan. 1973.

20 Cougar Brown interview by Mike Grenby, *Vancouver Sun* 17 Nov. 1969.

21 Cougar Brown interview with Jan Peterson, *Alberni Valley Times* 16 May 1984..

22 *West Coast Advocate* 19 April 1951.

23 See Brown interview with author.

24 Dick McMinn interview. The following account of McMinn's life

has been taken from the author's interview plus several other interviews, tapes and speeches, ADHSA.

25 *Canadian Geographic*, undated article, Tidal Wave file, L.4.4, ADHSA. See also B. C. Professional Engineer, Nov. 1995: 5.

26 Cannings, 30-31.

27 See B.C. Professional Engineer, 6.

28 Duncan Hay, P. Eng, "Tsunamis," undated.

29 *Daily Colonist* 21 June 1896: 5.

30 Sydney O. Wigen, "Tsunami Hazard evaluation on the Canadian West Coast," International Tsunami Symposium, 6 Aug. 1985, Victoria, B.C.

31 *Port Alberni News* 9 Feb. 1928.

32 *West Coast Advocate* 5 March 1936.

33 T. S. Murty, "Seismic sea waves: Tsunamis," 337.

34 See Tsunami Symposium, "A Reconstruction of the Tsunami of June 1946 in the Strait of Georgia," T. S. Murty and P. B. Crean, Institute of Ocean Science.

35 "Alberni District Suffers Heavy Earthquake Damage," *West Coast Advocate* 27 June 1946.

36 Ernest A. Hodgson, "Whole No. 357: British Columbia Earthquake, June 23, 1946."

37 See Tidal Wave File L.4.4, ADHSA.

38 May Luecke, "When Good Friday was Black Friday," *Islander* 20 April 1986: M1, M4.

39 McMinn interview with Jan Peterson, 16 Sept. 1996.

40 Minutes of the meeting of Alberni and Port Alberni Disaster Committee at Provincial Civil Defence Control Headquarters, Alberni Fire Hall, 31 March, 1964, Part II.

41 *Ibid*. Part I.

42 Raymon Kwok.

43 "District Escapes Damage from Tidal Wave," *Tofino Ucluelet Press (West Coaster)*, 2 April 1964: 1, 3, 4.

44 W. R. H. White, "The Alaska earthquake - its effect in Canada," ADHSA.

45 Report of the Alberni Tidal Wave Disaster, Department of the Provincial Secretary, Civil Defence Coordinator.

46 "Harbour Surveyed," *Twin Cities Times* 3 May 1964.

Chapter Twelve

1   Scott interview, BOHP.

2   "Officials to inspect Long Beach for Park Site," *Port Alberni News* 22 May 1930.

3   "Pulling hidden wires in Victoria against Long Beach Park site," *Port Alberni News* 6 Nov. 1930.

4   See Scott interview, BOHP.

5   "New Wickaninnish Inn begins operation July 4," *West Coast Advocate* 2 July 1964.

6   "Sadness around Wickaninnish Inn," *Vancouver Sun* June 30, 1972.

7   "Arrival of Jean Chrétien," *Alberni Valley Times* 20 Nov. 1968.

8   "Average Small Town Boy," *Ibid*. 2 Dec. 1968.

9   See Guppy, 51.

10 Untitled newspaper clipping, Pacific Rim National Park file, ADHSA.

11 Jim Hamilton, "Beauty in Peril," *Daily Colonist* 15 Feb. 1970.

12 *Vancouver Sun* 30 June 1972.

13 R. Bruce Scott, "Wreck of the Vanlene," *Daily Colonist* 4 June 1978.

14 Rollie Rose, "38 Rescued from grounded ship," *Alberni Valley Times* 15 March 1972.

15 *Ibid*. The following account of the grounding has been taken from several articles written by Rollie Rose, unless otherwise stated.

16 Meg Trebett, "His first voyage a rough one," *Alberni Valley Times* 15 March 1972.

17 "Freighter's Fate in Hands of Sea Gods," *Ibid*. 16 March 1972.

18 *Daily Colonist* 4 June 1978.

19 "Deadship waits for Ocean burial," *Ibid*. 21 March 1972.

20 McMinn interview with Jan Peterson.

21 John and Kay Monrufet interview, BOHP.

22 *Ibid*.

23 *Daily Colonist* 4 June 1978.

24 "Sedco 135-F dominates Port Alberni Harbor," *Twin Cities Times* 18 Oct. 1967.

25 *Vancouver Sun* 24 May 1969.

26 *Alberni Valley Times* November 8, 1977.

27 Carl Vesterback, "A tour of the Ocean Ranger," *Alberni Valley Times* 29 Dec. 1978.

28 *The Province* 21 Feb. 1982. Information about the voyages of the Ocean Ranger is from this source.

29 Michelle MacAfee, "Oil Rig Disaster Haunts Memories," *Vancouver Sun* 15 Feb. 1997.

30 "Ill-fated Rig Hailed as the Ultimate," *The Province* 21 Feb. 1982: G.

31 *Alberni Valley Times* 29 Dec. 1978.

32 *Vancouver Sun* 15 Feb. 1997.

BIBLIOGRAPHY

Books

Alberni District Historical Society. *Place Names of the Alberni Valley.* Port Alberni: ADHS, 1988.

Barman, Jean. *The West Beyond The West: A History of British Columbia.* Toronto: University of Toronto Press, 1991.

Bird, George. *Tse-wees-tah: One Man in a Boat.* Port Alberni, BC: Alberni District Historical Society, 1972.

Brown, Craig. *The Illustrated History of Canada.* Toronto: Lester & Orpen Dennys, 1987.

Cannings, Richard and Sydney Cannings. *British Columbia: A Natural History.* Vancouver: Douglas & McIntyre, 1996.

Carr, Emily. *Klee Wyck.* Foreword by Ira Dilworth. Toronto: Oxford University Press, 1941.

Dale, Bill. "George Fraser." *American Rhododendron Society.* Summer 1990: 125.

Dunn, Alex. *Presbyterianism in British Columbia.* New Westminster, BC: Columbian Company Ltd., 1905.

Forester, Joseph E. and Anne D. Forester. *B.C.'s Commercial Fishing History.* Surrey, BC: Hancock House Publishers, 1975.

Gibson, Gordon with Carol Renison. *Bull of the Woods: The Gordon*

Gibson Story. Vancouver: Douglas & McIntyre, 1980.

Goodall, Trevor. *Trevor Goodall's Memories of the Alberni Valley.* Port Alberni: Goodall Self-Publish, 1983.

Graham, Donald. *Keepers of the Light.* Madeira Park, BC: Harbour Publishing, 1985.

Green, Ruth. *Personality Ships of British Columbia.* Vancouver: Marine Tapestry Publication Ltd., 1969.

Guppy, Walter. *Clayoquot Soundings.* Tofino, BC: Grassroots Publication, 1997.

—. *Wet Coast Ventures.* Victoria, BC: Cappis Press, 1988.

Henderson, Vi. *Pipers Lagoon.* Nanaimo: Quadra Graphics, 1984.

Hines, Ben. *Pick, Pan & Pack: A History of Mining in the Alberni Mining Division.* Port Alberni: Alberni Valley Museum, 1976. Booklet by Local Initiatives program.

Hodgson, Ernest A. "Whole No. 357: British Columbia Earthquake, June 23, 1946." *Journal of the Royal Astronomical Society of Canada.* 40.8 (1946).

Howard, Oliver. *Godships.* Toronto: United Church Observer, 1984.

Jewitt, John Rogers. *White Slaves of the Nootka, 1783-1821.* Surrey, BC: Heritage House, 1987.

Johnson, Louise. *Not Without Hope: The Story of Dr. H. A. McLean & The Esperanze General Hospital.* Matsqui, BC: Maple Lane Publishing, 1992.

Kew, Della and P. E. Goddard. *Indian Art and Culture of the Northwest Coast.* Surrey, BC: Hancock House Publishers, 1974.

Kirk, Ruth. *Wisdom of the Elders.* Vancouver: Douglas and McIntyre, 1988.

Lamb, W. Kaye. "Early Lumbering on Vancouver Island, BC." *Historical Quarterly.* 2 (1938): 104.

Lyons, Cicely. *Salmon: Our Heritage, British Columbia Packers Limited.* Vancouver: Mitchell Press, 1969.

MacKay, Donald. *Empire of Wood: The MacMillan Bloedel Story.* Vancouver: Douglas & McIntyre, 1982.

McDonald, Herbert L. *British Columbia: Challenge in Abundance.* Victoria, BC: Canadian Confederation Centennial Committee of British Columbia, 1966.

McMillan, Alan D. and Denis E. St. Claire. *Alberni Prehistory.* Penticton, BC: Theytus Books for the Alberni Valley Museum, 1982.

Morris, Rob. *Coasters.* Victoria, BC: Horsdal & Schubart, 1993.

Moser, Chas. *Reminiscences of the West Coast of Vancouver Island.* Victoria, BC: Acme Press, 1926.

Murty, T. S. and P. B. Cream. "A Reconstruction of the Tsunami of June 1946 in the Strait of Georgia." International Tsunami Symposium. Victoria, 1985. Tsunami Workshop Abstracts. Victoria: Institute of Ocean Science.

Murty, T. S. "Seismic Sea Waves: Tsunamis." Ottawa: Department of Fisheries and the Environment, 1977.

Newsome, Eric. *Pass the Bottle: Rum Tales of the West Coast.* Victoria, BC: Orca Books, 1995.

Nicholson, George. *Vancouver Island's West Coast: 1762-1962.* Vancouver: George Nicholson's Books, 1965.

Paterson, T. W. *Encyclopedia of Ghost Towns & Mining Camps of British Columbia.* Vol 1. Langley, BC: Stagecoach Publishing Co. Ltd., 1979.

Peterson, Jan. *The Albernis: 1860-1922.* Lantzville, BC: Oolichan Books, 1992.

—. Peterson. *Twin Cities: Alberni-Port Alberni.* Lantzville, BC: Oolichan Books, 1994.

Pickard, T. A. "Gilbert Malcolm Sproat." *B.C. Historical Quarterly.* 1 (1937) : 21-32.

Pojar, Jim and Andy MacKinnon. *Plants of Coastal British Columbia.* Vancouver: Lone Pine Publishing, 1994.

Rushton, Gerald A. *Whistle Up The Inlet: The Union Steamship Story.* Vancouver: Douglas & McIntyre, 1974.

Sanger, C. W. and A. B. Dickson. *They were as Clannish as Hell.* Halifax, NS: Oceans Institute of Canada, 1990.

Saul, A. M. Kinnersley. *A Course was Laid: An account of the voyage of the Lady Sylvia from Glasgow to Vancouver.* Private log of guarantee-engineer Oates. Ashton-under-Lyne, Eng: Horrocks & Co., 1937. Publication No. 263.

Scott, R. Bruce. *Barkley Sound: A History of the Pacific Rim National Park area.* Victoria, BC: Sono Nis Press, 1972.

Shadbolt, Doris. *The Art of Emily Carr.* Vancouver: Douglas & McIntyre, 1987.

Sproat, Gilbert Malcolm. *Scenes and Studies of Savage Life.* N.p. [Eng]: Smith, Elder and Co., 1868.

Starkins, Ed. "Rum Running." White, Howard. 10-19.

Staude, Craig. "Amphipacifica." *Journal of Systematic Biology.* 1.1 (1995).

Swadesh, Morris. "Motivations in Nootka Warfare." *Southwestern Journal of Anthropology* [Albuquerque, New Mexico] 4.1 (1948) : 76-93.

Tennant, Paul. *Aboriginal Peoples and Politics: The Indian Land Question in British Columbia, 1849-1989.* Vancouver: University of British Columbia Press, 1991.

Van Asdell, Jon. "B.C. Whaling: The Indians." White, Howard. 20-28.

Walbran, John T. *British Columbia Coast Names 1592-1906.* N.p: J. J. Douglas Ltd., 1971.

Wallbank, Jean Buck. *Benson Island.* Mission, BC: Digital Communications Inc., 1991.

Webb, Robert Lloyd. *On the Northwest: Commercial Whaling in the Pacific Northwest, 1790-1967.* Vancouver: University of British Columbia Press, 1988.

White, Howard. Editor. *Raincoast Chronicles First Five.* Vol. 1. Madeira Park, BC: Harbour Publishing, 1976.

Wigan, Sidney O. "Tsunami Hazard evaluation on the Canadian West Coast." International Tsunami Symposium. Victoria, 1985. Tsunami Workshop Abstracts. Institute of Ocean Science.

Young, Charles H. and Helen R. Y. Reid. *The Japanese Canadians.* Toronto: University of Toronto Press, 1938.

Newspapers & Magazines

Alberni Advocate [Port Alberni].

Alberni District News [Port Alberni].

Alberni Pioneer News [Port Alberni].

Alberni Valley Times [Port Alberni].

American Rhododendron Society [Fortuna, CA].

British Columbia Historical Quarterly/News [Wasa, BC]. (BC Historical Federation).

Daily Colonist [Victoria, BC].

Daily Times [Victoria, BC].

Daily Victoria Gazette [Victoria, BC].

Harmac News [Nanaimo, BC]. (H. R. MacMillan Export Co. Journal).

Ha-Shilth-Sa [Port Alberni]. Nuu-chah-nulth Tribal Council newspaper.

Nanaimo Free Press [Nanaimo, BC].

Port Alberni News [Port Alberni].

The Northern Scot, [Elgin, Scotland].

The Province [Vancouver].

The Westcoaster [Tofino-Ucluelet, BC]. Also *West Coaster* [Tofino-Ucluelet].

Times Colonist, The Islander [Victoria, BC].

Twin Cities Times [Port Alberni].

Vancouver Sun [Vancouver, BC].

Waterfront News [Port Alberni].

West Coast Advocate [Port Alberni].

Diaries, Journals, Letters, Notes, Lectures

(All located within Alberni District Historical Society archives, unless otherwise stated.)

Bird, George. Notes.

Banfield letters and reports. Ethnology vol. 1. Also Alberni Valley Museum.

Brabant, Father. Journal.

Cox, Gus. Memoirs.

Guillod, Harry. Reports from 1881-1903. ADHSA.

Pioneer Parade. Radio script.

Sears, Cyrus. Letter. *Alberni Pioneer News* 24 Feb. 1912.

Sproat, Gilbert Malcolm. Alberni Lands correspondence, 1864.

Stuart, Charles Edward. Banfield Reports. Nanaimo Community Archives.

Thornberg, Frederick Christian. "Memoirs of Trader Thornberg of Clayoquot."

Transcribed by Les Hammer.

Tuttle, Grace. Journal. 1917—.

White, W. R. H. "The Alaska Earthquake: its effect in Canada."

Interviews

Baird, Mr. & Mrs. Arthur. By Larry and Grace Kreuger. 7 July 1973. Pacific Rim National Park Study. Vol 2. Alberni Valley Museum Library.

Brown, Cougar. By Jan Peterson. May, 1984.

—. By Shirley Culpin. *Alberni Valley Times* 24 Jan. 1973.

Brown, Grace. By Jan Peterson. 4 Sept. 1996.

Cashin, Irma. Bamfield Oral History Project. 23 Nov. 1994.

Clappis, Annie. By Jean McIntosh. Re: basket weaving. 1986. Alberni Valley Museum.

Dick, Agnes. By Jan Peterson. July, 1981.

Garcia, Joe. By Tanya Porter. Re: Bamfield. BOHP.

Hanna, Larry. By Jan Peterson. Re: Port Alberni Waterfront. Aug. 1996.

Joe, Angie. By Tanya Porter. Re: Bamfield. BOHP.

Karpoff, George. By Jan Peterson. At Toquart Bay, BC. 16 Oct. 1997.

Logan, Ardie. By Tanya Porter. Re: Bamfield. BOHP.

McDermid, Bill. By Edwin Hubert. Re: Bamfield. BOHP. 10 Jan. 1995.

McMinn, Dick. By Jan Peterson. Re: Marine career. 16 Sept. 1996.

Mead-Miller, Sheila. By Larry and Grace Kreuger. 18 July, 1973. Pacific Rim National Park study. Vol 2. Alberni Valley Museum Library.

Monrufet, John and Kay. By Edwin Hubert. Re: Bamfield and Marine career. BOHP. 3 Feb. 1995.

Ostrom, Roald. BOHP.

Scott, Bruce and Pauline. By June and Kirk Kerstetter. Re: Bamfield. 1979.

Stone, Douglas Jr. By Jan Peterson. Re: Stone Bros. 20 Aug. 1996.

Watson, Antony. By Mary Oliver. Transcript. ADHSA.

Theses & Manuscripts

Carmichael, Alfred. "In an Open Boat from Alberni to Ucluelet." Provincial Archives of British Columbia. Typescript F/62/SW2 A. With permission: Alberni District Historical Society Archives.

—. "My Friend Melvin Swartout." *Ibid.*

—. "Revenge of the Clallams." BCARS.

—. "To Village Island and Back: Narrative of a Journey from Ucluelet to Village Island, Barkley Sound, 1896." *Ibid.*

Evans, Laura. "To Carmanah Point on the Princess Macquinna." *Discovery.* Port Alberni, BC: Alberni Valley Creative Writers' Group, 1978: 17-24. With Permission.

Garrard, Frank. "Memoirs." Unpublished. ADHSA.

Hillier, E. A. "History of Ucluelet 1899 to 1954." Manuscript. Ucluelet Historical Society Archives.

Howe, Gwen. "Looking Back." ADHSA.

Kwok, Ramon. "Salal Joe is Missing." Private.

Littlefield, Loraine. "Gender, Class and Community." Thesis. University of BC. October 1995. Nanaimo Community Archives.

Pacific Rim National Park Human History study. Alberni Valley Museum Library.

Scott, R. Bruce. "Unsung Hero of the West Coast." ADHSA.

Government Records

Alberni 1871 survey. ADHSA.

Department of the Naval Service . Annual Report of the Fisheries Branch, 1919. Alberni Valley Museum.

Annual Mining Reports 1893, 1944. Alberni Valley Museum.

Barkley Sound Planning Strategy, January 1994. Alberni Clayoquot Regional District study.

British Columbia pamphlets. Ottawa: Parliamentary Library.

Department of Indian Affairs. Annual Report 1882.

Department of Mines. Report of the Alberni coal-field. 14 May 1922.

Indian Agent Reports (Alberni) 1881-1885.

Pattullo papers. BCARS. Add. Ms. 3. Box 21, File 8.

British Columbia. Royal Commission on Indian Affairs. Minutes of the West Coast Agency hearings. McKenna-McBride Commission. Nuu-chah-nulth Tribal Council.

The author also wishes to acknowledge assistance received from the following:

Alberni District Historical Society Archives
Alberni Valley Museum
British Columbia Archives and Records Service
Nanaimo Community Archives
Vancouver Island Regional Library, Port Alberni and Nanaimo
Pacific Biological Station, Nanaimo
Bamfield Oral History Project, Nanaimo
Ucluelet Historical Society
Alberni Clayoquot Regional District
Government Agent, Port Alberni

INDEX

California, 29, 46, 53, 74, 84, 107, 164, 171, 191-94, 249, 302, 307, 325
California Academy of Science, 171
Campbell River, 197, 277, 290
Canadian Fishing Company, 199, 201
Canadian Hydrographic Services, 189
Canadian National Railway, 203, 219
Canadian North Pacific Fisheries Limited, 118
Canadian Overseas Telecommunication Corporation, 273
Canadian Pacific Lumber Company, 202, 232
Canadian Pacific Navigation Company, 97, 216
Canadian Pacific Railway, 98, 135, 141, 148, 194, 295, 306. See also Esquimalt & Nanaimo Railway
Cape Beale, 30, 40-1, 51-5, 57, 63, 82-3, 136, 137, 148, 152-53, 167, 186,194, 224, 229, 243, 280, 294, 301, 309, 313
Cardinal, Jean, 170
Carmanah Point, 237, 238, 240, 241, 299, 308, 309, 324, 347
Carmichael, Alfred, 125, 126, 129, 130, 133
Carmichael, Herbert, 100
Carr, Emily, 124, 200
Cashin, Irma, 106, 233
Celebrations: Boat Days, 208, 215. Coronation, 71. Queen Victoria's Birthday, 38
Cherry Creek, 25, 138
China, 182, 319
China Creek, 24, 78, 80, 84, 86-90, 137, 203, 291, 327
Chinese, 67, 71, 84, 117, 162, 178, 182, 201, 211, 312
Chretien, Jean, 309-311
Chup Point, 25
Christ Community Church (Ucluelet Evangelical Church), 259
City of Alberni, 249
Clappis, Annie, 261
Clark, E., 169
Clarke Island, 285
Clarke, Dan Jr., 87
Clarke, Dan Sr., 46, 70
Clarke, George, 69, 70
Clayoquot Sound, 25, 31, 40, 50, 66-8, 81-3, 105, 179, 195, 198, 234, 237, 324
Cli-shin, Chief, 30, 152
Clo-oose, 133, 217, 233, 237-241, 313
Clutesi, George, 59, 267, 284
Comox, 66, 78, 82, 96, 190, 199, 300, 315
Comox Post, 63
Consolidated Whaling Company, 120, 162
Cooper, J.P., 196
Copper Island, 50, 54, 59, 84, 156
Coulson Forest Products, 202, 272
Courtney, 171, 218, 300
Cous Creek, 24, 226
Cox, Edward (Ed), 62, 117
Cox, Gus, 53, 59-61, 157, 186
Cox, Emanuel J., 52-7, 152
Creelman Brothers, 211
Croll, Captain J. A., 92

Deep Sea Fishermen's Union of the Pacific Coast, 186
Deer Group Islands, 24
Department of Indian Affairs, 61, 68, 70, 268, 305, 309

Commissioner), 47, 69

Pachena Bay/Point/Lighthouse, 40, 50, 51, 52, 59, 72, 153, 189, 262, 279, 280, 311
Pachena Fish Co. Ltd., 166
Pacific Biological Station, 120, 171
Pacific Cable Board, 147, 149, 150
Pacific Coast Militia Rangers, 62, 230
Pacific Geoscience Centre, 298
Pacific Rim National Park Reserve, 158, 277, 284, 308, 311
Pacific Whaling Company, 112, 114, 115, 118
Pamphlet, Captain Tom, 34, 36, 41, 104
Parksville, 138, 150, 248
Paterson, Thomas George, 52, 137, 153
Patterson, Jack, 83, 167, 168
Pattullo, Hon. T.D., 173-77
Pennsylvania, 145, 217
Peters, Harold, 81
Petersen, Jens, 158
Pipestem Inlet, 82, 85, 112, 188
Pocahontas, 39, 40. Rock, 136
Poett Nook, 327
Police, 40, 59-61, 66, 74, 196, 249, 293, 324
Polly Point, 150, 260, 261, 304
Porritt, Captain Richard, 223, 224
Porritt, Wright, 151
Port Alberni/Alberni, 24, 25, 31-2, 33. Anderson mill, 38, 39. CNR railway, 116, 134-41, 150-51. Coal mine, 98-101. Crofters, 173-76, 177. Early shipments & population, 40, 40-53, 56-57, 60, 63, 70-5. Earthquake & tsunami, 301-07, 318-22, 325-27. Mile 0 Post planting, 196, 282. Mining boom, 78, 79. Naming, 34, 35
Port Alberni Harbour Commission, 25
Port Alberni Shipyard. See Stone Bros.
Port Albion, 159, 198, 200-201, 219, 225, 234, 268, 286, 306
Port Desire, 32, 211
Port Renfrew, 30, 50, 63, 68, 136, 148, 197, 233, 238, 241, 308, 311
Prefontaine, Joseph-Raymond Fournier, 112
Presbyterians, 61, 72, 124, 133, 134, 137, 174, 325
Prince Rupert, 171, 193, 230
Prince Rupert Whaling Company, 118
Princess Maquinna, 60, 62, 106, **143**, 144, 198, 224, 228, 232-41, 295
Princess Norah, 105, 198, 236, 237

Qualicum, 66
Queen Charlotte Islands, 108, 114, 115, 118, 176, 193, 318, 320
Queen Charlotte Whaling Company Limited, 115, 118

R.B. McLean Sawmill, 294
Richards, Captain G.H., 32, 36, 39, 40, 154, 188, 196
Riley's Boat Service, 243-45
Riley, Alice and Reese, 223, 243-44
Riley, Douglas and Mickey,

243-44
Rissmuller, Dr. Ludwig, 114,
116
Ritherdon Bay, 159, 219
Rodgers, Reverend Roy, 254,
255
Rogers, Jeremiah (Jerry), 34,
209
Roff, William, 115, 150, 151
Roman Catholics, 50, 51, 66,
134, 325
Romeril, Reverend John, 255,
256
Rose, Rollie, 314-15
Royal Commission on Indian
Affairs, 60, 103
Ruck, Sidney, 162
Rumrunning, 189-94
Rum Row, 192, 193

Saggers, Walter, 197
Salal Joe, 283-85, 306
San Francisco, 40, 42, 53, 65,
78, 96, 97, 171, 194
San Mateo Bay, 159, 181, 219,
220, 250, 264
Santa Maria Island, 42, 84
Sarita/River, 24, 28, 51, 54, 91,
151, 152, 157, 159, 162,
179,181. Cannery, 185,
203, 211, 219, 225, 227,
234, 255, 308
Sarita River Logging Camp.
See Bloedel, Stewart &
Welch
Sareault, Mike, 56, 137
Saunders, Fred (brother of
Henry), 85, 137, 139
Saunders, Henry, 71, 87
Schools:
Alberni District Secondary,
262
A.W. Neill Junior Secondary,
262, 264
Bamfield, 153, 154, 279, 281

Beaver Creek, 71
C.T. Hilton, 62
Franklin, 204
John Howitt's School(Alberni),
62
Kildonan, 178
Port Albion, 124, 201
Redford, 268
Sarita, 206
Stapleby, 198
Ucluelet, 147, 197, 198, 201
School teachers, 62, 70, 90,
124, 125, 197, 201, 205,
208, 279
Schupp, William, 118, 119
Schwarz, Harry, 169-72
Scott, Bruce, 234, 273, 286,
309
Scottish Crofter Fishermen
Scheme, 173-176
Sears, Captain Cyrus, 39
Sea Serpent, 167-73
Sechart, 36, 85, 86, 91, 112-21,
131, 159, 185, 217, 219
Sedco drilling rigs, 317-18
Seghers, Right Reverend C.J.,
51
Shantymen's Christian Asso-
ciation, 256, 258, 325
Shewish, Chief (Tseshaht),
127-29
Shewish, Chief Adam, 260
Smallpox, 65, 68, 152
Smith, George, 81, 169
Smith, Teddy, 220
Snug Basin, 91, 92, 96
Somass Hotel, 139, 293, 303,
313
Somerville Cannery Company,
181
Southeastern Commonwealth
Drilling Ltd. 318
Spring, Captain William, 50,
51, 54, 56, 286
Sproat, Gilbert Malcolm, 34,